STRATEGIES FOR CRITICAL READING

A Text with Thematic Reader

Jane L. McGrath
Professor Emerita
Paradise Valley Community College

PEARSON

Prentice
Hall

Upper Saddle River, New Jersey 07458

Library of Congress Cataloging-in-Publication Data

McGrath, Jane L.
   Strategies for critical reading : a text with thematic reader / Jane L. McGrath.
   — 1st ed.
      p. cm.
   Includes index.
   ISBN 0-13-048875-5
1. College readers.   2. Reading comprehension—Problems, exercises, etc.
3. Reading (Higher education)—Problems, exercises, etc.   I. Title.

PE1122.M269 2005
428.6—dc22

2004000488

Senior Acquisitions Editor: Craig Campanella
Editor in Chief: Leah Jewell
Editorial Assistant: Joan Polk
Executive Marketing Manager: Rachel Falk
Marketing Assistant: Adam Laitman
Production Liasion: Fran Russello
Permissions Supervisor: Connie Golden

Manufacturing Buyer: Ben Smith
Cover Image: Frank Mortimer
Composition/Full-Service Project Management:
   Pine Tree Composition, Inc.
Printer/Binder: Courier Companies, Inc.
Cover Printer: Coral Graphics

Credits and acknowledgments borrowed from other sources and reproduced, with permission, in this textbook appear on pages 373–374.

Portions of this book were previously published in *Understanding Diverse Viewpoints: A Thematic Reader* by Jane McGrath. Copyright © 1999 by Harcourt Brace & Company.

Pearson Education LTD, London
Pearson Education Singapore, Pte. Ltd.
Pearson Education, Canada, Ltd
Pearson Education–Japan
Pearson Education Australia PTY, Limited

Pearson Education North Asia Ltd
Pearson Educación de Mexico, S.A. de C.V.
Pearson Education Malaysia, Pte. Ltd.
Pearson Education, Upper Saddle River,
   New Jersey

10   9   8   7   6   5   4   3   2   1
ISBN: 0-13-048875-5

CONTENTS

TO THE INSTRUCTOR

Strategies for Critical Reading: A Text with Thematic Reader is an effective primary text in college-level reading courses. It can serve as the common reader in paired courses and learning communities and is compatible with critical thinking texts and composition texts.

Strategies for Critical Reading is derived from my convictions that (1) adopting the skills, strategies, attitudes, and habits associated with critical reading are vital for success in college and in life and (2) those skills, strategies, attitudes, and habits can be developed and improved through instruction and practice. This text provides the foundation for that instruction and practice. Its thematic approach promotes a meaningful, connected understanding of topics that allows students to profit from more sophisticated material than is possible with isolated readings. Students become thoughtful readers who comprehend, analyze, and reach reasoned judgments rather than readers who simply accumulate bits and bytes of information.

This text, like the first two texts in this series, *Basic Skills and Strategies for College Reading* and *Building Strategies for College Reading,* is shaped by my premises:

- Reading is a complex, multidimensional cognitive activity with myriad interrelated skills—not fragmented, discrete tasks.
- Comprehension is a generative process with many factors contributing to the meaning the reader derives from print.
- Instructors play a vital role in helping readers become more successful.
- Examples and practice must be authentic.

ORGANIZATION

A list of "Common Assumptions about Reading" and my rationale about why the assumptions are false open the text.

The "Reading as a Process" instructional chapter reviews information about and examples of strategies successful readers use. The goal of the chapter is to remind students to build their own repertoire of strategies so they will be better able to accomplish various reading tasks. Next, using the annotated example, "On the Limits of Critical Thinking," I summarize how I used some of the strategies while working on this book. The chapter concludes with review questions, an opportunity to reflect and connect, and information about using Web resources to research various points of view. Two essays for guided or independent practice follow the chapter.

The main part of the text is the five thematically organized reading units. The purpose of the themes is to encourage students to practice logical, meaningful reading strategies on authentic text. Each theme opens with an introduction to the topic. Each selection begins with an idea to think about to help students place the topic in a context before they begin to read. The readings present diverse views on issues related to the theme's topic and are surrounded by apparatus that reinforces good reading strategies. Each theme concludes with reflective questions that encourage readers to think about and value diverse views.

The book includes a variety of writing styles and organizational structures. The emphasis is on reading exposition and argument; however, a poem and a myth are included. Paragraphs within a selection are numbered to make class discussion of specific ideas and phrases easier. Cartoons that touch on the topic are included in each Theme to promote additional discussion.

I realize there are more readings than needed for a quarter or even a semester course. However, I wanted to provide an abundant collection of authentic material so you would be able to select the topics and readings that meet the needs of your students.

SUPPORTING PRINT AND ELECTRONIC MATERIALS

For Instructors

An *Instructor's Manual* including course syllabus recommendations, presentation ideas, additional exercises, readability information for selections, and suggested answers for exercises is available.

The *Prentice Hall Reading Skills Test Bank* is available in print and electronic format. It has more than 1,000 exercises, covering word analysis, context clues, stated main idea, implied main idea, tone and bias, details, major vs. minor details, style, study reading, reading rate, and visual aids. Questions are multiple choice, matching, or true/false.

For Students

When you adopt *Strategies for Critical Reading,* your students gain access to Research Navigator™, Prentice Hall's one-stop research solution for students. It includes three databases of credible and reliable source material and extensive help on the research process. Once students log on to Research Navigator.com and enter their personal passcode, they have access to (1) EBSCO's *Content Select*™ Academic Journal Database, where they can search leading academic journals by keyword, topic, or multiple topics; (2) *The New York Times* Search-by-Subject Archive, organized by academic subject and searchable by keyword, or multiple keywords; and (3) Link Library, organized by subject, which offers editorially selected "best of the web" sites. Link Libraries are continually scanned and kept up to date to provide relevant and accurate links.

Your students can receive a free *New American Webster Handy College Dictionary* packaged with their text. This best-selling dictionary includes more than 115,000 definitions, including current phrases, slang, and scientific terms. It has more than 1,500 new words, boxed inserts on etymologies and language, foreign words and phrases, and an international gazetteer with correct place-name pronunciations.

Rather than the dictionary, you can have students receive a free *New American Roget's College Thesaurus* packaged with their text. This best-selling thesaurus is arranged alphabetically in an easy-to-read, double column format. It includes more than 5,000 new words and phrases and 2,000 new synonym entry words for efficient cross referencing.

Ask your Prentice Hall representative for information on any of these supplements.

IN APPRECIATION

Although my name appears on the cover, many wonderful people contributed to the development and production of this book. First, I am very grateful to my students. Their enthusiasm and perseverance have always been vital to our classroom successes. My thanks to my colleagues across the Maricopa Community Colleges and to the reviewers of this edition for their willingness to share their expertise to make this text more useful for students: Ann Wolf, Gonzaga University; Debbie Naquin, Northern Virginia Community College; Deborah O'Brien-Smith, Nassau Community College; Victoria Sarkesian, Marist College; Diane Bosco, Suffolk County Community College; Tamara Brawner, Coastal Georgia Community College; David Boles, Fordham University; and Elizabeth Price, Ranger College.

A special thank you to the cadre of dedicated professionals at Prentice Hall, especially my editor Craig Campanella and editorial assistant Joan Polk. They are undoubtedly the most creative and patient folks on the planet. My sincere thanks to Larry McGrath, my partner in all of life's adventures. Without his wisdom, good humor, technical expertise, and encouragement, this book would not exist.

And, thank *you* for inviting me into your classroom. I welcome your suggestions and will be delighted to hear your comments at Jellenjay@aol.com.

ABOUT THE AUTHOR

Jane L. McGrath earned her undergraduate degree and M.A. in education and mass communications and her Ed.D. in reading education from Arizona State University. During her more than 25 years with the Maricopa Colleges, McGrath has taught a variety of reading, English, journalism, and computer applications courses. In 1991, she was named *Innovator of the Year* by the Maricopa Colleges and the League for Innovation in Community Colleges for Project Read-Aloud, a college-community service program. McGrath's other books include *Building Strategies for College Reading: A Text with Thematic Reader* and *Basic Skills and Strategies for College Reading: A Text with Thematic Reader.* In addition to her work in reading education, McGrath and her husband Larry write for the high performance automotive industry. Their work has appeared in magazines such as *Drag Racing Today* and *Circle Track,* and their monthly column appears in *Performance Racing Industry.*

TEN COMMON ASSUMPTIONS ABOUT READING

An assumption is an idea we believe to be true—something we take for granted. Many of my students begin the semester with these assumptions. How many of them do you share?

1. Good readers need to read a text passage only once to understand it.
2. Information that appears in print, whether on paper or on the Internet, is true and worthwhile.
3. Every word and every sentence of an assignment are of equal importance.
4. It doesn't matter whether it's a biology lab manual, a contemporary short story, or a philosophy chapter—reading is reading.
5. The source of the writing (the author) guarantees its substance.
6. A question has only one right answer (and the teacher knows what it is).
7. Each essay, article, poem, novel, and play has only one correct interpretation.
8. All information can be neatly categorized as either fact or opinion. (And furthermore, we should believe only authors who use facts and disregard authors using opinions.)
9. Critical readers/thinkers cannot have any commitments to ideas, causes, people, or actions.
10. Reading—understanding what an author says and means—is easy for other people.

Continue reading to see why I believe all 10 assumptions are inaccurate.

Assumption 1: *Good readers need to read a text passage only once to understand it.* Rarely do I meet a student who can comprehend all he or she needs from a passage with a single reading. Depending on their purpose for reading, most successful readers read assignments at least twice and often reread difficult or key sections even more often.

Assumption 2: *Information that appears in print, whether on paper or on the Internet, is true and worthwhile.* Fortunately, or unfortunately, almost anyone can get something into print. It is up to the reader to objectively assess the value of the information.

Assumption 3: *Every word and every sentence of an assignment are of equal importance.* This is rarely true. Authors typically develop their thesis with a series of main ideas, each supported by a variety of major and minor details. Successful readers identify and concentrate on information that is relevant to their purpose.

Assumption 4: *It doesn't matter whether it's a biology lab manual, a contemporary short story, or a philosophy chapter—reading is reading.* Successful readers approach each assignment as a unique task. They consider variables such as the author's purpose, vocabulary, and method of organization/structure plus their own purpose for reading and background knowledge.

Assumption 5: *The source of the writing (the author) guarantees its substance.* Just because an author is a celebrity or an expert does not guarantee that everything he or she writes is beyond debate.

Assumption 6: *A question has only one right answer (and the teacher knows what it is).* Obviously, this statement is sometimes true. If I ask who succeeded John F. Kennedy to the presidency, or what was the date of America's first manned space flight, the answers are not matters of debate. However, many questions do have multiple interpretations and solutions. For example, if I ask who was the most effective president after Kennedy or which space flight was the most important, different people will offer different interpretations.

Assumption 7: *Each essay, article, poem, novel, and play has only one correct interpretation.* Like Assumption 6, this assumption is sometimes true. On the basis of information from the author, historians, researchers, or critics, there may be a compelling case for a particular interpretation. However, many works are open to several valid interpretations.

Assumption 8: *All information can be neatly categorized as either fact or opinion. (And furthermore, we should believe only authors who use facts and disregard authors using opinions.)* The two categories of fact and opinion are often useful. For example, much scientific, mathematical, and technical information can be agreed to as facts, and many items of personal taste and values can be labeled opinions. However, much of what we consider as we read is the author's reasoned judgment—his or her informed interpretation of the information. Critical readers consider facts, reasonable opinions, and reasoned judgments.

Ten Common Assumptions About Reading

Assumption 9: *Critical readers/thinkers cannot have any commitments to ideas, causes, people, or actions.* I believe the opposite is true: Critical readers/ thinkers can be passionate in their beliefs, commitments, and actions. The key is that they reach their position after an informed, careful analysis of all the available information. In addition, they remain open to new information.

Assumption 10: *Reading—understanding what an author says and means—is easy for other people.* Only a very few people can read everything from the mathematical concepts of Pythagoras to the history of rock and roll with equal ease and success. How "easy" or "difficult" a selection is for any reader depends on his or her background knowledge and purpose for reading as well as the difficulty level of the text.

Over the next few weeks I hope you will examine your assumptions about reading.

READING AS A PROCESS

Chapter at a Glance

CHAPTER FOCUS

Imagine that on the front page of the morning newspaper you read about a "horrible new battle in the jungles of Central America between hired guerrilla rebels and defending army personnel." Then this afternoon, another paper's editorial describes the same battle as an "on-going conflict between local freedom fighters and military militia." Tonight, the television news anchor describes the event as "yet another skirmish between warring drug factions." Which do you think is the most accurate description? How can you decide?

What would be your impression of the incident if you read or heard only one report?

Although I invented this example, we all read and hear a hodgepodge of information every day. Some of it is reliable, some of it is questionable, and some of it is inaccurate.

To be successful in school, work, and life, you cannot passively accept what you read, what an associate tells you, what you see on television, or what you download from the Internet. You must do more than just accumulate bits and bytes of information. You must be able to understand, analyze, synthesize, and use it. In other words, you must become a critical reader.

BECOMING A CRITICAL READER

Becoming a critical reader *does not* mean turning into a person who finds fault, or is critical of, everything you read. It is not negative thinking.

Becoming a critical reader *does* mean being willing and able to objectively evaluate what you read. It means that you reach reasoned judgments on the basis of the evidence presented rather than accepting or rejecting information based on assumptions, emotions, and anecdotes.

James Mursell provides an excellent explanation of critical reading in his book, *Using Your Mind Effectively* (New York: McGraw-Hill, 1951, pp. vi–vii):

> There is one key idea which contains, in itself, the very essence of effective reading, and on which the improvement of reading depends: *Reading is reasoning.* When you read properly, you are not merely assimilating. You are not automatically transferring into your head what your eyes pick up on the page. What you see on the page sets your mind at work, collating, criticizing, interpreting, questioning, comprehending, comparing. When this process goes on well, you read well. When it goes on ill, you read badly.

Critical Readers Are Critical Thinkers

Because reading is reasoning, many of the skills and strategies you use to read critically are commonly known in philosophy and psychology as critical thinking skills.

ARE YOU A CRITICAL THINKER?

Dr. Thomas A. Shipka,
Philosophy and Religious Studies, Youngstown State University,
Youngstown, OH

Most people that I encounter assume that they reason well, that they are "critical thinkers." Is this assumption justified? Take the following test of critical thinking skills I developed for my students and award yourself a mark as high as 5 or as low as 1 on each item.

I am a successful problemsolver.

I am an informed and responsible decision-maker. I gather as many relevant facts as time constraints permit and I anticipate the likely consequences of each option before I make a decision.

I strive for informed beliefs, that is, beliefs based on compelling evidence and strong arguments.

I use language with precision and clarity.

My beliefs are coherent; that is, some of my beliefs do not contradict others.

I can explain and defend my beliefs capably.

I am a good listener.

I am objective and even-handed in my assessments. I do not exaggerate the benefits or harms of a belief, an argument, a person, an organization, a life style, a movement, a product or a service.

I know that my perceptions can be distorted by my expectations, beliefs, biases and state of mind.

I know that my memory is selective and constructive, and seldom provides a literal report of past events.

I appreciate the important role of skepticism in my life, refusing to embrace a claim, however satisfying or intriguing, until I find reasonable grounds for it.

I am open-minded and flexible. I am willing to consider a different perspective on an issue than the one that I am used to taking, and I am willing to hear or read an elaboration and defense of a claim which strikes me initially as weird or far-fetched.

I am sensitive to my own fallibility, that is, my proneness as a human being to make mistakes. I have the courage to acknowledge the possibility that a long-cherished belief of mine may be mistaken.

I successfully detect bias, propaganda, special pleading, code words and exaggeration in what I hear and read.

I am aware that many television programs, films and publications deviate from the historical record and contradict well-established scientific laws and theories.

(continued)

1　I strive to stay intellectually alive. I regularly read books, newspapers, magazines and other publications. I balance my reading so that I expose myself to a variety of views and perspectives. I participate regularly in serious, civil conversations about significant issues in the news.

2　I understand and detect common fallacies in reasoning, including begging the question (assuming what one is supposed to prove); equivocation (using the same word in different senses); the appeal to ignorance (assuming the correctness of a claim because it has not been disproved); stereotyping and hasty generalization (jumping to a conclusion based upon one or few observations); post hoc ergo propter hoc (assuming that because one event preceded another the former caused the latter); ad hominem (disqualifying an argument because of its presenter and not its merit); the appeal to authority (sanctioning a claim based solely on its advocate or supporter); and the slippery slope (assuming that a modest change will necessarily trigger dire consequences).

2　I strive to avoid the use of such fallacies in my own reasoning.

____ TOTAL

The highest score possible is 90. How did you do?

Now if you are especially bold and brave, you might invite another person to evaluate your critical thinking skills on this test and then compare the two scores. Remember, good thinking, like good health, is a lifelong challenge.

Whether on Paper or on the Screen

When you read, in a print medium or on the Internet, you often find conflicting information. For example, suppose you are reading about the "problems associated with global warming." The author of the first journal article you read concludes that the problems of global warming have been "totally exaggerated and are of no concern." The next article reports that a group of scientists "urge immediate action on this escalating crisis." On the Web, your search locates more than 500 pages with information about global warming. Some pages provide information that seems to discredit the entire concept, some proclaim global warming is a precursor to global doom, and some pages provide tables and charts without interpretation.

As you read each article or Web page, the information seems reasonable and the examples appear plausible. Yet the selections contain different and sometimes contradictory information.

What do you do? Do you just keep searching until you find *the* journal or book or Web site that contains the "right" information? If you tried this approach on global warming, or most any other topic, your search would never end. This is so because most fields of study require humans to interpret information, make inferences, and reach reasoned conclusions. Therefore, it is quite common for even rational professionals to have different points of view.

To help you evaluate information, most of what you read in print-on-paper resources such as journals and textbooks is reviewed by an editor for content and style before it is published. This editorial process gives some assurance the material is valid and reliable. Or, at the very least, print resources provide author and source information you can review.

The Miami Herald
Distributed by King Features Syndicate

© Jim Morin 1997 King Features Syndicate. Reprinted by special permission.

Unfortunately, this traditional filtering system does not exist for most of the material you read on the Internet. For this reason, one of the great strengths of the Internet—that anyone anywhere can put up any information he or she wants—becomes its biggest weakness. Although you can run a Web search and locate hundreds of sites with information related to your topic, sources are not equally valuable or reliable. In cyberspace you are not just a reader; you are also the editor reviewing the information for legitimate content and understandable style. This means that you must be extra cautious when reading information on the Internet. For specific guidelines and checklists for evaluating web information, log on to one of these sites or run a search on "how to evaluate web information."

http://www.library.georgetown.edu/internet/eval.htm
http://www.walthowe.com/navnet/quality.html
http://www.hopetillman.com/findqual.html
http://libweb.uoregon.edu/guides/findarticles/credibility.html
http://credibility.stanford.edu/

Passively accepting any information as accurate and reliable makes you vulnerable to a variety of problems—from small inconveniences such as seeing a highly rated movie that you hate to major disasters such as submitting a report to your boss containing flawed information. To increase your chances of identifying and rejecting flawed information, use an active, strategic approach to reading.

APPROACHING READING AS A PROCESS

When you sit down to write a multiparagraph essay or report, you don't expect the first words you type, from the opening word of the introduction to the final word of the conclusion, to be your finished product. Because writing is a process, you expect to use a variety of prewriting, writing, revising, and editing strategies before you have a final document that meets your purpose.

Reading is also a process. Therefore, you should not expect to read straight through from the first word of an assignment to the last word and understand everything the author says and means. During the reading process, you need to use a variety of prereading, reading, analyzing, and reflecting strategies to help you meet your purpose. Strategies are the tools and techniques you select to accomplish a particular task.

Preparing to Read
Reading Actively and Accurately
Analyzing and Evaluating the Content
Reflecting on and Connecting What
   You Have Read

During the reading process you can use many strategies to help you better understand what you read. Although I've organized the strategies under these four categories, it does not mean that successful readers use a predictable, step-by-step sequence every time they read. Strategic readers select, adapt, combine, and repeat strategies as appropriate to their purpose. For some reading assignments you might use several strategies; for others you might use only one or two.

This chapter reviews skills and strategies you can use to be a more effective and efficient reader. As you read about these strategies, compare and contrast them with the strategies you use. The more aware you are of your current reading process, the easier it will be to add new strategies. And, the more strategies you have to select from, the more likely you will be able to match the appropriate tools to your reading tasks.

Strategies for Preparing to Read

Luck is what happens when preparation meets opportunity.
Seneca (5 BC–65 AD)

Taking time to prepare before you begin to read is like planning a route before a trip, warming up before a run, or preparing your menu before going to the grocery store. It helps you avoid major problems and keeps you from wasting time. When you spend a few minutes preparing you have time to think about things like what you already know about the topic, what you need to know when you finish reading, and what to do to increase your chances for success.

PREVIEW THE READING TO DETERMINE
AS MUCH AS POSSIBLE ABOUT THE CONTENT.

Ask yourself questions such as these:

- What do the title and subtitles tell me about the content?
- What major topics are discussed?
- What do I know about the topics?
- Are there graphics that can help me understand the content?
- In a text, do end-of-chapter questions ask about major topics? What other topics do the questions cover?
- Who is the intended audience?
- Is the material primary or secondary in nature?
- How long will it take me to read this assignment?

Previewing an assignment is not a random activity. When you preview, you read key structural organizers, such as titles and subtitles. Although the organizers in reading materials vary, these features highlight important information and are keys to understanding the selection's content.

For example, texts usually have chapter titles, subtitles, and bold or italicized type. They may also have learning objectives, unit summaries, and review questions. Magazine and journal articles often have a paragraph that appears before the article summarizing the content or giving author information.

Once you become familiar with how to preview, you should be able to preview a 30-page text chapter with clear structural elements in about 10 minutes.

A Note about Primary and Secondary Sources

Primary sources are first-hand forms of information; they are the raw material of the research process. Secondary sources are usually commentary, critical analyses, or explanations based on primary source material. For example, if you were researching former President Carter's role in the Mid-East peace process, Carter's writings would be a primary source. Other primary sources could include relevant government documents and some media articles. Most books, encyclopedia articles, Web pages, and scholarly journal articles interpreting Carter's role would be secondary sources. Read both primary and secondary sources when you have the opportunity.

KNOW YOUR PURPOSE FOR READING.

Ask yourself questions such as these:

- What do I need to know when I'm finished reading?
- Are there specific questions I need to answer from the information?
- What am I going to do with the information I read? For example, is it for class discussion, research for an essay, or to review for an exam?
- What information from lectures or other readings do I need to integrate with this new information?
- How soon will I be using the information?

Question: *If you don't know where you're going, how will you know what route to take or when you've arrived?*
Answer: *You won't!*

Without a purpose, you are saying that everything in the selection is of equal value and that you need to learn it all in complete detail. Although this total-mastery approach may be necessary in a few reading assignments each term, many times it just leads to frustration and information overload. Setting a personal purpose or goal for reading is how you focus your attention on specific aspects of a selection.

For Example

If your purpose for reading the second chapter of your psychology text is to prepare for a quiz over key vocabulary, you wouldn't need to read the chapter with the same emphasis on main ideas that you would need if you were preparing for a discussion group.

If, on the other hand, you were going to give an oral report on that chapter, you would read it with more attention to details than if you were preparing to listen to a lecture about it. Adjusting your reading to your purpose can make your reading more effective and efficient.

BRING OR DEVELOP THE KNOWLEDGE NEEDED TO GRASP THE SUBJECT.

Ask yourself questions such as these:

- What do I know about the topic?
- What references can I gather, such as articles or lecture notes, to help me develop basic knowledge?
- Whom can I can talk to about this topic?
- Are there differences of opinion about this topic?

Research confirms what most of us have figured out by trial and error: The more we know about the subject we're reading, the easier it is to understand.

IDENTIFY THE AUTHOR'S KNOWLEDGE AND CREDIBILITY AND THE TIMELINESS OF THE WRITING.

Ask yourself questions such as these:

- Has anything been mentioned in class or in other readings that gives me a hint about what to expect from this author?
- Is the author an expert or advocate?
- What do I know about the author's age, occupation, politics, or general beliefs?
- Does the author belong to any group that might influence his or her point of view?
- When was the selection written, and where has it been published?
- Does the author document his or her sources?
- What are the date and source of any reference material?
- Are the sources respected?

Critical readers are aware of the context as well as the content of what they read. By that I mean, you think about elements such as when the selection was written, who wrote it, and what you know about the author.

By putting their words on paper, authors allow us to hear their thoughts, their individual perspective. To fully understand the message, we must understand the messenger.

An expert is an authority, a specialist. Experts work to uncover the accuracy and exactness of a view or position. On the other hand, an advocate is a supporter or defender of a particular position or point of view. Advocates attempt to prove that their view or position is right. Experts and advocates can provide valuable information.

For Example

Before reading a selection on "current environmental policies," consider the perspective you would gain by knowing if the author was (1) an active member of the Sierra Club, a nonprofit conservation and outdoors organization dedicated to the exploration and preservation of the nation's wilderness and wildlife; (2) a logger in the Pacific Northwest who is out of work because of a ban on logging in order to preserve the spotted owl; or (3) the director of the Environmental Protection Agency (EPA), the federal agency that monitors environmental pollution and enforces environmental standards.

Knowing when a selection was written can provide additional context to help you understand the material. For example, a title such as "Living in an Electronic Age" would possibly suggest different issues if it were written in 1947, when television was just coming into homes, than if it were written in 2004, with the Internet spreading throughout the world.

Strategies for Reading Actively and Accurately

Reading furnishes the mind only with materials of knowledge;
it is thinking that makes what we read ours.
John Locke (1632–1704)

How would you contrast talking with someone and reading?

If you're like many people, one of the first differences on your list is that you have to be active and involved to take part in a conversation while reading is more passive. (That's why you don't fall asleep while talking but sometimes do while reading.) However, that difference does not exist for strategic readers who view reading as an active, thinking process that requires energy and focus.

Consider this analogy: If you were putting a bicycle together and a critical element such as the gear chain was missing, what would you do? You would undoubtedly stop and solve the problem. If you didn't, you would wind up investing hours of your time in a bike that didn't work.

Similarly, strategic readers don't wade through 20 pages of text and then say, "I missed something on page 4," or "I didn't understand what the author meant on page 10." When you run into problems such as words you don't understand or examples that don't make sense, develop the habit of stopping and solving the problem quickly.

UNDERSTAND THE AUTHOR'S LANGUAGE.

Ask yourself questions such as these:

- Do I understand the denotative and connotative meanings of the words?
- Can I replace jargon and unusual words with more common synonyms?
- Can I rephrase clichés into more meaningful language?
- Does the author use any euphemisms to soften a negative impact or harsh words to increase the negative impact of what he or she says?
- Does the author use any words and phrases that cause me to respond emotionally?
- Does the author intend this to be taken literally?

Words, even simple words such as run or hit, have many meanings. Depending on how, where, when, and why it's used, the same word can change meanings to be an active verb, a noun, or even a descriptive adjective. In addition to their dictionary definitions, words have implied definitions, connotative meanings, created by the feelings and images associated with them.

Authors select the words and phrases that best communicate their message, whether directly through the denotative meaning or indirectly through the connotative meaning.

Authors' words are the building blocks of their ideas. If you don't understand their words, you won't have a foundation for understanding their ideas.

For Example

Words take on meaning from their context: how they are used with the other words in the sentence. This is the reason it is usually best if you define unfamiliar words and phrases by using the context clues the author gives you. And the reason, even if you look a word up in the dictionary, you always need to fit the definition back into the sentence to be sure it fits the way it's being used in the sentence.

To see the impact of the connotative meanings of words, look for the meaning of "cheap" in these five sentences.

1. "Clara was wearing a gown of sequined silver. She looked cheap." E. L. Doctorow, *Loon Lake,* 1979.
2. We were very lucky to find a dress that looked beautiful and perfectly matched her shoes. The fact that it was cheap was an added bonus.
3. When our travel agent was able to find us cheap travel rates, we were able to extend our holiday an extra week.
4. Although my brother thought of himself as thrifty, I thought of him as cheap.

Explanation: Although the denotative meaning of the word "cheap" is similar in each sentence, the feelings and images associated with the word change in each sentence. The connotations of the words authors select can subtly influence your understanding of their message.

IDENTIFY THE AUTHOR'S PURPOSE FOR WRITING.

- Is the author reporting or explaining facts, events, or ideas without personal interpretation?
- Is the author painting a picture in words?
- Is the author telling a story?
- Does the author want me to believe or feel a certain way or take a particular action?

An author's purpose is his or her reason for writing. Knowing the purpose helps you understand what the author writes.

Although much of the material you read is expository—designed to report or explain facts, events, or ideas without personal interpretation—authors often have additional reasons for writing. These include description—to paint a picture in words; narration—to tell a story; persuasion/argumentation—to influence you by engaging your emotions or by presenting logical arguments to believe or feel a certain way or take a particular action.

And, just as in your own writing, authors often combine two or more purposes so they can clearly communicate their message. For example, an author can use vivid descriptions to tell a story's sequence of events or can give you facts about the consequences of inaction to persuade you to take some action.

Clarification of Terms

Used in this context, an argument is not a fight or disagreement between two people. In this context, an argument occurs when an author goes beyond just reporting or explaining information to wanting to persuade you to feel a certain way about the information or take a particular action. This type of writing is found in all forms of media from textbooks to newspapers to the Internet.

In writing, an argument consists of an author's thesis called a *conclusion* and the reasons supporting the conclusion, called *premises.* A conclusion is the main point the author wants you to accept. Reasons are the author's explanation of why we should accept the conclusion. Reasons can be any type of information from verified research data to personal testimonials.

Reading as a Process

Argumentation is not inherently bad or good. However, it does require that (1) you recognize the author's purpose is to persuade you; (2) you identify the conclusion and reasons; and (3) whether you agree with or disagree with the author's conclusion, you set aside your own views and analyze the evidence before you accept or reject the information.

IDENTIFY AND CLARIFY THE AUTHOR'S THESIS/CONCLUSION.

Ask yourself questions such as these:

- What is the topic of the entire selection?
- What does the author want me to know about the topic—the controlling idea?
- When I combine the topic and the controlling idea, what is the author's thesis/conclusion?
- Is there one sentence that directly states the idea I think is the thesis/conclusion or is it implied?
- Do the main ideas/reasons develop and support the idea I think is the thesis/conclusion?

Clarify *means to make clear, to explain. When you clarify your understanding of the thesis/conclusion, you make sure you understand the central message the author wants to deliver.*

The thesis/conclusion is the framework that holds the ideas of a multiparagraph selection such as an argumentative essay or text chapter together. It is the umbrella idea that unifies all the writer's main ideas. Although it is often stated in the opening paragraph, it can appear anywhere in the selection or it can be implied. If you don't identify the thesis/ conclusion or can't understand it, you will not fully comprehend the selection.

For Example

If 20 people in your English class decided to write a multiparagraph essay on the topic "reading," there would probably be 20 different thesis/ conclusion statements. This is because the topic is only part of an author's thesis/conclusion. The other part of the thesis/conclusion is the idea he or she wants to express about the topic. Thesis statements using the topic of reading could include ones such as: *Reading is critical for college success. How speed reading got me into trouble. Oprah's book club boosted the popularity of reading. Reading statistical tables is important in many careers. Reading transports me to far-away places. You can improve your reading comprehension.*

In the next three selections, the topic is the same: *success.* However, (1) the authors' purposes are different and (2) their controlling ideas are different.

Selection 1. Written by two college professors for their course syllabus:

Rarely can you get something for nothing. However, according to study skills expert David Ellis, students can get nothing for something—it happens when the only thing they invest in a course is their money.

We have no magic formulas, no new discoveries, no quick fixes that will assure your success. The reading and studying strategies we will present have been around, in one form or another, for a long time. Some of the strategies will work for you and some will not, but there is no way for you to know until you use them.

We can merely set the stage; you create learning through your energy and action. You control your success.

Selection 2. Written by a director of college research:

Student completion rates are one measure of student success. A review of student completion data for the 2002–03 fall and spring terms across state colleges indicates the highest course completion rates was for students in the 25–31 age group (87 percent). The lowest completion rate was found in the 18–24 age group (79 percent). Liberal arts and education majors had significantly higher completion rates across age groups (90 percent and 89 percent respectively).

Completion rates were slightly higher for females in all age groups for the fall semester (84 percent female, 82 percent male); however, the numbers reversed in the spring with more male (83 percent male, 81 percent female) completers.

Selection 3. Written by a college student:

This has been quite a week. And amazingly, surviving midterms and finally getting my car fixed weren't even the best parts. The greatest moment was my discovery: It doesn't take a million dollars, a Pulitzer Prize or fame to be a success. You see, I had always believed that there were only a few really successful people in the world. They were the ones whose faces filled magazine covers and whose words were captured in sound bites for the nightly news.

But I found out there are millions of successful people. Most of them aren't famous and they aren't rich. They don't have plaques and awards to hang on the wall. They don't have reporters calling them for their opinions.

Ah, but what they do have is better than all that; they have a sense of humanity. I know that because I met one of those really successful people this week. He was gently holding the small hand of a child. He was using his hours as a Hospice volunteer to make the child's hours less scary. He was a success. I think someday, in my own way, I will be a success.

Explanation: Although the topic is the same for all three writers, their purposes for writing and the ideas they want to communicate about success are very different. The college professors want to persuade students that success is up to them, the research director wants to report information on student completion rates as one measure of student success, and the student has a story to tell about what success means to him.

As you know, authors do not always directly state their thesis/conclusion. When the author does not directly state the thesis, you must infer it. An inference is your best reasoned conclusion based on the information you are given. Valid inferences follow logically from the information the author provides. As semanticist S. I. Hayakawa says in *Language in Thought and Action,* an inference is "a statement about the unknown made on the basis of the known."

IDENTIFY AND CLARIFY THE MAIN IDEAS/REASONS USED TO SUPPORT AND DEVELOP THE THESIS/CONCLUSION.

Ask yourself questions such as these:

- What is the topic of this paragraph?
- What is the controlling idea in this paragraph; what does he or she want me to understand about this topic?
- Is there one sentence that directly states the main idea or is it implied?
- Do the details support the idea I think is the main idea?
- Do the main ideas clearly support the thesis?

A main idea is the umbrella idea that unifies, or holds together, all the ideas and sentences of one paragraph. It is the primary thought the author wants you to understand in a paragraph. It may be directly stated or implied. If you don't identify the main idea, you will have only bits and pieces of details and examples and will not fully comprehend the paragraph.

Clarifying by Paraphrasing

Unlike the passive activities of highlighting a main idea or copying a thesis statement into your notes, paraphrasing is an active strategy to help you clarify your understanding of what the author says. It's an active strategy because it requires thought and action: You must understand what the author is saying completely enough to write it in your own words. Good paraphrasing is more than just copying the writer's sentence with a couple of synonyms inserted. In fact, your paraphrase should use a *substantially* different sentence structure and vocabulary than the original—one that is typical of your writing style.

A paraphrase is different than a summary. When you paraphrase, you include all the information in the original, whereas in a summary you include only the most important information. Paraphrase when you need a total, accurate restatement of short segments, such as a thesis or main idea, and summarize when you need the essence or gist of long segments, such as an essay.

Analyze these two paraphrases of a passage from Ellen Graham's *Wall Street Journal* article "Work May Be a Rat Race, But It's Not a Daily Grind."

Original: "Tumultuous changes have swept through American factories and offices in the past decade, and the way work gets done is being transformed. Workers are reeling, but they aren't alienated and demoralized."

Paraphrase 1: Difficult changes have swept through American work places in the past decade, and the way work gets done is being changed. Workers are disturbed, but they aren't alienated and discouraged.

Explanation: Instead of using a substantially different sentence structure and vocabulary than the original did, this writer just moved the words around and inserted some synonyms. Inappropriate paraphrases like this one are a form of plagiarism since you are using another author's structure and language pattern as your own. If you cannot make major changes in the structure and language, then use it as a direct quotation.

Paraphrase 2: American workers are adapting to and surviving the impact of the dramatic changes in the way they must now do their work.

Explanation: This is an appropriate paraphrase. The author of this paraphrase used a substantially different sentence structure and different vocabulary than the original did. Credit for the thought should be given to the original author, but it does not need to be in quotation marks.

One strategy for paraphrasing a thesis or main idea statement is to:

1. Identify the controlling thought, what the author really wants you to know or understand about the topic.
2. Restate that thought using your own words.
3. Weave your restatement into the sentence in a different order than the original.
4. Compare your paraphrase to the original to be sure the meaning is the same but that the structure and language are different.
5. Document the source as needed.

Two Useful Organizing Strategies

The dictionary says you organize something by "systematically arranging a collection of interdependent parts with relation to the whole." In other words, you introduce an overall order to things. When you organize the information you need from your reading, it becomes more accessible and understandable and helps your memory.

Annotating. Annotating is the strategy I recommend for marking important information in the text. When you annotate a selection, you write brief, useful notes in your own words in the margins. Annotating forces you to think about and clarify the author's words and ideas. You usually need to read a section more than once to annotate it accurately. How much you annotate depends on your purpose for reading.

Annotating is a useful strategy for at least three reasons: It requires you to be an active reader, it helps you monitor your comprehension, and it marks important information so you can easily return to it later.

I don't recommend using colored pens to highlight text because they make it too easy to passively mark everything that looks like it "might be important" with the promise to go back and read it later. In essence, you just postpone the reading assignment.

Example: Annotating

It is unlikely that two people would annotate an article exactly the same way. Even if they have the same general assignment, or purpose for reading, factors such as how much they know about the subject and how difficult the language is, will make the process slightly different for each person. This example does not mean you should always use just these strategies or annotate all your readings this way.

Getting Started: Read the title and subtitles and spend a couple of minutes thinking about what you believe today's employers might want from new employees. Clarify your purpose: to find out what employers want from job applicants.

WHAT DO TODAY'S EMPLOYERS WANT FROM JOB APPLICANTS?

Dr. Kenneth G. Heinemann is Director of Heald College, School of Business and Technology, San Jose, California. This selection is excerpted from his article for the T.H.E. (Technology in Higher Education) Journal.

simple answ: great job skills

The simple answer is this: employers want individuals who are *trained* in the skills of the job.

In the past, knowing the basic skill of the workplace was enough. Secretaries were expected to type. Repair people repaired. Electricians wired. But, increasingly, people with one-dimensional skills are not getting the better jobs. In fact, according to former N.Y. Governor Mario Cuomo, 61 percent of America's workers do not have the skills for today's jobs.

BUT job skills NOT enough

def: tempermental or arrogant person

This is especially true wherever technology is concerned. High-tech employers do not want prima donnas, no matter how skilled; the days of a soloist soldering a circuit board in a cubicle are long gone; and the near-genius who knows his electronics equations but can't tell others what they mean or how to apply them may have a difficult time finding employment.

Info especially for technology jobs

Do NOT want "show-off" or "hermit genius"

• job skills
• tmwk & comm skills

Need for People Skills

In the field of electronics and computer technology, the focus is on teamwork and communication. Employers still expect job applicants to understand the fundamentals of electronics, from which specific on-the-job training can follow. But almost of equal importance, employers expect the new field service technician, computer repair person or test technician to work well in groups and understand the necessity of telling co-workers about the status of projects verbally and in writing. It goes with the territory these days that the job applicant—particularly the one applying for a job in technology—knows what the job entails, and knows how to *talk* about and often *write* about the job.

• work well in groups
• comm w/cowkrs, oral, written

• know job + how to talk & write abt it

Further, the classic dividing lines between blue collar workers and white collar executives are fading fast. Today's high-tech line employees must often look as successful as the boss, project an image of professionalism by dress and language, and still be able to handle the technical requirements of his or her job.

• look (dress) &
• sound (talk) professional

"We're looking for people with good 'people skills,' " says John Tebbets, one of some 17 staffing specialists with Entex Information Services of Ryebrook, N.Y. "I can often tell within a few minutes if an applicant has what we want. Entex expects prospective employees to dress professionally. What I see is what our customers see. First impressions really count." And, "of course we expect applicants to have the job skills that are necessary," says Tebbets.

Good Grades and Attitude

Of course, good "people skills" alone can't take the place of solid electronics training proven by good grades.

• good grades
• work exp.

Kimberly Senise, a Human Resources representative with KLA Instruments, tells us that she looks first at a prospect's grade point average. "If I see a 3.5 to 3.8, then I'm definitely interested. But I'll consider a prospect with lower grades if that person has had work experience. *Any* work tells me the applicant has a measure of dedication and discipline. If the work has been in some aspect of technology, all the better."

• ability to think!

Like many employers we see, Senise wants an applicant who can think and who has thought about the job he or she is applying for. "I want to know if the prospective employee has a goal, has a sense of where he or she is going, whether that person is a 'worker bee' type or someone who aspires to become a leader."

• personal goals

What about teamwork? "Absolutely essential," says Senise. "During the interview process I'm listening carefully to see how the applicant describes school projects: is it 'I did this' or 'We did this'? Finally it's important that the applicant show some genuine enthusiasm," she says "I want to get a feeling that the person has thought about the interview, has selected KLA for good reasons, is eager to work in almost any capacity and at any time."

• be team player

• be enthusiastic

Final Words

What do employers want from today's job applicant? Everything they've wanted before . . . and a whole lot more.

Employers are more sophisticated and customers are more demanding. It's critical that the person who wants a rewarding career—especially in technology—be ready to extend him or herself, reach out beyond their basic skill or interest area, communicate effectively and work smoothly and efficiently with others.

Employers Want:
- *job skills*
- *people skills*
- *comm skills*
- *personal skills*
- *knowledge skills*

Remember, these annotations reflect my thoughts; your annotations would be similar but not the same.

Graphic Organizers. When you can't annotate in the text or if you learn better using visuals, you may want to use a graphic organizer, such as an information map or informal outline, to illustrate the important ideas you need from a selection. Creating such an organizer can help you see the relationships among ideas.

Accurately identifying the information you need such as the thesis, main ideas, and major supporting details is as critical to creating an effective graphic organizer on paper as it was to creating effective annotations in the text.

For a multiparagraph selection, start with the thesis as the central focus of your graphic. List the main ideas in a way that shows they support the thesis. Likewise, jot down the details you need in a way that demonstrates which main idea they support.

Example: Information Map

What Do Today's Employers Want from Job Applicants?
(according to Dr. Heinemann)

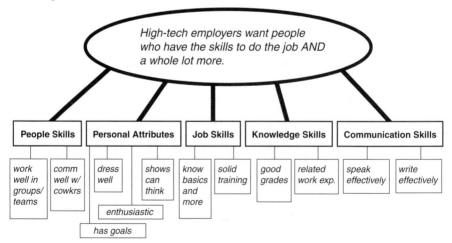

Your information map of the article would contain similar information but probably not look exactly the same.

When it's useful, let the writer's structure or method of development be a guide to creating your information map. For example, if the author has developed the thesis by giving the likenesses, the differences, or both the likenesses and differences between or among things, ideas, or people, you could use a graphic organizer with columns to easily see the comparisons and/or contrasts.

For example, in this paragraph Dr. Larry Long compares a computer system to the human body. The graphic organizer that follows it visually clarifies the likenesses.

A computer system can also be likened to the biological system of the human body. Your brain is the processing component. Your eyes and ears are input components that send signals to the brain. If you see someone approaching, your brain matches the visual image of this person with others in your memory (storage component). If the visual image matches that of a friend, your brain sends signals to your vocal cords and right arm (output components) to greet your friend with a hello and a handshake. Computer system components interact in a similar way. (Long, *Introduction to Computers and Information Processing.*)

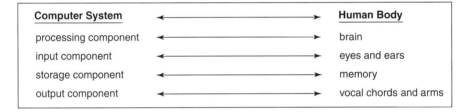

In an informal outline, you are not bound by the number and letter rules of formal outlining. An informal outline simply allows you to use differing amounts of indentation from the left margin to create a picture of the relationships among the ideas. The outline that opens this chapter is an example of an informal outline created from this chapter's headings. As you look back at it, you can quickly see which ideas are of the same level of importance and which ones—because of the amount of indentation—support and develop other ideas.

As with other types of organizers, the information you put in an informal outline of the article would be similar to this example, but not exactly the same.

Example: Informal Outline

What Do Today's Employers Want from Job Applicants?

(according to Dr. Heinemann)

High-tech employers want people who have the skills to do the job AND a whole lot more.

People Skills
    work well in groups and in teams
    communicate effectively with co-workers

Personal Attributes
    dress well
    show you can think
    be enthusiastic
    have personal work goals

Job Skills
    know basic job skills and more
    demonstrate solid training and background

Knowledge Skills
    good grades
    related work experience

Communication Skills
    speak effectively
    write effectively

UNDERSTAND THE GRAPHICS.

Ask yourself questions such as these:

- What are the topic and main idea of the graphic?
- How is the graphic organized?
- What trend(s), pattern(s), or relationship(s) does the graphic show?
- What is the source of the data?
- How does the information in the graphic compare/contrast with the text information?
- How does the graphic's information relate to my purpose for reading?

Graphics such as graphs, tables, diagrams, and cartoons are a unique fusion of images and words. I say they are a fusion because the images and words work together to communicate the information. Among the reasons authors use graphics are to clarify, simplify, emphasize, summarize, illustrate, and add details to their written material. Integrating the information from graphics with the text improves your overall comprehension.

For Example

Unlike most other graphics, an editorial cartoon is a unique form of graphic that expresses a point of view. It takes just seconds to read and understand, yet it encourages the reader to develop an opinion about someone or something in the news. It seems that the overall nature of sarcasm, satire, and parody inherent in cartoons makes the absurdities or truths more obvious than in written text.

Your strategy for understanding an editorial cartoon is a bit different than for other types of graphics:

- Determine the topic. What issue is addressed? Was there a specific event or issue that inspired the cartoon? What is the history of the topic or issue?
- Identify who is portrayed in the cartoon. Are there any real people?
- Identify any symbols used. What do the symbols represent?
- Determine which of these common components is used and why: stereotype, exaggeration, or caricature. (A caricature is a drawing that pokes fun at a well-known person by exaggerating his or her physical and facial characteristics.)
- Understand the information and impact of the caption or words in the cartoon. Is the caption in straightforward language, or does it contain features of satire, sarcasm or irony?
- Identify the cartoonist's point of view. What are the opposing or varying points of view on the issue?
- Clarify the cartoonist's purpose and intended audience. What does he or she want the reader to do or think after reading this cartoon?

Look back at the editorial cartoon by Jim Morin of *The Miami Herald* on page 5 with these questions in mind.

COMPARE AND CONTRAST YOUR KNOWLEDGE WITH THE WRITER'S IDEAS AND INFORMATION.

Ask yourself questions such as these:
- How are the writer's observations and interpretations the same as or different from those of other writers I've read?
- Which information presents new ideas for me to consider?
- How are examples in my life similar to and different from the ones the author uses? What might be a reason for the differences?
- How do the behaviors, attitudes, and ideas of people I know compare to those the author describes?

One of the best ways to guarantee being an active participant in the reading process is to connect this writer's ideas to what other authors have said and your own knowledge and experience.

Strategies for Analyzing and Evaluating the Content

"A great many people think they are thinking when they are merely rearranging their prejudices." William James

We know that writers put words on paper or screen to communicate ideas and information for a reason but that their purpose is not always straightforward and clear; sometimes it is hidden or vague. To fully understand what you read, you use of a variety of strategies to identify the writer's purpose and point of view. Then, especially when the purpose is argument, you need to analyze and evaluate the support (the reasons, sometimes called *evidence*) the author offers to persuade you to accept the conclusion.

Analyze means separating the parts—conclusion and reasons—and seeing how they fit together. Evaluate means to judge the merit of the parts and the whole.

CLARIFY THE AUTHOR'S POINT OF VIEW.

Ask yourself questions such as these:
- What is the author's tone—straightforward, emotional, humorous, ironic, sarcastic, positive, negative?
- Can I determine the author's attitude or opinion about the topic/issue?

An author's point of view is his or her fundamental attitude, position, or opinion about the topic/issue. Understanding the author's point of view gives you additional perspective on the author's message and is essential to comprehension

However, because an author doesn't often state his or her point of view, you must consider the information from all the sentences and infer the point of view.

For Example

Tone is the emotional feeling or attitude we create with our words. When you're talking with someone, you identify tone by listening to the pitch and volume of his or her voice and watching gestures and facial expressions. Using these clues, you determine whether someone is being serious, humorous, straightforward, or ironic—and knowing that helps you understand their meaning.

A writer, like a speaker, can create any emotion. Although you don't have a speaker's verbal or visual clues available when you are reading, you can understand the author's tone by watching for words and phrases that have special connotations and details the author chooses to include or to leave out.

Using these clues, along with what the author says directly and your own knowledge, will help you correctly infer the author's tone.

In some of your reading assignments you may need to narrowly define the author's tone (e.g., decide whether the tone is funny, witty, whimsical, or comical). However, most of the time you can place the tone of the writing into one of seven general groupings: straightforward, emotional, humorous, ironic, satire/sarcastic, positive, negative.

Irony. Some authors do not intend for their words to be taken literally. Sometimes, to make a point, an author says exactly the opposite of what he or she means. Such tongue-in-cheek writing is called *irony*. For example, consider this portion of a scientist's presentation to his colleagues:

The Principles of Good Writing

Write hurriedly, preferably when tired. Have no plans; write down items as they occur to you. The article will thus be spontaneous and poor. Hand in your manuscript the moment it is finished. Rereading a few days later might lead to revision—which seldom, if ever, makes the writing worse. If you submit your manuscript to colleagues (a bad practice), pay no attention to their criticisms or comments. Later, resist any editorial suggestions. Be strong and infallible; don't let anyone break down your personality. The critic may be trying to help you or he may have an ulterior motive, but the chance of his causing improvement in your writing is so great that you must be on guard.

Explanation: The scientist's title tells us that his purpose is to give information on techniques for good writing. However, when his first details (e.g., writing hurriedly, when tired, and without plans) seem to contradict what you know about good writing practices, you begin to question his real meaning. Then, in his third sentence when he actually says his advice will lead to a poor article—the opposite of his stated purpose—you know that he's being ironic.

Satire and Sarcasm. Although the terms *irony, satire,* and *sarcasm* may sound like they all describe the same kind of tone, they do not. They differ in the way they are used—what the author wants to accomplish.

Irony is simply intended to amuse or provoke thought.

Satire is intended to reform. It uses humor and ironic statements to poke fun at people and deride foolish or dishonest human behaviors or institutions. It is funny, even when it is painful. For example, political satire mocks politics and politicians in an effort to bring about public awareness or change.

Sarcasm is intended to deride, embarrass, or cause injury. Sarcasm is a much more aggressive device with a bitter, caustic quality.

Like understanding tone of voice and body language, you must understand the subtle clues of tone. If you misunderstand the tone, you are likely to misunderstand the message.

KEEP AN OPEN MIND—SET ASIDE YOUR POINT OF VIEW TO OBJECTIVELY EXAMINE WHAT THE AUTHOR SAYS.

Ask yourself questions such as these:

- Do I have opinions that agree or disagree with the writer's that might influence my understanding?
- Do my friends or family have strong feelings about this topic?
- Does my faith or religion encourage me to take a position on this topic?
- What else have I read about this topic that might influence my understanding?

To *objectively examine* means to evaluate in an impartial, unprejudiced manner—a very difficult task.

Because readers are as human as writers, you must be as aware of your assumptions and biases as you are of the writer's. You want to behave exactly opposite the old saying, "Don't confuse me with the facts; my mind's already made up." You want to evaluate information and then make up your mind.

For Example

Assumptions are personal beliefs we take for granted; *biases* are assumptions that keep us from considering the evidence fairly. Statements such as "I don't care what anybody says, I know it's not true" or "That's my opinion and nothing is going to change it" are prime examples of accepting or rejecting a conclusion based on our biases rather than evidence. A critical reader asks questions such as, "What are the author's assumptions? What are my assumptions? What evidence supports or refutes this argument? Is the evidence reliable?"

This does not mean, however, that asking questions—being open minded—means never accepting information, forming opinions or taking a position. "It's good to be open-minded," philosopher Jacob Needlerman once said, "but not so open that your brains fall out."

EXAMINE THE WRITER'S REASONS—THE FACTS, OPINIONS, AND REASONED JUDGMENTS.

Ask yourself questions such as these:

- What reasons, such as examples, statistics, or expert testimony, does the author provide to support and develop the argument?
- Does the author provide the original research or observations he or she used to form the opinion or reach the judgment?
- Are the reasons/evidence relevant to the conclusion? Is there a clear, compelling connection between the support and the thesis?
- Are the reasons consistent—does each piece work together to develop and support the conclusion?
- Are the reasons/evidence reliable—does each piece appear to be trustworthy and accurate?
- Are the reasons/evidence current?

A fact is an objective statement that can be proved true or false. It can be objectively verified through observation or experimentation; the interpretation doesn't change because of the view of the interpreter. However, it is wise to remember that knowledge is an ongoing process; facts are not frozen for all time.

An opinion can be very well thought out, but it cannot be verified. It is a subjective statement that cannot be proved true or false; the information can change depending on where you look or whom you ask.

Reasoned judgments are my label for thoughtful opinions. They are logical, coherent conclusions that informed individuals make from the available evidence.

Articles, essays, and even texts rarely use only facts, and most of the time we're grateful because it is the writer's insight, wisdom, and conclusions that we want. The difficult task is to differentiate among the facts, opinions, and reasoned judgments and weigh the merits of each.

For Example

As you examine the specific reasons/evidence that writers use to support their position, you want to determine if each is:

1. relevant—does it have a clear supportive connection to the thesis?
2. reliable—does it appear to be trustworthy and accurate?
3. consistent—does each piece work together to develop and support the thesis?

Then you must consider whether there is an adequate amount of relevant, reliable, consistent reasons/evidence to support the author's thesis/conclusion.

The following two selections provide examples of how writers use reasons/evidence to support their ideas. Although the writers use different language and writing styles, it is important to focus on the different kinds of reasons each author uses to support a conclusion.

Selection 1. *Reader Beware: The Need for an Internet Site Rating System* by Marty Mannor, freshman composition student:

> Unlike ideas and information you get out of books, magazines and journals in the library, you can't depend on material you download from Internet sites to be very good support for academic research papers. That's why I believe there should be an accuracy-ratings system for Internet sites.
>
> If there was a quality rating procedure, people would have a way to know the accuracy of the information being presented. For example, the first time I used the Internet I found two great sites with a lot of information for my psychology research paper, but when I used them I received a poor grade. Although my teacher said the problem was a "lack of relevant information," I know a rating system would have helped me to know not to use the Internet information. However, during another search I did find an excellent site for information about different brands of guitars and I know it is accurate.
>
> In addition, a rating system like the one used on television or in the movies would help parents know whether their children should be accessing it. Right now there is no way for anyone to know what is on a site until it comes up on the screen. If there was a rating system, that could come up first and users would know what kind of information they would get if they logged on to the site. . . .

Selection 2. *Testing the Surf: Criteria for Evaluating Internet Information Resources* by Alistair G. Smith of the School of Communications and Information Management, Victoria University, Wellington, New Zealand. Excerpted from "Testing the Surf: Criteria for Evaluating Internet Information Resources," *The Public-Access Computer Systems Review* no. (3): 8. (refereed article): 1998

> Users of the Internet were initially impressed that they found useful information of any kind. However, now that anyone with access to a server and a passing knowledge of HTML (Hypertext Markup Language) can put information on the Internet, the problem has become one of sifting through a mass of advertising material and vanity publications in order to find information of high quality. Matthew Ciolek expressed a concern that the WWW (World Wide Web) may become the MMM (Multi-Media Mediocrity).[1]
>
> For librarians and library users to make effective use of the Internet, they need criteria to use in evaluating the information found. As has been

noted by James Rettig, many Internet sites that select and review Internet information resources rely on subjective values of style and "coolness," instead of focusing on information content. . . .[2]

There exists a significant literature on the evaluation of print reference sources. Katz devotes a section of his influential textbook on reference work to "Evaluating Reference Sources," and lists as criteria purpose, authority, scope, audience, cost, and format.[3] Criteria for evaluating "traditional" material also appear on the Internet, as shown in guidelines published by Cornell University Library.[4]

Criteria for print materials can in most cases be applied to the Internet domain, but evaluation criteria may be more critical in the "vanity publishing" environment of the Internet. Print publishing involves a series of editorial checks that tends to reduce the appearance of low-quality information. On the Internet, these checks exist to a lesser degree. . . .

Notes

1. T. Matthew Ciolek, "Today's WWW—Tomorrow's MMM? The Specter of Multi-Media Mediocrity," *Computer* 29 (January 1996): 106–108.

2. James Rettig, "Beyond 'Cool': Analog Models for Reviewing Digital Resources," *Online* 20 (September 1996): 52–54, 56, 58–62, 64.

3. William A. Katz, *Introduction to Reference Work* (New York: McGraw-Hill, 1992).

4. Joan Ormondroyd, Michael Engle, and Tony Cosgrave, *How to Critically Analyze Information*

Sources: (Ithaca, NY: Cornell University Library, 20 January 1995).

Explanation 1: Mannor's conclusion appears to be "I believe there should be an accuracy-ratings system for Internet sites." As support, he offers the example of how he used information from two sites in a research paper and received a poor grade. However, he doesn't explain the implied cause-effect relationship. The guitar reference is unclear and probably irrelevant. He then leaves the accuracy issue and discusses type of content and in a later portion, not reprinted, discusses the need for a system to rate the use of graphics, sound, and animation. In this short excerpt, although the conclusion is valid and the examples are current, not all of his evidence is relevant and consistent. Its reliability may be questionable since it developed solely on the basis of getting a poor grade. In addition, there is a difference between the "relevance" of information and the "quality" of information that ratings would address.

Explanation 2: Smith provides examples, expert testimony, and reasoned judgments to support and develop his thesis that Internet users "need criteria to use for evaluating information." In this short excerpt, his evidence appears to be relevant, reliable, consistent, and adequate.

The more relevant, reliable, consistent, and adequate the reasons/evidence, the stronger the conclusion and thus the more convincing the argument.

What Does It Mean to Be "Logical"?

When we tell someone to "be logical—don't jump to conclusions," we are asking him or her to use a process of reasoning from evidence rather than making snap judgments or responding from emotion. Common labels for this process include terms such as *infer, deduce, surmise, conclude, gather,* and *generalize.* All these words imply arriving at a sensible, rational, reliable inference at the end of a chain of reasoning, reaching a statement about what isn't known or hasn't happened on the basis of what is known or has happened. In formal logic, each term has a distinct meaning, but in everyday language we often use these terms interchangeably.

Reliable inferences provide important support for arguments. Unreliable inferences, those with errors in reasoning, are called *fallacies* and are of little use.

In this excerpt from *Zen and the Art of Motorcycle Maintenance: An Inquiry into Values,* (New York: Quill William Morrow, 1974), p. 107. Robert Pirsig describes the reasoning processes we use to make inferences.

> . . . Two kinds of logic are used, inductive and deductive. Inductive inferences start with observations of the machine and arrive at general conclusions. For example, if the [motor]cycle goes over a bump and the engine misfires, and then goes over another bump and the engine misfires, and then goes over another bump and the engine misfires, and then goes over a long smooth stretch of road and there is no misfiring, and then goes over a fourth bump and the engine misfires again, one can logically conclude

that the misfiring is caused by the bumps. That is induction: reasoning from particular experiences to general truths.

"Deductive inferences do the reverse. They start with general knowledge and predict a specific observation. For example, if, from reading the facts about the machine, the mechanic knows the horn of the cycle is powered exclusively by electricity from the battery, then he can logically infer that if the battery is dead the horn will not work. That is deduction. Solution of problems . . . is achieved by long strings of mixed inductive and deductive inferences. . . .

We use those two processes to draw many conclusions or to make many inferences every day. For example, your co-worker has clocked in 30 minutes late four of the last seven days. The supervisor has yelled at her each time. Today you see her coming in 33 minutes late. You can logically conclude that the supervisor will yell at her. It hasn't happened yet, but based on what has happened in the past, it will likely happen. In addition, because she is an hourly worker and her pay is automatically calculated in 15-minute increments from time clock records, you can logically infer that her pay will be docked.

We also misuse those thinking processes and make unreliable inferences like Marty Mannor did in the excerpt from his *Reader Beware: The Need for an Internet Site Rating System* essay. His lines of reasoning seemed to be (1) I used the Internet and found two great sites with a lot of information for my psychology research paper, (2) I used them and I received a poor grade, (3) therefore, there should be an accuracy rating system for Internet sites. He didn't seem to consider other factors that could have caused the low grade, and he discounted his teacher's "lack of relevant information" comment, apparently not recognizing the difference between "accurate" and "relevant". In this case, it seems unlikely that "an accuracy rating system" would have helped him know whether or not to use the Internet information, since problems with accuracy and relevance call for different solutions.

It is crucial that the author *and* reader make reliable inferences.

Strategies for Reflecting on and Connecting What You Have Read

"There are two ways to slice easily through life: to believe everything or to doubt everything. Both ways save us from thinking."
Alfred Korzybski, Polish-American linguist (1879–1950)

I believe education is a process in which we learn to open our minds. It's where we gather, understand, analyze, and evaluate ideas from many people and places to help us develop informed opinions. To paraphrase Alan Kay, Distinguished Fellow at Apple Computer, understanding is not a state of being or destination you always arrive at, but a manner of traveling where the journey is the reward.

For Example

Read these two editorials on "the value of phased-in licensing programs for teen drivers" from *USA Today* September 29, 1997. Compare and contrast the author's ideas and points of view.

PHASED-IN LICENSES MAKE DRIVING SAFER FOR TEENS

USA Today editorial staff.

1   When it comes to worrying about the safety of their teen-agers, studies show that parents fear drug addiction the most. Only one in five realizes that driving is the No. 1 teen killer.

2   Such ignorance about the dangers of teen driving is deadly as more baby boomers turn over the car keys to their driving-age kids. More than 6,300 teens ages 15 to 20 died in crashes last year. Without changes, teen driving deaths are expected to jump to 7,500 by 2012.

3   Studies show the majority of teen crashes are caused by a lack of experience. Because it takes up to three years of practice to become a skilled driver, several states are embracing a sensible solution: phasing in teen driving privileges.

4   This step-by-step approach to driver training, known as graduated licensing, recognizes that inexperienced teen drivers are going to make mistakes. Crash rates for 16-year-olds are three times as high as for 19-year-olds, according to the AAA.

5   So instead of granting full driving privileges to any teen who passes a quickie driving course and a road test, the programs gradually increase teens' driving rights as they become more skilled.

6   Ten states have enacted limited forms of graduated licensing, including bans on night driving and required practice time with adults. But the Insurance

Institute for Highway Safety says that to reduce deaths, the laws should include a package of restrictions for drivers under 18, including:

- A prohibition on recreational night driving—since 42% of teen driving deaths occur between 9 p.m. and 6 a.m.   *7*
- Zero tolerance for alcohol use—because it is illegal for teens to drink.   *8*
- Restrictions on chauffeuring other teens unless an adult is along—since 66% of teens killed in crashes are riders.   *9*
- Required practice with adults—found to improve teens' driving skills.   *10*

One year after Ontario passed a similar, graduated licensing law for all   *11* new drivers in 1994, government studies showed a 66% drop in 16-year-olds' accident rates.

The AAA has launched a nationwide effort to pass comprehensive gradu-   *12* ated license laws in every state. And a "model" law awaits the governor's signature in California, the first to require a six-month wait before a young driver can carry teen passengers unless an adult is on board.

These laws won't stop young drivers from making dumb mistakes. Only   *13* age and experience can do that.

But by requiring teens to hone their skills under adult supervision, in the   *14* light of day, there's a better chance they'll be around to learn from their errors.

TRAIN, DON'T TINKER

Todd Franklin

Mr. Franklin, Communications Director of the National Motorists Association. According to its Web site, the NMA was "founded in 1982 and advocates, represents, and protects the interests of North American motorists." One of NMA's five major objectives is "to support improved driver training and education."

Spend a few minutes on the road and you'll realize that the driver educa-   *1* tion system in this country needs repair. Many drivers lack basic knowledge of driving courtesy, safe driving practices and crash-avoidance techniques.

The amount of training most teens receive before they drive is not suffi-   *2* cient considering the dense and intense driving environment many of them will face. Most teens think "driver's ed" is a joke.

In some respects, they're right. Teaching young drivers when to use turn   *3* signals and how to parallel park is simply not enough.

Now there is a growing clamor for graduated driver-licensing programs. The   *4* concept is to gradually phase in driving privileges for new licensees as they "demonstrate growth in driving skills and responsible operation of motor vehicles." The misguided premise for graduated licensing is that time is a substitute for training.

Studies in California and Maryland have credited such programs with re-   *5* ducing teen accidents by 5%, which means they would reduce teen accident involvement from 20% to 19% nationally. This minuscule reduction in accidents is due to the fact that teen drivers are logging fewer miles because of the graduated licensing restrictions. It's quite likely that the barely detectable reduction in accident involvement will simply be transferred in the form of increased accidents to the next-higher age group.

Reading as a Process   **33**

We're glad to see a growing interest in reducing accidents involving 6 teenagers, but the focus should be on improving driver programs. Let's teach young people such things as driver etiquette, handling a car under adverse conditions and avoidance techniques.

Graduated licensing programs will waste millions of dollars, complicate 7 the lives of millions of families and provide new excuses for traffic tickets and insurance surcharges. The programs will serve the insurance industry, federal agencies and "safety" groups by lowering the exposure of these higher-risk drivers. However, these programs will do nothing to improve young drivers' skills and will have no meaningful effect on highway safety.

Explanation: The editorial writer and Franklin agree that the rate of teen driving accidents is a significant problem, the amount and type of training most teens receive before they drive isn't sufficient, and changes are needed. It would also appear they agree that the majority of teen crashes are caused by a lack of experience.

They disagree on the solution(s) to the problem. The editorial writer proposes that practice under adult supervision, aging, and experience are the keys to reducing teen accidents. The writer suggests that graduated licensing programs work because they require practice with adults and gradually increase teens' driving rights over three years as they become more skilled. For support, the writer points to results of a government study in Ontario in which one year after a similar graduated licensing law was passed there was a 66% drop in 16-year-olds' accident rates.

Franklin believes that the premise "time is a substitute for training" is misguided and argues that the key to teens' safety is improved driver training

---

DRAW LOGICAL INFERENCES TO REACH A REASONED JUDGMENT.

Ask yourself questions such as these:

- Do my conclusions or inferences follow from the evidence and information?
- Do my conclusions or inferences make sense based on the writer's evidence and information?
- Can I outline the sequence of reasoning I used to reach my judgment? Is it logical?
- What other assumptions underlie my judgment?
- Do I have sufficient evidence to support my judgment?

You want writers to provide relevant evidence and reasoned judgments to support their argument. In the same way, you want to be certain the inferences you draw from the evidence are sensible and reasonable. This helps ensure that your conclusions are objective.

---

programs. He says that the tiny reduction of teen accidents reported in studies of graduated licensing programs is actually due to the fact that teens are driving fewer miles because of the programs' restrictions. In addition, he believes it's quite likely that such programs will just increase the accident rate for the next-higher age group.

After reading these two points of view, you could seek additional information to clarify and expand your knowledge until you felt you had sufficient evidence to reach your own reasoned conclusion about the value of phased-in licensing programs.

SUSPEND JUDGMENT WHEN THERE IS NOT ENOUGH INFORMATION AND SEEK ADDITIONAL INFORMATION.

Ask yourself questions such as these:

- Have I read several points of view on this issue?
- Do I understand all the points of view equally well?
- Am I missing critical evidence or information?
- Are there additional sources of information available to me?
- Do I have enough evidence to reach a reasoned judgment?

In 1859, John Stuart Mill, an English author and philosopher, advised "all who study any subject in order to arrive at the truth" that: "He who knows only his own side of the case, knows little of that. His reasons may be good, and no one may have been able to refute (disprove) them. But if he is equally unable to refute the reasons on the opposite side, if he does not so much as know what they are, he has no ground for preferring either opinion. The rational position for him would be suspension of judgment. . . ."

For Example

Most of the time you must search out diverse viewpoints. Sometimes, however, you can find newspaper and magazine editorial and op-ed pages that provide differing points of view. As an example, read these two editorials from THE COSTCO CONNECTION July 2002 on whether cities should use cameras at intersections to catch people who commit red-light violations.

As you read, consider the context and the content. Compare and contrast the facts, opinions and reasoned judgments the writers use to develop and support their thesis/conclusion.

NO: CITIES SHOULD NOT USE CAMERAS TO CATCH RED-LIGHT RUNNERS

Barry Steinhardt is Associate Director of the American Civil Liberties Union in Washington, D.C.

Many American cities are installing camera systems that photograph vehicles allegedly running red lights or stop signs and then use the license plate to look up the owner's address and mail him or her a ticket. The use of these sys-   *1* tems should be halted or delayed until the concerns they raise have been settled. Traffic cameras raise two fundamental issues that affect the right to due process. First, the tickets are sent to the car's owner, who was not necessarily the person committing the alleged violation. The burden of proof usually then falls on the owner to prove he or she was not driving. This is a violation of the bedrock American principle that the accused be considered innocent until proven guilty.

Second, many red-light camera systems have been installed under contracts that deliver a cut of ticket revenue to the contractor. The obvious incentive for contractors to "game" the system to increase revenue generates public cynicism and suspicion. Such bounty contracts make a mockery of the ideal of disinterested justice and undermine the pursuit of traffic safety.

Legitimate questions have been raised about the choice of intersections where these cameras have been installed and about the timing of the yellow lights at those intersections. Are cameras strategically placed to increase traffic safety or maximize ticket revenue? These concerns were underscored by a recent decision of the San Diego court holding that the evidence from the cameras there was unreliable.

These cameras also raise privacy issues. Will the data collected by these cameras be used for purposes other than tracking reckless drivers? Government and private industry surveillance techniques created for one purpose are rarely restricted to that purpose. Every expansion of data and every new use for the data opens the door to more privacy abuses. For example, cameras installed at the Texas-Oklahoma border have been used to capture the license-plate numbers of thousands of law-abiding persons who were subjected to inquiries about why they were crossing the border.

If red-light camera programs are to succeed, the public must be confident that such systems operate with unimpeachable fairness and that the information collected is used only for the authorized purpose indicated and is not sold, shared or otherwise abused.

YES: CITIES SHOULD USE CAMERAS TO CATCH RED-LIGHT RUNNERS

Brian O'Neill is President of the Insurance Institute for Highway Safety based in Arlington, Virginia.

As the familiar phrase goes, the bottom line is what matters, and in auto safety the bottom line is reducing deaths and injuries. High among dangerous driving practices that lead to deaths and injuries on U.S. roads is red-light running, which causes about 200,000 crashes and 850 deaths annually.

Red-light violations are not isolated events. A study of five busy intersections in the Washington, D.C., area found more than three violations an hour on average before camera enforcement began. That adds up to more than 70 chances a day for someone to become a crash victim.

Red-light cameras photograph the license plates of vehicles that enter intersections after signals have turned red. Pertinent information—including how long after the signal changed the violation occurred and the speed of the vehicle, also are recorded. After a review for accuracy, a ticket is sent to the vehicle owner.

One main argument against these cameras is that they invade motorists' 4
privacy. Driving, however, is a regulated activity on public roads. Cameras have
been used without objection to deter theft at banks and ATMs. Why should anyone be concerned about the alleged invasion of privacy of motorists who deliberately run red lights? After all, they kill more people every year—about 400
innocent motorists and pedestrians—than bank robbers.

Red-light cameras deter crime and they are effective. Studies in Oxnard, 5
California, and Fairfax City, Virginia, found a 40 percent drop in violations the
first year, with driver compliance spilling over to intersections without cameras.
Injury crashes at intersections with cameras dropped 29 percent in Oxnard.
Front-into-side collisions were reduced 32 percent, and those involving injuries
were reduced 68 percent.

Some critics have made the ridiculous claim that yellow lights have been 6
shortened to accommodate camera enforcement, causing motorists to run red
lights inadvertently. Do people really believe that traffic engineers around the
country are engaged in a conspiracy to deliberately make intersections more
dangerous by mistiming yellow lights?

Red-light cameras are making intersections safer. They are preventing 7
crashes and saving lives. And they are doing so without impinging on the privacy
of anyone who abides by traffic laws.

Explanation: A critic of using cameras to catch red-light runners, Mr.
Steinhardt says the approach raises legal questions about due process and privacy and that camera-system manufacturers may be reaping profits from the
tickets. Mr. O'Neill, a proponent, says that camera enforcement has successfully deterred red-light runners and drastically reduced accidents.

Have these authors provided enough information for you to reach a reasoned judgment about whether cameras should be used to catch red-light runners, or do you need to seek additional information?

USE THE IDEAS AND INFORMATION.

Ask yourself questions such as these:

- How do the new ideas and information fit with what I already know?
- How are these ideas similar to and
  different from my past beliefs?
- What meaning do these ideas have
  for me?
- How do these ideas impact issues in
  my life?
- How can I use this information?

*The worth of any reading, whether
you accept what the author said, reject
it, or suspend judgment and seek additional information, is the way it increases your knowledge. You think
about each idea—how it is similar to
old ideas and how it is different. You
connect it to issues and events in your
life; you use it. And, when you gather
new evidence and updated information,
you use the opportunity to review, rethink, and grow.*

A FINAL THOUGHT

Reading and thinking critically are not easy. As Richard Paul, Director of Research of the Center for Critical Thinking at Sonoma State University reminds us:

> . . . humans are not simply the only logical animals, they are also the only illogical ones. They are the only animals that use meanings—ideas, concepts, analogies, metaphors, models, theories, and explanations—to make sense of things and to understand, predict, and control things. They are also the only animals that use meanings to negate, contradict, and deceive themselves, to misconceive, distort, and stereotype, and to be dogmatic, prejudiced, and narrow-minded. Humans are the only animals whose thinking can be characterized as clear, precise, accurate, relevant, consistent, profound, and fair; they are also the only animals whose thinking is often imprecise, vague, inaccurate, irrelevant, superficial, trivial, and biased.
>
> Humans should not simply trust their instinct. They should not unquestioningly believe what spontaneously occurs to them. They should not accept as true everything that is taught as true. They should not assume that their experience is unbiased. They need to formulate, since they are not born with, intellectually sound standards for belief, truth, and validity. They need to cultivate habits and traits that integrate these standards into their lives. . . . Richard Paul, "Critical Thinking: What, Why, and How," New Directions for Community Colleges 77 (San Francisco: Jossey-Bass, 1992), p. 3.

Although cultivating the habits and traits of critical reading and thinking are difficult processes, they are worth the effort. For example, students who read and think critically become more engaged in the learning process, cope with new information and situations more easily, and have greater academic success. In the workplace and in society, adults who listen, read, and think critically are better able to take control of their lives, make worthwhile contributions at work and home, and positively influence their community.

The readings collected in this text's thematic units provide practice material to assist you in developing the strategies and habits needed to become a critical reader. The different styles, passions, backgrounds, and motives of the writers will, as Calvin said at the beginning of this chapter, give you a lot to think about and, perhaps, seem to complicate your life.

As Stephen Brookfield, Distinguished Professor, Graduate School of Education, University of St. Thomas says, however, "Thinking critically—reflecting on the assumptions underlying our and others' ideas and actions, and contemplating alternative ways of thinking and living—is one of the important ways in which we become adults. When we think critically, we come to our judgments, choices, and decisions for ourselves, instead of letting others do this on our behalf. We refuse to relinquish the responsibility for making the choices that determine our individual and collective futures to those who presume to know what is in our own best interests."

USING THE STRATEGIES: AN EXAMPLE
WITH ANNOTATIONS

Reading critically is not just a theoretical concept that educators, writers, and business executives promote but never really expect anyone to use. Actively seeking, understanding, and analyzing divergent points of view is a practical process adaptable to a variety of situations.

The following example is a result of my initial research for this textbook. Because my files contained articles on only the positive aspects of teaching critical reading and thinking skills, I ran a specific literature search to find writers with different points of view.

The search located "On the Limits of Critical Thinking," by Michael S. Roth, in the January–February 1996 issue of *Tikkun,* a scholarly journal that critiques politics, culture, and society. Dr. Roth revised that article for this text.

A Glimpse into My Reading Process

Before I Began Reading

I read the title and biography of Dr. Roth. I read the "Abstract," read the title again, and thought about what some of the "limits" of teaching critical reading and thinking might be and how it could "give students a reason not to learn."

I clarified my purpose: Find out (1) what Roth sees as limitations, (2) what he offers as ways to minimize the limitations, and (3) how I can use the information in my teaching and writing.

ON THE LIMITS OF CRITICAL THINKING

Michael S. Roth

Dr. Roth: scholar, historian, educator, writer

Formerly Director of European Studies at the Claremont Graduate School, Dr. Roth is now President of California College of Arts and Crafts. His publications include The Ironist's Cage: Memory, Trauma, and the Construction of History; Looking for Los Angeles: Architecture, Film, Photography; *and* Disturbing Remains: Memory, History, and Crisis in the Twentieth Century Urban Landscape *with Charles G. Salas.*

Abstract: Most young scholars have a tendency to criticize what is brought before them. Although this has its positive aspects, it could also give students a reason not to learn.

? Can crit thnkg emphasis discourage learning?

Working with graduate students in the humanities, I have noticed a trait common to young scholars in a variety of fields: They are really good at being critical. For many students today, being smart *means* being critical. To find the philosopher Emmanuel Kant's errors, to see the fashionable culture critic Gyatri Spivak's blind spots, or to pinpoint a young professor's failure to account for his own "politics of identity" is in our academic culture a mark of sophistication, a sign of one's capacity to participate in academic life as a full member of the tribe. While this is a common observation of many critics of university life, I find myself wondering both how this skill has developed out of our traditions, and how it has been absorbed into our culture. How have we come to prize this capacity for critical rejection?

Students think being smart = being critical

? how/why developed attitude finding fault is good?

This is not just an academic question. Many professionals think they have escaped academic culture when they leave the university to pursue careers in journalism, politics, law, or business. They can look back on their college or graduate school years with nostalgia, or, as is more often the case, with irony and condescension. But when we consider what they have taken with them, the capacity and taste for criticism looms large.

attitude continues after college

I do not want to minimize the importance of |analytical skill.| After all, we want to be able to see through shoddy arguments and to avoid being hoodwinked by deceptive rhetoric. |Critical skill| allows us to see that what looks like a coherent or compelling presentation might actually be an exercise in ideology, or the manipulation of the reader by emotion or prejudice. As students learn to unmask these practices, one hopes that they are better able to avoid using them in their own work: that

Crit skills ARE needed to:
• see through poor argument
• avoid being misled

AND
• think & write with more objectivity

def: mental sharpness to examine info objectively

def: stringent, accurate experiments/ observations

Q: When we reinforce smart = critical, do students become TOO good at finding fault?

they are better able to protect their own thinking from influences which are not based on rigorous empirical research or on reasonable theoretical speculation.

I fear, however, that as the goal of education has become the creation of a class of professional unmaskers, we have seriously limited our ability to make sense of the world. In overdeveloping the capacity to show how books fail to accomplish what they set out to do, we may be depriving students of the capacity to learn as much as possible from what they read. In an academic culture in which being smart often means being a critical unmasker, our students may become too good at showing how things don't make sense. That very skill may diminish their capacity to find or create sense, meaning, and direction in the books they read and the world in which they live. Once outside the university, our students continue to make points by displaying the critical techniques for which they were rewarded in school. They wind up contributing to a cultural climate that has little tolerance for finding or making meaning, whose intellectuals and pundits delight in ever more sophisticated unmaskings of somebody else's attempt at meaningful expression.

I am not here joining the chorus of right-wing commentators who bemoan the latest crisis in the humanities, often associating any departure from great old books as a nihilistic impoverishment of the nation's soul. Nor am I accusing deconstruction, postmodernism, or some other newfangled approach to texts of failing to give our students the virtues that would make them effective competitors in the marketplace. Instead, I am asking that we recognize that some of the most powerful traditions in modern humanist pedagogy have fed into the contemporary stress on unmasking, resulting in criticism that aims only at de-meaning. Right-wing attacks on the so-called "radicalism" or "anti-humanism" of professors, and on the general insignificance of the liberal arts in our country are themselves the latest expression of this concentration on de-meaning. Both within and outside the university, the critical thinking of which the liberal arts have been so proud has become a powerful defense against learning from the past, making meaning in the present, and imagining a livable future.

The problem of unmasking as a denial of meaning has been discussed since the modern version of critical thinking itself was formulated in the Enlightenment. The French eighteenth-century philosopher, Jean-Jacques Rousseau already posed these issues about the dangers of Enlightenment's powers of demystification, even as he participated in the movement's radical criticism of the politics and culture of his time. Rousseau worried that the attempt to unmask the follies of common belief would leave people with nothing at all in which to believe; that the pulling apart and examination of

HOWEVER

Does OVER-emphasis on crit skills:

• result in less ability to understand world?

• keep students frm lrng all they can?

• lessen ability to find/create meaning in bks & world?

• encourage creating world that finds fault everywhere w/everything?

NOT saying teaching other than classics will destroy America's soul

NOT saying new tchng approaches/ materials fail to prepare students

Q: Do I think too much emphasis on crit skills teaches students to criticize only to degrade/ humble?

def: The Age of Enlightenment: term describes major 18th cent. philosophical period. More than a set of fixed ideas, the E. was an attitude, a method of thought; a desire to reexamine/question all ideas/values

NOT being a "radical," but must consider possibility that some age-old tchng methods contribute to/reinforce undesirable student behavior:

• asking Qs just to hurt or humble rather than to clarify or enlighten

? Have we turned crit thnkg into justification to ignore past, stumble through present, view future as hopeless?

Scholars have ALWAYS discussed human pblms that occur if crit thnkg results only in finding fault morality, politics, and religion would leave people with only a lonely cynicism with which to confront the world.

In a workshop for dissertation writers in the humanities titled "The Modern and the Post-Modern," I began with Rousseau's questioning of the Enlightenment's unmasking powers. The students were at first very surprised to be starting with Rousseau rather than with the contemporary master of deconstruction, Paul de Man on Rousseau. They imagined that the earlier writer did not have access to the critical tools with which their own graduate education had been blessed. But they attacked the text with the tools they had been honing in school, and soon they were ready to uncover the philosopher's reliance on ideas that were no longer deemed respectable. In other words, they wanted to find in Rousseau the failure to write in the carefully guarded ways that their professors had apparently taught them was the professional norm.

Example: Roth's students anxious to prove they were smart = they were good at being critical (could unmask an unmasker)

The most obvious questions were in some ways the most difficult: Why had Rousseau written that way? Why not assume he could have asked himself questions at least as difficult as we were asking? What was he trying to teach his readers in writing as he did? My students were surprised; some of them seemed to think that I had asked them to take their shots at a moving target. But instead I had asked them to re-position themselves as readers: to turn themselves so that they could learn most from what they were reading. This request was in tension with the conventional practice of critical thinking that they had been taught in the good old Enlightenment tradition. After all, the typical practice which one can see in almost every question session following a public lecture at any university was to put themselves in a position to ask tough questions, to show a critical superiority to whatever it was they were examining.

Roth's goal— learn as much as possible from author— seemed to conflict with what students assumed goal was—to show they could question/criticize author

In training our students in the techniques of critical thinking, we may be giving them reasons not to learn rather than techniques for learning. The confident capacity to refuse to learn from those with whom we disagree seems to have infected much of our cultural life: from politics to the press, from ghettoized multi-culturalists to elitist believers in Grand Universals. But as teachers, we must find ways for our students to open themselves to the emotional and intellectual power of history and literature, since critical thinking is sterile without the capacity for empathy and comprehension.

Q: Does way we tch crit thnkg skills encourage students to think they "know it all" rather than value new/ different ideas?

One of the crucial tasks of higher education should be to help our students cultivate the willingness and ability to learn from material they might otherwise reject or ignore. Creating an academic culture that values the desire to learn from unexpected sources as much as it values the critical faculties to detect something illogical would be a crucial contribution to democratic life more generally.

Roth believes I must help students find ways to appreciate, understand, and learn from the past and everything they read!

Must tch how to be critical thinkers BUT outcome must be that rdg and thnkg help us make meaning of/in world we live in, not isolate us from it.

Reading as a Process

True critical thinkers question their own thinking!

We should not pass over critical thinking in favor of some form of humanities appreciation, feel-good mode of learning. But if education is to help us make meaning and find direction in the world and not just to detach us from it, we must be not only critical thinkers but capable of questioning the limits of critical thinking.

---

possible limits of crit thnkg:

- *discourage students from learning all they can*
- *make students think being smart = being critical*
- *diminish ability to understand world*
- *lessen ability to find/create meaning in books & world*
- *encourages finding fault everywhere*

to minimize limits:

Very impt. to teach how to be critical thinkers. BUT, must reinforce that purpose of crit thnkng/rdg is to help us make meaning and understand, not find fault.

As I Read

I first read the essay straight through, stopping only to put a small check next to terms I needed to clarify: *analytical skill, critical skill, rigorous empirical research, the Enlightenment.* I looked up the definitions and made those annotations.

During the second reading, as I made my text annotations, I looked for a clear connection between his facts, opinions, and reasoned judgments and his thesis. Next, I read through my annotations, rereading paragraphs and editing annotations as necessary, to make my notations accurately reflect Roth's text.

After I Read the Essay

The next day I read the essay and my annotations again. I concluded that Roth's reasoning did follow a logical path from his experiences to his thesis. Finally, I made the two summary annotations at the end to answer the "Read to Find" I had set as my purpose.

On the basis of the information I have at this time, I concluded we do create limitations/ problems when we overemphasize critical thinking and critical reading. By *overemphasis* I mean when we teach critical skills for the purpose of finding fault. In addition, I agree with Roth that the primary reason for me to teach critical reading is to help students find ways to appreciate, understand, and learn from the past and everything they read. I've used that reasoning as one of the foundations of this text.

CHAPTER REVIEW QUESTIONS

1. Describe what it means to be a critical reader. Include specific characteristics or behaviors that you believe a critical reader must have.

2. McGrath says it is dangerous to passively accept any information as accurate and reliable and recommends that readers exercise extra caution when reading information on the Internet. Explain why you agree or disagree with her cautions.

3. McGrath believes reading is a process. Explain why you agree or disagree with her view.

4. List the four categories McGrath uses to organize the reading strategies she presents. For each category, describe (a) one strategy you currently use and give an example of how you have used it and (b) one strategy that is new or different and an example of how you can use it.

REFLECT AND CONNECT

1. Think back to the scenario that opened the chapter: The morning newspaper describes a "horrible new battle in the jungles of Central America between hired guerrilla rebels and defending army personnel." The afternoon paper describes the same battle as an "on-going conflict between local freedom fighters and military militia." Tonight's television report describes the event as "yet another skirmish between warring drug factions." Discuss how you could find out which description is most unbiased. Also discuss why you should find out. Then extend your answer beyond this example to something important to you.

2. Think about an expensive item you would like to buy in the next year such as a car or a computer. To help you decide what model and brand to buy and where to buy it, describe (a) how much and what kind of information would you want to gather, (b) what resources you would use to gather the information, and (c) whether you would use an information source, such as a manufacturer's web site, that you knew would try to influence your decision.

INVESTIGATING WEB RESOURCES

One way to investigate a variety of points of view is through the resources of Research Navigator™. Once you log on to Research Navigator.com and enter your personal passcode (inside the front cover of this text), you have access to three databases of credible and reliable source material:

1. EBSCO's Content Select Academic Journal Database, organized by subject, contains leading academic journals. You can search the online journals by keyword, topic, or multiple topics. Articles include abstract and citation information.

2. *The New York Times* Search by Subject_ Archive, organized by academic subject and searchable by keyword, or multiple keywords, gives you access to full-text articles from *The New York Times.*

3. Link Library, organized by subject, offers editorially selected "best of the web" sites. Link Libraries are continually scanned and kept up to date to provide relevant and accurate links for your research.

In Addition to Research Navigator™ . . .

Exercise 1

Finding useful information can be challenging. To make sure your web searches yield a few applicable sites instead of hundreds of useless ones, take time to brush up on search techniques.

Log on to <http://www.searchenginewatch.com/facts/index.html> that offers (1) basic tips on using search engines, (2) how to use advanced commands to help you better control your searches, (3) links to articles and web sites that offer help with using search engines, (4) links to all types of search engines, and (5) links to articles that rank search engines against each other.

If the Search Engine Watch site is not available, log on to another web site that offers tips on how to use search engines.

Then, depending on your level of expertise, work through an informational section and summarize the most useful advice you discovered.

Exercise 2

IDEA is an organization of debate programs and organizations and individuals that support debate. It introduces debate to secondary schools and universities throughout Central and Eastern Europe, the Former Soviet Union, Central Asia, and Haiti. As part of its services, IDEA maintains the *Debatabase,* a searchable reference utility.

Log on to <http://www.debatabase.org/debatabase/> and enter a keyword in its search engine about a question/issue you want to research.

If the IDEA site and *Debatabase* are not available, run a web search on your question/issue.

Read two essays—with differing points of view—about the question/issue you are researching.

Summarize your readings.

USING YOUR STRATEGIES 1   IN DEFENSE OF SPLITTING UP

BARBARA EHRENREICH

Dr. Ehrenreich is a writer and social commentator. Her essays on contemporary issues have appeared in a diverse range of national publications including Time Magazine, The New York Times Magazine, Ms., Esquire, Mirabella, among others. She has received numerous fellowships and awards including a Guggenheim Fellowship and the Sydney Hillman Award for Journalism for a chapter of her recent book, Nickel and Dimed: On (Not) Getting By in America. Her other books include The Worst Years of Our Lives: Irreverent Notes from the Decade of Greed and Fear of Falling: The Inner Life of the Middle Class. She is at work on at least three new books.

IDEAS TO THINK ABOUT

Under what circumstances, if any, do you think it is in the best interest of the children for a couple to get a divorce? Under what circumstances, if any, do you think it is in the best interest of the children for a couple to stay together regardless of any problems?

WORDS TO KNOW

deprecating (¶3)—critical of themselves
restigmatize (¶6)—disgrace or defame again
rancorous (¶7)—bitter, hostile
e*nsues* (¶9)—follows

No one seems much concerned about children when the subject is welfare or   1
Medicaid cuts, but mention divorce, and tears flow for their tender psyches. Legislators in half a dozen states are planning to restrict divorce on the grounds that it may cause teen suicide, an inability to "form lasting attachments" and possibly also the piercing of nipples and noses.

But if divorce itself hasn't reduced America's youth to emotional cripples,   2
then the efforts to restrict it undoubtedly will. First, there's the effect all this antidivorce rhetoric is bound to have on the children of people already divorced—and we're not talking about some offbeat minority. At least 37% of American children live with divorced parents, and these children already face enough tricky interpersonal situations without having to cope with the public perception that they're damaged goods.

Fortunately for the future of the republic, the alleged psyche-scarring ef-   3
fects of divorce have been grossly exaggerated. The most frequently cited

study, by California therapist Judith Wallerstein, found that 41% of the children of divorced couples are "doing poorly, worried, underachieving, deprecating and often angry" years after their parents' divorce. But this study has been faulted for including only 60 couples, two-thirds of whom were deemed to lack "adequate psychological functioning" even before they split, and all of whom were self-selected seekers of family therapy. Furthermore, there was no control group of, say, miserable couples who stayed together.

As for some of the wilder claims, such as "teen suicide has tripled as divorces have tripled": well, roller-blading has probably tripled in the same time period too, and that's hardly a reason to ban in-line skates.   4

In fact, the current antidivorce rhetoric slanders millions of perfectly   5
wonderful, high-functioning young people, my own children and most of their friends included. Studies that attempt to distinguish between the effects of divorce and those of the income decline so often experienced by divorced mothers have found no lasting psychological damage attributable to divorce per se. Check out a typical college dorm, and you'll find people enthusiastically achieving and forming attachments until late into the night. Ask about family, and you'll hear about Mom and Dad . . . and Stepmom and Stepdad.

The real problems for kids will begin when the antidivorce movement   6
starts getting its way. For one thing, the more militant among its members want to "restigmatize" divorce with the cultural equivalent of a scarlet D. Sadly though, divorce is already stigmatized in ways that are harmful to children. Studies show that teachers consistently interpret children's behavior more negatively when they are told that the children are from "broken" homes—and, as we know, teachers' expectations have an effect on children's performance. If the idea is to help the children of divorce, then the goal should be to destigmatize divorce among all who interact with them—teachers, neighbors, playmates.

Then there are the likely effects on children of the proposed restrictions   7
themselves. Antidivorce legislators want to repeal no-fault divorce laws and return to the system in which one parent has to prove the other guilty of adultery, addiction or worse. True, the divorce rate rose after the introduction of no-fault divorce in the late '60s and '70s. But the divorce rate was already rising at a healthy clip *before* that, so there's no guarantee that the repeal of no-fault laws will reduce the divorce rate now. In fact, one certain effect will be to generate more divorces of the rancorous, potentially child-harming variety. If you think "Mommy and Daddy aren't getting along" sounds a little too blithe, would you rather "Daddy (or Mommy) has been sleeping around"?

Not that divorce is an enviable experience for any of the parties involved.   8
But just as there are bad marriages, there are, as sociologist Constance Ahrons argues, "good divorces," in which both parents maintain their financial and emotional responsibility for the kids. Maybe the reformers should concentrate on improving the *quality* of divorces by, for example, requiring prenuptial agreements specifying how the children will be cared for in the event of a split.

Reading as a Process   **47**

The antidivorce movement's interest in the emotional status of children   9
would be more convincing if it were linked to some concern for their physical
survival. The most destructive feature of divorce, many experts argue, is the
poverty that typically ensues when the children are left with a low earning
mother, and the way out of this would be to toughen child-support collection
and strengthen the safety net of supportive services for low-income families—
including childcare, Medicaid and welfare.

Too difficult? Too costly? Too ideologically distasteful compared with de-   10
nouncing divorce and, by implication, the divorced and their children? Perhaps.
But sometimes grownups have to do difficult and costly things, whether they
feel like doing them or not. For the sake of the children, that is.

QUESTIONS

Vocabulary

1. Explain what Ehrenreich means when she says, "you'll find people enthusiastically achieving and forming attachments until late into the
   night." (paragraph 5)
2. Explain what "the cultural equivalent of a scarlet D" means in paragraph
   6. What literary comparison is it suggesting?
3. What does the phrase "the goal should be to *destigmatize divorce*" mean
   in paragraph 6?
4. What does the phrase "sounds a little too blithe" mean in paragraph 7?

Comprehension and Analysis

5. State Ehrenreich's thesis/conclusion.
6. Ehrenreich says "the alleged psyche-scarring effects of divorce have been
   grossly exaggerated." How does she support this statement?
7. What is the "most destructive feature of divorce" according to Ehrenreich?
8. What is "a good divorce" according to sociologist Constance Ahrons?
   What does Ehrenreich suggest as one way to improve the quality of divorces?
9. In the last paragraph, Ehrenreich says, "But sometimes grownups have to
   do difficult and costly things, whether they feel like doing them or not."
   What does she mean?
10. In paragraph 7, Ehrenreich says "the divorce rate rose after the introduc-
    tion of no-fault divorce in the late '60s and '70s." Do you classify that as
    a fact, opinion, or reasoned judgment? How did you decide?

11. Is Ehrenreich divorced? Does she have children? Does this make her thesis any more or any less valid?

12. Do you believe Ehrenreich has presented a "defense" for splitting up? Why or why not?

Reflect and Connect

13. Your best friend and her husband have two school-age children. She tells you they are having marital problems and are considering getting a divorce. What are some of the factors you suggest she think about? What are some resources you suggest she investigate as she considers her options?

USING YOUR STRATEGIES 2   TELEVISION

JIM TRELEASE

An award-winning artist and writer for The Springfiled (MA) Daily News for more than 20 years, Mr. Trelease is now known for his international best-selling book, The Read-Aloud Handbook. In the book, Trelease encourages parents, teachers, grandparents, and siblings to discover the rewards—and the importance—of reading aloud to children. He now works full-time addressing parents, teachers, and professional groups on the subjects of children, literature and television. This is a portion of Chapter 8, "Television," of the fifth edition Trelease's The Read-Aloud Handbook.

IDEAS TO THINK ABOUT

What do you think makes television so appealing? How much time do you spend watching television? What would you be doing if you were not watching television?

WORDS TO KNOW

Luddite (¶2)—In early nineteenth century England, a group of Yorkshire weavers who lost their jobs because of the invention of mechanical weaving machines, named themselves followers of a mythical "King Ludd" and revolted against the mills by smashing the machinery. While some people saw the changes technology was bringing as generally positive—enabling increased production and reducing labor costs—the Luddites felt it was turning out inferior cloth and threatening their entire way of life. Modern-day Luddites fear that massive technological changes will create an ever-widening gap between the haves and have-nots, cause devastating economic ramifications, and lead to the destruction of our culture.

vindicated (¶10)—proven correct
pivotal moment (¶14)—critical turning point
nemesis (¶17)—something which must be defeated

> I believe television is going to be the test of the modern world, and that in this new opportunity to see beyond the range of our vision we shall discover either a new and unbearable disturbance of the general peace or a saving radiance in the sky. We shall stand or fall by television—of that I am quite sure. E. B. White, "Removal from Town," *Harper's* (October 1938)

Modern technology, if we use it instead of abusing it, can actually help us create lifetime readers. This chapter covers both the positive and negative aspects of the technology. . . . What helps and what hurts? . . . As for programs, I'll tell you what the research shows to be the best kind for children. 1

But this chapter is neither a hermit's nor Luddite's complaint. I own two television sets and a VCR, have favorite shows (*60 Minutes* and *Late Night with David Letterman*), watch videos with my grandsons, and enjoy being entertained. 2

Nothing exemplifies my television thesis better than the following story, which I've shared with every parent audience I've addressed in the last decade. 3

It begins with a woman named Sonya Carson, trying to raise two sons in inner-city Detroit as a single parent. One of twenty-four children, Mrs. Carson had only a third-grade education. A hardworking, driven woman, she worked as a domestic or child care-giver for wealthy families—sometimes working two or three jobs at a time to support her sons. Sometimes she worked so hard that she had to "get away to her relatives for a rest." Only years later did her sons discover that she was checking herself into a mental institution for professional help for depression. 4

Her sons, on the other hand, were not working themselves into any kind of frenzy. Both were on a slow ship to nowhere in the classroom. Bennie, the younger one, was the worst student in his fifth-grade class. The two brothers had done fine previously in a church school in Boston, but the change to Detroit public schools revealed the low standards of the earlier institution. As if raising two sons in one of the most dangerous cities in America were not enough, Mrs. Carson now had a new challenge—the boys' grades. She met it head-on. "Bennie—you're smarter than this report card," she declared, pointing to his math score. "First thing, you're going to learn your times tables—every one of them!" 5

"Mom, do you know how many there are? It would take me a whole year!" he replied. 6

"I only went through the third grade and I know them all the way through my twelves," his mother answered. "And furthermore, you are not to go outside tomorrow until you learn them." 7

Her son pointed to the columns in his math book and cried, "Look at 8
these things! How can anyone learn them?"

His mother simply tightened her jaw, looked him calmly in the eye, and 9
declared, "You can't go out until you learn your times tables."

Bennie learned his times tables—and his math scores began to climb. His 10
mother's next goal was to get the rest of his grades up. Her intuition pointed to
the television that never seemed to be off when the boys were home. "From
now on, you can only watch three television programs a week!" A week!
(What Sonya Carson lacked in book sense she made up for with common
sense—that would be vindicated nearly thirty years later when major research
studies showed a powerful connection between "over-viewing" and "under-
achievement.")

She next looked for a way to fill the free time created by the television 11
vacuum: She said, "You boys are going to the library and check out two books.
At the end of each week you'll write me a report on what you've read." (Only
years later did the boys discover she couldn't read well enough to understand
any of the reports.)

They didn't like it, of course, but they didn't dare refuse. And in reading 12
two books a week, then talking about them to his mother, Bennie raised his
reading scores. And because the entire curriculum is tied to reading, the rest of
the report card began to improve. Each semester, each year, the scores rose.
And by the time he was a senior in high school he was third in his class, scoring
in the ninetieth percentile of the nation.

With colleges like West Point and Stanford waving scholarships in his face 13
but only ten dollars in his pocket for application fees, Bennie let his choice fall to
whichever school won the College Bowl television quiz that year (Yale). He
spent four years majoring in psychology at Yale, then went on to the medical
schools at the University of Michigan and Johns Hopkins. Today, at age fifty,
Dr. Ben Carson is one of the world's premier pediatric brain surgeons. When
Johns Hopkins named him head of pediatric neurosurgery he was, at age thirty-
three, the youngest in the nation.

Ask Dr. Carson to explain how you get from a fatherless inner-city home 14
and a mother with a third-grade education, from being the worst student in
your fifth-grade class, to being a world-famous brain surgeon with a brother
who is an engineer. Again and again, Ben Carson points to two things: his
mother's religion (Seventh-Day Adventist) and the pivotal moment when she
limited their television viewing and ordered him to start reading. (For the
"complete" story, read *Gifted Hands: The Ben Carson Story* by Ben Carson
[Harper Collins/Zondervan].)

I have people in my audiences with three times the education of young 15
Mrs. Carson and ten times her income—but not half her common sense when
it comes to raising children. They can't bring themselves to "raise" children—
they can only "watch them grow up," and most of the watching occurs from
the couch in front of a television set.

Reading as a Process   **51**

There are two important factors to remember from the Carson family's 16 story: (1) Mrs. Carson didn't trash the set—she *controlled* it; and (2) she had high expectations of her children and demanded appropriate behavior from them.

WHAT EXACTLY IS SO WRONG WITH TELEVISION?

Nothing. There has never been a single TV set that caused brain damage 17 or committed a crime. Critics who assault TV as a nemesis of society are looking in the wrong corner of the room. People control it and use it; it is the over-viewing of television that causes the problem.

This chapter is largely a plea to control the *amount* of television viewed 18 within the home, not a petition to eliminate it. While there is no evidence to support the elimination of TV, there is some research to support the premise that students who have no television in their homes perform no better in school than those who watch a moderate amount. Moderation and the choice of programming appear to be significant factors, along with the age of the child. The American Academy of Pediatrics recommends children under two years of age should not watch TV at all and older children should not have sets in their bedrooms (more on that later). Part of the recommendation on babies was based on research that indicates developing brains need live interaction with people and objects, not passive viewing of TV.[1]

The Academy has called for a child limit of 10 hours of TV a week. This 19 was based on a research analysis of 23 TV-learning studies involving England, Japan, Canada, and five areas of the U.S., with 87,025 children, in a time period from 1963 to 1978.[2] The study's findings showed no detrimental effects on learning (and some positive effects) from TV viewing up to 10 hours a week, after which the scores begin to decline. It also found the most negative effects of heavy TV viewing occurred among girls and students of high IQ. Since the average child watches at least twice the recommended dosage, the research team cited that as "clearly a matter of concern."

WHAT ELSE DOES RESEARCH SHOW ABOUT "OVER-VIEWING" OF TV?

Scientific analyses of television and its impact on children over the last 20 forty years still leave many questions unanswered. We know for a fact that children who watch the most TV also have the lowest school scores, but why? To date no one has uncovered a biological explanation. It's definitely not brain or cognitive damage.[3]

One frequent argument is that television viewing takes away from read- 21
ing and homework time and thus lowers grades. The flaw in that reasoning is:
Would those same children in those same homes and families have been reading and doing homework if TV were not available? No research comes close to
answering that one way or another. Conversely, children who watch little TV
and do well in school usually watch educational TV and spend larger amounts
of time with print and educational experiences. Were they doing that because
TV was limited or would those parents have been actively involved in the children's lives anyway and provided an abundance of print in the home? More evidence points to parent behavior than to TV as the reason.

The only constant in the pros and cons of television is time. Those who 22
watch the most achieve the least in school. For more than three decades, the
National Assessment of Educational Progress (NAEP) has tested American
(and foreign) school children in major subject areas, thus giving us our only reliable "national report card."[4] Taking the home patterns they found in the scores
of thousands of students over the last three decades, the U. S. Department of
Education compared the scores of thirteen-year-old math students, based upon
how much TV they watched. As shown in the chart below, they found a clear
correlation between over-viewing of television in the home and underachieve-
ment in the classroom.[5]

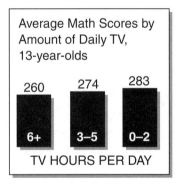

Is it the fault of TV viewing or the fault of families that allow children to 23
waste that much time in front of a plastic box? That's someone else's call. All I
can do is raise a warning flag: If you allow your child to watch too much TV,
you're asking for academic trouble, and there's ample evidence to prove it.

A 1996 study of 2,420 Asian and Latin American immigrants to Califor- 24
nia's San Diego area showed that eighth- and ninth-graders with the highest ra-
tios of homework-to-television-viewing hours had the highest grade-point
averages. Asian students did the most homework and Latin Americans did the
least. The more TV viewed by the student, the lower his grades and the lower
his aspirations for the future.[6] Did the home cause it or TV?

IF TIME IS THE PROBLEM, WHAT
ARE THE CURRENT DOSAGES?

We can get a quick gauge on the time problem by examining the rise in 25
total daily viewing per household:

- 1950—four hours, thirty-five minutes
- 1987—seven hours
- 1999—seven hours, twenty-four minutes[7]

A further sign of growth (or addiction) is the increase in the number of 26
channels now available to households: sixty-two, double that of 1988.[8]

The Henry J. Kaiser Family Foundation issues an annual media usage re- 27
port that examines the media environment of 3,155 children ages two through
eighteen, representative of the U. S. child population.[9] The 1999 report shows
that media usage usually fell along demographic lines: Children of higher-edu-
cated parents watched thirty minutes less TV each day, and children from
higher-income levels watched an hour less than lower-income peers. While
more than half of households watch TV during meals, less than half of college-
educated parents allowed the practice. (Awareness of the TV dangers apparently comes with more education, thus widening the education gap between
haves and have-nots.)

- 60 percent of households have three or more TV's
- 58 percent have 2 VCRs
- 58 percent have TV on during meals
- 50 percent have no TV rules
- two-to-seven-year-olds average 2 TV hours daily
- eight-to-eighteen-year-olds average 2 ¾ TV hours daily
- two-to-eighteen-year-olds average 29 video minutes daily
- 53 percent of children have a TV in their bedroom

The 1999 report expressed serious concerns about the last item on the 28
list and the isolated environment in which many children now experience
media. It conceded that while past forms of media (print, film, radio) have had
an impact on children, it usually was in the presence of others. The new forms
(TV, VCR, computers) are having their impacts on children in private, thus
lessening the chance of an adult or parent filtering what the media is streaming
into the child's mind. As the Kaiser Foundation Report notes, this greatly en-
larges the media power over the child.

A separate study involving the TV's presence in a child's bedroom sug- 29
gested part of the learning difficulties of children who watch large amounts of
television may be caused by sleep deprivation. In 1999, sleep researchers
working with parents and teachers of 495 students, kindergarten through

fourth grade, found that those with televisions in their bedrooms (25 percent) were far more apt to have difficulty falling asleep and woke up more often during the night. This made them more prone to sleepiness during the day, impeding their school performance. The study was prompted by the number of children visiting the Hasbro Children's Hospital Pediatric Sleep Disorder Clinic who had televisions in their bedrooms. The researchers strongly urged the rooms be cleared of both TVs and computers, especially if there are sleeping problems.[10]

30 The issue of TV demographics is explored further in a largely silent but smoldering issue in American education—the white-black test score gap—that appears to have a solid link to TV viewing, among other causes. Although there were considerable scoring gains made by African-American students following integration and the civil rights struggle, that upward movement hit a ceiling in the 1980s. During the 1990s it was an issue administrators worried over, but did so silently because of the issue's sensitive racial overtones.

31 A turning point came at decade's end when the standards movement demanded high-stakes testing and an end to social promotion, forcing national and state agencies to release students' scores to the public. The issue became the center of heated debate and then, finally, the subject of careful study in numerous communities throughout the nation.[11]

32 Although low-income families nearly always project lower scores for students, black children of parents with at least one graduate degree still score 191 points below their white counterparts in similar family circumstances.[12] A number of reasons are offered, based on research to date:

1. Their parents are the first generation of high education (college) and may not be seen studying or reading as often as they should be.
2. The grandparents of these children (an important support group in families) are still working class.
3. Middle-class black children watch twice as much TV as their white counterparts.

33 The aforementioned TV finding came from a study of an academically oriented high school in the middle-class white-black community of Shaker Heights, Ohio. Done by Harvard's Ronald F. Ferguson, the study showed black middle-class students made up only 9 percent of the top 20 percent of their classes and 83 percent of the bottom 20 percent. Ferguson's research shows this first generation of children of black achievers watches twice as many hours of TV as their white classmates: three hours a day compared to one and a half hours. The Kaiser Family Foundation study in 2000[13] showed national results almost identical to Ferguson's study, but also found black children were far more likely to have TVs in their bedroom, including ones with premium cable services.

DON'T KIDS NEED THE ENTERTAINMENT
BREAK THAT TV OFFERS?

Of course they do, and so do I—even the mindless kind. As I wrote ear- 34
lier, it's the number of TV hours filling a child's time that causes a problem. And
I'm not even addressing the subject of what they're watching; the bigger issue
is what are they not doing while they watch TV.

Paul Copperman, author of *The Literacy Hoax*, saw the interruption in 35
these terms: "Consider what a child misses during the 15,000 hours [from birth
to age seventeen] he spends in front of the TV screen. He is not working in the
garage with his father, or in the garden with his mother. He is not doing homework, or reading, or collecting stamps. He is not cleaning his room, washing
the supper dishes, or cutting the lawn. He is not listening to a discussion about
community politics among his parents and their friends. He is not playing baseball or going fishing, or painting pictures. Exactly what does television offer
that is so valuable it can replace these activities that transform an impulsive,
self-absorbed child into a critically thinking adult?"[14]

Based on the figures in the studies listed earlier, the average child will 36
view 1,200 hours of television and video this year. If that's a hard figure to comprehend, then think of 1,200 hours as the equivalent of watching "Gone With
the Wind" 307 times this year. Television has become an electronic pacifier for
entire families, putting them into states of semi-wakefulness.

Now let's compare a diet of sit-com watching with the experience of the 37
family of Mike and Sally Hard of Sarasota, Florida. They had four children, including a Down's Syndrome son named Jacob, who was eighteen. The others
were ages thirteen, ten, and six. In 1989, Mike and Sally came to hear me speak
at a local college, and as I spoke, Mike began to hear the echoes of his eighth-
grade teacher, Miss Marie Hunt, back in Metropolis, Illinois, as she read to the
classes every day for twenty minutes. "We'd hurry to class so we wouldn't
miss the next part of the story," Mike recalls. Coupling those powerful
memories with my remarks about the need to control television viewing in the
family, Mike and Sally made a resolution: No TV on school nights. Instead the
family would read aloud together.

That's not an easy thing to do with four children, especially Jacob. But 38
within three weeks, the reading-aloud had become both a habit and a magnet.
Jacob would hurry through the dishes and bring them the book to hear the next
chapter.

Mike also spent those evenings teaching his youngest, Andrew, how to 39
play chess. Six years later, Andrew tied for first in the Florida Scholastic Chess
Championship, and the family credited the long hours of listening to stories for
his remarkable concentration in chess tournaments. But even more credit must
be given to two parents who were intelligent and determined enough to control their TV before it controlled their children's futures.

ISN'T TV THE SAME AS READING: STORIES MADE OUT OF WORDS?

There are distinct differences between reading and TV viewing, includ- 40
ing:

Television is the direct opposite of reading. In breaking its programs into 41
eight-minute segments (shorter for shows like Sesame Street) it requires and
fosters a short attention span. Reading, on the other hand, requires and encourages longer attention spans in children. Good children's books are written
to hold children's attention, not interrupt it. Because of the need to hold viewers until the next commercial message, the content of television shows is almost constant action. Reading also offers action but not nearly as much, and
books fill the spaces between action scenes with subtle character development.

The use of the remote control only exacerbates the attention span prob- 42
lem: The average family "zaps" once every three minutes and twenty-six seconds, versus those who have no remote (once every five minutes and fifteen
seconds); and higher-income families zap three times more often than poorer
families.[15]

For young children television is an antisocial experience, while reading is a 43
social experience. The three-year-old sits passively in front of the screen, oblivi-
ous to what is going on around him. Conversation during the program is seldom
if ever encouraged by the child or by the parents. On the other hand, the three-
year-old with a book must be read to by another person—parent, sibling, or
grandparent. The child is a participant as well as a receiver when he engages in
discussion during and after the story.

Television deprives the child of his most important learning tool: questions. 44
Children learn the most by questioning. For the more than twenty hours a
week that the average five-year-old spends in front of the set (usually alone or
with siblings), he neither asks a question nor receives an answer.

Television interrupts the child's most important language lesson: family con- 45
versation. Studies show the average kindergarten graduate has already seen
nearly 6,000 hours of television and videos before entering first grade, hours in
which he engaged in little or no conversation. And with 58 percent of families
watching TV during dinner and 53 percent of preteens and teenagers owning
their own sets (and presumably watching alone in their rooms), the description
of TV as "the great conversation stopper" has never been more appropriate.

Television encourages deceptive thinking. In *Teaching as a Conserving Activ-* 46
ity, Neil Postman pointed out that implicit in every one of television's commercials is the idea that there is no problem that cannot be solved by simple
artificial means.[16] Whether the problem is anxiety or common diarrhea, nervous tension or the common cold, a simple tablet or spray solves the problem.
Instead of encouraging us to think through our problems, television promotes

the "easy way." The cumulative effect of such thinking is enormous when you consider that between ages one and seventeen the average child is exposed to 350,000 commercials (four hundred a week) promoting the idea that solutions to life's problems can be purchased.

The vocabulary of television is lower than nearly all forms of print, from 47 comic books to children's books and newspapers and magazines. A study of the scripts from eight programs favored by teenagers showed a sentence averaged only seven words (versus eighteen words in my local newspaper).[17] Since TV is a picture medium, a fair comparison would be with children's picture books:

- 72 percent of the TV scripts consisted of simple sentences or fragments.
- In *Make Way for Ducklings* by Robert McCloskey, only 33 percent of the text is simple sentences.
- In *The Tale of Peter Rabbit* by Beatrix Potter, only 21 percent of the text is simple sentences. Thus one can say even good children's picture books contain language that is at least twice the complexity of television's. Imagine how much more complex the novels are. . . .

IS THERE ANY DIFFERENCE BETWEEN EDUCATIONAL TV AND THE REST?

I've often said that educational TV is television from the neck up, while 48 the rest is from the neck down. Parent fans of PBS can take heart from numerous studies indicating I'm not far off the mark in my assessment—that PBS programs have a positive impact on children's intellect, and other programming (particularly cartoons and sitcoms) leaves a negative impression if consumed in heavy amounts. In small amounts, commercial programming is benign entertainment.

In a two-year study of 326 five- and seven-year-olds, viewing of educa- 49 tional television had a positive effect on children's reading, while non-informative shows (situation comedies) had a detrimental effect.[21] That same long-term project concluded that the biggest influence on children's reading development and skills was parent attitudes about reading and the availability of books in their homes. A follow-up study seven years later confirmed the original findings and showed the intellectual gains for at risk children were long-lasting.[22]

One of the things I respect about PBS is that it learns from its mistakes 50 (something seemingly beyond the grasp of other network and cable channels) and keeps improving its educational programs. For example, *Sesame Street,* as popular as it is, does not qualify as a great literacy lesson. When researchers studied ten episodes of *Sesame Street* in 1995, they counted 350 segments, of which 184 were literacy related and overwhelmingly related to letter sounds, not context.[23] Of those 184 segments, only 21, included print "in context," as

Reading as a Process

in signs, labels, posters, or logos. Even the impact of "role modeling" was missing most of the time in "Sesame's" instruction; only nine times in the ten hours were characters actually seen reading, and always to themselves. Not once in 350 segments did anyone read aloud to children or Muppets.

Recognizing the limitations of *Sesame Street's* format, PBS created two literacy shows targeting specific literacy issues—*Reading Rainbow* and *Between the Lions.* 51

Reading Rainbow, the award-winning PBS series on children's books, shows what can be accomplished when the industry sets its mind to educate and entertain. It is presently the most used television program in elementary classrooms, with more than four million students tuning in regularly. Once a book is spotlighted on the show, libraries and bookstores report an immediate positive response among children and their parents. It is not unusual for a book that normally sells twelve hundred copies to sell twenty thousand after being featured on *Reading Rainbow.* A complete list of books used on the hundreds of *Reading Rainbow* episodes can be found at http://gpn.unl.edu/rainbow/parents/mainlib.htm. 52

Between the Lions is a highly praised children's television program that is aimed at promoting reading skills and based on solid classroom and early childhood research. It's truly the best of its kind ever on national TV. 53

With the show's extensive Web site, www.pbskids.org/lions, PBS has shown that it is possible to marry TV to the Web in a meaningful way for families. Most of the entertainment industry's Web sites are intended purely to sell, seldom to educate, and never do either intelligently. This site's parent index points parents to ways they can teach literacy using story time, bath time, made-up stories, warning labels, television, food, errands, songs, newspapers, the dictionary, and airport or train signs. Each category offers almost ten simple literacy activities. . . . 54

NOTES

1. Lawrie Muffin, "Pediatricians Urge Limiting TV Viewing," *The New York Times,* August 4, 1999, p. Al, All.

2. Patricia A. Williams, Edward H. Haertel, Geneva D. Haertel, and Herbert J. Walberg, "The Impact of Leisure-Time Television on School Learning: A Research Synthesis," *American Educational Research Journal,* Spring 1982, vol. 19, no. 1, pp. 19-50.

3. Daniel R. Anderson and Patricia A. Collins, "The Impact on Children's Education: Television's Influence on Cognitive Development," U.S. Department of Education (Washington, DC: Office of Educational Research and Improvement, April 1988).

4. Jay R. Campbell, Catheriene M. Hombo, and John Mazzeo, *NAEP 1999 Trends in Academic Progress: Three Decades of Student Performance*, U.S. Department of Education (Washington, DC: National Center for Education Statistics, 2000); also available at http://nces.ed.gov/nationsreportcard.

5. Ibid.

6. Ruben G. Rumbaut, "The New Californians: Assessing the Educational Progress of Children of Immigrants," ERIC document: ED398 294, based upon chapter 2, *California's Immigrant Children: Theory, Research, and Implications for Education Policy*, Ruben G. Rumbaut and Wayne A. Cornleius, eds., San Diego, CA: Center for U.S.-Mexican Studies, University of California, April 1996.

7. "2000 Report on Television: The First 50 Years," New York, NY: Nielsen Media Research, 2000, p. 14.

8. Ibid., p. 16.

9. Donald Roberts, Ph.D., Ulla G. Foehr, Victoria Rideout, and Mollyann Brodie, Ph.D., Kids & Media @ The New Millennium, The Henry J. Kaiser Family Foundation, November 1999.

10. Judith Owens et al., "Television-Viewing Habits and Sleep Disturbance in School Children," *Pediatrics*, September 8, 1999, p. 552.

11. The single best exploration of the gap appeared in an award-winning newspaper series by Tim Simmons of the *Charlotte News & Observer*, reprinted in a special section, "Worlds Apart: The Racial Education Gap," December 27, 1999; see also Kate Zernike, "Gap Widens Again on Tests Given to Blacks and Whites," *The New York Times*, August 25, 2000, p. Al4: The article plots the racial gap in NAEP scores that has widened since the 1980s between white and black students in math, science, and reading, including a decline among students coming from the best-educated black families; Pam Belluck, "Reason Is Sought for Lag by Blacks in School Effort," *The New York Times*, July 4, 1999, pp. A2, A12; and Kate Zernike, "Racial Gap in Student Test Scores Polarizes Town," *The New York Times*, August 4, 2000, pp. Al, A25; Debra Viadero, "Lags in Minority Achievement Defy Traditional Explanations," *Education Week*, March 22, 2000, pp. 1, 18-22.

12. Pam Belluck, "Reason Is Sought for Lag by Blacks in School Effort," *The New York Times*, July 4, 1999, pp. Al, A12.

13. Donald Roberts, Ph.D., Ulla G. Foehr, Victoria Rideout, and Mollyann Brodie, Ph.D., Kids & Media @ The New Millennium, The Henry J. Kaiser Family Foundation, November 1999.

14. Paul Copperman, *The Literacy Hoax: The Decline of Reading, Writing, and Learning in the Public Schools and What We Can Do About It* (New York: Morrow, 1980), p. 166.

15. "Zapping of TV Ads Appears Pervasive," *The Wall Street Journal*, April 25, 1988. p. 29.

16. Neil Postman, *Teaching as a Conserving Activity* (New York: Delacorte, 1980), pp. 77-78.

17. Michael Liberman, "The Verbal Language of Television," *The Journal of Reading*, April 1983, pp. 602-9.

21. Rosemarie Truglio, Aletha Huston, John Wright, "The Relation Between Children's Print and Television Use to Early Reading Skills," Center for Research on the Influences of Television on Children, Department of Human Development, University of Kansas, 1988.

22. John C. Wright and Aletha C. Huston, "Effects of Educational TV Viewing of Lower Income Preschoolers on Academic Skills, School Readiness, and School Adjustment One to Three Years Later," Center for Research on the Influences of Television on Children, June 1995; the report can be obtained from Children's Television Workshop, 1 Lincoln Plaza, NY NY, 10023, (212) 595-3456; also at www.critc.he.utexas.edu/CRITC/Manuscripts/ effects-of education_tv_viewin.htm or www.cyfc.umn.edu/television/html; see also Mark Walsh, "Study Links Television Viewing, School Readiness," *Education Week*, June 7, 1995, p. 5.

23. Barbara Fowles Mates and Linda Strommen, "Why Ernie Can't Read: Sesame Street and Literacy," *The Reading Teacher*, January 1996.

QUESTIONS

Vocabulary

1. Explain what Trelease means when he says, "But this chapter is neither a hermit's nor Luddite's complaint."(paragraph 2)

2. Explain what Trelease means when he says, "They can't bring themselves to 'raise' children—they can only 'watch them grow up,' . . ." (paragraph 15)

3. Explain what Trelease means when he says, "Critics who assault TV as a nemesis of society are looking in the wrong corner of the room." (paragraph 17)

4. Explain the phrase, "a largely silent but smoldering issue in American education." (paragraph 30)

Comprehension & Analysis

5. State Trelease's thesis/conclusion.

6. How do paragraphs 4-14 support and develop paragraphs 1-3? How do paragraphs 37-39 develop and support paragraph 34-36?

7. According to Trelease, what is the problem with television? Please explain.

8. One frequent argument against television is that it takes time away from reading and homework. According to Trelease, what is the flaw in that reasoning?

9. According to Trelease, what is the only "constant" in the pros and cons of watching television?

10. Trelease believes the new forms of technology (TV, VCR, computers) are having a different impact on children than past forms such as print, film and radio. What does he see as the major difference in impact? Does he believe the impact of new technologies is primarily positive or negative? Why?

11. In paragraph 48, Trelease says "I've often said that educational TV is television from the neck up, while the rest is from the neck down." What does he mean? What impression of educational TV does he want to create? What impression of general broadcast TV does he want to create?

12. In paragraph 1, Trelease said "This chapter covers both the positive and negative aspects of the technology." Do you feel he fulfilled his promise? Cite specific examples to support your answer.

Reflect and Connect

13. In paragraph 46, Trelease says that instead of encouraging us to think through our problems, television promotes the concept that "solutions to life's problems can be purchased." If you disagree, discuss why you disagree and where you think Trelease's reasoning is faulty. If you agree with his analysis, discuss why you agree and one thing you could do in your family to counteract the idea.

THEME 1

EVALUATION
AND GRADES

How much time do you spend studying per week?

In the 1950s and 1960s, most freshman handbooks recommended that students study "three hours outside of class for every one hour spent in class," meaning nine hours of study for psychology class, another nine hours for English, and nine more for biology. So, a full-time student with a 12-credit hour load was hitting the books about 36 hours per week—the equivalent of a full-time job.

If you think that recommendation seems outdated, you aren't alone. According to survey data from UCLA's Higher Education Research Institute released in 2003, about 16 percent of college freshmen report studying "less than one hour per week" for all their classes combined, and the majority said they "don't spend nearly as much time as professors recommend."

Yet the survey shows that grades continue to improve: A record-high 45.7 percent of students across all types of U.S. colleges earned an A average, and only 10 to 20 percent received less than a B minus.

Do those high grades mean today's students are smarter, or are today's high GPAs more a result of grade inflation than exceptional braininess?

If today's grades don't really have any value, why don't we just eliminate them?

We don't eliminate grades because, as Rutgers sociology professor Jackson Toby says, "One of the main reasons for going to schools and colleges instead of being educated by one's parents is to find out how one compares with agemates in the ability to learn what society thinks it's important to know."

However, two assumptions suggested in Toby's writings are critical for an evaluation-grading system to provide that useful information: (1) Grades must be interpreted the same way by the professor who assigns them, the student who receives them, and the people who read the transcript, and (2) "the grading system has to be consistent for the competition [among students] to be fair. . . . An 'A' should encourage the student to continue studying; he is learning

Opening the Theme is the in-depth report on grade inflation and letters of recommendation published by the American Academy of Arts and Sciences. Authored by Henry Rosovsky and Matthew Hartley, *Evaluation and the Academy: Are We Doing the Right Thing?* examines both the causes and consequences of grade inflation.

In "All Shall Have Prizes; Grade-Inflation in Universities," *The Economist* looks at the controversy Harvard University's Professor Harvey Mansfield created when he declared he would give all his students two grades: an "ironic" grade that would go on their official records and a realistic grade that he would reveal to them only in private. Then cartoonist Garry Trudeau takes a look at grade inflation at the fictional Walden University.

Sally Abrahms asks, "Are all students 'above average'?" in "When 'A' Is for Anybody," and then *The Economist* reports in "An Eye for an A" that "economists are not the only ones who fret about inflation." However, in his *Christian Science Monitor* article "Amid Cries of Grade Inflation," Mark Clayton reports that "the mediocre grades of C-plus and lower are alive and kicking."

Next, we look at "the perennial conflict between those who want to spare students the stigma of failure and those who want to maintain standards." In "Why Any Grades at All, Father?" middle school principal Tina Juarez uses Bing Crosby's character, Father O'Malley, from the 1945 movie *The Bells of St. Mary's* to introduce the question, "Is a teacher's primary responsibility to give students a helping hand, or to measure their brains with a yardstick?"

Editorial cartoonist Brad McMillan explains his view of how the "real world" is going to react to the current trend in college and university grading, and Kurt Wiesenfeld, a physicist teaching at Georgia Tech, closes the Theme by encouraging us to look at how grade inflation affects society in "Making the Grade."

As you read the selections in this Theme and other articles and essays on evaluation and grades, answer questions such as these as a matter of course:

1. Do I understand the author's words and phrases?
2. What is the author's thesis (conclusion)?
3. What facts, opinions, and reasoned judgments does the author provide to support and develop the thesis?

4. Are the author's facts, opinions, and reasoned judgments respected sources?
5. Are there factual errors or misleading interpretations?
6. Has significant information been omitted or arbitrarily disco⌐
7. What new information does this author add to my understa⌐ issue?

SELECTION 1   EVALUATION AND THE ACADEMY: ARE WE DOING THE RIGHT THING?

HENRY ROSOVSKY AND MATTHEW HARTLEY

Dr. Rosovsky, the Geyser University Professor Emeritus and former Dean of the Harvard University College of Arts and Sciences, has been a Fellow of the American Academy of Arts and Sciences since 1969. Included in his numerous awards are 15 honorary degrees from institutions worldwide, the Order of the Sacred Treasure (Star) from the Emperor of Japan, and the Chevalier de la Legion d'Honneur from the French government. He is currently co-chairing the Task Force on Higher Education, sponsored by the World Bank and UNESCO.

Dr. Hartley is an Assistant Professor in the Graduate School of Education at the University of Pennsylvania. He served as a Teaching Fellow and Research Assistant at Harvard University and as Co-Chair of the editorial board for the Harvard Educational Review. His current research and writing focus on issues of organizational change at colleges and universities.

IDEAS TO THINK ABOUT

What do you want a grade to tell you? What do you want your grades to tell others? Do you believe the grades you receive this semester will accomplish those functions honestly and fairly?

WORDS TO KNOW

debasement (¶2)—corrupt, devalue
salutary (¶4)—positive, good
inexorably (¶17)—inevitably, undeniably

EVALUATION AND THE ACADEMY: ARE WE DOING THE RIGHT THING?

INTRODUCTION

It is a traditional and generally accepted role of teachers to evaluate their stu- 1
dents. We usually accomplish this task by assigning grades and writing letters of
recommendation. Informally, of course, we are constantly evaluating students
in conversations, office hours, and the like. As representatives of a discipline
and members of a larger academic community, we also evaluate peers as well
as younger colleagues: it is a well-established professional obligation that commonly takes the form of letters of recommendation. Evaluation is generally
considered to be a core function of our collegial life.

That all is not well in these domains is no secret: inside and outside col- 2
leges and universities there has been much discussion about grade inflation and
the debasement of letters of recommendation (we prefer the term "letters of
evaluation.") There is no unanimity about either the causes or consequences of
changed standards of evaluation. Even the very existence of a problem is
doubted by some observers. Nevertheless, there appears to be enough unease,
lack of consensus, and "noise" to justify a closer examination.

To that end, an informal group of academics from different fields and 3
backgrounds for the past year met at the American Academy of Arts and Sciences. We asked the same questions for both grades and letters of recommendation: what is the current situation, what are its consequences, and what
remedies, if any, are needed and possible? This Occasional Paper represents
the results of our discussions.

On all these issues we reached a general consensus, although individual 4
differences about some interpretations remain. Our hope is to start a discussion among our colleagues in all different types of institutions across the country. Such discussions could clarify the situation in each college and university
and lead to salutary changes. The quality of evaluation admits of no national
solution. Each institution has to determine and be responsible for its own standards, and the best beginning is awareness of the issues.

Current conditions have to be seen in the context of recent history. Since 5
World War II, colleges and universities—along with nearly all American institutions—have experienced major changes. A few examples will suffice. The
number of faculty members and the number and percentage of students seeking higher education have dramatically increased since that time. The 1950 census indicates that there were 190,000 academics; a decade later there were
281,000, and by 1970 the number had swelled to 532,000.[1] In 1998, according
to the latest figures from the U.S. Department of Education, there were
1,074,000 faculty members employed by institutions of higher learning. At the
turn of the twentieth century only about 1 percent of high-school students

attended college; that figure is closer to 70 percent today. Racial and gender diversity has also increased markedly over the past several decades. In 1975, there were 11 million students: 47 percent were women, 15 percent were minorities (Black, Hispanic, Asian, American Indian/Alaskan Native). By 1997, there were 12,298,000 students, the percentage of women had grown to 56 percent, and minorities represented 25 percent of the student population.

At the same time, the country's tertiary institutions have faced, and some are still facing, serious economic pressures and increased competition, and many are far less isolated from the outside world. All sectors of society clamor for access to knowledge and skills available in our laboratories and in other forms of faculty expertise. 6

These changes—largely external in origin—have had a variety of consequences for higher education. In what follows we begin by examining the implications of a specific and in our opinion undesirable practice that is part of these changes: grade inflation. At first glance, this practice may appear to be of little consequence, but we shall argue that its presence calls into question central values of academic life. 7

WHAT ARE THE FUNCTIONS OF GRADES?

Professors expect, and have received, a considerable measure of respect in our society. The privileges that flow from this status are related to the functions they perform and the values they bring to these performances. Consensus about these values has become diluted in recent years. For example, there is controversy in some institutions over the relative weight to be given to teaching and research, and over the role of political and ideological commitments in teaching and scholarship. The appropriateness of faculty unions is a matter of concern for other institutions. Nevertheless, whatever the balance of energies, commitments, and working arrangements, academics are only entitled to the respect they would like to command if they affirm some common standards. Among these, the least controversial—perhaps the most elementary—is the imperative for accuracy in evaluating their students' academic work. Yet, there is overwhelming evidence that standards regarding student grading have changed substantially over time. 8

Grades are intended to be an objective—though not perfect—index of the degree of academic mastery of a subject. As such, grades serve multiple purposes. They inform students about how well or how poorly they understand the content of their courses. They inform students of their strengths, weaknesses, and areas of talent. This may be helpful to students in making decisions about a career. They also provide information to external audiences: for example, to colleagues not only in one's own institution but to those in other institutions, to graduate schools, and to employers. We believe that this view of grades represents the consensus within the academy. 9

We recognize, of course, that a significant number of students who had 10 low grades in school were spectacularly successful in later life. That fact, however, does not weaken the rationale for grades. No one would claim that grades are a completely accurate index of the comprehension of subject matter, let alone a predictor of achievement in the world at large. Yet, they remain an efficient way to communicate valid information, but only if a meaningful range of grades exists.

Some professors hold the view that low grades discourage students and 11 frustrate their progress. Some contend it is defensible to give a student a higher grade than he or she deserves in order to motivate those who are anxious or poorly prepared by their earlier secondary school experiences. Advocates of this opinion contend that students ought to be encouraged to learn and that grades can distort that process by motivating students to compete only for grades. A few institutions have acted on this premise by using only written comments; for example, Hampshire College, Goddard College, and Evergreen State College (all small liberal arts colleges) and until recently U.C. Santa Cruz.[2] A more radical view holds that it is inappropriate for a professor to perform the assessment function because it violates the relationship that should exist between a faculty member and students engaged in the collaborative process of inquiry. Some critics of grades argue that it is a distorting, harsh, and punitive practice.

We doubt that these positions are espoused by large numbers in the aca- 12 demic community. Grades certainly are not harsh for those who do well, and empirical evidence for the hypothesis that lowering the anxiety over grades leads to better learning is weak. As for the inappropriateness of professors performing the assessment function, one must ask: who will perform this task? Relegating evaluation to professional or graduate schools and employers simply "passes the buck" and is unlikely to lead to more accurate and fair evaluations. Although the rejection of grading does not represent the academic mainstream, the criticisms are influential in some circles, and so we will return to them later in this paper.

DOES GRADE INFLATION EXIST: THE EVIDENCE

Grade inflation can be defined as an upward shift in the grade point average 13 (GPA) of students over an extended period of time without a corresponding increase in student achievement.[3] Unlike price inflation, where dollar values can—at least in theory—rise indefinitely, the upper boundary of grade inflation is constrained by not being able to rise above an A or a 100. The consequence is grade "compression" at the upper end.

We will begin by reviewing grading trends as described in the literature, 14 but will confine our sample to undergraduates. The situation in professional and graduate schools requires separate analysis. Relatively undifferentiated course grading has been a traditional practice in many graduate schools for a very long time. One justification for this may be the wide reliance on general examinations and theses.

Most investigators agree that grade inflation began in the 1960s[4] and continued through, at least, the mid-1990s. Several studies have examined the phenomenon over time, as illustrated in the following table:

Grade Inflation from 1960 to 1997

Author(s) and Years studied	Sample size	Findings
Arvo E. Juola 1960–1978[a]	180 colleges (with graduate programs)	From 1960 to 1974 the average GPA increased half a grade point (0.432). From 1974 to 1978, a leveling of grade inflation was detected.
Arthur Levine and Jeanette S. Cureton 1967, 1976, 1993[b]	Data from survey of 4,900 undergraduates at all institutional types	Grades of A- or higher grew from 7 to 26 percent. Grades of C or below fell from 25 to 9 percent.
George Kuh and Shouping Hu 1984–1987; 1995–1997[c]	52,256 student surveys from the Colleges Student Experiences Questionaire (CSEQ) at all institutional types	College grades increased over time in every institutional type on the average from 3.07 to 3.343

[a]Arvo E. Juola, "Grade inflation in higher education-1979. Is it over?" ED189129 (March 1980).

[b]Arthur Levine and Jeanette S. Cureton, *When Hope and Fear Collide: A Portrait of Today's College Student* (San Francisco: Jossey-Bass, 1998).

[c]George Kuh and Shouping Hu, "Unraveling the Complexity of the Increase in College Grades from the Mid-1980s to the Mid-1990s," *Educational Evaluation and Policy Analysis* (Fall 1999): 297–320.

Arvo Juola from Michigan State University was one of the earliest researchers to raise concerns about grade inflation.[5] His surveys of colleges and universities found that grade inflation continued unabated between 1960 and 1977.[6] From 1960–1974 the average GPA increased nearly half a letter grade (0.432) with the greatest annual increases occurring between 1968 and 1972.[7] Arthur Levine and Jeanette Cureton compared data from undergraduate surveys of 4,900 college students from all types of institutions in 1969, 1976 and 1993. Their research found that the number of A's increased nearly four fold during that time (from 7 percent in 1969 to 26 percent in 1993) and the number of C's declined by 66 percent (from 25 percent in 1969 to 9 percent in 1993).[8] Different estimates suggest that across all institutional types GPA's rose approximately 15–20 percent from the mid-1960s through the mid-1990s.[9] A recent study by George Kuh and Shouping Hu comparing the GPA's of 52,000 students—approximately half from the mid-1980s and half from the mid-1990s—found that student grades had risen from 3.07 in the mid-1980s to 3.34 in the mid-1990s.[10] By the mid-1990s, the average grade (formerly a C) resided in the B- to B range.[11] More recent research across all types of schools shows that only between 10 percent and 20 percent of students receive grades lower than a B-.[12]

Grade inflation moderated by the second half of the 1990s; its rate of growth has declined from the highs of the 1960s and 1970s. This result is to be expected because—as noted earlier—unlike price inflation, grade inflation is constrained by an immovable ceiling. An A is the upper limit, and, therefore, the recent decline in the growth rate is not an unambiguous indication of changed standards. Indeed, the seemingly mild degree of inflation in the table is, over time, very much magnified by compression at the top, which inexorably lessens the possibility of meaningful gradations. [17]

Patterns of grading show inflation to be more prevalent in selected disciplines. Grades tend to be higher in the humanities than in the natural sciences, where objective standards of measurement are enforced more easily.[13] This was probably always true, but the differences by discipline appear to have increased over time. It is not surprising that the "softer" subjects exhibit the severest grade inflation. [18]

Although higher grades appear in all types of institutions, grade inflation appears to have been especially noticeable in the Ivy League. In 1966, 22 percent of all grades given to Harvard undergraduates were in the A range. By 1996 that percentage had risen to 46 percent and in that same year 82 percent of Harvard seniors graduated with academic honors.[14] In 1973, 30.7 percent of all grades at Princeton were in the A range and by 1997 that percentage had risen to 42.5 percent. In 1997, only 11.6 percent of all grades fell below the B range.[15] Similarly, at Dartmouth, in 1994, 44 percent of all grades given were in the A range. [19]

When considered alongside indexes of student achievement, these increases in grades do not appear to be warranted. During the time period in which grades increased dramatically, the average combined score on the Scholastic Achievement Test (SAT) actually declined by 5 percent (1969–1993).[16] Since the SAT's recentering in 1995 (when the mean was reset to a midpoint of 500 in a range of 200 to 800) scores increased only slightly—the average combined score in 1995 was 1,010 and in 2000 it was 1,019. [20]

By one estimate, one third of all college and university students were forced to take remedial education courses, and the need for remediation has increased over time. One study found that between 1987 and 1997, 73 percent of all institutions reported an increase in the proportion of students requiring remedial education.[17] Further, from 1990 to 1995, 39 percent of institutions indicated that their enrollments in remedial courses had increased.[18] Currently, higher education devotes $2 billion a year to remedial offerings,[19] and faculty have noticed a shift in student ability and preparation. In 1991, a survey [21] conducted by the Higher Education Research Institute found that only 25 percent of faculty felt their students were "well-prepared academically."[20]

Discussions that led to standards-based reform also show that systems' administrators, regents, and state boards of education felt a growing unease about the competence of their students. Eighteen states have currently implemented competency tests that all high-school graduates must pass. Similar testing programs are being considered in several states for institutions of higher learning. The University of Texas System, Utah's State Board of Regents, and the sixty-four campus SUNY system are all considering implementing competency tests.[21]   22

Measures of average achievement are far from perfect, but the available evidence does support the proposition that grading has become more lenient since the 1960s. Higher average grades unaccompanied by proportionate increases in average levels of achievement defines grade inflation.   23

We have already mentioned that increases in average grades appear to have been especially noticeable in the Ivy League. Because admission into these institutions became increasingly competitive since the 1960s, it might be possible to argue that higher average grades merely reflected a more academically talented student body. There is some evidence for higher quality, but the magnitude of grade increases in Ivy League institutions seems to indicate inflationary pressures as well.[22]   24

EXPLANATIONS OFFERED FOR GRADE INFLATION

The dynamics of grade inflation are complex, and a variety of explanations have been offered.   25

The Sixties and the Vietnam War

Students played a prominent part in the turmoil of the 1960s and early 1970s. Their activities were dominated by resistance to the Vietnam War draft, and institutions of higher learning were challenged by the resulting social unrest. It has been suggested that faculty members were reluctant to give poor grades to male students during those years because forcing them to drop out of school would have made them subject to wartime military service.[23] In the words of one professor at the University of Florida: 26

> The upward shift started in the jungles of Vietnam, when those of us now at the full-professor level were safely in graduate school. We were deferred by virtue of being in school, which wasn't fair and we knew it. So when grading time came, and we knew that giving a C meant that our student (who deserved a D) would go into the jungle, we did one better and gave him a B.[24]

Eventually, the courtesies extended to draft-age males became the norm.

Specific incidents of campus unrest created particularly large inflationary 27
leaps in grades. In 1969–1970 many institutions cancelled final examinations following the U.S. Army invasion of Cambodia. At Harvard—to cite just one
case—students were allowed to designate *ex post facto* whether they preferred
a letter grade or pass-fail. The effects of this decision on GPA's are obvious.

The 1960s and the first half of the 1970s also witnessed rising student en- 28
rollments and therefore a great expansion of the faculty. Some three hundred
thousand new professors were hired between 1960 and 1970, doubling the size
of the professorate.[25] The new faculty members generally were young, anti-
war individuals who identified with the values of students, and this shifted the
faculty's ideological base. The ideals of these new "student centered" faculty
members, who were concerned with student development and protection, col-
lided with those "institutionally centered" faculty members, who were more
concerned with preserving the assessment function of higher education.[26]

Response to Student Diversity

During the past three decades, increasing numbers of students from varied so- 29
cioeconomic groups have attended institutions of higher learning. The preparation of these students has sometimes been inadequate. Some have argued that in
the interest of retaining these students, colleges and universities have been forced
to become more lenient.[27] It has been suggested that lower grades (C's and D's)
were effectively eliminated and grades became compressed into the upper (B
and A) range. However, as we have already shown, grade inflation began in the
1960s when poor and minority students represented a tiny proportion of the national student body.[28] Even as late as the early 1970s, for example, black students
represented only 8 percent of the total student population. Furthermore, fully 60
percent of these students attended historically black colleges and universities at
this time.[29] Thus, the role of minority students in starting grade inflation appears
specious. Most importantly, William Bowen and Derek Bok have demonstrated
that, on average, black students in their sample did somewhat less well in college
than white students who entered with the same SAT scores.[30] That finding does
not support the idea of faculty favoritism toward minorities.

New Curricular and Grading Policies

Certain curricular requirements, for example, foreign language, mathematics, 30
and science, were abandoned by many schools in the 1960s, giving students the
opportunity to avoid difficult courses that were less suited to their abilities.
Many colleges and universities adopted freer distribution requirements, which
gave students increased control over their curriculum and allowed them to
avoid more demanding courses and the risk of a poor grade.

Other policy changes with similar consequences allowed students to 31
withdraw from courses well into the semester (sometimes up to the final
week), removed "first attempt" grades (letting students take a class again and

substitute the higher grade), and presented pass-fail as an option.[31] Many institutions adopted "pluses" and "minuses" for the first time, which, some have argued, allowed grades to drift upwards.[32]

Student Evaluations

Another policy frequently linked to grade inflation is the widespread and growing use of student evaluations. Student evaluations have played a role (sometimes an important one, depending on the type of institution) in promotion, tenure decisions, and merit-pay increases.[33] Research has shown that grades were significantly correlated with student ratings of faculty performance—that is, courses with higher grades received higher evaluations.[34] For example, a study conducted at the University of Washington found that faculty members who were "easy graders" received better evaluations.[35] Thus, according to this source, good evaluations could be partially "bought" by assigning good grades.[36] On the other hand, low grades carried the risk of small enrollments, which might endanger a promising professional career in its early stages.[37]

Students as Consumers

Another force associated with grade inflation, particularly in the 1980s, is the rise in consumerism—universities operating like businesses for student clients. Demographic projections during the 1980s suggested that the pool of potential college applicants would decline. Although students of nontraditional age ultimately closed the anticipated gap for some institutions, colleges and universities began competing more fiercely for students and their retention. Students wanted good grades,[38] and because from their perspective a C was well below average,[39] institutions that resisted grade inflation found that their graduates had a more difficult time being accepted into graduate programs.[40] This fact made their graduates unhappy and their programs less attractive.

Former President Rudenstine applied a version of this reasoning to Harvard: "The faculty over the last thirty years have begun to realize that the transcript matters. . . . Often your degree as an undergraduate is not your last degree, so [students] are worried about their transcripts."[41] Rudenstine went on to imply that an increased demand for graduate education "led professors to give better grades so that Harvard students would not be disadvantaged."

Faculty practices have reinforced student expectations. Students counted on "good grades." For example, a 1999 study at one university found that large proportions of undergraduates in five different courses assumed grade inflation was the norm—even students who reported doing "average" work expected B's or A's.[42]

Watering Down Content

Another source of grade inflation is the watering down of course content at some institutions. As course content becomes less demanding, it is reasonable to see grade averages rise. But grade inflation cannot be accounted for by identifying faculty members who are especially lenient. Other faculty members may become party to the process by simply demanding less of students than they did in the past. The grades they assign may be valid, but students are required to master less content to earn them.[43]

The Role of Adjuncts

Even if some of the historical factors producing grade inflation have recently become less powerful—if only because of compression—there are other pressures that may sustain inflationary tendencies. One is the changing internal structure of the faculty in our colleges and universities. Currently, only about half of all faculty members are designated "tenured" or "tenure track." The other half are described as "adjuncts": an academic proletariat with few rights and benefits, frequently holding part-time jobs at more than one institution at the same time. Their position is vulnerable from below in the form of student pressure and from above in the form of the displeasure of administrators. They have little reason to be loyal to the institutions for which they work for they are often overworked and underpaid. This situation is likely to lead to more tolerant grading, a tendency that is exacerbated by high workloads that make it impractical to engage in careful student evaluation.

This pressure extends beyond adjuncts. A study conducted by Michael Kolevzon of Virginia Commonwealth University compared ten "high grade inflation" and ten "low grade inflation" departments at a four-year university with approximately 8,500 undergraduates. Three-quarters of the faculty from high grade inflation departments indicated that rising class sizes and more nonclassroom commitments (e.g., committee work, publishing, advising) detracted from time that could be devoted to evaluating students.[44]

RECAPITULATION, MECHANISM, AND CONSEQUENCES

The fact that grade inflation has existed between the late 1960s and the present is beyond dispute. The rate of inflation, however, has varied during these thirty-five years among institutions and departments. But again the phenomenon of inflation is undeniable unless one asserts that there has been an extraordinary improvement in the quality of students during this period, and for that there is very little evidence. Indeed, on a national level, most evidence goes in the opposite direction.

There is much less agreement about the causes of grade inflation. We have supplied the reasons found in the literature, and there is little doubt that the beginning of grade inflation was closely related to the Vietnam War and its consequences. Other cited causes are controversial and may or may not have played an important role. For the record, it should be noted that the most con-

37

38

39

40

troversial claim is rejected by almost all who have studied the subject: we refer to it as a "response to student diversity." When grade inflation originated in the 1960s there was virtually no "student diversity" in the sense in which that term is used today.

It is most important to stress that, once started, grade inflation has a self-sustaining character: it becomes systemic, and it is difficult for faculty to opt out of the system. When significant numbers of professors adjust their grades upwards so as to shelter students from the draft—as certainly happened during the Vietnam era—others are forced to follow suit. Otherwise, some students will be disadvantaged, and pressures from students, colleagues, and administrators will soon create conformity to emerging norms. (The analogy is not perfect, but when the economy experiences price inflation, the individual seller will adjust prices upwards, and in higher education there is no equivalent of government or the Federal Reserve that can arrest that process.) 41

We are describing an inflationary system in which the individual instructor has very little choice. Grade inflation is not the consequence of individual faculty failure, lowered standards, or lack of moral courage. It is the result of a system that is self-sustaining and that produces less than optimal results for all concerned. The issue is not to assign blame; rather, it is to understand the dynamics of grade inflation and its consequences. 42

Are there any adverse consequences? Quite a few can be deduced from what we have said. The present situation creates internal confusion giving students and colleagues less accurate information; it leads to individual injustices because of compression at the top that prevents discrimination between a real and an inflated A; it may also engender confusion for graduate schools and employers. Not to address these issues represents a failure of responsibility on the part of university and college faculties acting collectively: we have the obligation to make educational improvements when needed and when possible. Simply to accept the status quo is not acceptable professional conduct. We need, if possible, to suggest ways for institutions to initiate reforms that will allow as clear gradations as possible to replace the present confusion. 43

EXTERNAL VERSUS INTERNAL CONSIDERATIONS

Do inflated grades really hamper the selection process as carried out by those who normally rely on undergraduate transcripts? It is very difficult to answer that question with a desirable degree of certainty. We have found no large body of writings in which, for example, employers or graduate schools complain about lack of information because of inflated grades. Informal conversations with some employers and graduate schools lead us to believe that the traditional users of grades have learned to work around present practices: they 44 expect to find high and relatively undifferentiated grades, and therefore rely more heavily on other criteria.

Graduate schools use standardized tests (e.g., the GRE), recommenda- 45 tions, the ranking of particular schools, and interviews. Grade inflation invites admissions committees to place more emphasis on standardized test scores, which is not necessarily in our view a wise shift in emphasis. Corporations conduct their own evaluations—interviewing candidates, checking references, and in some cases testing the analytic skills of candidates. Grades remain an important criterion but their influence may be waning. For example, one survey of the Human Resource Officers (HRO) from Fortune 500 companies in 1978, 1985, and 1995 found that the percentage of HROs who agreed that transcripts of college grades ought to be included with an applicant's resume fell from 37.5 percent to 20 percent.[45] Judith Eaton, president of the Council for Higher Education Accreditation, asserts that employers have become dissatisfied with grading information, arguing that now "government and business want to know more specifically what kind of competencies students have."[46]

It is certain that a diminution in the use of grades increases the relative 46 weight of informal evaluations, and thus being in the proper network may become more valuable than personal achievement. As a matter of fairness, society should have an interest in counteracting this trend.

Suppose, just for the sake of argument, that the net negative impact of 47 working around grades is small, and in addition that grades are less important to those who—in some manner—choose our graduates. Should we then adopt the radical response either to give no grades at all, or—and it amounts to the same thing—award A's to all students? In other words, are there wholly internal justifications for formal evaluations of students that offer meaningful gradations? The answers have been given at the beginning of this essay. Grades, if they discriminate sufficiently, help and inform students in many different ways, and students are entitled to these evaluations.

For evaluations to accomplish their intended purpose we must question a 48 currently popular assumption in psychology and education that virtually all students can excel academically across the board—and in life as well. Accordingly, differences in performance are primarily attributed to levels of "self-confidence" or "self-esteem" because this is assumed to be the most important determinant of success; motivation and talent are relevant, though secondary. The enemy of high self-confidence is criticism, and that is how rigorous evaluation is perceived.

These sentiments may be powerful elements in grade inflation: praise 49 motivates accomplishment. There may even be a grain of truth in this proposition, but it is far from the whole truth. Talent as well as motivation remain powerful explanatory factors in achieving success. In fact, most studies do not support the connection between academic success and self-esteem. In a recent comprehensive review article, Joseph Kahne quotes Mary Ann Scheirer and Robert E. Kraut as follows:

The overwhelmingly negative evidence reviewed here for a causal connection between self-concept and academic achievement should create caution among both educators and theorists who have heretofore assumed that enhancing a person's feelings about himself would lead to academic achievement.[47]

THE NEED FOR AND THE POSSIBILITIES OF CHANGE

Is there a way to change the status quo? There is neither an easy nor a single 50 answer to that question. Since the term "inflation" originated in economics, we can refer to another concept from the same discipline in order to put the question in focus. Gresham's Law says that if two kinds of money have the same denomination but different intrinsic value—for example, gold coins versus paper money—the bad money (paper) will drive the good money (gold) out of circulation because the good money will be hoarded. The only solution is currency reform in which only a single standard prevails. In education, bad grading practices drive out good grading practices creating their own version of Gresham's Law. Can we devise the equivalent of currency reform in higher education? The obstacles are obvious. Currencies are controlled by a single authority, and generally a state can enforce uniform standards. None of this exists in the American system of higher education, nor would we favor anything of the sort. Each institution has to make its own assessment and find its own solutions. The best we can hope for is a series of small steps and individual institutional initiatives whose cumulative effects could amount to the beginnings of reform. Recognizing the problem is a meaningful place to start.

What are the characteristics of a good grading system? 51

- It should be rigorous, accurate, and permit meaningful distinctions among students in applying a uniform standard of performance.
- It should be fair to students and candid to those who are entitled to information about students.
- It should be supportive of learning and helpful to students in achieving their educational goals.

Short of a fundamental systemic overhaul or return to an earlier day, nei- 52 ther of which are realistic possibilities, we review various suggestions that are contained in the literature.

Institutional Dialogue

The academic profession is the only one that provides virtually no formal train- 53 ing or guidance to new entrants concerning one of their primary responsibilities: teaching and evaluation.[48] Expectations, responsibilities, and standards are rarely discussed or committed to paper.[49] It would be helpful if this type of dialogue occurred in departments or in faculties as a committee of the whole.[50] Greater comparability of standards and fairness could result.

It would also be a good idea to make students a part of the institutional dialogue. Their ideas about how the system might be made more supportive of their educational ambitions would be especially appropriate and valuable.

More Information

Faculty members ought to know how their grading standards compare to those of their colleagues. Some universities (Harvard and Duke are examples) provide such data. In Harvard's Faculty of Arts and Sciences each professor annually receives an index number for each course taught that compares individual grading practices with departmental averages. This practice has not eliminated grade inflation, but it may have slowed its progress and made the system more equitable.

Additional Information

Some schools have adopted the practice of providing additional information about course grades on student transcripts. These schools include Columbia,[51] Dartmouth, Indiana,[52] and Eastern Kentucky.[53] Typically information about the number of students in the class and the average grade is added to the letter grade on the transcript.[54] Grade inflation is not addressed directly, but the information does help those who wish to put the transcript in perspective.

Alternative Grading Systems

Various alternative or modified grading systems are in use that intend to mitigate aspects of grade inflation. For example, a reduction in the range of grades from A through E to a simpler honors, pass, and fail might perhaps help reestablish "pass" as the average. Providing comments along with letter grades is another method of contextualization. Still another strategy is to administer general examinations to seniors, perhaps using outside examiners, which is the practice at Swarthmore.[55] However, both written comments and general examinations are labor intensive and do not seem practical for mass higher education.

A Standard Grade Distribution

In large classes it seems appropriate for departments and/or instructors to establish a standard distribution (a curve) so that distinctions are both fair and maintained over time. The distribution need not be totally inflexible—exceptions can occur—but this would be a useful yardstick.

We are conscious of the fact that all suggestions for change are partial and not wholly persuasive. This is not a surprise because no single or easy solution exists. The main plea is to be clear about professional standards and obligations and to bring practices into line with these standards. The selection of a standard will necessarily be an individual matter—individual for each college or university, department, and faculty. The present system is flawed. The ethics of professional conduct demand that we—as faculty members—seek the best solutions for our institutions.

FACTORS LEADING TO INFLATED LETTERS OF RECOMMENDATION

Thus far, we have dealt in some detail with the most common form of evalua- 60 tion, namely, grades. The other major type of evaluation is letters of reference. Faculty members write letters on behalf of colleagues who are seeking promotion, tenure, and other positions, or who are competing for grants and fellowships.[56] They also provide references for students, which is an integral part of the graduate admissions and employment process.[57] This form of evaluation will receive less extensive treatment in this paper: the overlap with grade inflation is very large and problems related to letters are unfortunately much less well researched. What evidence is available—empirical, anecdotal, and experiential—leads us to conclude that letters of recommendation suffer from many of the same, or worse, weaknesses and problems as grades. A commentary on letters written for promotion and tenure decisions summarized well the prevailing view: "Puffery is rampant. Evasion abounds. Deliberate obfuscation is the rule of the day."[58] Letters for students are similarly flawed. A member of Cornell's admissions committee observed ruefully: "I would search applications in vain for even subordinate clauses like 'While Susan did not participate often in discussions. . . .' "[59] As experienced academics, all of us sense the accuracy of these observations.

LETTERS OF REFERENCE: EVALUATION OR ACCLAMATION?

We believe that since the late 1960s, academics have been less willing to ex- 61 press negative opinions—either about their students or their colleagues. Many reasons for this phenomenon are identical to the forces that have created grade inflation, such as a legacy of the 1960s, an absence of clear standards, pressures to accommodate student "customers," and the like. As with grade inflation, the problem is systemic: once inflationary rhetoric becomes normative, it is difficult for individual faculty members to do otherwise. As one faculty member remarked: "It becomes like a nuclear arms race. If Michigan is using lots of adjectives, U.C.L.A. better too."[60] It is even possible to think of compression at the top, just as was the case with grade inflation: if letters are largely positive, how can one indicate true distinction?

Some differences between letters and grades do exist. Letters are much 62 more personal. They use descriptive words about specific individuals and therefore it is easier to make an author of a letter accountable for his or her text. Some faculty members are concerned that their anonymity cannot be assured when they write a letter of recommendation. Many faculty members have had their recommendations inadvertently leaked to candidates and have reported being harassed because of their statements.[61] Other faculty members are uncomfortable criticizing colleagues. They may wish to help a colleague who failed to achieve tenure land on his or her feet.[62] They also have a desire to see their students succeed—for the sake of their students and for their own sake, since having students accepted into graduate school reflects well on their department.[63]

The most important difference between letters of recommendation and grades is the fear of legal action, which appears to have had a powerful influence on letters. In 1974 Congress passed the Family Educational Rights and Privacy Act that gave students legal access to their files, including letters of recommendation written on their behalf. The extent to which letters could remain confidential became—and has remained—uncertain, even if students "waive their rights."[64] In addition, states with "sunshine laws," such as California, provided little anonymity for letter writers.[65] At present, fear of litigation has a chilling effect on the candor of those writing letters of evaluation, even though such litigation is rare.[66]

To explore this important matter in more detail, and especially because it is the factor that most clearly separates grades and letters, we sought the most authoritative advice possible. Martin Michaelson, of Hogan and Hartson in Washington, D.C., and a leading expert on legal issues that affect the academy, was kind enough to offer his thoughts on the legal risks associated with letters of evaluation, and we include his important communication in its entirety.

In recent years, a distinct perception has taken hold among employers in the United States (by no means limited to colleges and universities) that candid disclosure of negative or even equivocal information about personnel, to prospective employers and others, entails considerable risk and hence is inadvisable. The factual and legal basis of that perception is not entirely clear. Plainly, however, underlying factors include increased litigiousness in our society, a heightened responsiveness of the law to workers' rights, and the belief of many thoughtful persons that even slight and subtle criticisms can sometimes harm reputations and severely derail careers.

Coincident with the perception that candid disclosures can be legally dangerous, a new level of concern had developed that an employer's failure to reveal pertinent personnel information, too, can have far-reaching implications. For example, the institution that declines to disclose a departing employee's serious, proven misconduct to a prospective employer (especially when the prospective employer seeks such information) should worry that the omission could have a range of unwholesome ramifications.

Pertinent law, which varies considerably among the 50 states, addresses those concerns in several ways. In some contexts, the law recognizes a qualified privilege that attaches to personnel evaluations communicated in good faith in response to a prospective employer's request. More basically, truth is a legal defense to alleged defamation. And—apart from the duty, sometimes recognized by courts, not to misrepresent in a recommendation by being false or misleading in context—judicial precedents generally limit employers' "duty to warn" to situations in which the law assigns the person who has the adverse information special obligations regarding it. (In some jurisdictions, for example, psychotherapists are required to take steps to prevent bodily harm to a person a patient threatens in the course of psychotherapy.) But the legal current does not flow reliably in a direction favorable to candid referees. For example, the Supreme Court in University of Pennsylvania v. EEOC (1990) declined to recognize a special privilege of confidentiality for faculty references subpoenaed in an EEOC proceeding.

Extensive law reform, to promote reliable disclosure of adverse (as well as favorable) information about personnel, may be desirable. But such reform would be beyond the capacity of the academy acting alone; a far wider consensus, entailing coordinated action by legislatures and courts throughout the nation, would be required. Colleges and universities can, however, promote candor in evaluations in valuable ways, such as these: 68

- Higher education institutions should be prepared to indemnify faculty, and other personnel, who in the course of performing their duties supply good faith candid appraisals that other institutions and non-institutional employers seek and need.
- Faculty members should have access, without charge, to the institution's attorneys for particularized advice on how to handle requests for references, appraisals, and the like, in the full range of circumstances germane to the faculty member's discharge of institutional duties.
- Institutions should carefully address and specify their policies on confidentiality of and, where indicated, access to letters of reference and similar materials, taking into account the relevant legal considerations.
- No less than in other delicate areas of legal regulations (such as sexual harassment, research-related conflicts of interest, or compliance with copyright law in the reproduction of course materials), faculty should regularly be supplied background information and general guidance on legal implications of appraisals of personnel, by experts engaged by the institution.

No single prescription is likely to address adequately all personnel reference and disclosure situations. But periodic written and oral guidance on this topic to faculty from university attorneys and others is bound to reduce risks in practice and foster a salutary candor in evaluations of faculty, students, and staff. 69

Michaelson's observations underscore the complexity of the problem both inside and outside the academy. Legal precedent neither entirely dispels concerns about potential litigation, nor does it substantiate undue concerns of those who fear writing candid letters. The law does provide the greatest 70 protection to the frank evaluator, because "truth is a legal defense to alleged defamation." Michaelson rightly points out that colleges and universities can do much to encourage a climate of candor by supporting faculty and staff who write candid appraisals, allocating resources to this end, providing background information, allowing consultation with the college or university counsel, and indemnifying those who supply good faith candid appraisals.

CONSEQUENCES

The consequences of inflated letters of recommendation are much the same as 71
for grade inflation: poorly differentiated and therefore less useful information.

* *Inflated recommendations do not help external audiences distinguish between candidates:* If too many candidates are described with superlatives, one might as well wonder about the use of recommendations at all.[67] Furthermore, inflation cheats those excellent candidates who deserve great praise[68] and gives less distinguished applicants an unfair and unearned advantage.[69] It may also cause the employer or educational institution to have unrealistic expectations of the candidate.[70]

* *Inflated letters create self-sustaining and systemic pressures that make this form of evaluation almost meaningless.[71] The evaluation process is driven into increasingly informal channels:* In some fields, grade inflation has created an increasing reliance on letters of recommendation.[72] However, if recommendations fail to provide useful information, people who need information about potential candidates will be forced to gather information in more informal ways (e.g., telephone calls to friends). This may result in a process where the real information is shared primarily in private channels and therefore is not open to outside scrutiny—a strengthening of the "old boy and girl" network.

A FEW RECOMMENDATIONS

Can anything be done? A few partial remedies have been suggested. For 72
example:

* *Avoid writing "general" letters of recommendation:* Whenever possible, evaluators ought to write recommendations regarding specific positions rather than writing a blanket "all purpose" letter. Research suggests that greater specificity results in less vague and lofty rhetoric.[73] Specificity also adds to the perceived credibility of a recommendation in the minds of employers,[74] and no doubt fellowship committees as well.

* *Discuss what you will and will not write with the candidate:* Before agreeing to write a letter, discuss with the candidate your assessment of him or

her. He or she will then be in a better position to decide whether to have you write on his or her behalf.[75]

- *Be clear about your expectations regarding confidentiality:* Confidentiality tends to produce more honest appraisals, and research suggests that confidential recommendations are less likely to be inflated.[76] Insisting on student waivers is desirable. Those in charge of admissions and job searches look more favorably on confidential letters.[77] Confidentiality can be breached in case of lawsuits, but those are rare events.

Faculty members who write letters of evaluation have a two-fold responsibility. First, the candidate deserves to have his or her unique qualities and qualifications accurately and carefully described. Second, evaluators also have a responsibility to the persons who are receiving the letter and using that information to make decisions. Those persons deserve a balanced account of all candidates. A rephrased Golden Rule is the best guide: Write to others the kind of letter of recommendation you would like to receive from them. To follow the rule is responsible professional conduct. Not to follow the rule perpetuates harmful practices in the academy. 73

CONCLUSION

The reluctance to engage in frank evaluation of students and colleagues has— as we have shown—many different sources. Individually, these are less important than the dynamics created by this reluctance. Once it starts, grade inflation and inflated letters are subject to self-sustaining pressures stemming from the desire not to disadvantage some students or colleagues without cause. This self-sustaining character eventually weakens the very meaning of evaluation: compression at the top before long will create a system of grades in which A's predominate and in which letters consist primarily of praise. Meaningful distinctions will have disappeared. 74

A system that fears candor is demoralizing. Much is lost in the current situation, primarily useful information for students, colleagues, graduate schools, and employers. Even if those who need accurate information have learned to "work around the system," the cost of what prevails today remains high. Instead of moving through formal and open channels, information is guided toward informal and more secretive byways. 75

We know of no quick or easy solutions; habits of thirty years' duration are not easily changed. But change has to begin by recognizing the many aspects of the problem, and that is why we urge discussion and education about professional conduct and responsibilities. Reform will have to occur institution by institution, and we hope that what we have presented in this paper will offer a good way to begin. 76

CONTRIBUTORS

Philip G. Altbach is J. Donald Monan, SJ, Professor of Higher Education, Boston College.

Sissela Bok is Senior Visiting Fellow, Harvard Center for Population and Development Studies.

Charles Fried is Beneficial Professor of Law, Harvard Law School.

Carmine Gibaldi is Associate Professor of Higher Education Administration, St. John's University.

Matthew Hartley is Lecturer, Graduate School of Education, University of Pennsylvania.

Jerome Kagan is Daniel and Amy Starch Research Professor of Psychology, Harvard University.

Henry Rosovsky is Lewis P. and Linda L. Geyser University Professor Emeritus, Harvard University.

Dean K. Whitla is Lecturer on Education, Harvard Graduate School of Education.

NOTES

1. Metzger, "The Academic Profession in the United States," 1987. Note: These figures include part-time faculty.
2. U.C. Santa Cruz did not use grades until its traditional practice was changed in March of 2000. At the same time, the faculty decided to continue the use of written comments.
3. Goldman, "The Betrayal of the Gatekeepers: Grade Inflation," 1985.
4. Juola, "Grade inflation in higher education: What can or should we do?" 1976.
5. Ibid.
6. Juola, "Grade inflation in higher education—1979. Is it over?" 1980.
7. Ibid.
8. Levine and Cureton, *When Hope and Fear Collide: A Portrait of Today's College Student,* 1998.
9. Basinger, "Fighting grade inflation: A misguided effort?" 1997; Stone, "Inflated Grades, Inflated Enrollment, and Inflated Budgets: An Analysis and Call for Review at the State Level." 1996.
10. Kuh and Hu, "Unraveling the Complexity of the Increase in College Grades from the Mid-1980's to the Mid-1990's," 1999.

11. Weller, "Attitude Toward Grade Inflation: A Random Survey of American Colleges of Arts and Sciences and Colleges of Education," 1986; Reibstein, "Give me an A, or give me death," 1994; Landrum, "Student Expectations of Grade Inflation," 1999.
12. Farley, "A is for average: The grading crisis in today's colleges," 1995.
13. Wilson, "The Phenomenon of Grade Inflation in Higher Education," 1999.
14. Lambert, "Desperately Seeking Summa," 1993.
15. Report of the faculty committee on examinations and standings on grading patterns at Princeton, 5 February 1998.
16. The College Board; Levine and Cureton, *When Hope and Fear Collide: A Portrait of Today's College Student*, 1998; Schackner in Nagle, "A Proposal for Dealing with Grade Inflation: The Relative Performance Index," 1998.
17. Levine, "How the Academic Profession is Changing," 1997.
18. National Center for Education Statistics, "Remedial Education at Higher Education Institutions, Fall 1995–October 1996," NCES-97-584.
19. Schmidt, "Colleges are starting to become involved in high-school testing policies," 2000.
20. Dey, Astin, and Korn, "The American Freshman: Twenty-Five Year Trends, 1966–1990," 1991.
21. Schmidt, "Faculty outcry greets proposal of competency tests at U. of Texas," 2000.
22. This is verified by data provided by C. Anthony Broh, director of research for COFHE.
23. Lamont in Goldman, "The Betrayal of the Gatekeepers: Grade Inflation," 1985.
24. Twitchell, "Stop Me Before I Give Your Kid Another 'A,' " 1997.
25. Goldman, "The Betrayal of the Gatekeepers: Grade Inflation," 1985.
26. Wilson, "The Phenomenon of Grade Inflation in Higher Education," 1999.
27. Mansfield, "Grade Inflation: It's time to face the facts," 2001.
28. Cross, "On scapegoating Blacks for grade inflation," 1993.
29. Lucas, *American Higher Education: A History*, 1994.
30. Bowen and Bok, *The Shape of the River*, 1998.
31. Goldman, "The Betrayal of the Gatekeepers: Grade Inflation," 1985; Bromley, Crow, and Gibson, "Grade inflation: Trends, causes, and implications," 1978; Edwards, "Grade inflation: The effects on educational quality and personal well being," 2000.
32. Potter, "Grade Inflation: Unmasking the Scourge of the Seventies," 1979.
33. Williams and Ceci, "How'm I Doing? Problems with Student Ratings of Instructors and Courses," 1997.

34. Aleamoni and Kennedy in Goldman, "The Betrayal of the Gatekeepers: Grade Inflation," 1985.

35. Wilson, "New Research Casts Doubt on Value of Student Evaluations of Professors," 1998.

36. Goldman, "The Betrayal of the Gatekeepers: Grade Inflation," 1985; Wilson, "The Phenomenon of Grade Inflation in Higher Education," 1999.

37. Beaver, "Declining college standards: It's not the courses, it's the grades," 1997.

38. Basinger, "Fighting grade inflation: A misguided effort?" 1997.

39. Walhout, "Grading across a career," 1997.

40. Perrin, "How Students at Dartmouth Came to Deserve Better Grades," 1998.

41. *Harvard Crimson*, 7 March 2001.

42. Landrum, "Student Expectations of Grade Inflation," 1999.

43. Crumbley in Basinger, "Fighting grade inflation: A misguided effort?" 1997.

44. Kolevzon, "Grade inflation in higher education: A comparative study," 1981.

45. Spinks and Wells, "Trends in the Employment Process: Resumes and Job Application Letters," 1999.

46. McMurtie, "Colleges are Urged to Devise Better Ways to Measure Learning," 2001.

47. Kahne, "The Politics of Self-Esteem," 1996.

48. Basinger, "Fighting grade inflation: A misguided effort?" 1997; Rosovsky with Ameer, "A neglected topic: Professional conduct of college and university teachers," 1998.

49. Stone, "Inflated Grades, Inflated Enrollment, and Inflated Budgets: An Analysis and Call for Review at the State Level," 1996.

50. Weller, "Attitude Toward Grade Inflation: A Random Survey of American Colleges of Arts and Sciences and Colleges of Education," 1986.

51. Archibald, "Just because the grades are up, are Princeton students smarter?" 1998.

52. McConahay and Cote, "The Expanded Grade Context Record at Indiana University," 1998.

53. Wilson, "The Phenomenon of Grade Inflation in Higher Education," 1999.

54. Basinger, "Fighting grade inflation: A misguided effort?" 1997; Grieves, "A Policy Proposal Regarding Grade Inflation," 1982; Nagel, "A Proposal for Dealing with Grade Inflation: The Relative Performance Index," 1998; Wilson, "The Phenomenon of Grade Inflation in Higher Education," 1999.

55. Whitla, personal communication, 12 July 2000.

56. Altshuler, "Dear admissions committee," 2000; Mitchell, "The college letter: College advisor as anthropologist in the field," 1996.

57. Ibid.

58. Schneider, "Why you can't trust letters of recommendation," 2000.

59. Altshuler, "Dear admissions committee," 2000.

60. Schneider, "Why you can't trust letters of recommendation," 2000.

61. Ibid.

62. Callahan, "When friendship calls, should truth answer?" 1978.

63. Schneider, "Why you can't trust letters of recommendation," 2000.

64. Fox, personal communication, 1 August 2000.

65. Schneider, "Why you can't trust letters of recommendation," 2000.

66. Ibid.; Ryan and Martinson, "Perceived effects of exaggeration in recommendation letters," 2000.

67. Ryan and Martinson, "Perceived effects of exaggeration in recommendation letters," 2000.

68. Ibid.

69. Ibid.

70. Ibid.; Bok, *Lying,* 1999.

71. Ryan and Martinson, "Perceived effects of exaggeration in recommendation letters," 2000.

72. Kasambira, "Recommendation inflation," 1984.

73. Hauenstein in Ryan and Martinson, "Perceived effects of exaggeration in recommendation letters," 2000.

74. Knouse, "The letter of recommendation: Specificity and favorability of information," 1983.

75. Fox, personal communication, 1 August 2000.

76. Ceci and Peters, "Letters of Reference: A Naturalistic Study of the Effects of Confidentiality," 1984; Shaffer et al. in Ryan and Martinson, "Perceived effects of exaggeration in recommendation letters," 2000.

77. Shaffer et al in Ryan and Martinson, "Perceived effects of exaggeration in recommendation letters," 2000.

REFERENCES

Aamodt, Michael G., Bryan, Devon A., and Whitcomb, Alan J. 1993. "Predicting performance with letters of recommendation." *Public Personnel Management* 22: 81–89.

Altshuler, Glenn C. 2000. "Dear admissions committee." *New York Times* (January 9): 4A.

Archibald, Randal C. 1998. "Just because the grades are up, are Princeton students smarter?" *New York Times* (18 February).

Basinger, David. 1997. "Fighting grade inflation: A misguided effort?" *College Teaching* 45 (3) (Summer): 81–91.

Baummeistr, R. F. 1996. "Should schools try to boost self esteem?" *American Educator* 22 (Summer): 14–19.

Beaver, William. 1997. "Declining college standards: It's not the courses, it's the grades." *The College Board Review* 181 (July): 2–7.

Bok, Sissela. 1999. *Lying,* 2d ed. New York: Vintage Books.

Bowen, W. G. and Bok, D. 1998. *The Shape of the River.* Princeton, N.J.: Princeton University Press.

Bromley, D. G., Crow, H. L., and Gibson, M. S. 1973. "Grade inflation: Trends, causes, and implications." *Phi Delta Kappan* 59 (10): 694–697.

Callahan, Daniel. 1978. "When friendship calls, should truth answer?" *Chronicle of Higher Education* (7 August): 32.

Ceci, Stephen and Peters, Douglas. 1984. "Letters of Reference: A Naturalistic Study of the Effects of Confidentiality." *American Psychologist* 39 (1) (January): 29–31.

Cole, W. 1993. "By Rewarding Mediocrity We Discourage Excellence." *Chronicle of Higher Education* (6 January): B1–B2.

Cross, Theodore L. 1993. "On scapegoating Blacks for grade inflation." *Journal of Blacks in Higher Education* (1) (Fall): 47–56.

Dey, Eric L., Astin, Alexander W., and Korn, William S. 1991. "The American Freshman: Twenty-Five Year Trends, 1966–1990," Higher Education Research Institute, Graduate School of Education, University of California, Los Angeles (September): 37–38.

Dreyfuss, Simeon. 1993. "My fight against grade inflation: A response to William Cole." *College Teaching* 41 (4) (Fall): 149–152.

Edwards, C. H. 2000. "Grade inflation: The effects on educational quality and personal well being." *Education* 120 (3) (Spring): 538–546.

Farley, Barbara. 1995. "A is for average: The grading crisis in today's colleges." Princeton, N.J.: Princeton University Mid-Career Fellowship Program. [BBB24000] ED384384.

Fox, John B., Jr. 2000. Personal communication (1 August).

Geisinger, K. F. 1979. "A Note on Grading Policies and Grade Inflation." *Improving College and University Teaching* 27 (3): 113–115.

Goldman, L. 1985. "The Betrayal of the Gatekeepers: Grade Inflation." *Journal of General Education* 37 (2): 97–121.

Grieves, R. 1982. "A Policy Proposal Regarding Grade Inflation." *Educational Research Quarterly* (Summer).

Juola, Arvo. 1976. "Grade inflation in higher education: What can or should we do?" ED129917 (April).

Juola, Arvo. 1980. "Grade inflation in higher education–1979. Is it over?" ED189129 (March).

Kahne, Joseph. 1996. "The Politics of Self-Esteem." *American Educational Research Journal* 33 (2) (Spring): 3–22.

Kasambira, K. Paul. 1984. "Recommendation inflation." *Teacher Educator* 20 (2) (Fall): 26–29.

Knouse, Stephen B. 1983. "The letter of recommendation: Specificity and favorability of information." *Personal Psychology* 36: 331–341.

Kolevzon, Michael S. 1981. "Grade Inflation in Higher Education: A Comparative Study." *Research in Higher Education* 15 (3): 195–212.

Kuh, George and Hu, Shouping. 1999. "Unraveling the Complexity of the Increase in College Grades from the Mid-1980s to the Mid-1990s." *Educational Evaluation and Policy Analysis* (Fall): 297–320.

Lambert, Craig. 1993. "Desperately Seeking Summa." *Harvard Magazine* (May/June): 37.

Landrum, R. Eric. 1999. "Student Expectations of Grade Inflation." *Journal of Research and Development in Education* 32 (2) (Winter): 124–128.

Levine, Arthur. 1997. "How the Academic Profession is Changing." *Daedalus* 126 (4): 1–20.

Levine, Arthur and Cureton, Jeanette S. 1998. *When Hope and Fear Collide: A Portrait of Today's College Student.* San Francisco: Jossey-Bass.

Lucas, Christopher J. 1994. *American Higher Education: A History.* New York: St. Martin's Press.

Mansfield, Harvey C. 2001. "Grade inflation: It's time to face the facts." *Chronicle of Higher Education* (6 April).

McConahay, Mark and Cote, Roland. 1988. "The Expanded Grade Context Record at Indiana University." *Cause/Effect* 21 (4): 47–48, 60.

McMurtie, Beth. 2001. "Colleges are Urged to Devise Better Ways to Measure Learning." *Chronicle of Higher Education* (24 January).

Metzger, Walter P. 1987. "The Academic Profession in the United States" in *The Academic Profession,* ed. Burton R. Clark. Berkeley: University of California Press.

Mitchell, Joyce Slayton. 1996. "The college letter: College advisor as anthropologist in the field." *Journal of College Admissions* 150 (Winter): 24–28.

Nagel, Brian. 1998. "A Proposal for Dealing with Grade Inflation: The Relative Performance Index." *Journal of Education for Business* 74 (1) (September/October).

Perrin, Noel. 1998. "How Students at Dartmouth Came to Deserve Better Grades." *Chronicle of Higher Education* (9 October).

Potter, William P. 1979. "Grade Inflation: Unmasking the Scourge of the Seventies." *College and University* 55 (I) (Fall): 19–26.

Reibstein, L. 1994. "Give me an A, or give me death." *Newsweek* 62 (13 June).

Rosovsky, Henry with Ameer, Inge-Lise. 1998. "A neglected topic; Professional conduct of college and university teachers" in *Universities and their Leadership*, ed. William E. Bowen and Harold Shapiro. Princeton: Princeton University Press.

Ryan, Michael and Martinson, David L. 2000. "Perceived effects of exaggeration in recommendation letters." *Journalism and Mass Communication Educator.* Columbia. (Spring).

Schackner, B. 1997. "Inflation in grades: a 1990s fact of life." *Pittsburgh Post Gazette* (24 August): 1.

Schmidt, Peter. 2000. "Colleges are starting to become involved in high-school testing policies." *Chronicle of Higher Education* (January 21).

Schmidt, Peter. 2000. "Faculty outcry greets proposal of competency tests at U. of Texas." *Chronicle of Higher Education* (October 6).

Schneider, Alison. 2000. "Why you can't trust letters of recommendation." *Chronicle of Higher Education* (30 June): A14–16.

Shils, Edward Albert. 1983. *The Academic Ethic*. Chicago: University of Chicago Press.

Spinks, Nelda and Wells, Barron. 1999. "Trends in the Employment Process: Resumes and Job Application Letters." *Career Development International*.

Stone, J. E. 1996. "Inflated Grades, Inflated Enrollment, and Inflated Budgets: An Analysis and Call for Review at the State Level." *Educational Policy Analysis Archives* 3 (11) (26 June).

Twitchell, James B. 1997. "Stop Me Before I Give Your Kid Another 'A.' " *The Washington Post* (4 June).

Walhout, Donald. 1997. "Grading across a career." *College Teaching* 45 (3) (Summer): 83–87.

Weller, L. David. 1986. "Attitude Toward Grade Inflation: A Random Survey of American Colleges of Arts and Sciences and Colleges of Education." *College & University* 61 (2) (Winter): 118–127.

Williams, Wendy M. and Ceci, Stephen J. 1997. "How'm I Doing? Problems with Student Ratings of Instructors and Courses." *Change* 29 (5) (September/October).

Wilson, Bradford P. 1999. "The Phenomenon of Grade Inflation in Higher Education." *National Forum* (Fall): 38–41.

Wilson, Robin. 1998. "New research casts doubt on value of student evaluations of professors." *Chronicle of Higher Education* (January 16).

Zander, Rosamund Stone and Zander, Benjamin. 2000. "The power of A." *Boston Globe Magazine* (27 August).

SELECTION 1 QUESTIONS

Vocabulary

1. Define "grade inflation." Include an explanation of "grade compression."

2. Explain what Rosovsky and Hartley mean when they say, "There is no unanimity about either the causes or consequences of changed standards of evaluation."

3. Explain what Rosovsky and Hartley mean when they say "the role of minority students in starting grade inflation appears specious."

4. Rosovsky and Hartley say, "Research suggests that greater specificity results in less vague and lofty rhetoric." Explain the meaning of this rationale for writing specific, rather than general, letters of evaluation.

Comprehension and Analysis

5. According to Rosovsky and Hartley, what is a grade is intended to be? What three purposes should a grade serve?

6. What are five common explanations for grade inflation?

7. Rosovsky and Hartley report that the probability that grade inflation began as a "response to student diversity" has been rejected by almost all who have studied it. Why has it been rejected?

8. What are two of the "adverse consequences" of grade inflation?

9. According to Rosovsky and Hartley, what do faculty see as the "most important difference" between writing letters of recommendation and assigning grades?

10. Do Rosovsky and Hartley believe grade inflation exists? Does their evidence convince you to believe as they do? If so, what evidence did you find most convincing? If not, what convinced you they are wrong?

11. Rosovsky and Hartley say that for "evaluations to accomplish their intended purpose we must question a currently popular assumption in psychology and education that virtually all students can excel academically across the board—and in life as well." Do you classify that as fact, opinion, or reasoned judgment? Please explain your reasoning.

12. Summarize Rosovsky and Hartley's conclusions.

Reflect and Connect

13. What influence, if any, do you think web sites such as RateMyProfessors.com has on grade inflation? Please explain. (RateMyProfessors.com has about half a million evaluations for about 115,000 professors at 2,500 colleges in the United States and Canada.)

14. Assume you are about to get a new job. However, to get the job, you must get an A grade in your computer applications course to demonstrate your competency in creating and manipulating databases. You don't really understand the database work all that well, but you can do enough extra-credit work to get you the A grade and the new job. Explain what you decide to do and your reasons.

SELECTION 2   ALL SHALL HAVE PRIZES; GRADE-INFLATION IN UNIVERSITIES

THE ECONOMIST STAFF

Since it began in London in 1845, The Economist *has been written by a collection of staff journalists, freelance writers, and subject experts from across Europe and the United States. However, no matter how famous the author, no article in* The Economist *is signed. The main reason for anonymity "is a belief that what is written is more important than who writes it." This article appeared April 14, 2001.*

IDEAS TO THINK ABOUT

Should grades establish relative merit—how you did compared to those around you—or show how you did against a set standard? Should different methods be used in different classes?

WORDS TO KNOW

belies (¶1)—disguises, camouflages
sullied (¶2)—soiled, dirtied
making divisive charges (¶5)—creating trouble or dissension
pernicious (¶6)—harmful, destructive

Every so often academic squabbles are worth treating as more than just up- 1
market versions of "The Jerry Springer Show". Harvard University is having exactly such a squabble at the moment. The instigator is Harvey C. Mansfield, a political philosopher whose soft-spoken manner belies a taste for public controversy; the subject is the rampant grade-inflation under which so many American students now take it for granted that they will be given an A for work that 20 years ago would have got a C; and the debate he has set off is challenging the cloying culture of self-esteem that stretches well beyond Harvard.

The whole thing started when Mr. Mansfield, whose tough grades 2 earned him the nickname "C-minus", declared that he was no longer willing to punish his students by giving them realistic grades. Henceforward he would give them two grades: an "ironic" grade that would go on their official records, and a realistic grade that he would reveal to them only in private. In this way Harvard students could enjoy the challenge of measuring themselves against real standards without having their gleaming resumes sullied.

"Ironic" is a gentle word for Harvard's grading system. About half of 3 Harvard's students get an A-minus or above. Only 6% receive a C-plus or lower. Some Harvard apologists justify this inflated system on the ground that their university selects the best and brightest. But aren't grades supposed to establish relative merits? Aren't "elite" institutions supposed to measure people against the highest possible standards? And aren't serious teachers supposed to point out their pupils' weaknesses as well as their strengths?

None of this would matter if Harvard were alone in taking the name of 4 excellence in vain. But grade-inflation is almost universal in American education. Outstanding students are compared with Einstein. Abject failures are praised as "differently abled." Even the hard sciences have started diluting their standards in order to compete with the humanities, where cheating is so much easier.

Why have academics allowed their standards to become so debased? Mr. 5 Mansfield provoked an outcry when he put some of the blame on affirmative action, the policy of providing places to some people on the basis of their race. University administrators accused him of making "divisive" charges without a "shred of evidence" to back them up. The divisive bit is certainly true, but Mr. Mansfield could hardly provide the proof when the university administration keeps the relevant student transcripts under lock and key. He was simply relying on the only tools at his disposal: personal experience (he has been on the Harvard faculty since 1962) and circumstantial evidence: grade-inflation followed the introduction of affirmative action.

The debate about affirmative action is arguably a red herring. Three less 6 controversial but much more pernicious things probably matter more. The first is the cult of self-esteem. For years fashionable educators have been arguing that the worst thing you can do to young people is to damage their sensitive egos with criticism. "If a child lives with criticism, he learns to condemn," goes a popular screed handed out to the parents of pre-schoolers. "If a child lives with praise, he learns to appreciate; if a child lives with approval, he learns to like himself."

This might be defensible when applied to the kindergarten. The trouble is 7 that this therapeutic philosophy is spreading throughout the educational system. The idea is at the heart of "constructivist mathematics" which emphasizes the importance of feeling good about mathematics rather than mastering basic techniques. It is at the heart of "Ebonics," which argues that black children should not be penalized for adopting "black speech patterns." And it is at the heart of the "I love me" sessions that proliferate in American elementary schools, in which children complete the phrase "I am . . ." with words such as "beautiful," "lovable" and "great," when "spoiled," "bored" and "violent" often seem more accurate.

Resisting this claptrap is made no easier by the fact that so many leftish 8 university professors routinely argue that traditional standards are little more than tools of western oppression. But the second mighty force behind grade inflation is something conservatives normally praise: the marketplace.

American universities are big businesses which can charge students in ex- 9 cess of $20,000 a year for the privilege of attending them. Students naturally gravitate towards institutions that are going to give them a return on their investment—the sparkling academic resume that opens the doors to Wall Street banks or prestigious law firms. Professors who resist the demand for grade-inflation may find themselves embarrassed by empty classrooms. Student course guides provide plenty of details about how generously teachers grade.

The third force is the lack of interest that high-flying academics show in 10 the humdrum business of teaching. People who care a great deal about something are obsessed with making precise judgments of quality: listen to the average sports fan, for example. But the road to success in modern academia lies through research rather than teaching. All too many academics are content to hand out A-grades like confetti in return for favourable teaching ratings and more time to devote to research.

Fixing grade-inflation will not be easy in a system in which professors 11 rightly value their autonomy. On the other hand, there are some signs of change. Graduate schools such as Harvard's Business School have manfully maintained their use of a rigorous grading curve. Some universities have experimented with putting two grades on report cards—the individual student's grade and the average grade for the class as a whole.

But perhaps the simplest argument for Mr. Mansfield's cause is that any- 12 body who has ever been well taught knows that he is right. People who work under demanding taskmasters usually learn to respect them. People who are coddled with unearned A-grades despise the system they are exploiting. Living on a diet of junk grades is like living on a diet of junk food. You swell up out of all decent proportions without ever getting any real nourishment. And you end up in later life regretting your disgusting habits.

SELECTION 2 QUESTIONS

Vocabulary

1. Explain what the authors mean by a "cloying culture of self-esteem." (paragraph 1) Does the phrase carry a positive or a negative connotation?

2. The authors say, "The debate about affirmative action is arguably a red herring." (paragraph 6) What is a "red herring"?

3. In paragraph 6, the authors label the phrase "if a child lives with criticism, he learns to condemn" a "popular screed." What do they mean? Do they want the label to evoke a positive or negative reaction to the phrase?

Comprehension and Analysis

4. State the authors' thesis/conclusion.

5. Why did Professor Mansfield declare he would start giving students two grades? Describe the two grades.

6. The authors describe three "less controversial but much more pernicious" reasons for grade inflation. List them.

7. Do the authors believe grade inflation is limited to Harvard? If not, how widespread do they believe it is?

8. How would you describe the article's overall tone? List two phrases or sentences that you believe contribute to and illustrate the tone.

9. The authors use an analogy to illustrate their thesis/conclusion. Explain the analogy. Do you think the analogy accomplished what the authors wanted? Why or why not?

Reflect and Connect

10. In *Evaluation and the Academy,* Rosovsky and Hartley say grades should (1) tell students how well or how poorly they understand the course content; (2) tell them their strengths, weaknesses, and areas of talent; and (3) provide information to external audiences. Do you think *The Economist* staff would agree or disagree? Please give an example to support your conclusion.

SELECTION 3 **DOONESBURY CARTOON**

GARRY TRUDEAU

Mr. Trudeau received his B.A. and an M.F.A. in graphic design from Yale University. He launched his signature comic strip Doonesbury *in 1970; it now appears in nearly 1,400 daily and Sunday newspapers in the United States and abroad. In 1975, Trudeau became the first comic strip artist ever to be awarded a Pulitzer Prize for editorial cartooning. He has contributed articles to publications such as* Rolling Stone, The New Republic, The New Yorker, *and*

The Washington Post. *He is currently a contributing essayist for* Time *magazine.*

IDEAS TO THINK ABOUT

How would you feel about a professor who happily accepted any answer for any question? What do you see as some of the positive and negative consequences of such behavior?

Doonesbury © G.B. Trudeau. Reprinted with permission of *Universal Press Syndicate.* All rights reserved.

SELECTION 3 QUESTIONS

Comprehension and Analysis

1. What is Trudeau's message?
2. Explain what the "pressure to pander" means. Who is "giving in to the pressure"? Who and/or what is exerting the pressure?

Reflect and Connect

3. In the article, "All Shall Have Prizes," the authors describe "constructivist mathematics" where the emphasis is on the importance of feeling good about math, rather than mastering basic techniques. What do you think would be an advantage of that approach to mathematics? What do you think would be a disadvantage of that approach to mathematics?

SELECTION 4   WHEN 'A' IS FOR ANYBODY

SALLY ABRAHMS

Ms. Abrahms has more than 20 years of experience writing and editing for national publications, including 7 years as a columnist for The Boston Globe. *She often writes about family issues and is the author of* Children in the Crossfire *and co-author with Gayle Rosenwald Smith, J.D., of* What Every Woman Should Know About Divorce and Custody.

AN IDEA TO THINK ABOUT

Would your behavior change in any way if you knew that your transcript would list the percentage of the class that earned the same grade as you did?

WORD TO KNOW

curmudgeons (¶1)—people who enjoy being negative and grouchy

When historians look back on the academic achievements of America's college 1
students, they'll see the late 1990s and early 2000s as a golden age—or an epic
boondoggle. For years campus curmudgeons have railed against the upward
drift of college grades. But lately "grade inflation" has come under new scrutiny
after *The Boston Globe* published an analysis of grades at Harvard.

The newspaper found that half of undergrads there receive an A or A- 2
minus in courses, and an astounding 91 percent of the class of 2001 graduated
with honors. In response, Harvard announced it will limit honors to 60 percent
of the class (only those with a B-plus or better need apply), and deans will encourage professors to hand out more B's. As the nation's flagship university
tightens its standards, other students may feel the ripple. "Harvard is a trend-
setter," says Bradford Wilson, executive director of the National Association of
Scholars, a faculty group. "If Harvard is doing stricter evaluations, other institutions will fall in line."

Grade inflation appears to be widespread. According to a 2002 report by 3
the American Academy of Arts and Sciences, A's accounted for 30.7 percent
of undergraduate grades at Princeton in 1973 but had risen to 42.5 percent by
1997. In a national survey, Arthur Levine, president of Teachers College at Columbia University, found that the percentage of grades that were A-minus or
better jumped from 7 percent in 1969 to 19 percent in 1976 to 26 percent in
1998. Despite lots of learned talk about why this is happening, no one is really
sure. Some observers say the laxity stems from Vietnam-era professors who
pumped up grades to keep students from getting caught in the draft; other

commentators say it's a side effect of affirmative action, and that professors are reluctant to give low grades to minority students. Others say the upward trend is justified because kids are just smarter today; admissions at top schools have become so competitive that it's no surprise students who make it through this gauntlet can earn A's.

Colleges are trying various tactics to stem the laxity. To give outsiders (like grad schools and corporate recruiters) a better sense of what achievement a student's grades represent, Dartmouth now includes median class grades for the courses on a student's transcript. Similarly, Columbia's transcripts show the percentage of each class that earned the same grade as the student. Neither move actually lowers student grades, a fix that administrators may have limited power to implement. "Faculty members have enormous freedom in how they grade," says Columbia's Levine. "To get them to simultaneously reduce the grades they give out would be like herding cats." 4

But by signaling which students are taking gut classes, colleges hope to reduce the prestige that accrues to undergrads who pad their schedules to boost grades. Experts who've studied the problem aren't sure those moves will change student behavior. "Grade inflation is not going to stop," says Valen Johnson, author of "College Grading: A National Crisis in Undergraduate Education." 5

As the debate continues, freshmen may arrive on campuses just as professors' expectations of what constitutes A-quality work are changing. Some students, such as those majoring in hard sciences like chemistry, may be less affected; grading in those disciplines is generally considered more stringent than in essay-based subjects like English or history. Some schools—MIT, Johns Hopkins, Reed College—boast of their tough grading system as a benefit to students. With no honors to compete for, "students study and work for the right reasons, to gain mastery of the material, instead of arguing between an A-minus and a B-plus," says Dean Robert Redwine of MIT, where the average grade is a B. 6

Unsurprisingly, students themselves seem rather muted among the calls for reform. Most don't seem to mind going home with report cards filled up with A's. "We've become an A-minus society," says Mark Oldman, founder of Vault, Inc., a career-research service for young job hunters. "We're numbers and ratings obsessed, and no one wants to be just average." Unless colleges find a way to bring grades down, students will continue enjoying the modern definition of average: the gentlemen's A-minus. 7

SELECTION 4 QUESTIONS

Vocabulary

1. Explain what President Levine means in paragraph 4, when he says that getting faculty to "simultaneously reduce the grades they give out would be like herding cats."

Evaluation and Grades

2. Explain what Abrahms means by "gut classes." (paragraph 5) Give an example of a "gut class" and a "non-gut class."

Comprehension and Analysis

3. What are Dartmouth and Columbia doing to try to stem grade inflation?
4. What does Abrahms believe is the "modern definition of average"?
5. In paragraph 7, Abrahms says, "Unsurprisingly, students themselves seem rather muted among the calls for reform." Explain what she means. Does her use of the word "unsurprisingly" influence you in any way? Please explain.
6. Does Abrahms view the academic achievements of America's college students during the late 1990s and early 2000s as a golden age or an epic boondoggle? Please explain. How would you characterize the period?

Reflect and Connect

7. In "All Shall Have Prizes" the authors say, "grade-inflation is almost universal in American education." Would Abrahms agree? Please explain.

SELECTION 5   AN EYE FOR AN 'A'

THE ECONOMIST STAFF

Since it began in London in 1845, The Economist has been written by a collection of staff journalists, freelance writers, and subject experts from across Europe and the United States. However, no matter how famous the author, no article in The Economist is signed. The main reason for anonymity is "a belief that what is written is more important than who writes it."

IDEAS TO THINK ABOUT

If your instructor told you the first day of class that everyone would get an 'A,' would this affect your behavior in the course? Would the effect be any different if your instructor told you the first day of class that 5 percent would get an 'A,' 15 percent would get a 'B,' 60 percent would get a 'C,' 15 percent would get a 'D,' and 5 percent would get an 'F'?

WORDS TO KNOW

eminent (¶1)—distinguished, well-regarded
pedantically (¶3)—being extremely picky to ensure accuracy

Gresham's Law (¶9)—a process by which inferior products or practices drive out superior ones
debauching (¶10)—abuse, corruption

Economists are not the only ones who fret about inflation. Lately, presidents of   1
some American universities have also added it to their worry list. One man
who is both an eminent economist and a university president—Larry Summers,
at Harvard—stirred up particular excitement over the subject recently. He is
concerned about inflation not of prices, but of academic grades, and he caused
a storm when he told one of the university's professors he didn't like it.

An internal study shows that nearly half the grades Harvard awards have   2
lately been A or A-minus—a lot more than in the 1980s. Surely, outsiders
mock, this grade inflation is but a symptom of a wider dumbing-down in America's universities: a symbol of the country's obsession with self-esteem, as opposed to self-improvement.

Without the benefit of a Harvard education, they would say that. But the   3
trend does seem a little odd. Is it such a bad thing, in fact? This column also
feels obliged to ask, pedantically, whether grade inflation really is "inflation."

To take the second question first, the answer is, No, not strictly speaking. If   4
you take the metaphor seriously, "inflation" in grades ought to mean that work of
a given standard would be awarded an ever higher grade, year by year. The highest permissible grade would therefore have to keep rising: A this year, A-star the
next, A-double-star and so forth thereafter, in a ceaseless procession of non-
improvement. Because in reality the top grade is fixed, the process is not so much
grade inflation as grade compression. This is worse: a distortion in relative prices
is more confusing than a uniform upward drift. Grade compression squeezes information out of the system. At the limit, when all Harvard's students get As all
the time, the university's grades will yield no information whatsoever.

Fixing the proportion of students awarded each grade would avoid grade   5
compression—but this might squeeze out information in another way. After all,
it may indeed be the case that the changing distribution of grades reflects improvements in the quality of students. Harvard has attracted record applications in the past few years. Some maintain, with straight faces, that each class
is cleverer than the last—a hard thing to disprove.

But is grade inflation necessarily a bad thing? The answer depends on   6
who you are. When students leave Harvard, they carry grades as a sort of currency: a pocketful of intellectual capital, to bid for jobs or places in graduate
schools against graduates from other universities with other currencies. These
positions go to those who can put the most academic cash on the table. Employers and graduate schools must decide on the exchange rate, as it were, between a Harvard C student (a rare thing, these days) and an A student from a
less distinguished place.

Again, overall grade inflation—the uniform devaluation of the students'   7
capital—would be relatively easy to cope with, working in principle neither to

the advantage or disadvantage of Harvard graduates. Recruiters, in a position to see the market for graduates as a whole, would simply adjust their exchange rate. Compression, however, has distributional consequences. The best Harvard students see their grades devalued relative to those of mediocre Harvard students. That is bad for incentives.

ENOUGH, ALREADY

In practice, adjustment to overall grade inflation is unlikely to be smooth: there may be gross exchange-rate misalignments, as well as relative-price distortions. As with workers and wages, one needs to think about how recruiters form their expectations about future grade inflation. If employers are "rational"—if the assumption is that Harvard is inflating its grades, and will continue to do so—then they can apply an appropriate deflation factor. If they are "adaptive"—how surprising, Harvard inflated its grades again last year (but surely won't do so again)—Harvard students will benefit, and keep on benefiting, from recurring episodes of grade illusion. 8

The possibility that grade illusion will deliver gains to students, as well as merely flattering their intellectual vanity, and the undoubted fact that it makes life less demanding for the faculty (less work, less irritation), create a strong incentive for universities to inflate and compress. Soon, inflated and compressed grades will be the norm and fair grades the exception: a kind of Gresham's Law, you might say, with bad grades driving out good. 9

Good, stable currencies are hard to create and should not be abandoned lightly. But once the debauching has begun, it is hard to stop—as Mr. Summers is discovering. Yet he and Harvard need not despair. Once the professors have reduced their grades to an absurdity, and rendered that particular currency worthless, other units of account will necessarily spring up to take its place: recommendations from professors, "personal essays", interviews, standardised tests—areas in which students from the most inflated universities happen to excel. The spur to competition will remain, the information will continue to flow. But watch out, faculty members: these alternative currencies sound as though they involve more work and trouble than simply giving true grades in the first place. 10

SELECTION 5 QUESTIONS

Vocabulary

1. The authors say many believe grade inflation is just another "symbol of the country's obsession with self-esteem, as opposed to self-improvement." Please explain.

Comprehension and Analysis

2. How is "grade compression" different than "grade inflation"? How does the Economist staff's explanation of these two terms compare with Rosovsky and Hartley's explanation in *Evaluation and the Academy*?
3. Why do the authors believe "grade compression" is even "worse" than grade inflation? What do they forecast as the end result of grade compression?
4. Why do the authors think grade inflation would be easier to deal with than grade compression?
5. Who do the authors believe is primarily responsible for grade inflation/compression? Cite an example to support your answer.
6. Is grade inflation necessarily a bad thing? Please explain.
7. The authors say that the increase in A grades at Harvard could be because "each class is cleverer than the last." Do they believe that is true? How do you know?
8. The authors propose that grades are a sort of currency. Do you think that is an appropriate analogy? Please explain.

Reflect and Connect

9. In *Evaluation and the Academy,* Rosovsky and Hartley say, "It is not surprising that the 'softer' subjects exhibit the severest grade inflation." Would these authors agree? Please explain.

SELECTION 6   AMID CRIES OF GRADE INFLATION, C'S STILL ABOUND

MARK CLAYTON

Mr. Clayton has been with the Christian Science Monitor since 1984, and has been its higher education reporter for the last six years. He has written on diverse subjects such as the influence of corporate cash in university research and fraternities' attempts to curb their own alcohol abuse. In 2001, he received the Iris Molotsky Award for Excellence in Coverage of Higher Education given by the American Association of University Professors for his two-part series, "The Gender Equation." This article appeared in the August 20, 2002, edition of the Monitor.

IDEAS TO THINK ABOUT

Are students who attend different types of colleges and universities—private, public, Ivy League, small, large—in different parts of the United States different from one another? Are professors at those different types of institutions different from one another?

WORD TO KNOW

spate (¶1)—a large number

When 9 out of 10 Harvard seniors graduated with honors last year, it was proof 1
to some that grade inflation was rampant in American higher education. A
spate of reports that followed affirmed the growing threat.

Now comes a new study by the US Department of Education suggesting 2
that the hand wringing may be much ado about not too much.

According to "Profile of Undergraduates in US Postsecondary Education 3
Institutions: 1999, 2000," a national study released summer 2002, the
mediocre grades of C-plus and lower are alive and kicking.

About 34 percent of the 50,000 undergraduates at 900 institutions sur- 4
veyed earned C's and D's or worse, the study reported. About 41 percent earned
B's and C's or mostly B's. Meanwhile, 26 percent earned A's and B's or mostly A's.

On its face, this breakdown may seem unremarkable. 5

Yet the study contradicts other reports, including one this spring by the 6
American Academy of Arts and Sciences, that say grade inflation is widespread. The AAAS report cites a raft of academic studies documenting grade
inflation back to 1960 and recounts estimates that just 10 to 20 percent of undergraduates get a B-minus or worse.

"There's been this series of reports all saying the same thing—that grade 7
inflation is running rampant—and now this [Education Department] report
makes that appear more questionable," says Jacqueline King, director of the
Center for Policy Analysis at the American Council on Education.

Others agree. A spokeswoman for the Association of American Colleges 8
and Universities told the *Chronicle of Higher Education* recently that the new
report "debunks all the furor over grade inflation."

Overall, the strength of the Department of Education report is its breadth. 9
But it's also a snapshot of just one year and does not track grades over time to see if
they ratchet upward, as have some smaller studies. Still, it is the proportion of students receiving high grades or poor grades that, on the face of it, doesn't appear to
be in sync with the more alarming findings in smaller studies, Ms. King says.

"It's typically been studies at a small number of institutions, primarily 10
highly selective research universities and liberal arts colleges, that have produced this belief that grade inflation is widespread," she says. "A lot of these
have been primarily surveys of faculty."

By contrast, she says, the [Education Department] study may be more 11
reliable because it is based on student transcripts or, where those were not
available, student reports of their own grades.

The AAAS report cited a steady rise in the proportion of students at 12 Princeton, Harvard, and Dartmouth who get A's.

Harvard, in response to this and other reports that pointed to grade infla- 13 tion, adopted some new policies this spring. The school decided to cap the number of honors degrees awarded and to cut the number of A's and B's professors give students.

Some experts suggest that grade inflation is indeed a problem at a few 14 elite institutions—but not necessarily across the board.

The Department of Education report did find that private four-year 15 doctorate-granting institutions give far fewer C's and D's—only about 21 percent, compared with 33 percent at public doctorate-granting institutions.

While certain schools may deserve scrutiny, these numbers don't have to 16 translate into a general problem of grade inflation at private schools, King says.

"These are highly selective institutions where it would be rather odd to 17 have a large proportion of C's and D's," she says.

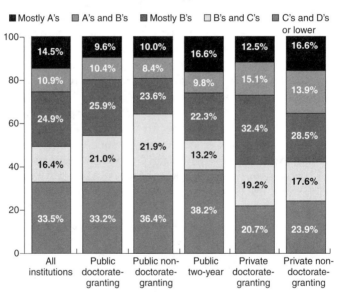

Distribution of Undergraduates by Grade-Point Average and Institution Type, 1999–2000

College-level grade inflation may not be as widespread as people believe, according to a new report from the U.S. Department of Education. About a third of undergraduates, in fact, earn C's and D's or lower.

Source: US Department of Education, National Center for Education Statistics, "Profile of Undergraduates in US Post Secondary Education Institutions: 1999, 2000."

Evaluation and Grades

WHO MAKES THE GRADE?

- Older students earn higher grades than their younger counterparts. For example, 38 percent of undergraduates in their 30s earned A's and B's or mostly A's, compared with 18 percent of students between the ages of 19 and 23.
- 43 percent of married undergraduates earn A's and B's.
- Grades rise with student income, but parents' education level does not seem to have a substantial effect on student grades.
- Almost 40 percent of men earn C's and D's or lower, compared with 30 percent of women.

Source: U.S. Department of Education, "Profile of Undergraduates in US Postsecondary Education Institutions: 1999, 2000."

SELECTION 6 QUESTIONS

Vocabulary

1. Explain what Clayton means in paragraph 2 when he says the "hand wringing may be much ado about not too much."
2. A spokeswoman for the Association of American Colleges and Universities said the new [Department of Education] report "debunks all the furor over grade inflation." (paragraph 8) What did she mean?
3. Jacqueline King from the American Council on Education said the "proportion of students [in the Department of Education report] receiving high grades or poor grades . . . doesn't appear to be in sync with . . . smaller studies." (paragraph 9) What did she mean?

Comprehension and Analysis

4. State Clayton's thesis.
5. According to Clayton, what is the strength of the Department of Education report? What is its limitation?
6. Why does Mrs. King believe the Department of Education study "may be more reliable"? Does her argument convince you? Please explain.
7. List and explain two reasons that different research studies about grade inflation have different findings.

8. Compare the grade inflation studies data Rosovsky and Hartley present in *Evaluation and the Academy* to the Department of Education data in this article. What factors could account for any differences?

9. Clayton presents information about studies that report there is widespread grade inflation, but the new study that reports there is not widespread grade inflation. Does he give equal weight and authority to all the information? Please explain.

Reflect and Connect

10. In "When 'A' Is for Anybody" Abrahms says, "Unless colleges find a way to bring grades down, students will continue enjoying the modern definition of average: the gentlemen's A-minus." Do you think Clayton would agree with Abrahms? Please explain.

SELECTION 7   WHY ANY GRADES AT ALL, FATHER?

TINA JUAREZ

Dr. Juarez is Principal of Walter Prescott Webb Middle School in Austin, Texas. A past president of the Austin Hispanic Public School Administrators Association, she serves on numerous advisory boards. Her most recent publication is The School at Box Canyon, *which she describes as "sort of* Animal Farm *of the American southwest. But whereas Orwell's allegory satirizes government, my book is a satire of education, especially the grading system." This is the introduction to her article for* Phi Delta Kappan *about "the perennial conflict between those who want to spare students the stigma of failure and those who want to maintain standards."*

IDEAS TO THINK ABOUT

Think of a time when you worked very hard for a test or project yet didn't perform well and therefore received a "low" grade. Should the grade have been higher because of the amount of effort? Now think of a time when you didn't study yet managed to perform well and received an A. Was the grade "fair"?

WORDS TO KNOW

jaunty (¶1)—jolly, happy
emanate (¶10)—come from

In the movie classic *The Bells of St. Mary's*, Bing Crosby portrays jaunty Father   1
O'Malley, a priest sent by his bishop to determine if the dilapidated St. Mary's

<u>parochial</u> school should be closed to make way for a parking lot.[1] Unaware of Father O'Malley's true mission, Sister Superior Mary Benedict (Ingrid Bergman) continues to run St. Mary's with a steady hand while dreaming of moving the school to a modern building being constructed across the street by a wealthy businessman.

Because Father O'Malley comes to admire how dedicated Sister Mary 2 Benedict and her faculty are to the welfare of students, he joins the effort to persuade the wealthy businessman to donate his new building to St. Mary's. In the meantime, the easygoing priest and the no-nonsense nun discover that they seem to subscribe to opposing educational philosophies. Their differences come to a head when Father O'Malley tries to persuade Sister Mary Benedict to raise a child's failing score on an exam to a passing one. Patsy, the child in question, is a troubled girl whom Father O'Malley has been trying to help. If her test score is not raised, she will fail the semester and be unable to graduate with her class.

A firm believer in maintaining "standards," Sister Mary Benedict rejects 3 Father O'Malley's reasons for raising Patsy's test score (which include his suggestion that Patsy should get extra points for spelling her name correctly). Exasperated, the nun asks, "Do you believe in just passing everybody, Father?"

"Maybe I do," Father O'Malley answers and then poses a question of his 4 own: "Aren't we here to give children a helping hand—or are we here to measure their brains with a yardstick?"

When the priest inquires why 75 is the passing score at St. Mary's, Sister 5 Mary Benedict responds, "You would put the standard at 65, Father?"

"Why not?" 6

"Then why not at 55? Why any grades at all, Father? Why don't we 7 close the school and let them run wild?"

After a thoughtful moment, Father O'Malley replies, "Maybe. Be better 8 than breaking their hearts."

Sister Mary Benedict informs Father O'Malley that she will pass Patsy if 9 ordered to do so, but she will not change the cutoff score, because to do so would lower the school's standards.

Though a fictional scene from a movie released half a century ago, the 10 dispute between Father O'Malley and Sister Mary Benedict over Patsy's grade could have been played out just this morning in virtually any school in the nation. Few issues in education have remained as constant over the years as the question of whether "grading" helps learners or hurts them. The debates over grading that emanate from the musty pages of the education journals published in the 19th century have a distinctly contemporary tone—and, for better or worse, the grading practices commonly employed today are little different from those found in the 19th-century schoolhouse.[2]

Endnote: Sister Mary Benedict had a change of heart when Patsy admitted that she had not tried as hard as she might on the test because she was distraught over her parents' troubled relationship. Sister Mary Benedict could have let Patsy's failing grade stand. But she was a teacher, and Patsy's well-being and learning were important to her. So Sister Mary Benedict decided to do something she had never done before, something that ran counter to conventional wisdom and to her own instincts. She quizzed Patsy a second time over the same material. Patsy's answers revealed that she had indeed mastered the material, so she was allowed to graduate with her class.

NOTES

1. *The Bells of St. Mary's* (Los Angeles: Republic Pictures Corporation, 1945).
2. John Laska and Tina Juarez, eds., *Trading and Marking in American Schools: Two Centuries of Debate* (Springfield, Ill.: Charles C Thomas, 1992): 3–4.

SELECTION 7 QUESTIONS

Vocabulary

1. Explain the two points of view Juarez wants us to understand in paragraph 2 when she says that Father O'Malley and Sister Mary Benedict "subscribe to opposing educational philosophies."
2. Explain the phrase "could have been played out just this morning in virtually any school in the nation." (paragraph 10)

Comprehension and Analysis

3. Although Sister Mary Benedict doesn't know it, what is Father O'Malley's "true mission"?
4. What does Sister Mary Benedict want to happen to St. Mary's?
5. Why does Father O'Malley decide to help get the new school building?
6. What event causes Sister Mary Benedict and Father O'Malley to disagree? Explain what each wants to happen.
7. Examine the words Juarez uses to describe Father O'Malley, such as "jaunty," and "easygoing," and the descriptors for Sister Mary Benedict, such as "with a steady hand," and "no-nonsense." How do these words contribute to your analysis of the characters?
8. At the end of paragraph 10, Juarez says that "the grading practices commonly employed today are little different from those found in the 19th-century schoolhouse." Do you classify that as fact, opinion, or reasoned judgment? How did you decide?

9. Why do you think Juarez began her article with the movie? Do you think it was effective? Why or why not?

Reflect and Connect

10. Answer this paraphrase of Father O'Malley's question: Is a teacher's primary responsibility to give students a helping hand or to measure their brains with a yardstick?

SELECTION 8   EDITORIAL CARTOON

BRAD MCMILLAN

Mr. McMillan began his art career in the early 1970s in Memphis, Tennessee, drawing cartoons and illustrations for alternative and underground publications. In 1981, he opened a gallery in downtown Memphis devoted to his

By McMillan, Brad

work and the work of other area cartoonists and illustrators. In 1983, he became staff illustrator and editorial cartoonist for The Memphis Business Journal. He retains that position today even though he has been based in Dallas, Texas, since 1986. In Dallas, McMillan has exhibited his paintings and drawings, freelanced, and done editorial cartoons and cartoon illustrations for many publications including The Dallas Morning News, The Dallas Business Journal, and Texas Catholic.

IDEAS TO THINK ABOUT

Pretend that your supervisor at work issues you a report card with grades for your on-the-job performance in the basics of reading, writing, speaking, computer skills, and applied mathematics. How would those grades match with the grades you would receive from your professors? What might account for any differences?

SELECTION 8 QUESTIONS

Comprehension and Analysis

1. In this cartoon, who and/or what is the "real world"?
2. State McMillan's thesis.

Reflect and Connect

3. How do you think McMillan would answer the paraphrase of Father O'Malley's question: Is a teacher's primary responsibility to give students a helping hand or to measure their brains with a yardstick? Please explain.

SELECTION 9 MAKING THE GRADE

KURT WIESENFELD

Dr. Wiesenfeld has been a Professor in the School of Physics at Georgia Tech since 1997. His research interests lie in the field of nonlinear dynamics. He is a member of the American Physical Society, the Society of Industrial and Applied Mathematics, and he currently serves as a member-at-large of the Executive Committee of the American Physical Society's Division of Biological Physics. This article was published in the "My Turn" section of Newsweek.

IDEAS TO THINK ABOUT

Do most of your teachers allow students to complete extra credit assignments to boost their grades? What do you see as some of the positive and negative outcomes of allowing extra credit work?

WORDS TO KNOW

tentative (¶1)—cautious, hesitant
declarative statements (¶1)—making a statement, not asking a question
intrinsically worthless (¶6)—having no value in itself
eccentric (¶7)—strange, off-beat
less blatant (¶9)—not as obvious

It was a rookie error. After 10 years I should have known better, but I went to 1 my office the day after final grades were posted. There was a tentative knock on the door. "Professor Wiesenfeld? I took your Physics 2121 class? I flunked it? I wonder if there's anything I can do to improve my grade?" I thought: "Why are you asking me? Isn't it too late to worry about it? Do you dislike making declarative statements?"

After the student gave his tale of woe and left, the phone rang. "I got a D 2 in your class. Is there any way you can change it to 'Incomplete'?" Then the e-mail assault began: "I'm shy about coming in to talk to you, but I'm not shy about asking for a better grade. Anyway, it's worth a try." The next day I had three phone messages from students asking *me* to call *them*. I didn't.

Time was, when you received a grade, that was it. You might groan and 3 moan, but you accepted it as the outcome of your efforts or lack thereof (and, yes, sometimes a tough grader). In the last few years, however, some students have developed a disgruntled-consumer approach. If they don't like their grade, they go to the "return" counter to trade it in for something better.

What alarms me is their indifference toward grades as an indication of 4 personal effort and performance. Many, when pressed about why they think they deserve a better grade, admit they don't deserve one but would like one anyway. Having been raised on gold stars for effort and smiley faces for self-esteem, they've learned that they can get by without hard work and real talent if they can talk the professor into giving them a break. This attitude is beyond cynicism. There's a weird innocence to the assumption that one expects (even deserves) a better grade simply by begging for it. With that outlook, I guess I shouldn't be as flabbergasted as I was that 12 students asked me to change their grades *after* final grades were posted.

That's 10 percent of my class who let three months of midterms, quizzes 5 and lab reports slide until long past remedy. My graduate student calls it hyper-rational thinking: if effort and intelligence don't matter, why should deadlines?

What matters is getting a better grade through an unearned bonus, the academic equivalent of a freebie T-shirt or toaster giveaway. Rewards are disconnected from the quality of one's work. An act and its consequences are unrelated, random events.

Their arguments for wheedling better grades often ignore academic performance. Perhaps they feel it's not relevant. "If my grade isn't raised to a D I'll lose my scholarship." "If you don't give me a C, I'll flunk out." One sincerely overwrought student pleaded, "If I don't pass, my life is over." This is tough stuff to deal with. Apparently, I'm responsible for someone's losing a scholarship, flunking out or deciding whether life has meaning. Perhaps these students see me as a commodities broker with something they want—a grade. Though intrinsically worthless, grades, if properly manipulated, can be traded for what has value: a degree, which means a job, which means money. The one thing college actually offers—a chance to learn—is considered irrelevant, even less than worthless, because of the long hours and hard work required.

In a society saturated with surface values, love of knowledge for its own sake does sound eccentric. The benefits of fame and wealth are more obvious. So is it right to blame students for reflecting the superficial values saturating our society?

Yes, of course it's right. These guys had better take themselves seriously now, because our country will be forced to take them seriously later, when the stakes are much higher. They must recognize that their attitude is not only self-destructive, but socially destructive. The erosion of quality control—giving appropriate grades for actual accomplishments—is a major concern in my department. One colleague noted that a physics major could obtain a degree without ever answering a written exam question completely. How? By pulling in enough partial credit and extra credit. And by getting breaks on grades.

But what happens once she or he graduates and gets a job? That's when the misfortunes of eroding academic standards multiply. We lament that schoolchildren get "kicked upstairs" until they graduate from high school despite being illiterate and mathematically inept, but we seem unconcerned with college graduates whose less blatant deficiencies are far more harmful if their accreditation exceeds their qualifications.

Most of my students are science and engineering majors. If they're good at getting partial credit but not at getting the answer right, then the new bridge breaks or the new drug doesn't work. One finds examples here in Atlanta. Last year a light tower in the Olympic Stadium collapsed, killing a worker. It collapsed because an engineer miscalculated how much weight it could hold. A new 12-story dormitory could develop dangerous cracks due to a foundation that's uneven by more than six inches. The error resulted from incorrect data being fed into a computer. I drive past that dorm daily on my way to work, wondering if a foundation crushed under kilotons of weight is repairable or if this structure will have to be demolished. Two 10,000-pound steel beams at the new natatorium collapsed in March, crashing into the student athletic complex. (Should we give partial credit since no one was hurt?) Those are real-world consequences of errors and lack of expertise.

But the lesson is lost on the grade-grousing 10 percent. Say that you 11 won't (not can't, but won't) change the grade they deserve to what they want, and they're frequently bewildered or angry. They don't think it's fair that they're judged according to their performance, not their desires or "potential." They don't think it's fair that they should jeopardize their scholarships or be in danger of flunking out simply because they could not or did not do their work. But it's more than fair, it's necessary to help preserve a minimum standard of quality that our society needs to maintain safety and integrity. I don't know if the 13th-hour students will learn that lesson, but I've learned mine. From now on, after final grades are posted, I'll lie low until the next quarter starts.

SELECTION 9 QUESTIONS

Vocabulary

1. Explain what Wiesenfeld means by the phrase "rookie error." Give an example of a rookie error in another setting, such as basketball. (paragraph 1)
2. What is a "tale of woe"? (paragraph 2)
3. What analogy does Wiesenfeld use to make his point in paragraph 3?
4. Wiesenfeld refers to our society as "saturated with surface values" in paragraph 7. Give an example of what he means.

Comprehension and Analysis

5. State Wiesenfeld's thesis.
6. How does he develop and support his thesis?
7. Does Wiesenfeld believe that grades themselves have worth? What can they be used for?
8. According to Wiesenfeld, what do colleges "actually offer"? Why does he believe students consider that offering "less than worthless"?
9. What happens, in Wiesenfeld's opinion, when a student's "accreditation exceeds their qualifications"?
10. Explain what Wiesenfeld means when he says that students believe "an act and its consequences are unrelated, random events." Why does he think that?
11. Is Wiesenfeld in favor of extra credit projects? Why or why not?
12. What are two actions you think Wiesenfeld would like students to take?

Reflect and Connect

13. How do you think Wiesenfeld would respond to this paraphrase of Father O'Malley's question: Is a teacher's primary responsibility to give students a helping hand or to measure their brains with a yardstick? Please explain.

INVESTIGATING OTHER POINTS OF VIEW . . .

One way to investigate a variety of points of view on evaluation and grades is through the resources of Research Navigator™. Once you log on to Research Navigator.com and enter your personal passcode (from inside the front cover of this text), you have access to three databases of credible and reliable source material: 1) EBSCO's Content Select Academic Journal Database with content from the leading academic journals, 2) *The New York Times* Search by Subject™ Archive with full-text articles from *The New York Times*, 3) Link Library providing editorially selected "best of the web" sites. For more information about Research Navigator™ and how to use it efficiently, see "Introducing Research Navigator™" starting on page RN–1.

AFTER CONSIDERING SEVERAL POINTS OF VIEW . . .

A. One of the major issues in the debate surrounding grading is related to Father O'Malley's question: Is a teacher's primary responsibility to give students a helping hand or to measure their brains with a yardstick? Discuss the importance of a student's performance on classroom assessment devices in the awarding of grades. Include any other factors, if any, that should be given serious consideration when computing grades and the value you think should be placed on extra credit.

B. Writers have differing opinions as to whether significant "grade inflation" occurs in all colleges and universities or if it is just a phenomenon at a few elite institutions. Discuss your analysis of whether grade inflation exists. Include your working definition of grade inflation and some of the factors that are responsible for the inflation or the perception of the inflation.

C. Some people view students' ability to withdraw from classes without grade or transcript penalty as a major problem with long-term effects. Discuss what you believe are the effects of withdrawing from classes without grade or transcript penalty. Include both the immediate and long-term positive and negative effects of such policies.

THEME 2

FAMILIES

The photo of the "New American Family" on the February 2000 cover of *Rolling Stone* magazine erased all doubt that times—and the American family—have changed. Included in the familial group were David Crosby and his spouse, Jan; Melissa Etheridge and her life partner, Julie Cypher; and two children, the biological offspring of a test-tube union of Mr. Crosby and Ms. Cypher.

Although that group represents a small percentage of today's families, so does the Ozzie and Harriet model family from the '60s. During the last two decades, we have seen an increase in divorce rates, a decline in marriage rates, a rise in cohabitation, and fertility rates declining to a historic low point. Such changes have created a greater diversity in household structures: a steady increase in the proportion of one-parent families, two-career couples with children, homosexual couples with children, blended families, grandparents raising grandchildren, and communal families. According to figures released from the 2000 census, the number of U.S. single-person households increased to 26 percent while households with married couples and children under 18 dropped to 23.5 percent from 25.6 percent in 1990, and 45 percent four decades ago.

Are these changes cataclysmic? Are the changes evolutionary? Are we in crisis?

Many do see a crisis and urge a return to and/or preservation of traditional family values. Brigitte Berger, professor of sociology at Boston University, says, "More than a decade of research compellingly demonstrates that a particular type of family, namely the nuclear type . . . continues to be the single most important key to a child's success in school and in life beyond. . . . If this proposition is correct—and I think it is—it follows that the fate of the family and modern society are inexorably intertwined."

Others suggest that if the family isn't working, perhaps there is something wrong with its structure and that we are finally experiencing a long-needed revolution in the family structure. Dr. Pamela Kinnear, Research Fellow at the Australia Institute of Family Studies, says in her *New Families for Changing Times* discussion paper (2002) that although contemporary families have their failings, and new family forms have their shortcomings, we should view the changes as attempts by modern people to construct family forms that work for them, not as a matter of people being selfish individualists who do not care about the consequences of their actions for others.

The authors in this Theme tackle the complex changes and challenges for today's families.

To provide an overview of the topic, "Family Life," a chapter from John Macionis's *Social Problems* text opens the Theme. He considers a broad range of issues about families including the debate over definitions of "family" and problems of family life.

John Leo's column "Marriage on the Rocks" advises that "marriage is in trouble" and so are families and society; then Sam Gross provides a possible definition of family in one of his classic *New Yorker* cartoons.

Next, Bridget Maher looks at the "suffering caused by family break-down" and how "marriage counselors, educators, social workers, religious leaders, judges, divorce lawyers, and scholars are banding together to develop family-strengthening strategies" in "Patching Up the American Family."

In "Nostalgia As Ideology" Stephanie Coontz says that while she does agree that family life and marriage have irreversibly changed that "there is no way to reverse this trend short of a repressiveness that would not long be tolerated even in today's patriotic climate."

Liz Caile submits that "Families Suffer from Delamination" [between generations] as much as they do from the high rate of divorce or the decision to go parenting alone." Richard Weissbourd closes the theme with "Moral Parent, Moral Child" and his premise that "family structure matters less to a child's development than the quality of the parenting."

As you read the selections in this theme and other articles and essays on families, answer questions such as these as a matter of course:

1. Do I understand the author's words and phrases?
2. What is the author's thesis (conclusion)?
3. What facts, opinions, and reasoned judgments does the author provide to support and develop the thesis?
4. Are the author's facts, opinions, and reasoned judgments derived from respected sources?
5. Are there factual errors or misleading interpretations?
6. Has significant information been omitted or arbitrarily discounted?
7. What new information does this author add to my understanding of the issue?

SELECTION 1   FAMILY LIFE

JOHN J. MACIONIS

Dr. Macionis is Professor and Distinguished Scholar of Sociology at Kenyon College in Gambier, Ohio. During his many years at Kenyon, he has chaired the Anthropology-Sociology Department, directed the multidisciplinary program in humane studies, and presided over the campus senate. He says he is "first and foremost a teacher." He has authored and co-authored many sociology textbooks and articles on community life in the United States, interpersonal intimacy in families, effective teaching, humor, and the importance of global education.

AN IDEA TO THINK ABOUT

How would you describe a "traditional" American family to someone unfamiliar with our culture?

WORDS TO KNOW

Key terms appear in bold-faced type with definitions immediately following the term in italic type.

The Washington, D.C., courtroom was crowded and tense as the prosecutor   1
hammered away at Latrena Pixley, a twenty-five-year-old mother in a custody case who sat emotionless on the witness stand. "You carried your first child for nine months, held him in your arms, but then you gave him away. You carried your second child for nine months, held him in your arms, and you haven't seen him for six years. You carried your third child for nine months, held her in your arms, and then you killed her. Isn't this right?" Pixley looked up blankly, paused, and then answered "Yes" (Donnelly, 1998:28).

No one in the courtroom doubted that Pixley had utterly failed as a   2
mother. Even so, the judge had to decide whether to allow Pixley to take custody of her fourth child—a two-year-old boy named Cornelius—or to allow another woman, who had been raising the boy, to keep him. The verdict: Latrena Pixley would remain in prison for killing her daughter, but she would be moved to a new facility where she could take custody of her young son, Cornelius.

Laura Blankman, the woman raising Cornelius, was heartbroken. Having   3
befriended Pixley after she had killed her daughter, Blankman had come to think

of the boy as her own. Convinced that she could provide a better home for the boy, she had filed for custody. But Pixley objected, and the court case ended with the judge ordering Blankman to give the boy back to the woman who admits she did not want two children and killed a third.

It is easy to see that Latrena Pixley has not been up to the task of raising 4 children. She has made some terrible choices, and she is in prison as a result. But she also has been poor all her life, she has had no support from the men who fathered her children, and she never even met a social worker until after the death of her third child. Her case forces us to wonder what responsibility we have as a nation to ensure that people have the knowledge and the means to provide for themselves and their families.

This chapter examines many questions and controversies about family 5 life in the United States. Why are so many children poor? Why is single parenting twice as common today as it was in 1960? Why do half of all U.S. children live with a single parent at some time before age eighteen? We begin by defining some basic terms.

WHAT IS A FAMILY?

The **family** is *a social institution that unites individuals in cooperative groups that* 6 *care for members, regulate sexual relations, and oversee the bearing and raising of children.* **Kinship,** a related concept, refers to *a social bond, typically based on blood, marriage, or adoption, that joins individuals into families.*

Keep in mind that the form families take has varied over time and from 7 place to place. In modern, high-income societies, such as the United States, most people focus on the **nuclear family,** *one or two parents and their children.* In low-income nations around the world, however, people typically belong to an **extended family,** *parents and children, plus grandparents, aunts, uncles, and cousins, who often live close to one another and operate as a family unit.*

Everywhere, families form around **marriage,** *a lawful relationship—* 8 *expected to be lasting—involving economic cooperation, sexual activity, and, usually, childbearing.* Marriage, too, varies around the world. Most societies link marriage and having children, a connection evident in the fact that the word *matrimony* comes from Latin words meaning "the state of motherhood." This is why many people around the world may define a child born to an unwed mother as "illegitimate," although this attitude has become far less common in the United States.

Debate over Definitions

With so much change surrounding the family, we should not be surprised to find 9 disagreement over what the term "family" ought to mean. In the United States, the traditional view is that a family consists of a married couple and their children. Many people still support this view, claiming that marriage provides a secure setting that benefits children. From a more liberal point of view, such a narrow view of the family amounts to judging everyone by a single moral standard. Today, more people acknowledge the increasing diversity of family forms and favor recognizing **families of affinity,** that is, *people, with or without legal or blood ties, who feel they belong together and wish to define themselves as a family.*

Does it matter how we define "families"? The answer is *yes,* because this 10 question involves moral concerns (Are some kinds of relationships morally right or wrong?) as well as practical concerns (Is one kind of relationship better or worse for children?). The remainder of this chapter will explore all of these questions.

A Sociological Approach to Family Problems

Worth emphasizing at the outset is the approach sociologists take when study- 11 ing family problems. When most people speak about "family problems" or "problems at home," they usually have in mind conflicts between individuals or, perhaps, a situation involving a family member who is struggling with alcohol or some other drug.

Sociologists realize that problems of this kind are common enough. But, 12 as the story of Latrena Pixley in the opening to this chapter suggests, the sociological perspective looks beyond the behavior of individuals to how the organization of society creates certain challenges for families. Poverty, for example, results in an insecure family life for millions of people. Moreover, the fact that most women as well as men work for income today goes a long way toward explaining why so many families struggle to balance work and family responsibilities and find good, affordable child care.

PROBLEMS OF FAMILY LIFE

Few people doubt that U.S. families are changing. The number of people living 13 together without being married is rising; an increasing share of children are born to single mothers; mothers are joining fathers in the labor force in record numbers, so more young children spend the day in child-care programs; the divorce rate is now far higher than it was fifty years ago, creating new "blended families"; gay men and lesbians are coming closer to winning the right to legally marry; and new medical technology has raised miraculous new possibilities for reproduction. In the following sections, we examine each of these trends in turn.

Living Together: Do We Need to Marry?

Fifty years ago, most people took it for granted that couples married before 14 moving in together. But a recent trend favors **cohabitation,** *the sharing of a household by an unmarried couple.* From about 500,000 couples in 1970, the number of cohabiting couples in the United States has reached about 6 million today, representing 10 percent of all couples. Gay men and lesbians—who cannot legally marry someone of the same sex—account for almost 2 million cohabiting couples; the remaining 4 million couples are heterosexual (Miller, 1997; U.S. Census Bureau, 2000).

In some countries—especially Sweden and other Scandinavian nations, cohabitation is very common, even for couples having children. On the other hand, this practice is rare in more traditional (and Roman Catholic) nations such as Italy. The United States represents something of a middle case, with almost half of people between twenty-five and forty-four years of age cohabiting at some point. About one-third of cohabiting couples also live with at least one child under eighteen (Gwartney-Gibbs, 1986; Popenoe, 1988, 1991, 1992; Bumpass & Sweet, 1995; Raley, 1996).

Critics of cohabitation—typically conservatives—contend that marriage rather than cohabitation provides the more stable setting in which to raise children. In addition, they claim, cohabiting puts women and children at risk, since men can more easily abandon them. Then, too, men in informal unions run the risk of losing legal rights to children, should the couple split up. Indeed, about 60 percent of cohabiting couples do eventually split up without marrying. Some researchers caution that living together appears to discourage marriage because partners get used to relationships with little commitment (Popenoe & Whitehead, 1999).

Supporters of cohabitation—typically liberals—argue that decisions about sexual relationships are private matters that should be left to individuals. Moreover, there is little reason to expect that one relational form—monogamous marriage—will meet the needs of everyone in a large and diverse population. On the contrary, some argue, cohabitation better reflects U.S. cultural values of choice and freedom and encourages a more equal relationship between a woman and a man. What about the well-being of children? Supporters of cohabiting argue that all parents who separate—whether married or not—must take responsibility for the support and care of their children (Anapol, 1998; Kramer, 1998; Brines & Joyner, 1999).

Delaying Marriage

The trend toward cohabitation is one reason that more people in the United States, on average, are delaying marriage today than ever before. Back in 1950, as Figure 2–1 shows, the median age at first marriage in the United States was 20.3 years for women and 22.8 years for men. By 1998, these figures had jumped about five years, to 25.0 years for women and 26.7 years for men (U.S. Census Bureau, 1999).

Why are people putting off marriage? One important reason is that a larger proportion of young people are attending college and graduate school; after graduation, moreover, a rising share of women enter the labor force. In addition, economic insecurity delays marriage, since most young people between eighteen and twenty-four are still living with parents rather than setting up households of their own. Finally, improvements in birth control technology

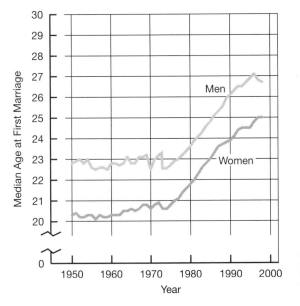

Figure 2–1 The Trend toward Later Marriage (*Source:* U.S. Census Bureau [1999].)

as well as legal abortion play a part, since an unexpected pregnancy does not force a couple to marry, the way it often did in the 1950s.

Is this delay in marriage a problem itself? Not necessarily, but it does have 20 some important consequences. For one thing, couples who marry later in life are also likely to have children later in life; the share of women having children in their forties, jumped dramatically in the decades after 1950. Older parents may not always be able to match the energy level of parents who are twenty years younger, but they typically have more time to offer their children, and they earn much more money (Chandler, Kamo, & Werbel, 1994). Delayed marriage is also linked to a drop in overall childbearing: The total number of children the typical U.S. woman bears has declined from 3.0 in 1976 to 1.9 in 1998 (U.S. Census Bureau, 2000). Other patterns that go along with delayed marriage include a rising share of couples who have no children (up from 9 percent in 1970 to 14 percent in 1998) and a rising proportion of the population that remains single (up from 11 percent in 1950 to 28 percent in 1998). In later life, remaining single is more common for women than for men, since U.S. culture encourages men (but not women) to marry someone younger than they are.

PARENTING: IS ONE ENOUGH?

In 2000, about one in three families with children under 18 years of age had just 21 one parent in the household, a share that has doubled since 1970. This means that half of U.S. children will live with a single parent at some point before reaching the age of eighteen.

There is no doubt that many children raised by a single parent turn out 22 just fine; similarly, having two parents in the home is no guarantee of a child's well-being. Still, evidence is mounting that growing up in a one-parent family disadvantages children in various ways. Some studies indicate that a father and a mother each make a distinctive contribution to a child's social development, so one parent alone cannot do as good a job as two working together. But the biggest problem confronting one-parent families—especially if the parent is a woman, which is true in 80 percent of all cases—is poverty. Children in one-parent families begin with a one-in-three chance of being poor and, on average, end up with less education and lower incomes. Such disadvantages often take the form of a vicious cycle, as boys and girls raised by single parents grow up to become single parents themselves (Astone & McLanahan, 1991; Li & Wojt-kiewicz, 1992; Biblarz & Raftery, 1993; Popenoe, 1993; Shapiro & Schrof, 1995; Webster, Orbuch, & House, 1995).

Parenting: Race and Poverty

There are many reasons that children live with a single parent. Among white 23 families, divorce is the most common reason; among African American fami-lies, most women who have children have never married. Therefore, while the risk of poverty is great for all children living with a single parent, it is especially high for African American children. In the United States, about 30 percent of families headed by white women are poor but 46 percent of families headed by African American women are poor, which contributes to the fact that one-third of all African American youngsters grow up in poverty (U.S. Census Bureau, 2000).

The Moynihan Report In 1965, U.S. Senator Daniel Patrick Moynihan 24 sounded an alarm that the African American family was in crisis because of a growing number of absent fathers who leave single mothers to struggle against poverty at the same time that they are trying to care for their children. In Moynihan's view, single motherhood threatened the African American com-munity with a cycle of poverty spilling from mothers to children.

When Moynihan issued his warning, 20 percent of African American 25 children were born to single mothers; today the figure is 69 percent. Thus, for some people, the African American family itself has become a matter of con-troversy (Lemann, 1991; U.S. National Center for Health Statistics, 2000). But critics charge that Moynihan set up one traditional type of family as the ideal and rejected anything different as "dysfunctional." From their point of view, there is nothing wrong with a female-headed household, at least nothing that adequate income cannot solve (Norton, 1985; Angelo, 1989). In other words, for African Americans, single-parent families and poverty are not so much *family* problems as they are *economic* problems. Eleanor Holmes Norton (1985) argues that the "breakdown" of the African American family is the result of long-term racism as well as discrimination in education, jobs, and housing. Sociologist William Julius Wilson (1987, 1996) adds that African Americans in the disadvantaged urban "underclass" find that there are simply not enough jobs to allow men and women to support a family. To claim that African Americans *choose* their family patterns (much less choose to be poor) amounts to blaming the victim (Hewlett & West, 1998).

African American Families: A Closer Look   Stereotypes abound 26 about African American families. A widespread attitude in the United States describes the average "welfare mother" as an unmarried African American woman. However, most people who receive public assistance are white.

In the end, the reason that these stereotypes are wrong is that African 27 American families take *many* forms, and no single description accurately portrays them. Indeed, U.S. families—black families, white families, rich families, and poor families alike—are much more diverse than most people realize.

Strengths of African American Families   There is little doubt that 28 African American families deal with more problems—including low income as well as racial prejudice and discrimination—than white families do. Research shows that African American families—especially those struggling with poverty—have real strengths. These families adapt to their situation in a number of ways, building strong kinship bonds, drawing strength from traditional religious beliefs, and utilizing the resources of grandparents (especially grandmothers) to form three-generational households. In addition, many poor households band together in networks of mutual assistance that help everyone get by (Stack, 1975; Littlejohn-Blake & Darling, 1993).

Conflict between Work and Family Life

For much of U.S. history, work and family life were very much the same thing, 29 since families lived and labored together on farms. With the Industrial Revolution, however, people (primarily men) went off to work in factories, which set the home apart from the workplace.

With the rapid entry of women, too, into the labor force after 1950, 30 people began to feel greater tension between work and family life. On average, today, families in the United States have two people working for income, and women, more than men, still perform almost another full-time job's worth of housework (Hochschild, 1989). As a result, marriage and family life often come down to the interaction of tired people trying to juggle all their responsibilities.

The Information Revolution has again changed the nature of work, with 31 about one-third of people in the labor force now spending at least some time each week working at home. For many of them, doing so helps to reduce work-family tensions. At the same time, however, as more people work at home or maintain home offices, workplace activities and concerns are likely to further intrude into family life (McGinn & McCormick, 1999; Macionis, 2001).

Child Care

A century ago, most families considered that a mother's job was child care, 32 which was performed in the home. Today, 60 percent of U.S. women are in the labor force working for income. Moreover, a majority of women with children (59 percent of women with infants, 62 percent of women with preschoolers, and 76 percent of women with school-age children) are employed outside the home (U.S. Census Bureau, 2000).

With so many women and men working, child care is a major concern 33 across the United States. Who cares for the children of the majority of mothers who are in the labor force? Figure 2–2 provides the answer. One-third of children under age five remain in the home, and most receive care from the father, grandparent, or another relative. Another one-third receive care in another person's home, and this segment is evenly divided between the home of a relative and the home of a non-relative. The final one-third of children go to a child-care facility, that is, a day-care center or a preschool facility.

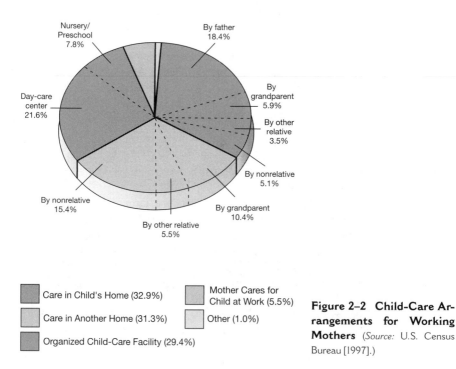

Care in Child's Home (32.9%)

Care in Another Home (31.3%)

Organized Child-Care Facility (29.4%)

Mother Cares for Child at Work (5.5%)

Other (1.0%)

Figure 2–2 Child-Care Arrangements for Working Mothers (*Source:* U.S. Census Bureau [1997].)

Families

Which option a family chooses has a lot to do with income. Parents with higher incomes can afford to hire a nanny or to send their children to day-care programs that emphasize learning and enrichment activities that foster early childhood development. Those with lower incomes, by contrast turn to relatives or friends, piece together a patchwork of babysitters, or send their children to less costly day-care centers (often overcrowded "tot-lots"), whose staff may lack training in early childhood education and provide only minimal attention to children. 34

Older children, of course, spend most of the day at school. But, after school, about 2 million youngsters (13 percent of all five- to fourteen-year-olds) are "latchkey" kids who fend for themselves until a parent returns from work (Capizano, Tout, & Adams, 2001). Some children adapt well to being alone after school, becoming more self-reliant. But, especially when families live in poor neighborhoods, unsupervised children are at high risk for problems involving drugs, crime, and sexual exploitation. 35

In short, caring for children is not a problem for some families but it *is* a problem for millions of others. We might then ask what role the government should play in ensuring that everyone's needs for child care are met. In most other high-income nations, the government uses tax money to operate child-care centers. In the United States, many working parents can deduct child-care costs on their income tax returns; in addition, states do provide some financial assistance to poor families who need child-care. But this nation, with its strong culture of self-reliance, has yet to offer child-care programs on a large scale. 36

Those who favor expanded government child-care programs point out that many low-income families would welcome them; moreover, in this way the government could do more to ensure that children receive high-quality care. Then, too, most child-care centers operate only during business hours from Monday to Friday, which makes them of little help to parents who work night shifts or "swing" shifts that change from week to week. 37

Can employers, too, play a part in providing child care? Employers know that workers who worry about their children's care are not very productive. Therefore, more employers now offer on-site child-care programs. In most cases, employees pay for this care, but some employers provide this service as a workplace benefit. Such programs are usually of good quality and have two added advantages: First, parents have a chance to visit their children during breaks throughout the day and, second, companies that provide workplace child care have the edge in attracting and retaining the best employees. 38

Divorce

Many people recite marriage vows that they will stay together "till death do us part." But the reality in the twenty-first century is that divorce—not death—ends most marriages. In the United States, more than four in ten of today's marriages will end in divorce (among African Americans, the rate is six in ten). 39

The divorce rate today is ten times higher than it was a century ago. Then, 40 family members (almost half of whom worked on farms) depended on one another to get by; therefore, there was strong economic pressure to remain married. In addition, women had yet to enter the labor force in large numbers, so that, unless they could turn to other kin for support, divorce often meant becoming poor. Then, too, many people viewed divorce as somehow sinful; thus, moral pressure kept couples together, even people who were not happily married.

During the twentieth century, the share of women working for income 41 rose steadily, while the average number of children a woman bore declined steadily. These trends made divorce more realistic, and public attitudes toward divorce became more accepting (Weitzman, 1985; Furstenberg & Cherlin, 1991; Etzioni, 1993).

As Figure 2–3 shows, the divorce rate soared for a time after World War 42 II (the war forced millions of couples to live apart for years), dropped during the 1950s, and began a steady climb from about 1965 to 1980. Since then, the divorce rate has eased downward, but not by much. Figure 2–4 shows the percentage of the population that is divorced across the United States.

No-Fault Divorce Certainly the growing economic independence of 43 women played an important part in the rising divorce rate after 1965. But changes in law also helped make divorces easier to get. In 1969, California became the first state to implement a policy of "no-fault" divorce, which spread across the country by 1985.

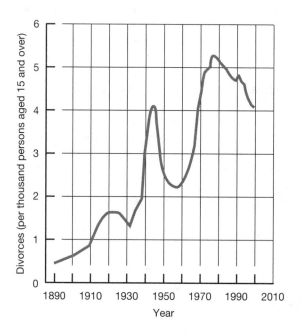

Figure 2–3 The U.S. Divorce Rate, 1890–1999
(*Source:* U.S. Census Bureau [2000] and U.S. National Center for Health Statistics [2001].)

Families

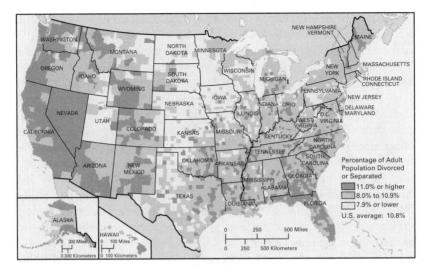

Figure 2–4 Divorce across the United States The map shows the share of the population that is divorced for all counties across the country. Overall, about 12 percent of U.S. adults over the age of fifteen are divorced. But divorce is far more common on the West Coast (and especially in Nevada, a state with very liberal divorce laws), somewhat less common in the East, and much less common in the middle of the country. Research suggests that divorce is more likely among people who are younger, who have weaker religious ties, and who move away from their parents' hometown. Can you apply these facts to make sense of this map? (*Source: American Demographics*, October 1992, p.5. Reprinted with permission. © 1992, *American Demographics*, Ithaca, New York. Data from the 1990 decennial census.)

What does no-fault divorce mean? Before no-fault, for a couple to di-   44
vorce, one partner had to claim in a court that the other was "at fault" for ruining the marriage, typically through abandonment, adultery, or physical or emotional cruelty. More than just blame was at stake, because courts took "fault" into account when dividing a couple's property and assigning custody of any children.

No-fault divorce laws did away with the idea that one person was neces-   45
sarily to blame for the collapse of a marriage. Now, couples simply declare their marriage is over and cannot be resumed due to "irreconcilable differences." The court then tries to divide property fairly and places children where they seem best off. In addition, the court assigns child support according to the custodial parent's needs, the noncustodial parent's ability to pay, and both parents' ability to work. Rarely does no-fault divorce involve alimony.

By greatly reducing cases of alimony, no-fault divorce ended the historical   46
idea that men ought to take care of women. But this does not mean that women are better off. Lenore Weitzman (1985) found that, after divorce, the

living standard of men went up while the living standard of women and their children went down, a pattern confirmed by other researchers (Faludi, 1991; Holden & Smock, 1991; Weitzman, 1996). Why the difference? Allen Parkman (1992) explains that no-fault divorce harms women because it ignores cultural capital, which includes skills and schooling that increase a person's chances to succeed. In traditional marriages, a wife puts little or no time into paid work, instead devoting herself to helping her husband develop his career. In doing so, she assumes she will stay married and that her husband's success will benefit her as well. But after divorce, the husband still has his job (a financial asset) while, in most cases, the stay-at-home wife has the children (a financial liability).

In the end, then, is no-fault divorce a problem? A slight majority of U.S. adults take the view that, today, it is too easy for people to get a divorce (NORC, 1999:233). And what of the fairness of the current system? Some people support no-fault divorce because it is in keeping with the times—more women and men are now working, so the law should treat them as equals. On the other hand, critics of current divorce policy call for going back to the old system of widespread alimony, by which the person with the greater earning power (usually the man) helps support the partner who stayed at home (usually the woman). Still others argue that the solution to this problem lies in giving women equal economic standing so they do not rely so much on men in the first place.

Too Much Divorce? Whatever one's view of no-fault divorce, there remains the question of whether today's high divorce rate should be considered a problem. Almost everyone recognizes that divorce is often necessary and may be preferable to remaining in an unhappy relationship. Liberals, especially, point to the value of easy divorce for women who must free themselves from abusive relationships. Conservatives, however, are more critical of a high divorce rate, suggesting that it signifies a "me-first" attitude that places individual needs and desires over obligations to others (Whitehead, 1997; Popenoe, 1999).

In global perspective, as shown in Figure 2–5 on the next page, the United States has more divorces (measured here in relation to the number of marriages) than most (but not all) nations in the world. In the United States, there are 49 divorces for every 100 marriages annually; Sweden has somewhat more divorce (64 divorces for every 100 marriages), while Italy has fewer (12 divorces for every 100 marriages) (United Nations Development Programme, 2000).

In recent years, a few states—notably Louisiana and Arizona—have responded to high divorce rates by enacting "covenant marriage" laws. These laws allow couples, when they marry, to choose a conventional marriage or a covenant marriage, which is harder to dissolve. Couples who choose a covenant marriage agree, first, to seek marital counseling if problems develop during the marriage. Second, they agree to seek divorce only for very limited reasons, including one spouse committing adultery or being convicted of a felony that results in a long prison sentence or the death penalty; abandonment

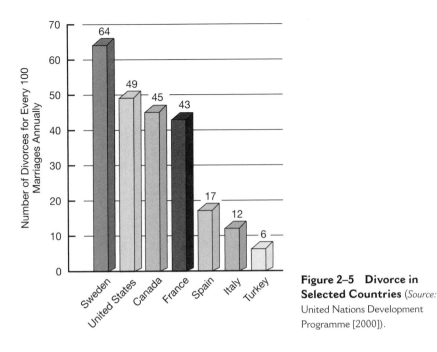

Figure 2–5 Divorce in Selected Countries (*Source:* United Nations Development Programme [2000]).

for at least one year or living separately for at least two years; habitual drug or alcohol abuse by a spouse; or physical or sexual abuse of the spouse or a child. In practice, then, couples who enter a covenant marriage reject the idea of divorcing simply because one spouse no longer wants to stay married (Nock, Wright, & Sanchez, 1999).

Covenant marriage has both supporters and critics. Supporters (who 51 tend to be conservatives) praise the covenant marriage law, claiming that making marriage harder to end will push down the divorce rate. Furthermore, such laws may make people think more carefully about who, why, and when they choose to marry. That is, if one partner balks at the idea of a covenant marriage, the other partner has good reason to question the whole relationship.

But critics (typically, liberals) worry that making divorce more difficult 52 may end up trapping women—and also young children—in abusive and perhaps violent relationships. In fact, the risk of being battered often rises for a woman who has declared her desire to end a marriage.

Some twenty other states are considering covenant marriage laws. But, 53 to date, only a small share of people in states that permit covenant marriages are choosing them. In short, this policy may have more symbolic importance than practical significance.

Finally, many couples try to spell out the terms of any future divorce by 54 writing a prenuptial (premarital) agreement. Is this a good idea?

Child Support

Given the high rate of divorce in the United States, many children do not receive 55
adequate financial support from parents. Indeed, the failure of parents to provide financial support is one cause of high poverty rates among U.S. children.

The problem of nonsupport occurs after parents separate or divorce and 56
the non-custodial parent fails to make court-ordered payments. Statistics show
that, after divorce, courts order support for about 56 percent of children. Yet,
of the children who should receive support, 60 percent receive partial payments or no payments at all (U.S. Census Bureau, 2000).

After divorce, courts usually award custody of children to mothers. For 57
this reason, most parents who fail to support their children are men, which explains the national attention given to the problem of "deadbeat dads." But,
comparing just noncustodial parents, mothers are actually less likely than fathers to make child-support payments, probably because single women have
lower incomes (U.S. Census Bureau, 2000).

What can be done about parents who do not support their children? The 58
law requires an employer to withhold money from the earnings of a parent
who fails to pay up. However, many parents manage to duck their responsibilities by moving or switching jobs (Weitzman, 1985; Waldman, 1992). In 1998,
therefore, Congress passed the "Deadbeat Parents Punishment Act," making
it a felony to refuse to provide support payments to a child residing in another
state or to move to another state in order to avoid making such payments. In
addition, many states have adopted the strategy of publishing "Wanted"
posters of delinquent parents, in hopes that such publicity will shame them
into paying up.

Remarriage: Problems of Blended Families

While divorce is common in the United States, so is remarriage. In fact, four 59
out of five people who divorce remarry, and most do so within five years. Nationwide, about half of all marriages are *remarriages* for at least one partner.

For women and men who already have children from a previous relation- 60
ship, remarriage creates **blended families,** *families in which children live with
some combination of biological parents and stepparents.* In the United States,
one-fifth of all white and one-third of all African American married-couple
households are blended families. Blended families with two parents offer children the advantages of higher average income and more parental attention. But
blended families also have a number of special problems. For one thing, children
who become part of a new family must learn new household rules and routines
as well as build relationships with new siblings. Stepparents, too, must make
adjustments, establishing relationships with children as well as a spouse. Most
couples in blended families also have to maintain a relationship with a child's
other biological parent (and, perhaps, that person's new partner).

Most blended families manage to cope with these challenges. But re- 61
search shows that blended families carry some special risks. Children suffer a
relatively high rate of physical and sexual abuse from stepparents. And, for
spouses, the likelihood of divorce (especially those who remarry at a younger
age) is higher than for those in first marriages (Finkelhor, 1984; Holden &
Smock, 1991; Ahlburg & De Vita, 1992; Fleming, Mullen, & Bammer, 1997).

Gay and Lesbian Families

Not all couples even have the choice of whether to marry. Across the entire 62
United States, gay men and lesbians are banned by law from marrying a same-
sex partner. Nonetheless, about 2 million gay couples have formed committed
partnerships, about 250,000 of these couples have children. Typically, these
children are offspring from a previous heterosexual relationship, although many
gay couples adopt children of their own (U.S. Census Bureau, 1998).

Many gay men and lesbians view the right to legally marry someone of 63
the same sex as an important measure of society's acceptance of their sexual
orientation. Beyond symbolic importance, gay marriage has practical value,
since many employers and government agencies extend benefits to both individuals and their legal spouses, including health insurance, tuition payments,
and retirement pensions.

At present, only four nations—Denmark (1989), Norway (1993), Sweden 64
(1995), and the Netherlands (2001)—have lawful gay marriage. But none of
these countries allows homosexual couples to adopt children, which is legal in
the United States. Many cities (including San Francisco and New York) register
"domestic partnerships" and, in 2000, Vermont became the first state to do so
(Trischitta, 2000). Domestic-partnership laws confer some—but not all—of the
legal benefits of marriage.

Should any state enact a gay marriage law, it would affect the entire 65
country because, according to the "Full Faith and Credit" clause of the U.S.
Constitution, a contract (including marriage) performed in one state must be
recognized by *all* states. For this reason, in 1996 congressional opponents of
gay marriage passed the "Defense of Marriage Act," which states that marriage
must involve one man and one woman, and that no state or other jurisdiction
has to recognize a same-sex marriage law enacted by any other state or jurisdiction. The passage of a gay marriage law in any one state would undoubtedly
open this act to legal challenge; whether or not the "Full Faith & Credit" clause
would be upheld would be resolved by the courts.

The gay marriage debate brings us again to the question of how to define 66
a "family." In general, liberals tend to think of "families" as people who share
their lives and wish to be defined that way. Such beliefs lead may liberals to
support gay marriage. Conservatives, by contrast, argue that gay marriage goes
against the traditional definition of families and, further, does not offer the best
setting in which to raise children (Knight, 1998). In this debate, however, the

lines are not clearly drawn: Some people who believe in the importance of "family values" also think all people—whatever their sexual orientation—benefit from marriage.

What about Gay Parenting? About 250,000 gay couples in the 67 United States are raising young children. Therefore, the diversity of families in this country also includes cases of children with two "moms" or "dads." Gay parenting is a controversial issue: While no federal or state laws ban this practice, in a number of recent custody disputes courts have declared that children are better off with heterosexual parents.

Public opinion is divided on whether gay parenting is in the best interests 68 of children. Some people fear that children living with homosexual parents are at higher risk of sexual abuse; research, however, does not support such fears. On the contrary, research does show gay and lesbian parents to be capable of the same supportive and effective parenting as heterosexual couples. Nor is there any evidence to suggest that children raised by homosexual parents are, for that reason, any more likely to be gay themselves. In short, gay and lesbian families face problems, but they come more from the stigma society attaches to homosexuality than from the family form itself (Harris & Turner, 1985; Bozett, 1987; Barret & Robinson, 1990; Peterson, 1992).

Brave New Families: High-Tech Reproduction

In 1978, Louise Brown became the world's first "test-tube baby." She was con- 69 ceived in a laboratory in England where doctors fertilized a human ovum with a sperm cell in a glass dish and implanted the embryo in a woman's womb. In 1991, in the United States, forty-two-year-old Arlette Schweitzer became the first woman to bear her own grandchildren. Because her daughter was unable to carry a baby to term, Schweitzer agreed to have her daughter and son-in-law's embryos surgically implanted in her own womb. Nine months later, she bore healthy twins—a boy and a girl (Kolata, 1991). These births illustrate how new reproductive technology has created new choices for families—and sparked new controversies as well.

In Vitro* Fertilization** So-called "test-tube babies" result from the 70 process of ***in vitro (that is, "in glass") **fertilization,** which means *uniting eggs and sperm in a laboratory.* Once a fertilized embryo is produced, doctors may implant it in a woman's body or they can freeze it for use at a later time.

Because as many as 3 million couples in the United States are unable to 71 conceive children in the normal way, *in vitro* fertilization offers an exciting new possibility to become parents. At the same time, however, the procedure is very expensive, so that only about 50,000 couples a year actually undertake it, resulting in about 10,000 births annually (Peres, 1998). Those who have the child they want, of course, view this procedure as nothing short of miraculous. Critics, however, point out that the cost places this procedure out of reach for a majority of people. Just as important, critics raise serious moral and ethical questions about whether what is now scientifically possible is always ethically desirable.

Surrogate Motherhood As it has solved the problem of infertility for 72 many couples, new reproductive technology has also created controversy over the issue of **surrogate motherhood,** *an arrangement by which one woman carries and bears a child for another, usually in exchange for money.* In the case of Arlette Schweitzer, she agreed to be implanted with an embryo from her daughter and son-in-law. Most of the controversy over surrogate motherhood involves women who agree to serve as surrogate mothers not for family members but for money.

In 1986, the case known as "Baby M" brought surrogate motherhood to 73 the nation's attention. In that case, William Stern, whose wife was unable to bear children, agreed to pay Mary Beth Whitehead $10,000 plus medical expenses to bear a child conceived with his own sperm. Although Whitehead would be the baby's biological mother, she agreed to give up all claims to the child. Within a year, Whitehead gave birth to a healthy baby girl. But, by that time, Whitehead had changed her mind, and wanted to keep "her" baby. The Sterns reacted by filing a court case seeking custody of "their" baby and pointing to the signed agreement with Whitehead. Although the lower court found in favor of the Sterns, the New Jersey Supreme Court in 1988 declared surrogacy contracts of this kind illegal in that state; further, the court ruled that the natural mother (in this case, Whitehead) should share custody of a child born from such an arrangement. Other states, however, have honored such contracts, so the future of surrogate motherhood is, at present, unclear.

Cases of surrogate parenthood also raise questions about who has re- 74 sponsibility for child support. In California, John and Luanne Buzzanca, a married couple unable to have children, enlisted a woman to serve as a surrogate mother. In this case, both the egg and sperm came from unknown donors. In 1995, the surrogate mother gave birth to a baby who had no biological ties to either her or the Buzzancas. A month before the child's birth, however, John Buzzanca filed for divorce from his wife. His wife Luanne took custody of the child and sought child support from her ex-husband. But the husband refused, claiming he was not the child's father.

In the court suit that followed, a California judge ruled that, while the 75 child had no biological parents, both John and Luanne Buzzanca were the child's "intended parents." Thus, the court ruled that both parties who engage a surrogate mother are responsible for a child born in this way. In the end, Luanne Buzzanca received custody, and her ex-husband John was ordered to pay monthly child support.

Cases such as these show that, while new reproductive technology has 76 obvious benefits for some couples, we have yet to devise clear laws to guide its application. This pattern illustrates what sociologists call *cultural lag,* a case of scientific discoveries occurring faster than our ideas develop about the proper ways to use them. This analysis of new reproductive technology raises the question of whether what is scientifically possible is always morally right.

THEORETICAL ANALYSIS OF FAMILY PROBLEMS

We can sharpen our understanding of issues surrounding the family by applying 77 sociology's three major theoretical paradigms: structural-functional analysis, symbolic-interaction analysis, and social-conflict analysis. We look at each in turn.

Structural-Functional Analysis: Family as Foundation

The structural-functional paradigm views the family as the most important 78 unit of social organization. Families exist everywhere in the world, claims George Murdock (1949), because they perform four major tasks essential for society to operate. First, families regulate reproduction, encouraging the birth of "legitimate" children to partners who have made a public commitment to one another. Second, families provide a secure setting for the socialization of the young. Third, families are units of economic cooperation between husband and wife, and, when necessary, couples look for economic assistance from other kin. Fourth, and finally, families provide a setting in which people provide affection and emotional support to one another.

Because they consider these functions so vital to any society, structural- 79 functional analysts hold that families are the backbone of society, so that any threat to family life is a social problem in itself. Thus, a structural-functional approach views many of the trends discussed in this chapter—including living together, single parenting, and high divorce rates—as serious threats to U.S. society.

Critical Evaluation The strength of the structural-functional ap- 80 proach lies in highlighting the many ways in which families contribute to the operation of society. There is evidence that families do matter: Children living in single-parent (versus two-parent) households, for example, grow up completing less schooling and are at higher risk of poverty. Furthermore, it is difficult to see how other social institutions could step in to perform the various functions that families perform now.

At the same time, the structural-functional approach comes in for criti- 81 cism for overlooking the extent of conflict and violence in families. In addition, critics point out that today's families also contribute to social inequality, typically supporting the dominance of men over women and perpetuating class inequality as parents pass along wealth and privileges to children. Then, too, the structural-functional approach takes a macro-level view of the family as a system, saying little about how people experience family life on the micro-level of everyday life. This concern brings us to the symbolic-interaction paradigm.

Symbolic-Interaction Analysis: The Experience of Family Life

The symbolic-interaction paradigm views the family less as an institution and more as the ongoing interaction of individuals. From this perspective, we see that family life has a great deal to do with the ways children learn to think about themselves. That is, parents who raise children with love and steady guidance help them to develop a positive self-image and to make decisions confidently as they move through life. By contrast, parents who continuously call their children's behavior into question end up fostering self-doubt in young people as they grow.

A symbolic-interaction approach also highlights how the experience of family life varies from one family to another. Ideally, for example, marriage helps a couple build a relationship that is *intimate* (a word with Latin roots meaning "free from fear"), one in which each partner finds comfort and support in the presence of the other. But the same marital ties that offer the promise of intimacy can work in the opposite direction to rigidly script the behavior of males (who, thus, act "just like men") and females (who feel constrained to act in feminine ways), with the result that the two sexes can have trouble opening up to one another (Macionis, 1978). This fact helps explain why, to the extent that people conform to cultural ideas about gender, women and men often report very different perceptions of the same marriage (Bernard, 1982).

Critical Evaluation   To its credit, the symbolic-interaction paradigm shows the varied ways in which individuals actually experience family life. A husband, wife, and child typically experience the same family quite differently, and all these experiences change over time.

Critics of this approach point out that, while family life is variable, a number of common patterns appear. Gender stratification, for example, is built into almost all families. The social-conflict paradigm offers a look at how the family is linked to various dimensions of social inequality.

Social-Conflict Analysis: Family and Inequality

As a macro-level approach, the social-conflict paradigm shares with the structural-functional paradigm the idea that the family plays an important part in the operation of society. But rather than highlighting ways in which family life benefits everyone, social-conflict theory explains that the family operates to benefit some and disadvantage others. Put another way, families *reproduce* social inequality in each new generation.

An early social-conflict theory of family life was developed by Friedrich Engels (1902; orig. 1884). As Engels saw it, the family actually came into being among the wealthy, mostly so men could be reasonably sure who their offspring were and could pass their property from father to son. In this way, the family (along with the legal system that protects inheritance) ensures that the class structure stays much the same from one generation to another.

Perpetuating the class structure is only one way in which the family sup- 88 ports inequality. In addition, Engels explained, by making men the heads of households, the family gives men power over women. For men to know who their heirs are, they must control the sexuality of women. To Engels, such concerns went a long way toward explaining the concern that women be virgins before they marry and faithful wives afterward. The family, in short, transforms women into the sexual and economic property of men.

Critical Evaluation   The strength of the social-conflict paradigm lies in 89 explaining how the family is bound up with a society's system of inequality. From this point of view, the path toward making a society more egalitarian is to think about ways of eliminating the family, at least in its current form (Mare, 1991).

Of course, this approach, too, is subject to criticism. For one thing, it 90 overlooks the fact that a large majority of people in the United States claim to get a great deal of satisfaction from family life (NORC, 1999:174). In addition, if society were to eliminate the family for the reasons Engels suggests, it is far from clear how important tasks such as raising children would be accomplished.

POLITICS AND FAMILY LIFE: CONSTRUCTING PROBLEMS AND DEFINING SOLUTIONS

Theory provides helpful ways to think about families, but exactly what people 91 consider to be family problems and what they think we ought to do about them depends on their values and politics. We conclude this chapter by applying conservative, liberal, and radical perspectives to issues surrounding families and family life.

Conservatives: Traditional "Family Values"

Conservatives see the family as the core of a society—the social institution 92 that does the most to improve human well-being and to instill the basic values that define a way of life. For this reason, conservatives support what they call a "family-values agenda," which emphasizes the importance of committed marriages, opposes divorce, and defends the two-parent family as the best setting in which to raise children.

From a conservative point of view, the rise in cohabitation is a trend that 93 spells trouble for U.S. society. Indeed, many conservatives do not approve of living together because such a relationship carries less commitment than legal marriage. The steady rise in the popularity of cohabitation, then, is a sign of a "me-first" culture in which people favor individualism over commitment. The greatest losers in this situation are children who, say the conservatives, have a higher chance of ending up in a single-parent family, which, in turn, raises their risk of poverty right away and of divorce later on as adults (Popenoe & Whitehead, 1999).

Conservatives see the rising rate of divorce after the 1960s as a serious 94 problem. Can anything be done to turn things around? Claiming that no-fault divorce laws simply made divorces too easy to get, conservatives applaud recent "covenant marriage" laws. They also advocate a broad change in our thinking about relationships—a shift from an individualistic "culture of divorce" to a pro-commitment "culture of marriage." Such a change is possible, they believe—after all the public's attitude toward cigarette smoking has changed dramatically in recent decades—and would benefit everyone. It would improve the mental—and financial—health of men and women, and would ensure that more children grow up in stable two-parent families. In addition, conservatives criticize the popular notion that parents need to stake out "quality time" with their children; in their view, this amounts to little more than an excuse for not spending enough time with children. Conservatives recognize that many households depend on the earnings of both mothers and fathers. Still, they suggest, couples with young children should consider limiting their total workweek to sixty hours so that they can spend enough time with the kids (Popenoe, 1988, 1993, 1999; Broude, 1996; Whitehead, 1997).

Liberals: Many Kinds of Families

Because liberals celebrate individual freedoms, their take on today's families and 95 family problems is very different from that of conservatives. Liberals claim that conservatives only recognize one type of "real" family as the best for everyone. But, as liberals see it, this is not the case; rather, different people favor different kinds of families (or no families at all). A wide range of families is found in U.S. history, and this diversity continues today (Kain, 1990; Koontz, 1992).

Therefore, liberals support any and all family forms, including living to- 96 gether, single-parent families, blended families, and even living single. For liberals, such family patterns are not the problems they are to conservatives. This is not to say that liberals see no family problems at all—poverty and violence are two quite serious problems. But liberals argue that trying to impose a single model of the family on everyone would not make these problems better. On the contrary, locking people in "traditional families" is likely to limit the opportunities of women as well as trapping some women in abusive relationships.

From a liberal perspective, then, the greater diversity in family forms is a 97 solution to the historical problem of women remaining in the home under the control of men (Stacey, 1990, 1993). But what do liberals say about the fact that single-mother families do have higher rates of poverty for women and children? The liberal solution to this problem is to increase the availability of quality child-care programs, so that more women can work, and to combat gender stratification so that working women are paid as much as working men. Similarly, liberals support raising the minimum wage and perhaps even setting a guaranteed minimum income; they see these as sound policies that are likely to promote the strength of U.S. families.

Radicals: Replace the Family

The radical left view begins with the close link between the family and social 98
inequality. From this perspective, the family (at least in its current form) perpetuates inequality in at least three ways.

First, according to Friedrich Engels's analysis, noted earlier, the family 99
helps perpetuate class stratification. That is, through the family, individuals pass private property from one generation to the next, reproducing the class system.

Second, Engels also explained that the family helps perpetuate gender 100
stratification. To be sure that they know who their heirs are, men must control the sexuality of women. Furthermore in order for men to leave home for the workplace, women are left behind as homemakers, placed in charge of housework and children.

Third, because legal marriage is restricted to partners of the opposite sex, 101
the current family system does not accept homosexual couples, pushing them to the margins of society. The family, therefore, also perpetuates stratification based on sexual orientation.

Taken together, these arguments give radicals who advocate an egalitarian 102
society good reason to support an end to the family as we know it. But what would be the radicals' practical solutions to the "problem" of the family? To eliminate class inequality, society would have to treat all children in the same manner, probably by making child care a collective enterprise. Similarly, to eliminate gender inequality, it would have to redefine marriage as a partnership with shared responsibility for housework and child care as well as earning income. Perhaps, too, collective living arrangements might enable people to share housework and child care even more efficiently. Finally, radical feminists envision a future in which new reproductive technology allows women to break the bonds of biology that now define them as the only ones who can carry children.

GOING ON FROM HERE

The twentieth century was a time of remarkable change for families in the United 103
States. That century opened with women having, on average, five children, no jobs, and no right to vote. The last century closed with women having, on average, two children, an ever-wider range of jobs, and growing political power.

In the twenty-first century, families will continue to change. For one 104
thing, the share of women working for income has been rising steadily at the same time that the birth rate is falling. As the lives of women and men become more alike, conventional ideas about marriage and family life are giving way to a greater diversity in relationships. It seems likely that, even if the divorce rate continues to edge downward, marriage will never be, for most people, a

lifetime commitment. On the contrary, many family patterns—conventional marriage, living together, living alone, and raising children outside of marriage—will all remain a part of U.S. society.

One issue that is likely to remain a topic of controversy is the rising share 105 of children living in poverty. As conservatives see it, the solution to this problem is a return to the traditional two-parent family; as liberals see it, the solution lies in policies that increase women's economic opportunities.

A second important question is whether gay men and lesbians should 106 have access to legal marriage. Although, up to this point, opponents of gay marriage have had the upper hand, there can be no question that the tide is turning in favor of such a change, which seems likely to occur in this century.

Third, and finally, developments in reproductive technology will continue 107 to raise new—and sometimes troubling—issues. Undoubtedly, our scientific ability to alter reproduction and even to clone individuals will increase; we will be left with the ethical dilemma as to whether doing so helps or harms society.

For all these reasons, debate over problems of family life will surely con- 108 tinue. Indeed, a century from now, people may still be lining up on different sides as they try to answer the question, "What is a family?"

SELECTION 1 QUESTIONS

1. How does Macionis define the "family"? Does everyone agree what the term "family" ought to mean? Please explain.
2. According to Macionis, does it matter how we define "families"? Please explain his reasoning.
3. Describe a "nuclear" and an "extended" family. Why do you think people in modern high-income societies focus on the nuclear family while people in low-income nations focus on an extended family?
4. What are three reasons Americans are putting off marriage?
5. Approximately what percentage of today's marriages end in divorce? How does that percentage compare to the divorce rate a century ago?
6. According to Macionis, "what people consider to be family problems and what they think we ought to do about them," depends on two things. List those two things.
7. Briefly compare and contrast how conservatives, liberals, and radicals define family and how each group views the problems of today's families.

Reflect and Connect

8. Of the issues discussed in this chapter—cohabitation, single parenting, child care, conflicts between work and family, and new reproductive technology—which do you think is the most serious? Please explain your reasoning.

SELECTION 2 MARRIAGE ON THE ROCKS

JOHN LEO

Mr. Leo is a columnist and contributing editor at U.S. News & World Report. *Before joining* U.S. News *in 1988, he covered the social sciences and intellectual trends for* Time *magazine and* The New York Times. *He also served as an associate editor for* Commonweal *magazine, a book editor of the sociology magazine* Society, *and a deputy commissioner of New York City's Environmental Protection Administration. His books include* How the Russians Invented Baseball and Other Essays of Enlightenment *and* Incorrect Thoughts: Notes on Our Wayward Culture. *This essay appeared in* U.S. News & World Report *December 16, 2002.*

AN IDEA TO THINK ABOUT

What do you think are the major strengths and weaknesses of "traditional" families?

WORDS TO KNOW

ponderous—(¶ 1)—massive, weighty
deconstructed—(¶ 4)—torn down

In modern journalism, radical change is often announced by a yawn-inducing 1
headline. For instance, "Legal Group Urges States to Update Their Family Law" (*New York Times,* November 29). The headline, one step up from "Don't Bother to Read This," refers to a ponderous 1,200-page commentary and set of recommendations by the American Law Institute, a group of prominent judges and lawyers. The proposals, "Principles of the Law of Family Dissolution," may seem like dry, technical suggestions about custody, alimony, and property distribution. But what this "update" really amounts to is a devastating legal assault on marriage.

The institute report says that in many important ways, domestic part- 2
nerships should be legally treated like marriage. It defines domestic partners as "two persons of the same or opposite sex, not married to one another, who for a significant period of time share a primary residence and a life together as a couple." When breaking up, the report says, cohabitants are entitled to a division of property and alimonylike payments, just like married people who divorce. And after a relationship ends, the cohabiting partner of a legal parent may share custody and decision-making responsibility for the legal parent's child.

The report validates homosexual relationships and gives them a status   3
comparable to that of marriage. If accepted, this idea would lead immediately
to the next legal argument: If gay and straight commitments have the same status in state law, isn't it picky and discriminatory to withhold the word marriage
from the gay version? Heterosexual couples who live together would also get
the same status as husbands and wives, blurring or eliminating another line between marriage and serial affairs.

WAR ON TRADITION

The most drastic notion embedded in the suggestions is that marriage is just   4
one arrangement among many. Marriage is being deconstructed here, down-
graded and privatized. It is no longer the crucial building block of the social
order and makes no special contribution to civil society that justifies any distinctive honor or status. "This report," says Lynn Wardle, professor of law at
Brigham Young University, "continues the war on the traditional family and traditional sexual morality that has been waged for over three decades."

Wardle has a point. Marriage is in trouble for a lot of reasons, but surely   5
one important factor is the relentless hostility unleashed by the 1960s counter-
culture, which portrayed marriage as oppressive, patriarchal, outmoded, and
destructive to children. The attitudes of today's elites reflect that never-ending
campaign. Now we have lots of "marriage" counselors who never use the word
marriage and textbooks on families bristling with hostility to the nuclear family.
As I wrote in this space several years ago, "One of the problems in trying to
shore up the institution of marriage is that so many of the professionals who
teach and write about it—counselors, therapists, academics, and popular authors—really don't support marriage at all."

What they do tend to support is known as "close relationship theory," the   6
idea that sexual and emotional satisfaction comes from intense, fragile, and
often short-term relationships that aren't necessarily going anywhere. One advocate calls them "microwave relationships," cooked up fast, served, and consumed, presumably with other similar meals to come. It all seems like the dream
world of a randy adolescent chasing cheerleaders. Marriage is knocked off its
pedestal, and the family itself fades away. Children tend to fade away, too, in
close-relationship theory, as emphasis comes down hard on adult fulfillment.

To get an idea of where this theory and our legal elites may take us, take a   7
look at last year's report of the Law Commission of Canada: "Beyond Conju-
gality: Recognizing and Supporting Close Personal Adult Relationships."
Canada's elites are usually earlier and franker than ours in presenting socially
destructive ideas. The report says flatly that the state must remain neutral in
relationships—no promoting marriage or giving it any edge. Registering partnerships of any kind "could be used to replace marriage as a legal institution,"
the commission said. "Religious marriage ceremonies would continue to exist,
but they would no longer have legal consequences."

These are the marriage-hating ideas of the most radical countercultural-   8
ists, circa 1969, now surfacing on the agenda of U.S. and Canadian legal elites.
At a time when efforts to bolster marriage are gaining some traction, the elites
are telling us marriage is defunct and almost any kind of short-term, self-serving
relationship will do. Can these people be taken seriously?

SELECTION 2 QUESTIONS

Vocabulary

1. Explain the meaning of the phrase "the most drastic notion embedded in
   the suggestions. . . ." (paragraph 4)
2. Explain the meaning of the phrase "efforts to bolster marriage are gaining
   some traction" (paragraph 8)

Comprehension and Analysis

3. What caused Leo to write this column?
4. Describe the tone of the column. Use an example to support your answer.
5. List two of the groups/types of people Leo thinks are responsible for the
   destruction of traditional marriage and family life.
6. Summarize Leo's point of view about marriage and family. Use an example to support your answer.
7. At the end of paragraph 8, Leo asks a rhetorical question. How do you
   think he would answer the question? How do you answer the question?

Reflect and Connect

8. In the text chapter "Family Life," Macionis said the family is a "social institution that unites individuals into cooperative groups that care for
   members, regulate sexual relations, and oversee the bearing and raising
   of children." Do you think Leo would agree with that definition? Please
   explain.

SELECTION 3   EDITORIAL CARTOON

SAM GROSS

Mr. Gross's cartoons appear in magazines such as The New Yorker, Harvard
Business Review, Esquire, Cosmopolitan, *and* Good Housekeeping. *He is the
former Cartoon Editor of* National Lampoon *and* Parents Magazine. *He has
edited more than 15 cartoon anthologies, and numerous collections of his*

work have been published in the United States, England, Germany, France, and Australia. In the past several years, he has been involved in electronic publishing ventures including screen savers and advertising web promotion with cartoons. This cartoon was originally published in The New Yorker.

AN IDEA TO THINK ABOUT

What do you think are the most important characteristics of a family?

"I guess we'd be considered a family. We're living together, we love each other, and we haven't eaten the children yet."

SELECTION 3 QUESTIONS

Comprehension and Analysis

1. What message does Gross want to communicate?
2. Why do you think Gross used fish rather than people to illustrate his message?

Reflect and Connect

3. How do you think Leo would react to this "definition" of a family? Please explain.

SELECTION 4 PATCHING UP THE AMERICAN FAMILY

BRIDGET MAHER

Dr. Maher is Marriage and Family Policy Analyst at the Family Research Council, a Washington, D.C., think tank. She edited the organization's new publication, The Family Portrait.

AN IDEA TO THINK ABOUT

What are some reasons people are "scared" of marriage?

"Marriage scares both of us, because of the statistics," remarked Ty Murray,   1
boyfriend of singer Jewel, when asked why he and the celebrity aren't married after four years of dating. Hollywood actress Sandra Bullock also admits her hesitancy about marriage. In an interview with *Parade* magazine, she revealed, "My biggest fear is marriage."

Their anxieties over marriage are not surprising, considering current statis-   2
tics on matrimony and divorce. The marriage rate (8.6 marriages per 1,000 citizens in 1999) is near an all-time low, while the current divorce rate (4.1 per 1,000 population in 1999) is nearly twice that of 1960. Researchers project that married couples have about a 50 percent chance of divorce. According to the U.S. Census Bureau, 20 percent of first marriages end within 5 years and 33 percent within 10 years. Over one million children annually experience their parents' divorce.

Cohabitation and out-of-wedlock births have also increased dramatically.   3
In 2000, there were 4.7 million cohabiting couples, compared with 500,000 in 1970. Married couples who have previously cohabited have a much higher incidence of divorce, domestic violence, and communication problems than couples who do not live together before marriage. Today, one-third of all births are out of wedlock. Although the teen birthrate has declined during the 1990s, the nation logged a record 1.35 million extramarital births in 2000.

COSTS OF FRACTURED FAMILIES

Children have suffered tremendously from America's explosion of family break-   4
down. Youngsters with divorced, never-married, or cohabiting parents are likely to suffer emotionally, academically, and economically. The psychological impact of divorce on children is especially devastating. In her extensive research on children of divorce, Judith Wallerstein found that these youngsters experience feelings of rejection, loneliness, anger, guilt, anxiety, fear of abandonment, and a deep yearning for the absent parent. Five years after the divorce, 37 percent of the children she studied were moderately or severely depressed.

These emotional and behavioral effects often last through the teen years 5 and into adulthood. Several studies have shown that children of divorce are far more likely to be delinquent, engage in premarital sex, and bear children out of wedlock during adolescence and young adulthood. A 33-year study published in 1998 in the *American Sociological Review* revealed that children whose parents divorced in their childhood or adolescence were likely to be afflicted with emotional problems such as depression or anxiety well into their twenties or early thirties.

Family breakdown has dire economic consequences for children, single parents, and society. Children living with a single mother are six times more likely to live in poverty than are children with married parents. A 1999 study found that women who have children out of wedlock are likely to have a much lower income than married women do; they are six times more likely to be on welfare and 40 percent less likely to be working full time. When divorce or separation occurs, women experience on average a 50 percent decline in family income.

Teen unwed childbearing directly costs U.S. taxpayers an estimated $7 billion per year in social services and lost tax revenue. The costs also include diminished productivity of these mothers and the child welfare and criminal-justice costs associated with high rates of child abuse and delinquency.

TACKLING THE PROBLEMS

Alarmed by these statistics, grassroots activists, policymakers, and others who 8 have witnessed the suffering caused by family breakdown are making a concerted effort to buttress the institutions of marriage and family. Federal and state legislation has been enacted to strengthen marriage and make divorce more difficult. Communities and churches have implemented many programs to encourage premarital sexual abstinence, marriage preparation, and communication skills.

Happily, these efforts are not isolated instances of reform, but part of a 9 growing movement. Marriage counselors and educators, social workers, religious leaders, judges, divorce lawyers, and scholars are banding together to develop family-strengthening strategies. The annual Smart Marriages conference, under the auspices of the Coalition for Marriage, Family, and Couples Education, has grown from 600 attendees in 1996 to 1,700 in 2002.

The federal government's efforts to revitalize families are most evident in 10 the areas of welfare reform, sexual abstinence education, profamily tax credits, and reducing the marriage tax penalty, which forced married couples to pay higher taxes simply because they were married. The 1996 Welfare Reform Act, which meant to encourage the formation and maintenance of two-parent families and reduce illegitimacy, authorized $250 million over five years, ending in 2001, for premarital abstinence programs. Congress extended the funding to the end of 2002. . . .

COVENANT MARRIAGE

Among the states' efforts to encourage marriage and reduce divorce are 11 covenant marriage laws. In 1997, Louisiana became the first state to enact such a law, followed by Arizona the following year and Arkansas in 2001. Covenant marriage laws give couples a choice between two types of marriage licenses: the standard one, which allows virtually unrestricted access to no-fault divorce, and the covenant marriage license, which requires premarital counseling and places restrictions on no-fault divorce.

In Louisiana, the premarital counseling required of couples who choose 12 covenant marriage must include discussion in the following areas:

- The seriousness of covenant marriage.
- The fact that it is a lifelong commitment.
- The requirement to seek counseling when marital difficulties arise.

A divorce or separation may be obtained in a Louisiana covenant mar- 13 riage only after a couple has lived apart for two years or if there is proof of adultery, a felony conviction with a death or imprisonment sentence, abandonment by either spouse for one year, physical or sexual abuse of a spouse or child, or (for purposes of legal separation only) cruel treatment or habitual intemperance.

Steven Nock, a sociologist at the University of Virginia and principal au- 14 thor of a large-scale study on covenant marriage, says that only about 3 percent of new marriages in Louisiana fall into the covenant category. But he still sees the new institution as worthwhile, because couples may be helped by the premarital and predivorce counseling, and because it has sparked a national debate. "The day after the [Louisiana] law passed," says Nock, "it was front-page news in the *Wall Street Journal* and *New York Times*. Nationally, people are discussing marriage, divorce, and cohabitation, and that's a wonderful thing."

In addition to enacting covenant marriage laws, states are using Tempo- 15 rary Assistance to Needy Families (TANF) money to fund promarriage activities. Oklahoma is a leading example. After learning that the state's economic problems were rooted in high rates of divorce and out-of-wedlock childbearing, Gov. Frank Keating announced in 1999 the goal of reducing divorce rates in Oklahoma by one-third by 2010. That same year, he and his wife hosted a major marriage conference that included leaders from business, government, religion, health care, universities, and the media. The governor's statewide Marriage Initiative, which was launched at the conference, conducts an advertising campaign on the importance of matrimony, trains state workers in marriage education, and has established a wedlock resource center. It uses $10 million of Oklahoma's unspent federal TANF welfare money. Also, 800 religious leaders joined the governor in pledging to establish premarital education and matrimony mentoring programs in their congregations.

EDUCATING SPOUSES

In 1998, Gov. Mike Leavitt of Utah formed a statewide commission on mar- 16
riage, tasked with gathering information on marriage-strengthening programs.
Each February, the governor presides over an annual Marriage Week; throughout the year he and his wife are featured at marriage conferences around the
state. In 2000, Utah earmarked $600,000 of TANF money for promoting mari-
tal education, presented through a video for couples applying for a marriage license, a Web site, and a pilot project focusing on low-income families.

Arizona and Arkansas also have marriage initiatives. In 2000, Gov. Jane 17
Dee Hull of Arizona signed a law authorizing the state to spend $1 million of
TANF funds to develop marriage education programs for low-income couples.
Gov. Mike Huckabee of Arkansas, besides supporting the covenant marriage
law in his state, promotes community marriage policies mandating that pastors
and judges marry only couples who have attended marriage preparation
courses. In 1997 and '99, Huckabee hosted conferences on the family, with notable speakers such as Gary Smalley and Michael Medved, covering such topics
as fatherhood, financial management, and communication skills. According to
Chris Pyle, the governor's director of family policy, the conferences were held
"to give people the tools [they could take with them] to strengthen their own
marriages."

Some states have passed marriage education laws. Florida was the first, 18
with its Marriage Preservation Act of 1998, requiring high school students to
receive marriage skills education; additionally, it gives a discount on the fee for a
marriage license for couples who undergo a minimum of four hours of marriage
preparation. These couples are also exempt from the three-day waiting period
before marriage.

In 1999, Oklahoma passed similar legislation reducing the marriage license 19
fee for those who receive premarital education, followed by Maryland and
Minnesota in 2001 and Tennessee in 2002. Doug Stiegler, executive director of
the Family Protection Lobby in Annapolis, Maryland, notes that the reduction
in the marriage license fee is minimal and not the most important part of the
law. "It's not the dollar amount but the fact that couples recognize the need for
having good information before entering marriage," he says.

COMMUNITY PROMARRIAGE INITIATIVES

Many community organizations and churches are implementing programs to 20
encourage marriage and reduce divorce. Marriage Savers, founded by Mike
and Harriet McManus, developed the Community Marriage Policy (CMP) in
such an effort. Clergy who sign a CMP agree to require engaged couples to
undergo at least four months of marriage preparation, which includes a premarital inventory.

The inventory, administered by older married couples who are trained as 21 mentors, helps to identify the strengths and weaknesses in the engaged couple's relationship. Both couples meet four to six times before the marriage and agree to continue afterward. So far, about 5,500 pastors, priests, and rabbis in about 150 cities have adopted CMPs, and the results are promising. In Modesto, California, the first city in which a CMP was signed (by 1 rabbi and 95 priests and pastors from 19 denominations), the number of divorces has dropped nearly 56 percent since 1986, and Kansas City, Kansas, has experienced a 46 percent drop since 1996.

Chattanooga, Tennessee, is the home of First Things First (FTF), a community-based nonprofit organization "dedicated to strengthening families 22 through education, collaboration, and mobilization," according to its mission statement. Civic leaders formed FTF in 1997, after deciding that their community and economy would be strengthened by building up the family, since Tennessee then had the second-highest divorce rate in the country and high illegitimacy, too. Working to promote healthy marriages and to reduce out-of-wedlock births, FTF has collaborated with numerous social service agencies, churches, businesses, schools, and media outlets.

"We've partnered with just about everyone in town," says Julie Baum- 23 gardner, who encourages her staff to "act outside the box" in promoting their message. FTF raised nearly $50,000 by partnering with over 25 organizations in a "Ride for Families," which involved more than 225 motorcyclists and 150 bicyclists. The group also staffs the local Marriage Savers initiative and has held a "fatherhood summit."

Also working to strengthen the family are abstinence educators who 24 teach young people the benefits of saving sex until marriage. These programs have been very successful in lowering the teen out-of-wedlock birth rate. According to the Consortium of State Physicians Resource Councils, which represents thousands of doctors, the decline in the adolescent birth rate is due to the fact that fewer teens are having extramarital sex.

A 1991 Pediatrics study found that teens who engage in premarital sex 25 are likely to engage in other risky behaviors such as drug abuse and delinquency. By helping teens to delay sex until marriage, these abstinence programs are encouraging teens to avoid these negative behaviors and to live healthy lifestyles that make them more solid husbands, fathers, wives, and mothers in the future.

Thousands of abstinence programs have been developed throughout the 26 United States, including Project Reality, True Love Waits, Sex Respect, Pure Love Alliance, and the Virginity Pledge Movement. Abstinence educators teach young people the skills to avoid risky behavior, resist peer pressure, and build self-esteem. Studies have shown the effectiveness of abstinence programs. For example, a Northwestern University study of Project Reality, an Illinois-based abstinence program, found that 54 percent of sexually active teens decided to become abstinent after a year in the program.

These are only a handful of the many initiatives that aim to shore up the American family. Hundreds of other organizations are also helping couples keep their marriages together and teaching young people the benefits of sexual abstinence. Because this movement has grown so quickly in recent years, it's likely to continue its upward trajectory—leading to a vastly strengthened family life in America and a consequently stronger social fabric, greater economic productivity, and better quality of life.

SELECTION 4 QUESTIONS

Vocabulary

1. Explain what Maher means when she says many are "making a concerted effort to buttress the institutions of marriage and family." (paragraph 8)
2. In a Louisiana covenant marriage, a divorce may be obtained if there is proof of "habitual intemperance." What does that mean?

Comprehension and Analysis

3. How does the title of the article relate to Maher's thesis?
4. Is Maher surprised that so many people are scared of marriage? What does she use to support her point of view?
5. List and explain two of the "costs" of "fractured families."
6. List and explain two of the states' and/or communities' efforts to encourage marriage and reduce divorce.
7. Why does researcher Steven Nock think covenant marriages are important even though they are not popular?
8. What does Maher predict will result from the initiatives to support and assist American families?

Reflect and Connect

9. Do you think Leo, author of "Marriage on the Rocks," would support covenant marriages? Please explain.

SELECTION 5   NOSTALGIA AS IDEOLOGY

STEPHANIE COONTZ

Dr. Coontz, Co-chair of the Council on Contemporary Families, and author of The Way We Never Were: American Families and the Nostalgia Trap, *teaches at The Evergreen State College in Olympia, Washington.*

AN IDEA TO THINK ABOUT

What do you think are the goals of marriage?

WORD TO KNOW

aberration (¶6)—exception, unusual occurrence

The more I listen to debates over whether we should promote marriage, the more I am reminded of one of my father's favorite sayings: "If wishes were horses, then beggars would ride." Yes, kids raised by married parents do better, on average, than kids raised in divorced- or single-parent homes. Yes, the long-term commitment of marriage confers economic, emotional, and even health benefits on adults as well. Certainly, we should remove marriage disincentives from government programs—16 states, for instance, still discriminate against married couples in welfare policy. We should expand health coverage to include "couples counseling" for all who wish it. With better support systems, we may be able to save more potentially healthy marriages and further reduce rates of unwed childbearing among teenagers. 1

But there is no way to re-establish marriage as the main site of child rearing, dependent care, income pooling, or interpersonal commitments in the modern world. Any movement that sets this as a goal misunderstands how irreversibly family life and marriage have changed, and it will inevitably be dominated by powerful "allies" who are not interested in supporting the full range of families that exist today and are likely to in the future. 2

For more than 1,000 years, marriage was the main way that society transferred property, forged political alliances, raised capital, organized children's rights, redistributed resources to dependents, and coordinated the division of labor by age and gender. Precisely because marriage served so many political, social, and economic functions, not everyone had access to it. Those who did almost never had free choice regarding partners and rarely could afford to hold high expectations of their relationships. 3

During the last 200 years, the growth of bureaucracies, banks, schools, hospitals, unemployment insurance, Social Security, and pension plans slowly but surely eroded the political and economic roles that marriage traditionally had played. It increasingly became an individual decision that could be made independently of family and community pressures. By the early 1900s, love and companionship had become not just the wistful hope of a husband or wife but the legitimate goal of marriage in the eyes of society. But this meant that people began expecting more of married life than ever before in history—at the exact time that older methods of organizing and stabilizing marriages were ceasing to work. The very things that made marriage more satisfying, and increasingly more fair to women, are the same things that have made marriage less stable. 4

The outlines of the problem were clear by the early twentieth century. 5 The more that people saw marriage as their main source of intimacy and commitment, the less they were prepared to enter or stay in a marriage they found unsatisfying. Divorce rates shot up so quickly that by the 1920s many observers feared that marriage was headed for extinction. Books warned of "The Marriage Crisis." Magazines asked, "Is Marriage on the Skids?"

During the 1930s and 1940s, these fears took a backseat to more immedi- 6 ate survival issues, but abandonment rates rose during the Great Depression, out-of-wedlock sex shot up during the war, and by 1946 one in three marriages was ending in divorce. At the end of the 1940s, politicians and other concerned Americans began a campaign to reverse these trends. For a while it looked as if they would succeed. During the 1950s, the divorce rate dipped, the age at which people initially married plummeted, and fertility rates soared. But most historians agree that this decade was an aberration stimulated by the most massive government subsidization of young families in American history. And below the surface, the underpinnings of traditional marital stability continued to erode. Rates of unwed motherhood tripled between 1940 and 1948. The number of working mothers grew by 400 percent in the 1950s.

By the late 1960s, divorce rates were rising again, and the age of first mar- 7 riage began to rise, too. The divorce rate peaked in the late 1970s and early 1980s, and has fallen by 26 percent since then. But the marriage rate has dropped at the same time, while the incidence of unmarried couples cohabiting, singles living alone, delayed marriage, and same-sex partnerships continued to increase throughout the 1990s.

Though welfare-state policies diverge, these trends are occurring in every 8 industrial country in the world. Where divorce remains hard to get and out-of-wedlock birth is stigmatized, as in Italy and Japan, rates of marriage have plunged, suggesting that the historical trends undermining the universality of marriage will, if blocked in one area, simply spill over into another.

There is no way to reverse this trend short of a repressiveness that would 9 not long be tolerated even in today's patriotic climate (and that would soon wipe out many of the benefits people now gain from marriage). Divorced families, step-families, single parents, gay and lesbian families, lone householders, and unmarried cohabiting couples will never again become such a minor part of the family terrain that we can afford to count on marriage as our main institution for allocating income or caring for dependents.

I don't believe that marriage is on the verge of extinction—nor that it 10 should become extinct. Most cohabiting couples eventually do get married, either to each other or to someone else. Gay men and lesbians are now demanding access to marriage—a demand that many marriage advocates perversely interpret as an attack on the institution. And marriage continues to be an effective foundation for interpersonal commitments and economic stability. Of course we must find ways to make marriage more possible for couples who want it and to strengthen the marriages they contract. But there's a big difference between supporting concrete measures to help marriages succeed and supporting an organized marriage movement.

Despite the benefits associated with marriage for most couples, unhappily 11
married individuals are more distressed than people who are not married. Women in bad marriages lose their self-confidence, become depressed, develop lowered immune functions, and are more likely to abuse alcohol than women who get out of such marriages. A recent study of marriages where one spouse had mild hypertension found that in happy couples, time spent together lowered the blood pressure of the at-risk spouse. In unhappily married couples, however, even small amounts of extra togetherness led to increases in blood pressure for the at-risk spouse.

For children, living with two cooperating parents is better than living with a 12
single parent. But high conflict in a marriage, or even silent withdrawal coupled with contempt, is often more damaging to children than divorce or growing up in a single-parent family. According to the National Center on Addiction and Substance Abuse at Columbia University, teens who live in two-parent households are less likely, on average, to abuse drugs and alcohol than teens in one-parent families; but teens in two-parent families who have a fair to poor relationship with their father are more likely to do so than teens who live with a single mother.

The most constructive way to support modern marriages is to improve 13
work-life policies so that couples can spend more time with each other and their kids, to increase social-support systems for children, and to provide counseling for all couples who seek it. But many in the center-right marriage movement resist such reforms, complaining that single parents and unmarried couples—whether heterosexual or of the same sex—could "take advantage" of them. If we grant other relationships the same benefits as marriage, they argue, we weaken people's incentives to get married.

But that is a bullet we simply have to bite. I am in favor of making it easier 14
for couples to marry and to sustain that commitment. But that cannot substitute for a more far-reaching, inclusive program to support the full range of relationships in which our children are raised and our dependents cared for.

SELECTION 5 QUESTIONS

Vocabulary

1. Explain the cliché, "If wishes were horses, then beggars would ride." (paragraph 1)
2. Explain what Coontz means by "there is no way to reverse this trend short of a repressiveness that would not long be tolerated even in today's patriotic climate." (paragraph 9)
3. Explain what Coontz means by "a demand that many marriage advocates perversely interpret as an attack on the institution." (paragraph 10)

Comprehension and Analysis

4. State Coontz's thesis.

5. In paragraph 2, Coontz says, "movement . . . will inevitably be dominated by powerful 'allies' who are not interested in supporting the full range of families. . . ." Who are the allies? Please explain.

6. According to Coontz, what were some of the original "purposes" of marriage? Why have those purposes changed in recent years?

7. By the early 1900s, what had become the legitimate goals of marriage? Why have these goals made marriage "less stable"?

8. Does Coontz believe the current "marriage crisis" is a new phenomenon? What does she use to support her point of view?

9. If a couple with children were hopelessly unhappily married, do you think Coontz would support them in getting a divorce? Please explain your reasoning.

Reflect and Connect

10. Which, if any, of the efforts to encourage marriage and reduce divorce that Maher describes in "Patching Up the American Family" would Coontz be likely to support? Please explain.

SELECTION 6   FAMILIES SUFFER FROM DELAMINATION

LIZ CAILE

Ms. Caile was a reporter and columnist for The Mountain Ear *newspaper in Nederland, Colorado, near Boulder, for 20 years. She wrote about the natural world for many publications, published a book of her poetry, and reviewed books for* The Bloomsbury Review. *She was 53 when she died in 1998. This essay is from the book,* Liz Caile: A Life at Treeline, *a collection of her columns published by her friends and colleagues after her death.*

AN IDEA TO THINK ABOUT

Think about the oldest people and the youngest people you see and interact with regularly. Think about how their perspectives, opinions, and attitudes are similar to and different from those of you and your agemates.

WORD TO KNOW

encumbered (¶2)—burdened

I ran into a childhood neighbor at a wedding recently, in the midst of other familiar Boulder faces. Fay is in her 70s, but, my son Billy and I agree, she seems not to have aged in the last 20 years, when she has with good humor seen many of us through many changes.

We were standing in one of the rooms of the University Club in Boulder, where I can remember being one of the younger set at such occasions (10 years old, flitting restlessly between the drink- and food- and conversationally-encumbered adults). Fay broke into a smile and sighed. "Oh, I wish we could go back 40 years! We all lived in the same block and there were 26 children," she told my husband, "and two of the lots didn't even have houses on them!"

The Sixth Street crowd—newcomers to a new land, our homes breaking up the prairie-clay soil at the base of the Flatirons, in the shadow of Flagstaff. Flocks of children, with so much to look forward to, so little apparently lacking in our lives. But looking back, I see we were lacking one thing on a consistent, daily level: grandparents. We were contained by the neat, nuclear American family, with other relatives in distant states.

I have to grope to remember my grandparents' names, separated from my childhood by death or the Atlantic Ocean. Few of my schoolmates had grandparents to whom they were close or large families that swallowed them up like an ocean, tranquil or stormtossed. My generation had a distorted view of its own importance, uninformed by the tides of other family members birthing and dying. Other people aged, old people existed in the world, but our day-to-day reality was compressed into the nuclear family, and youth seemed the definite norm.

How quaint the concept of many generations in one place seemed—comparable to a nostalgic picture of family farms or the layered, immigrant communities in large cities. Now, from the same, self-centered point of view, I am awed with my own discovery of vertical layers of family. It seems a privilege, a rarity, to have as many close family members as I have, with an age range of 1 to 80 plus, on the local phone exchange.

As much as anything, I love the impromptu exchange of stories that takes place with frequent visiting. We easily go back to other times, comparing notes and rediscovering each other at different stages. Then, we return with a laugh to the present, weaving in and out of time: "Gotta go don't forget. . . ." I love the history written in my grandson's big, four-tooth smile, a smile that reminds me of Fay's stories of my son at the age: "He was the smartest child I've ever known!" (No wonder we're fond of Fay!)

When certain factions get out the drum and start beating a death knell for the American family, blaming single parents for its demise, I think, that's not the problem. There is so much resentment in the charge—as if single parents weren't nestled within families of their own. The American family is weakened as much by the delamination between generations as it is by the high rate of divorce or the decision to go parenting alone.

Moving away from one's parents creates a more subtle loss, complicated by the search for economic opportunity. It creates a more subtle fragmentation that affects our knowledge of history and our respect for place. We pay a high price for our treasured and unexamined mobility, fleeing the places and people who shaped us.

And Fay—how does she stay so young? Would the fact that several of 9 her children and grandchildren live today within a stone's throw of Sixth Street have anything to do with it?

SELECTION 6 QUESTIONS

Vocabulary

1. Explain Caile's word picture, "families that swallowed them up like an ocean, tranquil or stormtossed." (paragraph 4)
2. Caile said her "generation had a distorted view of its own importance." (paragraph 4) What did she mean?

Comprehension and Analysis

3. Explain Caile's thesis and how it relates to the title of her essay.
4. As she was growing up, how did Caile feel about the concept of multiple generations living close together? How did she feel about the concept when she wrote this essay? Please explain.
5. Caile says, "We pay a high price for our treasured and unexamined mobility." Please explain what she means.

Reflect and Connect

6. In "Patching Up the American Family" Maher says children have suffered tremendously from America's explosion of family breakdown—youngsters with divorced, never-married, or cohabiting parents. How do you think Caile would respond to that statement?

SELECTION 7   MORAL PARENT, MORAL CHILD: FAMILY STRUCTURE MATTERS LESS TO A CHILD'S DEVELOPMENT THAN THE QUALITY OF THE PARENTING

RICHARD WEISSBOURD

Dr. Weissbourd teaches at Harvard's Graduate School of Education and the Kennedy School of Government. His publications include The Vulnerable Child.

AN IDEA TO THINK ABOUT

Who has been influential in helping you develop your moral and ethical "code of conduct"?

WORDS TO KNOW

abhor (¶10)— despise, hate
narcissistic (¶11)— self-centered, egotistic

These days there is once again a great deal of hand-wringing about the sorry moral state of America's children. All the usual suspects have been rounded up: parents who lack values, schools that neglect "character" education, and—conservative pundits' favorite culprit—family breakdown. As William Bennett puts it in *The Broken Hearth: Reversing the Moral Collapse of the American Family,* "Most of our social pathologies—crime, imprisonment rates, welfare . . . alcohol and drug abuse . . . sexually transmitted diseases— are manifestations, direct and indirect, of the crack-up of the modern American family."   1

Concern about single parenthood is legitimate. But single parenthood is not primarily responsible for children's moral troubles. The bigger problem is that our country fails to support good parenting, and it dramatically fails to cultivate critical moral qualities in adults—qualities that are critical to children's moral development—in part because of wrong-headed notions about the fundamental nature of adult's moral lives.   2

Children in single-parent families, to be sure, face obstacles to developing important moral qualities. Ethical development is rooted in emotional development, and children in single-parent families may suffer more persistently from those feelings—shame, distrust, cynicism—that commonly eat away at children's capacities for caring, responsibility, idealism, and other important moral qualities. In the wake of a divorce, for example, adolescents frequently suffer sharp disillusionment—a loss of idealized images of their parents and of the ideals these parents represent. After a divorce, large numbers of children both suffer the shame of poverty and are abandoned by their fathers (10 years after a divorce, two-thirds of children haven't seen their father in a year and have effectively lost contact with their fathers). This is not the soil out of which idealism and a sense of responsibility for others can easily grow.   3

But the reality is that most children in single-parent families are not morally defective. They are growing up to be quite good people. Moreover, the notion that single parenthood accounts for Bennett's slew of moral problems is bizarrely ahistorical. Many of these problems were prevalent before 1960, when single parenthood began to rise, and increases in these problems have not followed closely, as Bennett's argument suggests, the steady increase in single   4 parenthood between 1960 and 1990. From the mid-1970s to the late 1980s, for example, both violent crime and teen alcohol abuse declined. That's because single parenthood is only one of many factors that determine the prevalence of these moral problems.

What's more, whether children are somehow less moral in single-parent   5
families depends crucially on other options. How do kids fare when their parents do not divorce but simply remain in miserable marriages, or when their mothers elect to enter shotgun marriages rather than parenting solo? Studies show that children suffer high rates of behavior troubles before their parents' divorce. Locked into decaying marriages, parents who are angry, moody, and withdrawn are less likely to provide models of fairness, respect, compassion, and other virtues for their children. They are also less likely to provide the consistent expectations and encouragement that reduce cynicism and build trust.

All of which points to the big hole in the family breakdown argument of   6
Bennett and company. The focus on the structure of families has ignored what is most important to any child's ethical development: an ongoing, trusting relationship with at least one adult who is ethical and mature, and who listens and encourages without shying away from his or her moral authority. A mountain of research now shows that it is the content of adult-child interactions, not the structure of families, that most strongly determines the shape of children's ethical development. That's what makes parenting a profoundly moral act, and learning to parent well a profound moral achievement.

Can public policy positively influence these parent-child interactions?   7
This country desperately needs to provide high-quality parent-education programs through hospitals and various community organizations. Parents who were not parented well themselves often simply need to learn basic strategies for building trust and promoting their children's empathy and generosity.

This country also needs a public-health campaign focused on parental de-   8
pression. Parental depression is widespread—as many as 25 percent of children will grow up with a depressed parent—and parental depression undermines almost every key aspect of parenting. Depressed parents are far more likely to be moody, to lash out unexpectedly, and to criticize unfairly. Parental depression is strongly correlated with child neglect and abuse. Children of depressed parents are more likely to struggle by almost every measure; they are, for example, more likely to suffer behavior troubles and they are almost five times as likely to abuse drugs. Fortunately, many forms of depression are both preventable and treatable—as many as 80 percent of victims are helped by treatment. We need to be far more proactive in getting depressed parents access to effective treatment.

But something else may be equally important, although it is almost en-   9
tirely ignored: getting adults interested in their own ethical development. Because children's ethical development hinges on trusting relationships with respected, mature adults, it's hard to imagine that children will become more ethical if adults do not become more ethical and mature. But we have the peculiar notion in this country that our moral natures are by and large decided at

some point in childhood—that we as adults are left to simply live out the die that is cast.

It's not that we have no faith in adult development. Entire sections of our 10 chain bookstores are devoted to self-help—empowering adults to tame fears, dispatch obsessions, and deal with other people whom they abhor. (The book I'm dying to read is *Emotional Healing at Warp Speed*.) The adult personality appears to be entirely plastic. But what's hard to find is an "other-help" book, a book about how adults can become better people.

The point is not simply that adults need to be less narcissistic. The ambi- 11 tious cultural shift I am hoping for is this: that adults come to view appreciating and being generous to others, acting with fairness and integrity, and formulating mature and resilient ideals as evolving and subtle capacities. This shift is especially important for adults who are becoming parents. For parenting itself is clearly a prime instance when adults are faced squarely with hugely complex challenges to their core moral qualities: their capacity for empathy and fairness, their ability to disentangle their own interests from those of others, their generosity. For tenuously connected fathers, fundamental questions of responsibility hang in the balance.

Responding to parental depression, improving parent education, and help- 12 ing adults whether parents, teachers, or religious leaders—view their own moral development as connected to children's is obviously a tall order. It will mean, among other things, building on the success of some workplaces and parent-education programs (and many faith-based organizations) that actively value and support ethical development. But it will be far more productive, and surely no taller, than what Bennett and the Bush administration want: a return to a romanticized era of two-parent families.

SELECTION 7 QUESTIONS

Vocabulary

1. Explain the sentence, "This is not the soil out of which idealism and a sense of responsibility for others can easily grow." (paragraph 3)
2. Explain what Weissbourd means when he says, "the notion that single parenthood accounts for Bennett's slew of moral problems is bizarrely ahistorical." (paragraph 4)
3. Explain what Weissbourd means when he says "we as adults are left to simply live out the die that is cast." (paragraph 9)

Comprehension and Analysis

4. Who and what are the "usual suspects" responsible for the "sorry moral state of America's children"? What does Weissbourd think is a bigger problem than the usual suspects?

5. Does Weissbourd believe all children in single-parent families are doomed? According to Weissbourd, are all children in two-parent families guaranteed a bright future? Please explain his reasoning.

6. According to Weissbourd, what factor(s) most strongly determines the shape of children's ethical development?

7. Does Weissbourd think public policy can have a positive influence on parent-child interactions? Please explain.

8. Why does Weissbourd think it is critical to get adults interested in their own ethical development?

9. State Weissbourd's thesis.

Reflect and Connect

10. In "Patching Up the American Family" Maher says that "grassroots activists, policymakers, and others who have witnessed the suffering caused by family breakdown are making a concerted effort to buttress the institutions of marriage and family." What would Weissbourd probably think about this approach? Please explain.

INVESTIGATING OTHER POINTS OF VIEW . . .

One way to investigate a variety of points of view on the issues surrounding the complex changes and challenges for today's families is through the resources of Research Navigator™. Once you log on to Research Navigator.com and enter your personal passcode (from inside the front cover of this text), you have access to three databases of credible and reliable source material: 1) EBSCO's Content Select Academic Journal Database with content from the leading academic journals, 2) *The New York Times* Search by Subject™ Archive with full-text articles from *The New York Times*, 3) Link Library providing editorially selected "best of the web" sites. For more information about Research Navigator™ and how to use it efficiently, see "Introducing Research Navigator™" starting on page RN–1.

AFTER CONSIDERING SEVERAL POINTS OF VIEW . . .

A. There is no single, agreed-upon definition of a "family." Discuss what you think defines a family and any arrangements and people that do not constitute a family. Describe some of the factors that have influenced your view.

B. You have read about a variety of programs designed to encourage marriage, reduce divorce, support children, and/or strengthen parenting skills. Describe a specific program or a type of program you think will have the most positive effects for families and one program or type of program that you see as detrimental to families. Discuss what you think would be the most effective way to implement and promote the positive program.

C. One of the authors stated that it is not family structure but "an ongoing, trusting relationship with at least one adult who is ethical and mature, and who listens and encourages without shying away from his or her moral authority" that is most important to any child's ethical development. Discuss your view of what and who influences a child's ethical development, including the role of family structure. Include how you reached your decisions.

THEME 3

IMMIGRATION

In March 2003, the U.S. Census Bureau released a report showing that more than 3 million immigrants had arrived in the previous two years. That brought the number of foreign-born people living in U. S. households to 32.5 million, an all-time high. "Despite the recession, despite 9/11, the number of immigrants who came into the country of working age rose as fast as it did during the 1990s," said economist Andrew Sum, the report's lead author.

Sum believes that "many, if not most, of these workers are undocumented." The Immigration and Naturalization Service (INS) estimates that the undocumented population could grow by as much as half a million new arrivals a year. Other authorities, including the Census Bureau, say that number is too low.

For some Americans, the actual numbers are not important. They believe that the United States is threatened by hordes of immigrants who increase the crime rate, take jobs from local workers, and burden all our social services. Ardent restrictionists such as Patrick Buchanan say controlling and reducing both legal and illegal immigration are critical to America's survival.

However, others believe immigrants are living examples of American democracy in action. They believe that our immigrant population brings benefits such as adding vitality and culture to our national fabric, a willingness to do jobs that native citizens don't want to do, and offsetting middle-class flight by settling in cities with declining populations.

In her article "Fear Eats The Soul" for the *New Internationalist Magazine* (2002), Vanessa Baird says refugees, asylum seekers, undocumented aliens, and unauthorized economic migrants create several interconnected fears in the rich world:

Fear one: *Numbers.* There are too many refugees trying to come into our countries. It's a crisis. We are being invaded.

Fear two: *Resources.* Refugees fill our hospitals, classrooms, take our jobs, use our social welfare systems. What will be left for us?

Fear three: *Crime.* We don't know who these people are. Many have entered without documents. They might be criminals—or, worse, terrorists.

Fear four: *Disbelief.* Many claiming asylum may not be real refugees. How do we know we are not being duped?

Fear five: *Culture.* They are different from us. They don't share our values or customs or language or religion. They will swamp our own culture.

But, she adds, "that does not mean the fears are rational—or wired into the reality of today's world."

The battle over immigration policy is especially tense in the Arizona desert. In 2002, the Border Patrol said it arrested 156,950 undocumented immigrants who crossed into Arizona illegally, and that at least twice that number may have made it through successfully. In addition, 133 illegal immigrants died attempting to enter Arizona—most from dehydration after becoming lost in the desert. Humanitarian organizations such as Humane Borders set up water stations to aid illegal immigrants while self-described "gun-toting patriots" try to catch people crossing the border illegally and have them arrested.

The authors in this Theme delve into the complex issue of immigration.

The Theme opens with a character in a Wiley Miller cartoon asking, "What's the worst that can happen if we loosen up our immigration policy?" Next we look at "The Changing Face of Ethnicity in America" through a series of "Immigration and Community" excerpts from Faragher, Buhle, Czitrom and Armitage's American history text *Out of Many—A History of the American People.*

Then, in "Immigration Policy" from *A Nation of Immigrants* by President John F. Kennedy, we gain insight into the reasons for the immigration reform that was realized in the Immigration Bill of 1965.

In response to the question "Should Washington stem the tide of both legal and illegal immigration?" Dirk Chase Eldridge presents the case for his "yes" answer, and Daniel T. Griswold presents his reasons for saying "no."

Next cartoonist Clay Bennett adds some "fine print" to the Statue of Liberty's offer.

The next two selections focus on Hispanic immigration and the Arizona-Mexico border. However, similar observations, points of view, and realities are found across immigrant populations and geographic locations. In an article based on his best-selling book, *The Death of the West: How Dying Populations and Immigrant Invasions Imperil Our Country and Civilization,* Patrick Buchanan describes how the "Hispanic Immigration Threatens U.S. Values." Then Jim Seckler introduces us to a real immigrant in "He Crossed Border for a Better Life."

O. Ricardo Pimentel proposes that we "Rip Up Illegalities by the REAL Roots," and the Theme closes with "Opening the Door," an article by *The Economist* making a case for managed immigration in the rich countries of the world.

As you read the selections in this Theme and other articles and essays on immigration, answer questions such as these as a matter of course:

1. Do I understand all the author's words and phrases?
2. What is the author's thesis (conclusion)?
3. What facts, opinions, and reasoned judgments does the author provide to support and develop the thesis?
4. Are the author's facts, opinions, and reasoned judgments derived from respected sources?
5. Are there factual errors or misleading interpretations?
6. Has significant information been omitted or arbitrarily discounted?
7. What new information does this author add to my understanding of the issue?

WORDS TO KNOW

alien—Any person who is not a citizen of the United States.

asylee—Alien who is found to be unable or unwilling to return to his or her country of nationality, or to seek the protection of that country because of persecution or a well-founded fear of persecution.

border crosser—Alien resident of the United States reentering the country after an absence of less than six months in Canada or Mexico, or a nonresident alien entering the United States across the Canadian border for stays of no more than six months or across the Mexican border for stays of no more than 72 hours.

conditional resident—Any alien granted permanent resident status on a conditional basis (e.g., a spouse of a U.S. citizen; an immigrant investor), who is required to petition for the removal of the set conditions before the second anniversary of the approval of his or her conditional status.

derivative citizenship—Citizenship conveyed to children through the naturalization of parents or, under certain circumstances, to foreign-born children adopted by U.S. citizen parents, provided certain conditions are met.

emigrate—To go out, to leave one's country to settle in another; the opposite of *immigrate*. (For example, when people move from the United States to establish residency in another country.)

exchange visitor—Alien coming temporarily to the United States as a participant in a program approved by the Secretary of State for the purpose of teaching, instructing or lecturing, studying, observing, conducting research, consulting, demonstrating special skills, or receiving training.

illegal alien—Person, not a citizen or national of the United States who is residing the in the U.S. unlawfully.

immigrant—See *permanent resident alien*.

immigrate—To come into; to enter and establish permanent residence in a country of which one is not a native; the opposite of emigrate. (For example, when people from other countries come into the United States).

Immigration and Naturalization Service (INS)—Agency of the U.S. Department of Justice empowered to administer the federal laws relating to the admission, exclusion, and deportation of aliens and to the naturalization of aliens lawfully residing in the United States. As of March 1, 2003, the INS was eliminated and the Department of Homeland Security took over its duties.

Lawful Permanent Resident (LPR)—Person not a citizen of the United States who is residing the in the United States under legally recognized and lawfully recorded permanent residence as an immigrant. Also known as *permanent resident alien, resident alien permit holder,* and *green card holder.*

legalized aliens—Certain illegal aliens who were eligible to apply for temporary resident status under the legalization provision of the Immigration Reform and Control Act of 1986.

migration—Movement of people, especially of whole groups, from one place, region, or country to another, particularly with the intention of making permanent settlement in a new location.

nativist—Person who favors policies that give preference to native inhabitants over immigrants.

naturalization—The conferring, by any means, of citizenship on a person after his or her birth.

permanent resident—Any person not a citizen of the United States who is residing in the United States under legally recognized and lawfully recorded permanent residence as an immigrant. Also known as *permanent resident alien, lawful permanent resident, resident alien permit holder,* and *green card holder.*

permanent resident alien—Alien admitted to the United States as a lawful permanent resident. Permanent residents are also commonly referred to as *immigrants;* however, the Immigration and Nationality Act (INA) broadly defines an immigrant as any alien in the United States except one legally admitted under specific nonimmigrant categories.

refugee—Any person who is outside his or her country of nationality and is unable or unwilling to return to that country because of persecution or a well-founded fear of persecution.

remigration—Immigrants who return to their homeland to live. (For example, many of the "New Immigrants" to the United States in the early 1900s stayed only a few years to earn money and then returned home.)

repatriated—Describes a person who went back to his or her country of origin, allegiance, or citizenship.

resident alien—Non-United States citizen currently residing in the United States.

temporary worker—Alien coming to the United States to work for a temporary period of time.

undocumented alien/undocumented immigrant—Person who is not a citizen or national of the United States, and is in the United States unlawfully.

xenophobia—Hatred of foreigners.

SELECTION 1 EDITORIAL CARTOON

WILEY MILLER

Mr. Miller had worked as a cartoonist for three different newspapers when he made his big breakthrough: Playboy *bought a series of "bartoons"—drawings he had made on cocktail napkins. In 1991 he won the prestigious Robert F. Kennedy Journalism Award for editorial cartooning. That same year he created "Non Sequitur," his "wry look at the absurdities of everyday life," which is now syndicated in 500 newspapers in 20 countries.*

AN IDEA TO THINK ABOUT

How might your life be different if the British had not established colonies in "America"?

Comprehension and Analysis

1. Who are the people on the shore? Who is on the ships?
2. Why did Wiley select these people to convey his message?
3. What is Wiley's message?

Reflect and Connect

4. Then or now: What is an example of the "worst that can happen" when immigration policies are loosened? What is an example of the "best that can happen" when immigration policies are loosened?

SELECTION 2   IMMIGRATION AND COMMUNITY: THE CHANGING FACE OF ETHNICITY IN AMERICA

JOHN MACK FARAGHER, MARI JO BUHLE, DANIEL CZITROM, AND SUSAN H. ARMITAGE

Dr. Faragher is Arthur Unobskey Professor of American History at Yale University. Dr. Buhle is Professor of American Civilization and History at Brown University. Dr. Czitrom is Professor and Chair of History at Mount Holyoke College. Dr. Armitage is Professor of History at Washington State University.

These selections, from their American history text Out of Many—A History of the American People, *highlight the impact of the immigrant experience on the formation of American communities. The first selection covers the colonial period through 1800, the second 1800 to 1860, the third 1860 to 1930, and the last selection covers the period since 1930. Each selection opens with an overview of the character of immigration during the period followed by a section called "In Their Own Words" written by immigrants or by native-born Americans in response to the new arrivals.*

AN IDEA TO THINK ABOUT

How many people do you know who have immigrated, or whose relatives have immigrated, to the United States within the last 50 years? How was their journey?

THE CHANGING FACE OF ETHNICITY IN AMERICA

To 1800

Immigration contributed to the growth of the population of the colonies that 1 became the United States of America more than any other factor. Seventeenth-century migration to these colonies was mostly from England, although small but important groups of Dutch, Swedes, and French settled areas of New York, New Jersey, and Maryland.

By 1700 the population of British colonial North America had reached 2 250,000. The high levels of fertility characteristic of all the colonial societies of North America—British, Spanish, and French—contributed to the growth of population. But only the British encouraged immigration. The French and the Spanish adopted highly restrictive immigration policies. Dedicated to keeping its colonies exclusively Catholic, France turned down the requests of thousands of Protestant Huguenots who desperately sought to emigrate to Canada. The Spanish, fearful of depleting their population at home, severely limited the migration of their own subjects to their colonies and absolutely forbade the immigration of foreigners, with the exception of African slaves.

Yet a veritable flood of immigrants came to British North America during 3 the eighteenth century. Scots, Scots-Irish, Germans, and French joined the English in the trans-Atlantic crossing. Slave traders also brought tens of thousands of Africans to the southern colonies. By 1750 European and African migrants and their descendants outnumbered the Indian population of the continent, and by 1800 had grown to more than 5.3 million, an increase of more than twenty times the population in 1700 over the course of one hundred years.

William Penn was the first British colonial official to encourage the immi- 4 gration of non-British western Europeans, in the 1680s sending agents to recruit settlers in Holland, France, and the German principalities along the Rhine River. His experiment proved so successful that the leaders of other British colonies soon were employing recruiting agents of their own in Europe. Further encouraging this development, most of the British colonies enacted liberal naturalization laws in the early eighteenth century, allowing immigrants who professed Protestantism and swore allegiance to the British crown to become free "denizens" with all the freedoms and privileges of natural-born subjects. In 1740 Parliament passed a general Naturalization Act that extended these policies to all the colonies. The new legislation continued to prohibit the naturalization of Catholic and Jewish immigrants, however, and these groups remained tiny minorities in the British colonies.

Still, immigration to what would become the United States was charac- 5 terized by extraordinary ethnic diversity. The two largest migrating groups were the English and the Africans, each totaling, according to good historical

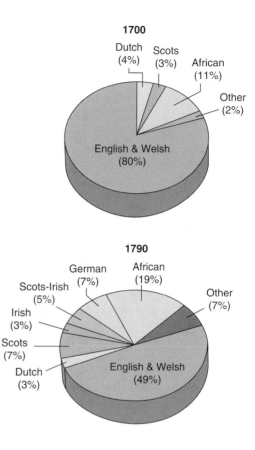

1700

Dutch (4%)
Scots (3%)
African (11%)
Other (2%)
English & Welsh (80%)

1790

German (7%)
African (19%)
Scots-Irish (5%)
Other (7%)
Irish (3%)
Scots (7%)
Dutch (3%)
English & Welsh (49%)

The Ancestry of the British Colonial Population The legacy of eighteenth-century immigration to the British colonies was a population of unprecedented ethnic diversity. *(Source:* Adapted from Thomas L. Purvis, *"The European Ancestry of the United States Population, 1790".* William and Mary Quarterly 61 (1984): 85–101. Copyright © 1984 by the Institute of Early American History and Culture. Reprinted with the permission of the publishers.)

estimates, perhaps 400,000 to 500,000 immigrants during the colonial period. There was also substantial emigration from the northern British Isles. Squeezed by economic hardship, an estimated 250,000 Highland Scots and Protestant Irish from the Ulster region (known in America as the "Scots-Irish") emigrated to North America during the eighteenth century. The Germans were another significant group; at least 100,000 of them settled in the British colonies, where they became known as the "Dutch" (from *Deutsch,* the German-language term for German). It should be noted that from half to two-thirds of Europeans came to British North America as indentured servants, or "redemptioners," or else convicts transported to the New World to serve out their sentences laboring on plantations. The Africans were not the only people to come involuntarily to America. A majority of immigrants during the colonial period came in a state of bondage.

The first federal census, conducted in 1790, provides a snapshot of the consequences of eighteenth-century immigration. Forty-nine percent of the population of the thirteen United States was English in origin, and nearly 20 percent was African; 15 percent were Irish or Scots, 7 percent German, 3 percent Dutch, and 2 percent French.

Many of the founders of the American republic worried that the different languages and traditions of these diverse peoples would fracture the nation. In the 1750s, for example, Benjamin Franklin wrote of his fears that German immigrants would not assimilate to English ways. "Why should Pennsylvania," he asked, "founded by English, become a colony of *aliens* who will shortly be so numerous as to Germanize *us* instead of Anglifying them?" Thomas Jefferson worried that immigrants from monarchical countries, untutored in the ways of democracy, would "warp and bias" the direction of American political development. Reflecting such fears, the nation's first Naturalization Act, passed in 1790, required a residency period of five years (a kind of probation period) before immigrants could apply for citizenship, and limited applications to "free white persons." In the nineteenth and early twentieth centuries this clause would be used to bar the naturalization of immigrants from Africa and Asia.

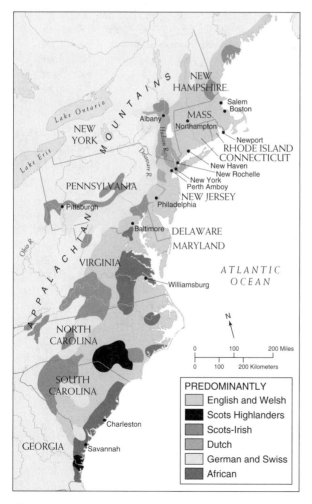

Ethnic Groups in Eighteenth-Century British North America The first federal census, taken in 1790, revealed remarkable ethnic diversity. New England was filled with people from the British Isles, but the rest of the colonies were a patchwork. Most states had at least three different ethnic groups within their borders, and although the English and Scots-Irish were heavily represented in all colonies, in some they had strong competition from Germans (eastern and southern Pennsylvania) and from African peoples (Virginia and South Carolina).

IN THEIR OWN WORDS

Judith Giton (ca. 1665–1711) was twenty years old when she and many other 8
Protestant Huguenots escaped French persecution to settle in South Carolina
in 1685. In the following letter to her brother, written from America, she described the harrowing experience of immigration.

We were detained in London for three months, waiting for a vessel ready 9
to sail for Carolina. Once embarked, we were miserably off indeed. The
scarlet fever broke out in our ship, and many died, among them our aged
mother. . . . Our vessel put in [at Bermuda] for repairs, having been badly
injured in a severe storm. Our captain . . . was thrown into prison, and the
ship was seized. It was with the greatest difficulty that we secured our passage in another ship, for our money had all been spent. After our arrival in
Carolina, we suffered all sorts of evils. Our eldest brother died of a fever,
eighteen months after coming here. . . . We ourselves had been exposed,
since leaving France, to all kinds of afflictions, in the forms of sickness,
pestilence, famine, poverty, and the roughest labor. I have been for six
months at a time in this country without tasting bread, laboring meanwhile
like a slave in tilling the ground. Indeed, I have spent three or four years
without knowing what it was to eat bread whenever I wanted it. God has
been very good to us in enabling us to bear up under trials for every kind.[1]

Gottlieb Mittelberger came to Pennsylvania from Germany in 1750 and 10
served as a schoolmaster and organist in Philadelphia for three years. In this famous account, written after his return to Europe, he paints a horrid picture of
the voyage to America, the conditions for indentured servants, and warns his
countrymen to remain content at home.

Both in Rotterdam and in Amsterdam the people are packed densely, like 11
herrings so to say, in the large sea vessels. One person receives a place of
scarcely 2 feet width and 6 feet length in the bedstead, while many a ship
carries four to six hundred souls; not to mention the innumerable imple-
ments, tools, provisions, water-barrels and other things which likewise oc-
cupy much space.

When the ships have landed at Philadelphia after their long voyage, 12
no one is permitted to leave them except those who pay for their passage or
can give good scrutiny; the others, who cannot pay, must remain on board
the ships til they are purchased, and are released from the ships by their
purchasers. The sick always fare the worst, for the healthy are naturally
preferred and purchased first; and so the sick and wretched must often remain on board in front of the city for 2 or 3 weeks, and frequently die,
whereas many a one, if he could pay his debt and were permitted to leave
the ship immediately, might recover and remain alive. . . .

Many parents must sell and trade away their children like so many 13
head of cattle; for if their children take the debt upon themselves, the par-

ents can leave the ship free and unrestrained; but as the parents often do not know where and to what people their children are going, it often happens that such parents and children, after leaving the ship, do not see each other again for many years, perhaps no more in all their lives. . . .[2]

Thomas Jefferson had doubts concerning the effect of mass immigration 14 on American institutions. These comments come from his extended essay, *Notes on the State of Virginia*, published in 1784.

The present desire of America is to produce rapid population by as great 15 importations of foreigners as possible. But is this founded in good policy? . . . Are there no inconveniences to be thrown into the scale against the advantage expected from a multiplication of numbers by the importation of foreigners? It is for the happiness of those united in society to harmonize as much as possible in matters which they must of necessity transact together. Civil government being the sole object of forming societies, its administration must be conducted by common consent. Every species of government has its specific principles. Ours perhaps are more peculiar than those of any other in the universe. It is a composition of the freest principles of the English constitution, with others derived from natural right and natural reason. To these nothing can be more opposed than the maxims of absolute monarchies. Yet, from such, we are to expect the greatest number of emigrants. They will bring with them the principles of the governments they leave, imbibed in their early youth, or, if able to throw them off, it will be in exchange for an unbounded licentiousness, passing, as is usual, from one extreme to another. It would be a miracle were they to stop precisely at the point of temperate liberty. These principles, with their language, they will transmit to their children. In proportion to their numbers, they will share with us the legislation. They will infuse into it their spirit, warp and bias its direction, and render it a heterogeneous, incoherent, distracted mass.[3]

In contrast to Jefferson, the French immigrant J. Hector St. Jean de 16 Crèvecoeur celebrated the American cultural blending that resulted from immigration. In his famous *Letters of an American Farmer* (1782), Crèvecoeur was the first to discuss the process by which immigrants were "melted" into a new kind of person, the American.

Whence came all these people? They are a mixture of English, Scotch, 17 Irish, French, Dutch, Germans, and Swedes. From this promiscuous breed, that race, now called Americans, have arisen. . . .

What then is the American, this new man? He is either an Euro- 18 pean, or the descendant of an European; hence that strange mixture of blood which you will find in no other country.

Here individuals of all nations are melted into a new race of men, 19 whose labours and posterity will one day cause great change in the world. Americans are the western pilgrims, who are carrying along with them that great mass of arts, sciences, vigour, and industry, which began long since in the east; they will finish the great circle. The Americans were once scattered all over Europe, here they are incorporated into one of the finest systems of population which has ever appeared, and which will hereafter become distinct by the power of the different climates they inhabit.[4]

SOURCES

1. Ruth Barnes Moynihan, Cynthia Russett, and Laurie Crumpacker, eds., *Second to None: A Documentary History of American Women* (Lincoln: University of Nebraska Press, 1993), 1, 54. Reprinted with permission of the publisher.

2. Gottlieb Mittelberger, *Journey to Pennsylvania in the Year 1750 and Return to Germany in the Year 1754*, trans. Carl Theo. Eben (Philadelphia: John Jos. McVey, 1898), 19–20, 22, 24–31.

3. Thomas Jefferson, *Notes on the State of Virginia* in *Thomas Jefferson: Writings* (New York, 1984), 210–212.

4. J. Hector St. Jean de Crèvecoeur, *Letters from an American Farmer* (London, 1782).

THE CHANGING FACE OF ETHNICITY IN AMERICA

1800–1860

Between 1790 and 1820, the rate of immigration to the United States was low, held in check by the Napoleonic Wars in Europe. It began to pick up in the 1820s, increased sharply in the 1830s, and reached a record 430,000 in 1854. As immigration increased, the ethnic composition of the immigrant stream changed. Most of the new immigrants were Irish, driven from home by the Potato Famine of 1845, and German, driven by economic and political unrest in the German Principalities.

Until the 1880s, the task of receiving immigrants fell completely on cities and states, not the federal government. New York City, by far the largest port of entry, did not even establish an official reception center until 1855, when Castle Garden, at the bottom of Manhattan Island (near present-day Battery Park), was so designated.

The influx of mostly poor, mostly Catholic foreigners provoked nativist hostility among many Protestant, native-born Americans, including many leaders of the major reform movements. It would be a mistake, however, to think that immigration was unwelcome to everyone. Industries needed willing workers, and western states were eager for settlers. In 1852 Wisconsin appointed a commissioner of emigration with responsibility for attracting Europeans to the state. Soon Iowa and Minnesota joined Wisconsin in advertising widely in Europe for settlers.

Immigrant labor fueled the nation's expanding economy and helped turn wilderness into farmland. Many of the changes in industry and transportation that accompanied the market revolution would have been impossible without immigrants. Irish contract workers, for example, were essential to the completion of the Erie Canal in 1825. And Irish women and men kept the mills at Lowell operating when the mill operators, facing increasing competition sought cheaper labor to replace their original labor force of farm women. 4

Irish immigration to the United States dated from colonial times. Many of Ireland's young people, with no hope of owning land at home, had long looked to America for better opportunities. But in 1845 Ireland's green fields of potato plants turned black with blight, and for five years a catastrophic famine ravaged the land. The Irish had two choices: starve or leave. One million people died, and another 1.5 million emigrated, most to the United States. The Famine Irish were America's first major refugee group. Starving, suffering from disease (thousands died of typhus during the voyage), and destitute, hundreds of thousands disembarked in the east-coast ports of New York, Philadelphia, Boston, and Baltimore. Lacking the money to go inland, they remained in the cities. Crowded together in miserable housing, desperate for work at any wages, foreign in their religion and pastimes (drinking and fighting, their critics said), tenaciously nationalistic and bitterly anti-British, they created ethnic enclaves of a kind new to American cities. 5

The largest number of Irish immigrants settled in New York. Fewer settled in Boston, but that city, smaller and more homogeneous than New York, was overwhelmed by the influx. By 1850, a quarter of Boston's population was Irish. The home of Puritanism and the center of American intellectualism, Boston was not welcoming. All over the city in places of business and in homes normally eager for domestic servants the signs went up. "No Irish Need Apply." The Irish were able to get only the worst and poorest-paying jobs and could afford housing only in an area of East Boston that was described by a health committee in 1849 as "a perfect hive of human beings, without comforts and mostly without common necessaries; in many cases, huddled together like brutes, without regard to sex or age or sense of decency." 6

Despite poverty and local hostility, the Irish created within their neighborhoods an impressive network of Catholic churches and schools, mutual aid societies, and religious and social clubs. And almost from the moment of their arrival, the Irish sent huge sums of money back to Ireland so that relatives could join them in America. For however bad the conditions in the adopted country, they were better than those in Ireland. As one newcomer wrote, "There is a great many ill conveniences here, but no empty bellies." 7

Irish immigrants changed American urban politics. In Boston, they quickly 8 took over the local Democratic Party, opposing that city's traditional, Whig-dominated power structure. Irish political strength lay at the neighborhood level. Many politicians were saloonkeepers, for the saloon was the secular center of Irish society—much to the horror of temperance reformers. One Irish saloonkeeper, Patrick Joseph Kennedy, founded one of America's most famous political dynasties. Barely a century after Patrick's birth into a poor immigrant family in Boston, his grandson John Fitzgerald Kennedy was elected the first Irish Catholic president of the United States.

The typical German immigrant was a small farmer or artisan dislodged by 9 the same market forces that were at work in America: the industrialization of manufacturing and the commercialization of farming. The first two major ports of embarkation for the Germans were Bremen (in northern Germany) and Le Havre (in northern France), which were also the main ports for the importation of American tobacco and cotton. The tobacco boats bore the Bremen passengers to Baltimore, and the cotton ships took them to New Orleans, a major entry point for European immigrants until the Civil War. From these ports, many Germans made their way up the Mississippi and Ohio valleys, where they settled in

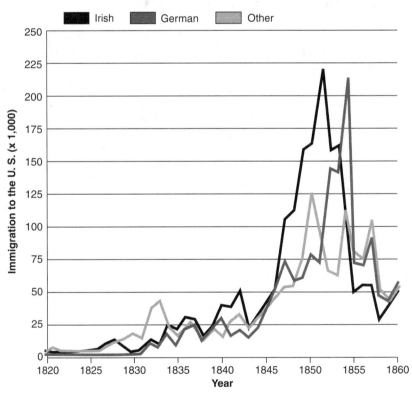

Immigration to the United States, 1820–1860

Milwaukee, Pittsburgh, Cincinnati, and St. Louis and on farms in Ohio, Indiana, Missouri, and Texas. In Texas the nucleus of a German community began with a Mexican land grant in the 1830s. Few Germans settled in the South.

German agricultural communities took a distinctive form that fostered cul- 10 tural continuity. Immigrants formed predominantly German towns by cluster- ing, or taking up adjoining land. A small cluster could support German churches, German-language schools, and German customs and thereby attract other Ger- mans, some directly from Europe and some from other parts of the United States. Non-German neighbors often sold out and moved on, but the Germans stayed and passed on their land to succeeding generations. They used soil con- servation practices that were unusual for the time. German cluster communities still endure in Texas, the Midwest, and the Pacific Northwest, and more Ameri- can farm families are today of German origin than of any other background.

Other areas attracting immigrants in the early nineteenth century were 11 Gold Rush California, which drew, among others, many Chinese, and Utah Territory, where the Mormon Church recruited many former English factory workers to its new Zion. In Texas and Mexico, a high proportion of residents listed as foreign-born in 1860 were in fact native-born Mexicans who had be- come foreigners only by virtue of the conquest of their homeland by the United States in the Mexican-American war.

The Chinese who came to California in the 1850s following the Gold 12 Rush worked in the mines, most as independent prospectors. Other miners dis- liked their industriousness and their clanishness. One reporter noted groups of twenty or thirty "Chinamen, stools, tables, cooking utensils, bunks, etc., all huddled up together in indiscriminate confusion, and enwreathed with dense smoke, inhabiting close cabins, so small that one would not be of sufficient size to allow a couple of Americans to breathe in it." In 1852 the California legisla- ture enacted a Foreign Miner's Tax aimed at the Chinese. By the time the tax was repealed in 1870, it had cost Chinese miners five million dollars. By the mid-1860s, Chinese workers made up 90 percent of the laborers building the Central Pacific Railroad, replacing more expensive white laborers and sowing the seeds of the long-lasting hostility of American workers toward Chinese. In the meantime, however, San Francisco's Chinatown, the oldest Chinese ethnic enclave in America, became a well established, thriving community. In the years to come, as hostility against the Chinese broke into violence, Chinatowns in San Francisco and elsewhere served a vital function as safe refuges for the Chinese who remained in the United States.

IN THEIR OWN WORDS

The unprecedented immigration of the 1840s and 1850s evoked the first orga- 13 nized nativist (antiforeign) movement in American history. As immigration swelled the country's previously small Catholic population, Protestant ministers became alarmed. One of them was Reverend Lyman Beecher, who equated

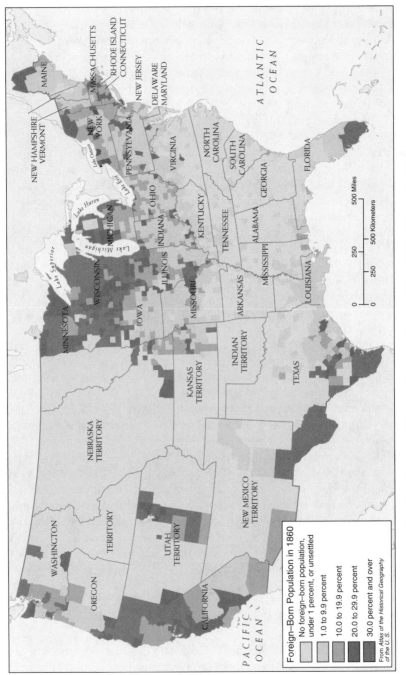

The distribution of foreign-born residents of the United States in 1860.

Foreign–Born Population in 1860

- No foreign-born population, under 1 percent, or unsettled
- 1.0 to 9.9 percent
- 10.0 to 19.9 percent
- 20.0 to 29.9 percent
- 30.0 percent and over

From *Atlas of the Historical Geography of the U. S.*

Catholicism with the antidemocratic powers of Europe and suggested that Catholic immigrants followed their bidding. Despite his disclaimer, Beecher viewed immigration as a religious as well as a political threat.

> Catholic Europe is throwing swarm on swarm [of immigrants] upon our shores. There is evidently a supervision abroad—and one here—by which they come, and set down together, in city or country, as a Catholic body, and are led or followed quickly by a Catholic priesthood, who maintain over them in the land of strangers and unknown tongues an ascendency as absolute as they are able to exert in Germany itself. 14
>
> In the beginning this eruption of revolutionary Europe was not antici- 15
> pated, and we opened our doors wide to the influx and naturalization of foreigners. But it is becoming a terrific inundation; it has increased upon our native population from five to thirty-seven percent, and is every year advancing. It seeks, of course, to settle down upon the unoccupied territory of the West, and may at no distant day equal, and even outnumber the native population.
>
> But what if this emigration, self-moved and slow in the beginning, is 16
> now rolling its broad tide at the bidding of the powers of Europe hostile to free institutions, and associated in holy alliance to arrest and put them down? Is this a vain fear? Are not the continental powers alarmed at the march of liberal opinions, and associated to put them down? . . . A tenth part of the suffrage of the nation, . . . condensed and wielded by the Catholic powers of Europe, might decide our elections, perplex our policy, inflame and divide the nation, break the bond of our union, and throw down our free institutions . . . .[1]

Compelled by the Potato Famine to migrate to America, many Irish felt an 17 enduring longing for their homeland, as the following song of lament reflects.

> *Farewell to thee, Erin mavourneen,*
> *Thy valleys I'll tread nevermore,*
> *This heart that now bleeds for thy sorrows,*
> *Will waste on a far distant shore.*
> *The green sods lie cold on my parents,*
> *A cross marks the place of their rest,—*
> *The wind that moans sadly above them,*
> *Will waft their poor child to the West.*[2]

The large German immigrant population was more geographically dis- 18 persed than either the Irish or the Chinese. Many German immigrants brought farming skills with them to America and put them to use, often in company with kin and friends, in rural ethnic clusters. Wilhelmina Stille, her brother Wilhelm Stille, and her fiance Wilhelm Krumme settled together along the Ohio River near Wheeling, Virginia (now West Virginia). The following letter, written in October 1838, is from Wilhelmina Stille to her mother.

We got married on August 10th. We've bought 80 acres of land and our brother has too, they are next to one another but his is so much better it cost 400 talers and ours 300 talers, we paid 200 talers of it since we didn't have any more. So we're asking you, dear mother and brothers in the name of the Lord, send me the rest of my money, please don't fail me because we have nowhere else to turn. I also want to tell you that my brother Wilhelm left his boss last fall and went down the river on a boat that was loaded with all kinds of goods, flour, potatoes, string beans, cabbage, onions, apples and two others had a quarter of it each. The city is called Neuoliens [New Orleans] which is 15 hundred miles away it's in South America there they can't grow such things. When he got back he started to work on his land, he's built himself a house and has already cleared 3 acres of farmland. We live 3 hours away from Wilingen [Wheeling] right on the road and are very happy for I have a happy marriage and live in peace.[3]

19

Carl Schurz, who emigrated from Germany in 1852 when the nativist political movement was at its height, gained great prominence in the United States, becoming a general in the Union Army, a senator from Missouri, and secretary of the interior in the administration of Rutherford B. Hayes. In this letter to a German friend, he reflects with pride on some of his accomplishments in his adopted country.

20

Here in America I lived for several years quietly and unobtrusively in an ideally happy family circle until at last in the year '56, when the movement against slavery developed magnificently, I found myself drawn into public life. I knew that I should accomplish something. America is the country for ambitious capability, and the foreigner who studies its conditions thoroughly, and with full appreciation, can procure for himself an even greater field of activity than the native. My success surprised even myself; I found my boldest expectations outdone. I flung myself with all my heart into the Antislavery Movement and thus showed the Americans something new . . . It is said that I made Lincoln President. That is certainly not true; but the fact that people say it indicates that I did contribute something toward raising the wind which bore Lincoln into the presidential chair and thus shook the slave system to its very foundations.[4]

21

SOURCES

1. Lyman Beecher, *Plea for the West* (1835)
2. "The Emigrant's Farewell," *Boston Pilot,* August 16, 1862
3. Walter D. Kamphoefner, Wolfgang Helbich, and Ulrike Summer, eds., *News from the Land of Freedom: German Immigrants Write Home* (1991)
4. Letter from Carl Schurz to Theodor Petrasch, Bonn, September 24, 1863, quoted in A. E. Zucker, ed. *The Forty-Eighters, Political Refugees of the German Revolution of 1848* (1950)

THE CHANGING FACE OF ETHNICITY IN AMERICA

1860–1930

Annual immigration to the United States, which had declined during the late 1850s from a peak of more than 400,000 in 1854, dropped sharply at the onset of the Civil War. But even before the war ended, the pace of immigration revived. From the late nineteenth century until World War I, as America's unprecedented industrial expansion created an unprecedented demand for labor, the rate of immigration increased dramatically, surpassing 1,000,000 in 1905. At the same time, the ethnic background of the immigrants changed, creating a corresponding change in the nation's ethnic landscape.

Before the Civil War most immigrants came from Ireland and Germany. After the war immigrants from Germany and northwestern Europe continued at first to predominate, but by 1896 they had been overtaken by the so-called "New Immigrants" from the countries of southern and eastern Europe. Immigration from Latin America and many Asian countries, although far lower than that from Europe, also increased. Immigration from China, however, slowed considerably after the passage of the Chinese Exclusion Act of 1882.

Overall, between 1860 and 1920 about 28.2 million people immigrated to the United States, and by 1920 these immigrants and their children represented more than one-third of the nation's population. The vast majority of New Immigrants sought better lives for themselves and their families. Driven by economic dislocation, political turmoil, and overpopulation at home, millions of people left their village for opportunity in distant lands, including Canada, Argentina, Brazil, Australia, and New Zealand as well as the United States. Italians were the largest group among the New Immigrants between 1880 and 1930 nearly 5 million came to the United States. Of them, 80 percent were peasants from southern Italy left landless by an agricultural depression.

Religious and ethnic persecution combined with economic hardship to drive the Jews of Russia, Poland, and other eastern European countries to emigrate. Laws in Russia dictated where Jews could live and restricted their opportunities for employment and education. Beginning in 1881, the Russian government encouraged violent attacks known as *pogroms* on Jewish communities. These hardships made the United States appear a beacon of salvation. As a result, the Jewish population of the United States grew from 250,000 in 1877 to more than 4 million in 1927.

Most New Immigrants settled in the nation's urban manufacturing centers, not on farms. Generally poorly educated and lacking industrial skills, they entered the bottom ranks in factories, mines, mills, slaughterhouses, and garment shops. Employers benefited from their numbers to reorganize the workplace and reduce their reliance on highly paid skilled workers. Jews, however, were an exception to this pattern. Many had come from cities and were skilled in craft work and business. Nearly 77 percent of immigrant Jewish men qualified for skilled work in such specialized trades as cigar manufacturing, printing, carpentry, and garment manufacturing. Japanese immigrants—more than 111,000 by 1920—likewise fared well. They had a literacy rate of 99 percent and were able to translate the agricultural experience they brought from Japan to establish themselves as successful farmers of market garden crops in California, where the majority settled.

Most New Immigrants were unmarried young men, and many did not intend to settle permanently in the United States. They hoped instead to earn enough money to return home and buy land or set up a small business. Italian immigrants, nearly 80 percent of them male, and Greek immigrants, more than 90 percent male, had the highest rate of remigration—almost 50 percent. Jews, facing persecution at home, were the least likely to return home. Only 5 percent remigrated. Instead, they saved their wages to bring other family members to the United States. As a result, Jews were the most evenly distributed by sex of the New Immigrants. Only among the Irish did women form the majority of newcomers.

Whether they planned to remigrate or stay, the New Immigrants quickly established distinctive communities, mainly in the nation's large cities or along the West Coast. In 1920 three-quarters of the foreign-born lived in cities. The vast majority of Italians, for example, entered through the port of New York, and nearly one-quarter of them settled nearby. By 1920, 400,000 Italian immigrants were living in sizable communities in Manhattan, Brooklyn, the Bronx, Queens, and Staten Island. In Chicago, one-third of all Italians lived in a single neighborhood on the city's West Side. Across the continent in California, where Italians represented the single largest immigrant group, they gave North Beach in San Francisco a special ethnic flavor.

In many cities the New Immigrants became the numerical majority and dominated political and social institutions. By 1910 in Passaic, New Jersey, for example, 52 percent of the population was foreign-born, most from Russia, Austria-Hungary, or Italy; 32 percent was second-generation (the children of foreign-born); and only 14 percent native-born whites. The immigrant population reshaped Passaic's political landscape, eventually forcing a sweeping reorganization of city government.

Although all New Immigrants tended to concentrate in neighborhoods near the factories or the steel mills where they worked, Italians were the most likely to cluster in so-called ethnic ghettos. Here, in "Little Italy," they spoke their native language, ate familiar foods, and helped their compatriots find jobs and housing. As immigrant communities grew, they sought to recreate Old World cultural patterns through schools, businesses, mutual-aid societies, and fraternal orders. Religious institutions—church and temple—provided the most important link to cultural traditions. Foreign-language newspapers—Germans and Jews produced the largest number—likewise helped forge community solidarity.

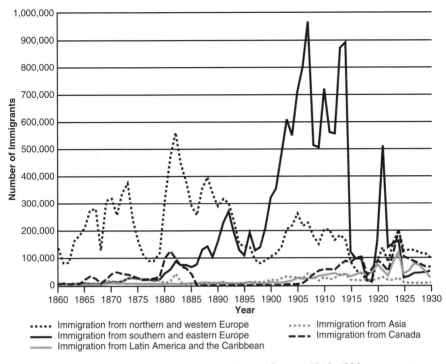

····· Immigration from northern and western Europe	····· Immigration from Asia
—— Immigration from southern and eastern Europe	▬ ▬ Immigration from Canada
—— Immigration from Latin America and the Caribbean	

Annual Immigration to the United States, 1860–1930

Although most old-stock Americans welcomed immigrant labor, many 10
feared the "alien" cultural values and mores of the immigrants themselves. Before the Civil War, nativist, or anti-immigrant, sentiment was directed primarily against Catholics; shortly after the war, its focus was the Chinese. As the new immigration gathered steam in the 1880s, nativist sentiment increasingly turned against *all* immigrants. The nativist reaction to the new immigration found justification in certain intellectual currents of the late nineteenth century. So-called "scientific racism" purported to demonstrate that some racial groups were inherently superior to others, with western Europeans, especially Anglo-Saxons, inevitably ranked at the top, Africans at the bottom, and southern and eastern Europeans not much above them. Social Darwinism similarly claimed to justify social ranking with evolutionary theory.

Until the late nineteenth century, the federal government did little to reg- 11
ulate immigration and instead allowed state governments to set their own policies. But a turning point was reached with the Immigration Act of 1882, which gave the federal government the right to regulate immigration in cooperation with the states. The act laid the foundation for the kind of selective immigration based on race or ethnicity that the Chinese Exclusion Act, also passed in 1882, put into practice. The Immigration Act of 1891 gave the federal govern-

ment the exclusive power to regulate immigration. The following year, in 1892, the newly centralized immigration reception center opened on Ellis Island.

In 1896, in the midst of a severe economic depression, a bipartisan majority in Congress passed a law requiring all immigrants to pass a literacy test, but it was vetoed by President McKinley. Subsequent efforts to enact such a law met a similar fate until 1917, when fear that the nation would face a wave of immigrants fleeing Europe at the end of World War I generated enough support for Congress to override President Wilson's veto and enact the Immigration Act of 1917. This landmark legislation implemented a literacy test and created an "Asiatic Barred Zone" to deny admission to people from India, Burma, Siam, Afghanistan, Arabia, the Malay Islands, and Polynesia. Foreshadowing the Red Scare that followed World War I, it also tightened restrictions on radicals to exclude members of anarchist and revolutionary organizations. 12

The era of open-door immigration came to a decisive end in the 1920s. Bills were introduced in Congress to suspend immigration altogether, but legislators compromised on a quota plan based on national origins, which was incorporated into the emergency restriction law passed in 1921. After a series of modifications and heated debates, Congress enacted a law on May 26, 1924, limiting immigration of specific groups to 2 percent of the number recorded by the 1890 census. The consequences were dramatic. European immigration dropped from more than 800,000 in 1921 to less than 150,000 by 1929. In that year, Congress passed the National Origins Act that put the quota system in place on a permanent basis, which, along with the Great Depression, reduced immigration to the United States in the 1930s to the lowest level since 1820. 13

IN THEIR OWN WORDS

In 1910 the U.S. Immigration Commission opened the Angel Island detention center, off the coast of San Francisco, for the few Chinese who were allowed to enter the United States following a loosening of the Exclusion Act of 1882. Modeled after Ellis island, the point of entry for most European immigrants, Angel Island housed new arrivals until U.S. immigration inspectors determined whether they were eligible to settle in the United States. The experience made a lasting, often unpleasant impression on the nearly 175,000 Chinese who were detained there before 1940, when the center shut down. In the following passage, a woman immigrant recalls her detention at Angel Island in 1913 when she was nineteen years old. 14

15

There was not much for us to do on the island. In the morning we got up and washed our faces. Afterwards, we had breakfast. After we ate, we napped or washed our own clothes. At lunch time we had congee in a large serving bowl with some cookies. Then at night we had rice with a main dish. You picked at some of it . . . and that was that. We ate in a huge dining hall. . . . They allowed us to go outside to the yard or even out to the dock, where there were grass and trees, tall and fan-like. The women were allowed to wander around, jump around, and stick our hands or feet into the water to fish out seaweed. Otherwise, the day would have been hard to pass. . . .

I was interrogated one day for several hours. They asked me so much, I broke out in a sweat. Sometimes they would try to trip you: "Your husband said such-and-such and now you say this?" But the answer was out already and it was too late to take it back, so I couldn't do anything about it. If they said you were wrong, then it was up to them whether to land you or not. Later, upon landing, I noticed a white man kept coming around to my husband's laundry and looking at me through the glass window. That was how they checked you out to make sure you didn't go elsewhere.[1]

Rose Schneiderman (1882–1972), who became a prominent trade union organizer, emigrated from Russia with her family. In this account, published in a popular magazine, *The Independent,* in 1905, she recounts with pride the ups and downs of her family's fortunes and her response to the burdens that fell upon her.

My name is Rose Schneiderman, and I was born in some small city of Russian Poland. I don't know the name of the city, and have no memory of that part of my childhood. When I was about five years of age my parents brought me to this country and we settled in New York.

So my earliest recollections are of living in a crowded street among the East Side Jews, for we also are Jews.

My father got work as a tailor, and we lived in two rooms on Eldridge Street, and did very well, though not so well as in Russia, because mother and father both earned money, and here father alone earned the money, while mother attended to the house. There were then two other children besides me, a boy of three and one of five.

I went to school until I was nine years old, enjoying it thoroughly and making great progress, but then my father died of brain fever and mother was left with three children and another one coming. So I had to stay at home to help her and she went out to look for work. . . .

I was the house worker, preparing the meals and looking after the other children—the baby, a little girl of six years, and a boy of nine. I managed very well, tho the meals were not very elaborate. I could cook simple things like porridge, coffee and eggs, and mother used to prepare the meat before she went away in the morning, so that all I had to do was to put it in the pan at night. . . .

I was finally released by my little sister being taken by an aunt, and the two boys going to the Hebrew Orphan Asylum, which is a splendid institution, and turns out good men. One of these brothers is now a student in the City College, and the other is a page in the Stock Exchange.

When the other children were sent away mother was able to send me back to school, and I stayed in this school (Houston Street Grammar) till I had reached the Sixth Grammar Grade.

Then I had to leave in order to help support the family. I got a place in Hearn's as a cash girl, and after working there three weeks changed to Ridley's, where I remained for two and a half years. I finally left because the pay was so very poor and there did not seem to be any chance of advancement, and a friend told me that I could do better making caps.[2]

SOURCES

1. Him Mark Lai, Genny Lim, and Judy Yung, eds., *Island: Poetry and History of Chinese Immigrants on Angel Island, 1910–1940* (Seattle: University of Washington Press, 1980), 72, 117

2. Rose Schneiderman, "A Cap Maker's Story," *The Independent, 58* (April 27, 1905), pp. 935–936

THE CHANGING FACE OF ETHNICITY IN AMERICA

Since 1930

During the last three quarters of the twentieth century, the character and 1
sources of immigration to the United States changed radically. With America's growing power and prominence in the international arena, the laws governing immigration became increasingly tools of foreign policy. The social devastation of World War II and the ideological battles of the cold war created whole new categories of immigrant, such as that of political refugee. Recent immigration has also reflected the dynamic transformations in the economies of the United States and of the rest of the world. The national quotas established in the 1920s severely limited the flow of immigrants from Europe. But lawmakers, responding to the labor needs of industry and agriculture, had placed no barriers to newcomers from the Western Hemisphere. Thus, Canadians and Mexicans grew into the two largest national immigrant groups. Circular migration shaped the experience of these peoples; they were "transborder peoples," going frequently back and forth between their homelands and the United States. Dividing their political and cultural loyalties between the United States and their homelands, Mexicans and Canadians developed an ambiguous identity. As a result, they were slower to adopt U.S. citizenship than were other immigrants.

Some 1.4 million Canadians arrived in the United States between 1920 2
and 1960, with three quarters from British Canada (Ontario, Nova Scotia, New Brunswick) and one quarter from French Canada (Quebec). They settled close to the border, primarily in New England cities such as Boston, Lowell, Nashua, and Holyoke, as well as in the Great Lakes region. During the same period, more than 840,000 Mexicans arrived as permanent settlers and 4.7 million more as temporary guest workers. They headed mainly for the rich agricultural areas of southern California and the lower Rio Grande Valley of Texas. Many, however, looking for factory work, settled in big Midwestern industrial centers such Chicago, Detroit, and Kansas City. In the Southwest, Mexicans tended to cluster in isolated *barrios.* In the midwest, in contrast, following the

pattern of older European immigrant communities in big cities, they tended to assimilate more.

Perhaps more than any other group, Mexican immigrants were subject to the vagaries of the U.S. economy. The Great Depression drastically reduced the need for their labor and spurred a mass reverse migration. As many as half a million Mexicans were repatriated during the 1930s, often at the urging of local American officials who did not want Mexican aliens on public relief rolls. The onset of World War II brought a new demand for Mexican labor in agriculture and transportation. In 1942 the U.S. and Mexican governments revived the guest worker program of World War I. The *bracero* (farmhand) program admitted agricultural workers on short-term contracts; they were classified as foreign laborers, not immigrants. By 1947, some 200,000 *braceros* worked in twenty-one states, including 100,000 in California. Congress renewed the program after the war ended. By 1960 Mexicans made up more than one quarter of the nation's farm labor force. 3

Puerto Ricans, the third largest group of immigrants to the U.S. mainland from the Western Hemisphere, were a special case because, as U.S. citizens since 1917, they could come and go without restriction. Like Canadians and Mexicans, they helped fill the labor demand caused by the restriction of European immigration. Between 1945 and 1965 the Puerto Rican-born population jumped from 100,000 to roughly 1 million. The majority headed for New York City and surrounding communities. 4

Another growing class of immigrants consisted of refugees uprooted by World War II and the emergence of Communist regimes in Eastern Europe. A series of laws combined the historical notion of America as a haven for the world's oppressed with the new reality of cold war power politics. The Displaced Persons Act of 1948 was the first law in American history to set refugee policy as opposed to immigration policy. It provided 202,000 visas over a two-year period, allowing permanent settlement in the United States for refugees from fascist and Communist regimes. A 1950 amendment upped the number of visas to 341,000 annually. The Refugee Relief Act of 1953 authorized admission of 205,000 "nonquota" refugees, but limited these to people fleeing persecution from Communist regimes. In practice, this policy gave priority to refugees from the Baltic states and Eastern European Communist nations; only a minority admitted under the act were Jews or other victims of Hitler. Indeed, hundreds of former Nazis, including many scientists, were allowed in under the act in the interest of "national security." 5

In 1952, as a conservative counterpoint to the growth of refugee legislation, Congress passed the McCarran-Walter Act. Reaffirming the 1920s principle of discriminatory quotas based on national origin, the act specified that 85 percent of those admitted annually were to come from Northern and Western European countries. Yet McCarran-Walter also contained some important liberal innovations. It revoked the denial of admission based on race, and it allowed for small, token quotas for immigrants from China and Japan, ending the long-standing policy of Asian exclusion. 6

The Immigration Act of 1965, passed almost unnoticed in the context of   7
the egalitarian political climate created by the Civil Rights movement, had revolutionary consequences, some of them unintended. The act abolished the discriminatory national origins quotas that had been in place since the 1920s. But
it also limited immigration from the Western Hemisphere for the first time, allowing 120,000 annual visas from that region, compared to 170,000 from the
Eastern Hemisphere. It continued the policy of selective admissions, but with
important exceptions. Exempted from numerical quotas were immigrants
seeking family reunification with American citizens or resident aliens. In addition, preferences to those with specialized job skills and training were extended
to people from the nations of the Eastern Hemisphere.

The high priority given family reunification greatly increased the "chain   8
migration" of people seeking to join relatives already in the United States. After
1965, Asian immigrants made up the fastest growing ethnic groups, with more
than 1.5 million arriving during the 1970s, as opposed to roughly 800,000 from
Europe. The new Asian migration included many professionals and well-
educated technical workers. For example, immigrants from the Philippines and
India included a high number of health care professionals, and many Chinese
and Korean immigrants found work in professional and managerial occupations.
At the same time, low-skilled and impoverished Asians poured into the "Chinatowns" and "Koreatowns" of cities like New York and Los Angeles, seeking
work in restaurants, hotels, and garment manufacturing. The end of the In-
dochina War brought new refugees from Cambodia, Laos, and Vietnam. The
1965 act also created conditions that increased undocumented immigration
from Latin America. The new limits on Western Hemisphere migration, along
with simultaneous ending of the *bracero* program, tempted many thousands to
enter the United States illegally. The Immigration and Naturalization Service
arrested and deported 500,000 illegal aliens each year in the decade following
the act, most of them from Mexico, Central America, and the Caribbean.

During the 1980s the rate of immigration accelerated. The estimated 6   9
million legal and 2 million undocumented immigrants who entered the United
States during that decade was second only to the 8.8 million who had arrived
between 1900 and 1910. By 1990, one out of every five immigrants living in the
United States was Mexican-born, and Mexican Americans accounted for more
than 60 percent of all Hispanics. Demographers predicted that by 2050 Hispanics would replace African Americans as the largest minority group in the
nation. The number of Asian Americans more than doubled during the 1980s,
from 3.5 million to 7.3 million. Nearly two out of every five Asian Americans
lived in California, with 300,000 in Los Angeles, "Koreatown." Among recent
immigrant groups, Asians—Vietnamese, Filipinos, Koreans, and Chinese—
gained naturalization (citizenship) at the fastest rate. Asians totaled nearly 50
percent of all people naturalized in the 1980s. Unlike early-twentieth-century
Asian migrants, the post-1965 newcomers were mostly intent on settling here
permanently, and they migrated in family units. The new Asian immigrants also

remade the small ethnic enclaves from earlier migrations, reinvigorating them with new energy, new capital, and a more explicit ethnic consciousness.

By the mid-1980s, growing concern over "illegal aliens" had become a 10 hotly debated political issue, particularly in the Southwest. The Immigration Reform and Control Act of 1986 marked a break with past attempts to address this problem. Instead of mass deportation programs, the law offered an amnesty to all undocumented workers who had entered the country since 1982. Although opening the "front door" of admissions wider, the law also tried to shut the "back door" by imposing sanctions on employers who knowingly hired or recruited undocumented aliens. Yet no matter what Congress did, the desperate economic realities in Mexico and Central America continued to enlarge the flow of undocumented aliens. At the century's end, both American immigration policy and the immigrants now arriving look radically different than they did 75 years ago. Nativist sentiment and calls for greater immigration restriction are still powerful voices on the political scene, especially during economic downturns and within those states absorbing the bulk of new immigrants. Nativist appeals and campaigns will likely remain part of the American political landscape—but they have been defeated by the fundamental idea that immigration has ultimately strengthened America's economy, culture, and society. At the dawn of the new millennium, a glance at almost any American city, school, or workplace reinforces that point clearly.

IN THEIR OWN WORDS

In 1984 Rosa Maria Urbina, a thirty-one-year-old widow from Juárez, Mexico, 11 crossed the Rio Grande looking for work as a housecleaner in El Paso. She had hoped to earn enough money to take her three children out of an orphanage. José Luis, a Juárez farm worker, moved to El Paso permanently in 1981 at the age of twenty-two. The two married and made their life among El Paso's fifty thousand illegal immigrants, known in Mexican slang as *mojados,* or "wets," the river people.

JOSÉ: The majority of the people in our apartment building have the 12 same problem as my family. All of us are in El Paso without legal papers. I have been living here since 1981.

ROSA: I came in 1984, to find work. After José and I were married and 13 we found a place to live, I brought my children from my previous marriage. We lived across the river in Juárez. But I was born further south, in Zacatecas.

JOSÉ: My hometown is Juárez. Since I was nine years old, I've been 14 coming to El Paso to work. At first I did gardening in people's yards, but I have stayed in El Paso constantly since 1981, going out to the fields to do farm work. I used to go to Juárez to visit my relatives at least one day each month. But in the last year, I haven't gone, because of the immigration law. To visit Juárez I have to swim across the river. I can't cross the bridge or the *migra* [Border Patrol officers] can catch me right there. . . .

ROSA: When I was a teenager, I worked as a hairdresser in a beauty salon, cutting hair. My first husband was a mechanic, fixing cars. We made a good living. But my husband spent the money he made drinking in the *cantinas.* And after a while, he wouldn't let me work, because I had young children to take care of. When he died in 1984, he left me with nothing at all. . . . My children were nine, seven, and three years old. I had to find a way to pay rent and feed them.

At that time, the economy in Mexico had become horrible. Inflation was going crazy. The peso jumped to 500 per dollar. Today it is still climbing at 1,000 per dollar. I found a job working on an assembly line at a factory. We produced rubber gloves for hospitals and medical supplies like caps for syringes. I would go into work at 4:30 in the afternoon and stay until 2:00 A.M. I was paid only 7,000 pesos [$14] each week. That was not enough to feed my kids. And I didn't have any relatives or friends to watch the kids while I worked. So I had no other choice but to put them in a special institution, like an orphanage, for children without parents. This upset me very much. But with my husband dead, and no other form of support, there was nothing I could do.

My only hope was to cross the river to the United States. If I could find a job that paid enough money, my children could join me. I wanted them to have an education and a proper life . . . to be someone. . . .

Before I met José, I crossed back and forth across the river five days each week to my housekeeping jobs in El Paso. On weekends, I took my children out of the orphanage. Then I had to reluctantly return them to the orphanage on Sunday evenings and prepare to go back across the river.[1]

Wing Ng, a Cantonese woman born into a poor family, emigrated to California in 1975 at the age of twenty-three. She came alone, but had the sponsorship of her sister's friend in Los Angeles, as well as financial help from the YMCA for the airfare from Hong Kong. She soon relocated to New York's Chinatown.

The reason I wanted to come to the United States is that I heard it is really freedom. That's the first thing. And the second was the education. It's hard to get an education in China. Only the United States can support you to get a good education and a good life. My childhood was not happy. Too many children. Poor. I don't want that again. I graduated from high school but nothing can get you into college. Even though you have good grades and a good record you can never get into college in China. I don't know how it is now but in my experience, when I was young, during the Cultural Revolution, there were no colleges to get into. Every student who graduated from high school in 1968, 1970, around that time, was sent to work in the countryside, to become a farmer. . . .

I came first to California. Los Angeles. Then I came here to New 21
York. I had some friends. They told me there were more opportunities to
find a good job in New York. To learn English. In Los Angeles everything is
far away. You have to drive in a car for hours to get anywhere. There's not
that much chance to get an education, to go to school, because of the distance between places. I stayed there just two weeks and then I came to
New York.

When I got here I worked as a babysitter. I had a green card and I 22
could have gotten another kind of job but I wanted to learn English. Even
though you go to school, you are just listening a lot of the time, and I
wanted a job where I could talk English. So I found a job with an American
family. They talked to me and corrected me. Told me how to do things. I
took care of their little boy. He was seven years old and very easy to take
care of. I took him to the park on his bicycle or to the museum. For me it
was very interesting. . . .

In February 1978, I started at City University, New York City Com- 23
munity College. There are many Chinese people there, many different
races. Many, many. I have helped about twenty people go there myself.
Told them it was a very good college, especially for data processing. I
promised myself I will go on to a four-year college when I graduate but I do
not know how long it will take. First I will get a job and then ask the boss to
help me with my education. . . . That first year back in college was very difficult for me. I had to take any kind of job, just to get money. Type. Work in
a restaurant. Whatever I could find.[2]

SOURCES

1. "Mojados (Wetbacks)", from *New Americans: An Oral History* by Al
   Santoli. Copyright © 1988 by Al Santoli. Used by permission of Viking
   Penguin, a division of Penguin Putnam, Inc.
2. From *Today's Immigrants, Their Stories: A New Look At The Newest Ameri-
   cans* by Thomas Kessner and Betty Boyd Caroli, Copyright © 1982 by
   Thomas Kessner and Betty Boyd Caroli. Used with permission of Oxford
   University Press.

SELECTION 2 QUESTIONS

Comprehension and Analysis

1. The authors say that "immigration to what would become the United
   States was characterized by extraordinary ethnic diversity." Identify four
   major immigrant groups during the colonial period. Did the majority of
   these immigrants come of their own free will? Please explain.

2. According to the authors, the immigration of the 1840s–1860s created the first organized nativist movement in American history. What was/is the nativist movement? Describe two factors you think helped to created this movement.

3. Before the Civil War most immigrants came from Ireland and Germany, but by 1896 they had been overtaken by the so-called "New Immigrants." Identify the major groups known as "New Immigrants."

4. Compare and contrast the reasons that the "New Immigrants" left their homelands for the United States to the reasons that today's immigrants leave their homelands for the United States.

5. What were the major changes in immigration law during the period between 1860 and 1930?

6. During the last portion of the twentieth century, the character and sources of immigration changed radically. Explain the concept of "transborder peoples." How are these immigrants similar to or different from previous immigrant groups?

7. What were two major consequences of the Immigration Act of 1965?

8. What effect(s) do the "In Their Own Words" sections have on your view of immigration? Please give an example to illustrate your view.

9. Do the authors believe that immigration has primarily strengthened or weakened America's economy, culture, and society? Please give an example to support your answer.

Reflect and Connect

10. Are the controversies surrounding immigration unique to the present generation? Please explain.

SELECTION 3 IMMIGRATION POLICY

JOHN F. KENNEDY

President Kennedy was working on the final draft of the book A Nation of Immigrants *when he was assassinated November 22, 1963, and it was decided the book should be published posthumously in 1964. According to his brother Robert F. Kennedy, the book is "essentially a cogent brief for immigration reform along the lines J. F. K. had long advocated, reform which was realized in the Immigration Bill of 1965." The 1965 amendments to the Immigration and Naturalization Act abolished the national-origin quotas and established an annual limitation of 120,000 visas for immigrants from western hemisphere countries. This selection is the sixth Chapter in the book.*

AN IDEA TO THINK ABOUT

President Kennedy said, "Little is more extraordinary than the decision to migrate, little more extraordinary than the accumulation of emotions and thoughts which finally leads a family to say farewell to a community where it has lived for centuries, to abandon old ties and familiar landmarks, and to sail across dark seas to a strange land." Can you imagine it?

WORDS TO KNOW

Mr. Dooley (¶17)—"Mr. Dooley," an opinionated first-generation Irish-American proprietor of a bar on Archey Road in Chicago, is a character created by writer Finley Peter Dunne (1867–1936) for his Chicago newspaper column. Mr. Dooley could criticize the nation and its powerful people without offending. (You can find more on Dunne, including the 1902 column on immigration Kennedy refers to, on the web.)
anachronism (¶22)—outdated, old-fashioned

From the start, immigration policy has been a prominent subject of discussion 1
in America. This is as it must be in a democracy, where every issue should be
freely considered and debated.

Immigration, or rather the British policy of clamping down on immigra- 2
tion, was one of the factors behind the colonial desire for independence. Restrictive immigration policies constituted one of the charges against King
George III expressed in the Declaration of Independence. And in the Constitutional Convention James Madison noted, "That part of America which has encouraged them [the immigrants] has advanced most rapidly in population,
agriculture and the arts." So, too, Washington in his Thanksgiving Day Proclamation of 1795 asked all Americans "humbly and fervently to beseech the kind
Author of these blessings . . . to render this country more and more a safe and
propitious asylum for the unfortunate of other countries."

Yet there was the basic ambiguity which older Americans have often 3
shown toward newcomers. In 1797 a member of Congress argued that, while a
liberal immigration policy was fine when the country was new and unsettled,
now that America had reached its maturity and was fully populated, immigration should stop—an argument which has been repeated at regular intervals
throughout American history.

The fear of embroilment in the wars between Britain and France helped 4
the cause of the restrictionists. In 1798 a Federalist Congress passed the Alien
Act, authorizing the expulsion of foreigners "dangerous to the peace and safety
of the United States" and extending the residence requirement for naturalization from five to fourteen years. But the Alien Act, and its accompanying Sedition Act, went too far. Both acts were allowed to expire in 1801; the

naturalization period went back to five years; and President Thomas Jefferson expressed the predominant American sentiment when he asked: "Shall we refuse to the unhappy fugitives from distress that hospitality which the savages of the wilderness extended to our fathers arriving in this land? Shall oppressed humanity find no asylum on this globe?"

But emotions of xenophobia—hatred of foreigners—and of nativism—the policy of keeping America "pure" (that is, of preferring old immigrants to new)—continued to thrive. The increase in the rate of immigration in the 1820's and 1830's set off new waves of hostility, directed especially against the Irish, who, as Catholics, were regarded as members of an alien conspiracy. Even Ralph Waldo Emerson could write to Thomas Carlyle about "the wild Irish element . . . led by Romanish Priests, who sympathize, of course, with despotism." Samuel F. B. Morse, the painter and inventor of the telegraph, wrote an anti-Catholic book entitled *A Foreign Conspiracy Against the Liberties of the United States.* Some alarmed Americans believed that every Catholic was a foreign agent dispatched by the Pope to subvert American society. In 1834 a mob burned down the Ursuline Convent school in Charlestown, Massachusetts. Though the leading citizens of Boston promptly denounced this act, anti-Catholic feeling persisted.

In the 1850's nativism became an open political movement. A secret patriotic society, the Order of the Star-Spangled Banner, founded about 1850, grew into the American party, whose members were pledged to vote only for native Americans, to demand a twenty-one-year naturalization period and to fight Roman Catholicism. When asked about their program, they were instructed to answer, "I know nothing about it," so people called them the Know-Nothings. Coming into existence at a time when the slavery issue was dissolving the older party allegiances, the Know-Nothings for a moment attracted considerable support.

They elected six state governors and seventy-five Congressmen in 1854 and got almost 25 percent of the vote for their candidate, former President Millard Fillmore, in 1856. But soon they, too, were split by the slavery issue, and the party vanished as quickly as it had appeared.

The legacy of the Know-Nothings lived beyond its life as an organization. The seeds of bigotry, fear and hatred bore fruit again in the years after the Civil War. The Ku Klux Klan launched a campaign of terrorism against the Negroes, and in the 1890's the American Protective Association tried to revive popular feeling against Catholics. Other nativists began to turn their attention to the Jews. In the meantime, agitators on the West Coast denounced the "yellow peril," and Congress in 1882 passed the first of a number of laws banning Oriental immigration. Yet, except for Oriental exclusion, Congress ignored the nativist clamor, and most Americans regarded nativism with abhorrence. When a Protestant clergyman supporting James C. Blaine in 1884 denounced the Democrats as the party of "rum, Romanism and rebellion," he provoked a reaction which may well have lost the election for Blaine, who himself had a mother of Irish Catholic descent.

The First World War led to another outbreak of nativism. A new group, 9
adopting the program of the Know-Nothings and the name of the Ku Klux Klan,
came into being, denouncing everything its members disliked—Negroes,
Catholics, Jews, evolutionists, religious liberals, internationalists, pacifists—in
the name of true Americanism and of "Nordic superiority." For a season, the
new KKK prospered, claiming five million members, mostly in the South but also
in Indiana, Ohio, Kansas and Maine. But, like the other nativist movements, the
fall of the Klan was as dramatic as its rise. It died when a genuine crisis, the
depression, turned people's attention away from the phony issue of racism to the
real problems facing the nation. In later years, the Jew succeeded the Catholic
as the chief target of nativist hysteria, and some Catholics, themselves so recently persecuted, now regrettably joined in the attack on the newer minorities.

America had no cause to be smug about the failure of these movements 10
to take deep root. Nativism failed, not because the seeds were not there to be
cultivated, but because American society is too complex for an agitation so
narrowly and viciously conceived to be politically successful. That the nativist
movements found any response at all must cause us to look searchingly at ourselves. That the response was at times so great offers cause for alarm.

Still it remains a remarkable fact that, except for the Oriental Exclusion 11
Act, there was no governmental response till after the First World War.

Not only were newcomers allowed to enter freely, but in some periods 12
they were actively sought after.

Inevitably, though, this mass influx of people presented problems which the 13
federal government was forced to recognize. In 1882, recognizing the need for a
national immigration policy, Congress enacted the first general legislation on the
subject. The most important aspect of this law was that, for the first time, the
government undertook to exclude certain classes of undesirables, such as lu-
natics, convicts, idiots and persons likely to become public charges. In 1891 certain health standards were added as well as a provision excluding polygamists.

From time to time additional laws were added. The only deviation from 14
the basic policy of free, nondiscriminatory immigration was the Oriental Exclusion Act.

Under a special treaty arrangement with China, nationals of that country 15
had been guaranteed free and unrestricted immigration to the United States.
At the peak of that immigration, in 1882, there were only forty thousand arrivals; even in 1890 there were but 107,000 Chinese in America. Most of them
lived in California and had proved good and useful workers and citizens. Although they had originally been welcomed to America for their services in
building railroads and reclaiming the land, the conviction began to grow that
Chinese labor was undermining the standards of "American" labor. This became virtually an obsession with many people. In the early 1870's antiChinese
agitation in California became organized and focused under the leadership of
Denis Kearney, who was, ironically, an immigrant from Ireland. A campaign of
organized violence against Chinese communities took form, and the hysteria

led to political pressure too violent to be resisted. President Hayes vetoed an act of Congress restricting Chinese immigration, but he did force renegotiation of the Burlingame Treaty under which the government of China agreed to restrict emigration voluntarily. Not satisfied with this remedy, Congress then enacted and the President signed into law a series of measures shutting off almost completely immigration from China.

Shameful as these episodes were, they were, however, only an exception 16 to the prevailing policy. A more serious warning of things to come was sounded in 1897 when Congress, for the first time, provided a literacy test for adult immigrants. President Cleveland vetoed the measure. Presidents Taft and Wilson vetoed similar bills on the ground that literacy was a test only of educational opportunity and not of a person's ability or his potential worth as a citizen. In 1917, with tension high because of the war, Congress overrode President Wilson's veto and the literacy test became law.

The twenty-year fight over the literacy test can now be seen as a signifi- 17 cant turning point in immigration policy. Indeed, many saw it as such at that time. Finley Peter Dunne, creator of the immortal Mr. Dooley, devoted one of Mr. Dooley's dissertations in 1902 to the subject of the test and immigration. With magnificent irony the Irish bartender says, "As a pilgrim father that missed the first boat, I must raise me claryon voice again' the invasion iv this fair land be th' paupers an' arnychists in Europe. Ye bet I must—because I'm here first. . . . In thim days America was th' refuge iv th' oppressed in all th' wurruld. . . . But as I tell ye, 'tis diff'rent now. 'Tis time we put our back again' th' open dure an' keep out th' savage horde."

But there is no denying the fact that by the turn of the century the opin- 18 ion was becoming widespread that the numbers of new immigrants should be limited. Those who were opposed to all immigration and all "foreigners" were now joined by those who believed sincerely, and with some basis in fact, that America's capacity to absorb immigration was limited. This movement toward restricting immigration represented a social and economic reaction, not only to the tremendous increase in immigration after 1880, but also to the shift in its main sources, to Southern, Eastern and Southeastern Europe.

Anti-immigration sentiment was heightened by World War I, and the dis- 19 illusionment and strong wave of isolationism that marked its aftermath. It was in this climate, in 1921, that Congress passed and the President signed the first major law in our country's history severely limiting new immigration by establishing an emergency quota system. An era in American history had ended; we were committed to a radically new policy toward the peopling of the nation.

The Act of 1921 was an early version of the so-called "national origins" 20 system. Its provisions limited immigration of numbers of each nationality to a certain percentage of the number of foreign-born individuals of that nationality resident in the United States according to the 1910 census. Nationality meant country of birth. The total number of immigrants permitted to enter under this system each year was 357,000.

In 1924 the Act was revised, creating a temporary arrangement for the 21
years 1924 to 1929, under which the national quotas for 1924 were equal to
2 percent of the number of foreign-born persons of a given nationality living in
the United States in 1890, or about 164,000 people. The permanent system,
which went into force in 1929, includes essentially all the elements of immigration policy that are in our law today. The immigration statutes now establish a
system of annual quotas to govern immigration from each country. Under this
system 156,987 quota immigrants are permitted to enter the United States
each year. The quotas from each country are based upon the national origins of
the population of the United States in 1920.

The use of the year 1920 is arbitrary. It rests upon the fact that this sys- 22
tem was introduced in 1924 and the last prior census was in 1920. The use of a
national origins system is without basis in either logic or reason. It neither satis-
fies a national need nor accomplishes an international purpose. In an age of
interdependence among nations such a system is an anachronism, for it dis-
criminates among applicants for admission into the United States on the basis
of accident of birth.

Because of the composition of our population in 1920, the system is 23
heavily weighted in favor of immigration from Northern Europe and severely
limits immigration from Southern and Eastern Europe and from other parts of
the world.

To cite some recent examples: Great Britain has an annual quota of 24
65,361 immigration visas and used 28,291 of them. Germany has a quota of
25,814 and used 26,533 (of this number, about one third are wives of service-
men who could enter on a nonquota basis). Ireland's quota is 17,756 and only
6,054 Irish availed themselves of it. On the other hand, Poland is permitted
6,488, and there is a backlog of 61,293 Poles wishing to enter the United
States. Italy is permitted 5,666 and has a backlog of 132,435. Greece's quota is
308; her backlog is 96,538. Thus a Greek citizen desiring to emigrate to this
country has little chance of coming here. And an American citizen with a
Greek father or mother must wait at least eighteen months to bring his parents
here to join him. A citizen whose married son or daughter, or brother or sister,
is Italian cannot obtain a quota number for them for two years or more. Meanwhile, many thousands of quota numbers are wasted because they are not
wanted or needed by nationals of the countries to which they are assigned.

In short, a qualified person born in England or Ireland who wants to emi- 25
grate to the United States can do so at any time. A person born in Italy, Hun-
gary, Poland or the Baltic States may have to wait many years before his turn is
reached. This system is based upon the assumption that there is some reason
for keeping the origins of our population in exactly the same proportions as they
existed in 1920. Such an idea is at complete variance with the American traditions and principles that the qualifications of an immigrant do not depend upon
his country of birth, and violates the spirit expressed in the Declaration of Independence that "all men are created equal."

One writer has listed six motives behind the Act of 1924. They were: 26
(1) postwar isolationism; (2) the doctrine of the alleged superiority of Anglo-Saxon and Teutonic "races"; (3) the fear that "pauper labor" would lower wage levels; (4) the belief that people of certain nations were less law-abiding than others; (5) the fear of foreign ideologies and subversion; (6) the fear that entrance of too many people with different customs and habits would undermine our national and social unity and order. All of these arguments can be found in Congressional debates on the subject and may be heard today in discussions over a new national policy toward immigration. Thus far, they have prevailed. . . .

SELECTION 3 QUESTIONS

Vocabulary

1. Explain what Washington wanted to happen when he said "to render this country more and more a safe and propitious asylum for the unfortunate of other countries." (paragraph 2)
2. Explain what Kennedy meant when he said, "America had no cause to be smug about the failure of these movements to take deep root." (paragraph 10)

Comprehension and Analysis

3. Prior to 1917, what had been America's only discriminatory immigration Act? What factors caused that Act to be passed?
4. What happened in 1917 to limit immigration? Trace the path of that law.
5. Briefly explain how the "Act of 1921" and its 1924 and 1929 revisions changed America's approach to immigration.
6. Compare and contrast how Americans have viewed aliens and immigration through the years.
7. List some of the "groups" that have been targeted by nativists through the years.
8. Why was Kennedy urging the country to rethink using a national origins system based on the 1920s census?

Reflect and Connect

9. In paragraph 26, Kennedy lists six motives behind the Act of 1924. Which of these reasons do you hear in today's discussions about immigration? Do you find that surprising? Please explain.

SELECTION 4 YES: WASHINGTON SHOULD STEM THE TIDE OF BOTH LEGAL AND ILLEGAL IMMIGRATION

DIRK CHASE ELDRIDGE

Mr. Eldridge is the author of Crowded Land of Liberty—Solving America's Immigration Crisis. *He writes about national policy issues from Long Beach, California. This article was printed in* Insight on the News, *March 11, 2002.*

AN IDEA TO THINK ABOUT

What are some reasons we should enact legislation to restrict immigration into the United States?

WORD TO KNOW

exacerbate (¶ 2)—intensify, make worse

The United States will double its population in the next 60 years unless we take prompt, aggressive action. The doubling will be caused almost entirely by immigration; more than 90 percent of our population growth since 1970 has come from recent immigrants and their children born here. Only Congress and the president can prevent this calamity, but so far neither has taken preventive action. Like Nero, they are fiddling while Rome burns. 1

To exacerbate matters, Congress legalized nearly 3 million illegal immigrants with amnesties in 1962, 1986 and 1997. Another is being considered for the 8 million to 11 million illegals we now host. This must be stopped. 2

In 1981, the Rev. Theodore Hesburgh, then-president of Notre Dame University, chaired a congressional commission to study immigration policy. The commission told President Ronald Reagan that our population was 200 million, which it labeled "already ecologically unsustainable," and recommended an immediate freeze on immigration. The commission found the root cause of our dramatic population growth to be chain immigration, a concept created by the 1965 amendments to the Immigration and Naturalization Act. The Hesburgh Commission studied chain immigration in detail, concluding that it allowed such aberrations as a family of five immigrants, if all became naturalized citizens, to grow in a relatively short period to 84 immigrants. Other studies found the multiplier to be somewhat less, but all agreed it was substantial. The study was reported more than 20 years ago, yet nothing has been done to halt population growth or reduce the dramatic effects of chain immigration. From the "ecologically unsustainable" 200 million in 1981, our population now is 281 million—and growing. 3

This growth has not occurred in a vacuum, but rather in the midst of the world's population exploding around us. It took from Adam and Eve to 1800 for the world to accumulate its first billion inhabitants. The pace of growth then accelerated, and the world added 2 billion people in the next 160 years. Then the really frightening growth began: It took only 40 years for Earth to double its population from 3 billion in 1960 to 6 billion by the year 2000! 4

This accelerating rate of growth created tremendous external pressure on the United States from people in the Third World, where most of this growth occurred. They are desperate to better their lot by moving to more-advanced countries such as the United States, Canada and Australia and those in Western Europe. 5

Excessive immigration, both legal and illegal, resulting from the amendments of 1965, has exacted a tremendous price from the American people, paid in the coin of overcrowded schools, congested highways, deteriorating ecology and lagging infrastructure. California, for instance, would require the completion of one new school each day to keep pace with the growth of the student populations. Of course, no state is able to finance and build schools that rapidly. This shortfall causes increasingly crowded classrooms and a deteriorating quality of education. Nor is the problem limited to California. Other high-immigration states such as New York, Florida and Texas face similar demands. 6

Inadequate highways are another manifestation of excessive immigration. Licensed drivers in the United States have increased by 64 percent since 1970, and vehicle miles by 131 percent. Yet during that period the nation's road mileage has grown a scant 6 percent. Remember that deficit next time you are stuck in traffic. 7

Recently we have experienced power shortages resulting in brownouts and rolling blackouts caused by too many people using a sometimes inadequate power supply. Because in today's politically correct climate it would be considered career suicide, no political leader has admitted that excessive immigration is a major contributor to these problems. 8

On the ecological front, in spite of impressive progress in some areas, 40 percent of Americans live in cities where the Environmental Protection Agency deems air quality substandard. Thirty-five of our states are withdrawing groundwater faster than it's being replenished. Forty percent of our lakes and streams are unfit for fishing or swimming. Our shortage of convenient open space is a national tragedy. Americans need tranquility more than ever, as overcrowding in our nation's population centers makes the mere absence of cell-phone babble a luxury. 9

The numbers tell why the United States suffers from immigration indigestion. During the 1960s we were absorbing 300,000 immigrants annually. Resulting from the aforementioned amendments to our immigration laws, the inflow of immigrants by the 1990s had ballooned to an average of more than 1 million per year. The dramatic change in the rate and ethnic composition of 10 immigration brought fundamental changes to our nation, with failure of assimilation being the most profound.

The United States has a proud tradition of assimilating immigrants into 11 the mainstream of our variegated population. Today, however, balkanization has replaced assimilation. Increasingly in America we see ethnic enclaves of recent immigrants making no effort to assimilate. Mexicans are the slowest to assimilate, perhaps because of their homeland's proximity. Alejandro Carrillo Castro, a former Mexican consul general in Chicago, says Mexicans in the United States are especially slow to naturalize, the ultimate act of assimilation. On average they take 22 years; others take seven.

Disturbing examples of balkanization are found in California and Florida, 12 to name just two trouble spots. The Hispanic former mayor of Miami, Maurice Ferre, once declared Spanish the official language of his city and predicted that soon people either would speak Spanish or leave. Fortunately, his abrasive 1981 forecast has yet to materialize. Many Miamians would say the issue still is in doubt. Southern California's Huntington Park and Garden Grove are cities staunchly balkanized by Hispanics and Asians, respectively. Some former Garden Grove residents expressed their frustration through a bumper sticker, widely displayed in the 1990s, that read: "Will the last American out of Garden Grove please bring the flag?"

The Houston Chronicle reported a jarring example of non-assimilation: "At a 13 soccer game against Mexico in February [1988], the American national team listened in frustration as a chorus of boos erupted during 'The Star-Spangled Banner.' Thousands of fans threw cups and bottles at the U.S. players, often striking them. They also attacked someone in the stands who tried to unfurl an American flag. The match didn't take place in Mexico City but in Los Angeles."

Failure of assimilation weakens America's social fabric and makes it diffi- 14 cult for immigrants to succeed here by participating fully in our economy. When immigration takes place at a reasonable rate, assimilation is more likely to occur. Adding to the problem of nonassimilation are more affordable airfares between the United States and immigrants' homelands, and such conveniences as reasonable long-distance telephone rates. In 1965 it cost $10.59 to call the Dominican Republic for three minutes and $15 to call India; now those rates are $1.71 and $3.66 respectively.

Through concerned, engaged leadership, the United States can stem the 15 tide of immigration and prevent the statistically inevitable doubling of our already-too-large population in the next 60 years. First, a 10-year moratorium for all immigration would provide time for us to assimilate and acculturate the torrent of immigrants of the last three decades. Second, it would give our underclass a chance to improve their incomes and working conditions absent the flood of cheap, immigrant labor with which they now compete for entry-level jobs. And, finally, it would give us time thoughtfully to plan future immigration policies. What characteristics will we seek in future immigrants? What level of education, what skills, what ages and how many will we admit? The moratorium would provide time to develop a consensus on future immigration, supplanting today's "policy-by-pressure-group" approach.

For national-security and other reasons, our borders must be bolstered 16 against today's silent invasion by illegal immigrants, 40 percent of whom enter with temporary visas and simply stay, melding into our society as did 13 of the September 11 terrorists. Other illegals sneak across our porous borders and shorelines. There currently is no downside to breaking U.S. immigration laws. If illegal aliens are apprehended, they often are simply taken back across the border and released. Hispanics at the border say: "Es un juego." Translation: It's a game.

We should put teeth into our laws by incarcerating apprehended illegals in 17 military facilities made available in recent rounds of base closures; 90 days for the first offense, six months for the second and a year for the third.

It's also time to demagnetize the magnet drawing them here: jobs. By re- 18 placing the easily counterfeited Social Security card every working American now must have with one containing a biometric representation of the carrier's fingerprints, we could make it simple to determine who is legally in our country and who is eligible for welfare and unemployment. Sanctions on employers who hire illegals should be part of the new paradigm.

A free, quality education is another element of the magnet. The simulta- 19 neous states of illegal immigrant and legal student are an affront to common sense and the rule of law and should be discontinued.

"There is nothing so permanent as a temporary farm worker" is more 20 than a clever turn of phrase; it is a truism. This should be recognized and such programs discontinued. They simply perpetuate economically unsound arrangements where U.S. farmers produce labor-intensive crops that cannot be grown and harvested profitably without cheap immigrant labor, the availability of which discourages development of automated methods. If we cannot grow such crops profitably, their production should be left to countries that can. That's how a free market, unfettered by a flow of unrealistically cheap labor, efficiently allocates its resources.

SELECTION 4 QUESTIONS

Vocabulary

1. Explain the cliché, "Like Nero, they are fiddling while Rome burns." (paragraph 1)
2. In paragraph 3, Eldridge says the commission found "the root cause of our dramatic population growth to be chain immigration." Explain the concept of chain immigration.
3. Explain what Eldridge means when he says that today, "balkanization has replaced assimilation." (paragraph 11)

Comprehension and Analysis

4. How does Eldridge develop and support his thesis? Give two examples of his evidence.
5. How does Eldridge feel about the "1965 amendments" that were championed by Kennedy and subsequently passed? Include specific examples to support your answer.
6. What does Eldridge mean by the phrase "immigrant indigestion"? What does he say has been the result of this phenomenon?
7. Why does Eldridge think a 10-year moratorium on all immigration would be a positive step?
8. What are three steps Eldridge thinks the United States should take to reduce illegal immigration?

Reflect and Connect

9. Kennedy listed six motives behind the Immigration Act of 1924. Would Eldridge see any of these reasons as valid? Please explain.

SELECTION 5   NO: WASHINGTON SHOULD NOT STEM THE TIDE OF BOTH LEGAL AND ILLEGAL IMMIGRATION

DANIEL T. GRISWOLD

Mr. Griswold is Associate Director of the Cato Institute's Center for Trade Policy Studies. His articles on trade and immigration issues have been widely published. This article was printed in Insight on the News, *March 11, 2002.*

AN IDEA TO THINK ABOUT

What are some reasons we should not enact legislation to restrict immigration?

Immigration always has been controversial in the United States. More than two centuries ago, Benjamin Franklin worried that too many German immigrants would swamp America's predominantly British culture. In the mid-1800s, Irish immigrants were scorned as lazy drunks, not to mention Roman Catholics. At the turn of the century a wave of "new immigrants"—Poles, Italians, Russian Jews—were believed to be too different ever to assimilate into American life. Today the same fears are raised about immigrants from Latin America and Asia, but current critics of immigration are as wrong as their counterparts were in previous eras.

Immigration is not undermining the American experiment; it is an integral 2
part of it. We are a nation of immigrants. Successive waves of immigrants have
kept our country demographically young, enriched our culture and added to
our productive capacity as a nation, enhancing our influence in the world.

Immigration gives the United States an economic edge in the world econ- 3
omy. Immigrants bring innovative ideas and entrepreneurial spirit to the U.S.
economy. They provide business contacts to other markets, enhancing America's ability to trade and invest profitably in the global economy. They keep our
economy flexible, allowing U.S. producers to keep prices down and to respond
to changing consumer demands. An authoritative 1997 study by the National
Academy of Sciences (NAS) concluded that immigration delivered a "significant positive gain" to the U.S. economy. In testimony before Congress last
year, Federal Reserve Board Chairman Alan Greenspan said, "I've always argued that this country has benefited immensely from the fact that we draw
people from all over the world."

Contrary to popular myth, immigrants do not push Americans out of 4
jobs. Immigrants tend to fill jobs that Americans cannot or will not fill, mostly
at the high and low ends of the skill spectrum. Immigrants are disproportionately represented in such high-skilled fields as medicine, physics and computer
science, but also in lower-skilled sectors such as hotels and restaurants, domestic service, construction and light manufacturing.

Immigrants also raise demand for goods as well as the supply. During the 5
long boom of the 1990s, and especially in the second half of the decade, the national unemployment rate fell below 4 percent and real wages rose up and
down the income scale during a time of relatively high immigration.

Nowhere is the contribution of immigrants more apparent than in the 6
high-technology and other knowledge-based sectors. Silicon Valley and other
high-tech sectors would cease to function if we foolishly were to close our borders to skilled and educated immigrants. These immigrants represent human
capital that can make our entire economy more productive. Immigrants have
developed new products, such as the Java computer language, that have created employment opportunities for millions of Americans.

Immigrants are not a drain on government finances. The NAS study 7
found that the typical immigrant and his or her offspring will pay a net $80,000
more in taxes during their lifetimes than they collect in government services.
For immigrants with college degrees, the net fiscal return is $198,000. It is true
that low-skilled immigrants and refugees tend to use welfare more than the
typical "native" household, but the 1996 Welfare Reform Act made it much
more difficult for newcomers to collect welfare. As a result, immigrant use of
welfare has declined in recent years along with overall welfare rolls.

Despite the claims of immigration opponents, today's flow is not out of 8
proportion to historical levels. Immigration in the last decade has averaged
about 1 million per year, high in absolute numbers, but the rate of 4 immigrants
per year per 1,000 U.S. residents is less than half the rate during the Great Mi-

gration of 1890–1914. Today, about 10 percent of U.S. residents are foreign-born, an increase from 4.7 percent in 1970, but still far short of the 14.7 percent who were foreign-born in 1910.

Nor can immigrants fairly be blamed for causing "over-population." America's annual population growth of 1 percent is below our average growth rate of the last century. In fact, without immigration our labor force would begin to shrink within two decades. According to the 2000 Census, 22 percent of U.S. counties lost population between 1990 and 2000. Immigrants could help revitalize demographically declining areas of the country, just as they helped re-vitalize New York City and other previously declining urban centers.

Drastically reducing the number of foreigners who enter the United 10 States each year only would compound the economic damage of Sept. 11 while doing nothing to enhance our security. The tourist industry, already reeling, would lose millions of foreign visitors, and American universities would lose hundreds of thousands of foreign students if our borders were closed.

Obviously the U.S. government should "control its borders" to keep out 11 anyone who intends to commit terrorist acts. The problem is not that we are letting too many people into the United States but that the government has failed to keep the wrong people out. We can stop terrorists from entering the United States without closing our borders or reducing the number of hard-working, peaceful immigrants who settle here.

We must do whatever is necessary to stop potentially dangerous people 12 at the border. Law-enforcement and intelligence agencies must work closely with the State Department, the Immigration and Naturalization Service (INS) and U.S. Customs to share real-time information about potential terrorists. Computer systems must be upgraded and new technologies adopted to screen out the bad guys without causing intolerable delays at the border. More agents need to be posted at ports of entry to more thoroughly screen for high-risk travelers. We must bolster cooperation with our neighbors, Canada and Mex-ico, to ensure that terrorists cannot slip across our long land borders.

In the wake of Sept. 11, longtime critics of immigration have tried to ex- 13 ploit legitimate concerns about security to argue for drastic cuts in immigration. But border security and immigration are two separate matters. Immigrants are only a small subset of the total number of foreigners who enter the United States every year. Only about one of every 25 foreign nationals who enter the United States come here to immigrate. The rest are tourists, business travelers, students and Mexican and Canadians who cross the border for a weekend to shop or visit family and then return home with no intention of settling perma-nently in the United States.

The 19 terrorists who attacked the United States on Sept. 11 did not 14 apply to the INS to immigrate or to become U.S. citizens. Like most aliens who enter the United States, they were here on temporary tourist and student visas. We could reduce the number of immigrants to zero and still not stop ter-rorists from slipping into the country on nonimmigrant visas.

To defend ourselves better against terrorism, our border-control system 15
requires a reorientation of mission. For the last two decades, U.S. immigration
policy has been obsessed with nabbing mostly Mexican-born workers whose
only "crime" is their desire to earn an honest day's pay. Those workers pose no
threat to national security.

Our land border with Mexico is half as long as our border with Canada, 16
yet before September 11 it was patrolled by 10 times as many border agents.
On average we were posting an agent every five miles along our 3,987-mile
border with Canada and every quarter-mile on the 2,000-mile border with
Mexico. On the Northern border there were 120,000 entries per year per
agent compared with 40,000 entries on the Southwestern border. This is out of
proportion to any legitimate fears about national security. In fact terrorists
seem to prefer the northern border. Let's remember that it was at a border-
crossing station in Washington state in December 1999 that a terrorist was apprehended with explosives that were to be used to blow up Los Angeles
International Airport during the millennium celebrations.

At a February 2000 hearing, former Sen. Slade Gorton (R-Wash.) 17
warned that "understaffing at our northern border is jeopardizing the security
of our nation, not to mention border personnel, while in at least some sections
of the southern border, there are so many agents that there is not enough work
to keep them all busy."

We should stop wasting scarce resources in a self-destructive quest to 18
hunt down Mexican construction workers and raid restaurants and chicken-
processing plants, and redirect those resources to track potential terrorists
and smash their cells before they can blow up more buildings and kill more
Americans.

For all these reasons, President George W. Bush's initiative to legalize and 19
regularize the movement of workers across the U.S.-Mexican border makes
sense in terms of national security as well as economics. It also is politically
smart.

In his latest book, *The Death of the West*, Pat Buchanan argues that op- 20
posing immigration will be a winning formula for conservative Republicans. His
own political decline and fall undermine his claim. Like former liberal Republican Gov. Pete Wilson in California, Buchanan has tried to win votes by blaming
immigration for America's problems. But voters wisely rejected Buchanan's
thesis. Despite $12 million in taxpayer campaign funds, and an assist from the
Florida butterfly ballot, Buchanan won less than 0.5 percent of the presidential
vote in 2000. In contrast Bush, by affirming immigration, raised the GOP's
share of the Hispanic vote to 35 percent from the 21 percent carried by Bob
Dole in 1996. If conservatives adopt the anti-immigrant message, they risk following Buchanan and Wilson into political irrelevancy.

It would be a national shame if, in the name of security, we closed 21
the door to immigrants who come here to work, save and build a better life
for themselves and their families. Immigrants come here to live the Ameri-

can Dream; terrorists come to destroy it. We should not allow America's tradition of welcoming immigrants to become yet another casualty of September 11.

SELECTION 5 QUESTIONS

Vocabulary

1. Explain the meaning of the phrase "Contrary to popular myth . . . ." (paragraph 4)
2. Explain what Griswold means in paragraph 4 when he says, "Immigrants are disproportionately represented" in certain jobs.
3. What is Griswold recommending in paragraph 15, when he says that "our border-control system requires a reorientation of mission"?

Comprehension and Analysis

4. How does Griswold develop and support his thesis? Give two examples of his evidence.
5. Compare and contrast the views of Griswold and Eldridge on the number of immigrants coming into the United States and their role in America's population growth.
6. Griswold says, "Border security and immigration are two separate matters." Explain what he means.
7. Compare and contrast the views of Griswold and Eldridge on the importance of security at our borders.
8. Griswold says that "immigrants are not a drain on government finances." How does he support his position? Would Eldridge agree or disagree? Please explain.

Reflect and Connect

9. Eldridge recommends "a 10-year moratorium for all immigration." How would Griswold probably respond to the recommendation? What would be his rationale?

SELECTION 6   EDITORIAL CARTOON

CLAY BENNETT

Pulitzer Prize–winning Editorial Cartoonist Bennett has been with The Christian Science Monitor *since 1998. In addition to producing five full-color car-*

toons each week for The Christian Science Monitor, *he produces fully animated editorial cartoons for the Internet and draws cartoons for distribution through King Features Syndicate.*

AN IDEA TO THINK ABOUT

In 1901, the last five lines of the sonnet "The New Colossus" by the U.S. poet Emma Lazarus were inscribed on a bronze plaque at the base of The Statue of Liberty:

> *Give me your tired, your poor,*
> *Your huddled masses yearning to breathe free,*
> *The wretched refuse of your teeming shore.*
> *Send these, the homeless, tempest-tossed to me,*
> *I lift my lamp beside the golden door!*

What do you think Lazarus and the people responsible for inscribing the sonnet wanted to communicate?

Immigration

SELECTION 6 QUESTIONS

Comprehension and Analysis

1. What message does Bennett want to communicate?
2. Do you think Bennett is in favor of more restrictive immigration laws? Please explain.

Reflect and Connect

3. Could this cartoon and message have appeared at any other time in our history? Please explain.

SELECTION 7   HISPANIC IMMIGRATION THREATENS U.S. VALUES

PATRICK J. BUCHANAN

Mr. Buchanan was Senior Adviser to three American presidents, ran for the Republican nomination for president in 1992 and 1996, and was the Reform Party candidate for president in 2000. He is the author of several books, including Right from the Beginning *and* A Republic Not an Empire, *is a syndicated columnist, and is a founding member of three television public affairs shows:* The McLaughlin Group, The Capital Gang, *and* Crossfire. *This article, which appeared in the Viewpoints section of the* Arizona Republic *newspaper on March 24, 2002, is based on his 2002 best-selling book* The Death of the West: How Dying Populations and Immigrant Invasions Imperil Our Country and Civilization.

IDEAS TO THINK ABOUT

How would you feel in this situation: If you stay inside your home there is a good chance that someone will break in and rob you, yet if you go outside someone may attack you? How would you cope? What would you want the authorities to do to help you?

Two years ago, while campaigning in Arizona, I drove south from Tucson to   1
Douglas, the border town of 18,000 that had become a major avenue of invasion of the United States. In March 1999, the Border Patrol had apprehended 27,000 Mexicans crossing illegally.

While in Douglas, I visited Theresa Murray, an 82-year-old widow living in the Arizona desert she grew up in. Her ranch house was enveloped by a chain link fence topped with coils of razor wire. Every door and window had bars and was wired to an alarm. As she had been burglarized 30 times, Theresa slept with a pistol on her bed table. Her guard dogs were dead—bled to death when someone tossed meat with chopped glass in it over her fence.

This American lady was living out her years in a maximum-security prison in her own home because her government lacked the fortitude to defend the borders of the United States. And still does.

If America is about anything, it is freedom. But as Theresa Murray told a reporter: "I can't ever leave the house unless I have somebody watch it. . . . It used to be fun to live here. Now, it's hell. It's plain old hell. . . . I've lost my freedom."

And as Murray lived unfree in a hellish existence on the U.S. border, U.S. soldiers defended the borders of Kuwait, Korea and Kosovo. Yet, nothing is at risk there to compare with what is at risk on our border with Mexico, over which pass the armies of the night as they trudge endlessly north to the great cities of America.

Our country is being invaded, and a morally and politically paralyzed White House refuses to halt that invasion. Each year, the Border Patrol turns back 1.5 million illegal aliens breaking into our country, but an estimated 500,000 succeed.

Comes the angry retort: "What are you, a nativist? Immigrants from Mexico are just like your Irish and Scot-Irish ancestors of a century ago. They come to do the jobs Americans refuse to do."

But this new immigration is radically different from the old.

First, it is huge. From 2 million Hispanics in 1960, the United States is now home to 36 million.

Second, much of it is illegal. By one estimate, there are 11 million illegal aliens in the United States, a number equal to the total population of Connecticut, Massachusetts and Rhode Island combined.

Third, it is concentrated in one region, the Southwest. So overwhelming is that presence that "Anglos" are now a minority in California and will be a minority in Texas in three years. Native-born Americans are fleeing California at the rate of 100,000 a year.

Fourth, unlike the Irish who came here to become Americans, millions of Mexicans consider themselves patriots of Mexico. Many have no desire to assimilate and are determined to maintain their culture and language as a separate people, a nation within a nation. Moreover, they are coming to an America whose melting pot is broken, whose elites preach not assimilation but multiculturalism, a society that is breaking down on racial and ethnic lines as the integrationist ethos of the 1960s gives way to a separatist ethos.

Much of this Mexican population is hostile to the host country. A third of the early arrests of criminals who pillaged and burned Los Angeles in 1992 were illegal. Illegal aliens have twice the crime rate of Americans. In the U.S.-

Mexico soccer game in the Los Angeles Coliseum in 1998, 90,000 Mexicans booed the U.S. national anthem, tore down our flag and showered debris and garbage on the U.S. fans and U.S. team.

In the Texas town of El Cenizo, Spanish has been declared the official language, and any city official who helps the Immigration and Naturalization Service run down illegal aliens is fired. 14

At Berkeley, conservative students who objected to a Latino student organization, MEChA, calling them "gringos," were threatened with death and saw their student newspaper edition seized and destroyed. 15

"The American Southwest seems to be slowly returning to the jurisdiction of Mexico without firing a shot," exulted *Excelsior,* Mexico's national newspaper. 16

"Even though I am saying this part serious, part joking, I believe we are practicing La Reconquista in California," said Mexican consul Jose Pescador Osuna in 1998. 17

Now President Bush has persuaded the House to grant amnesty to a million Mexican illegal aliens, putting them on the fast track to U.S. citizenship. Said Sen. Robert Byrd: This is "lunacy." 18

On Sept. 11, we Americans found that our open borders had been exploited by crazed killers who slaughtered 3,000 members of our family. We must wake up. This is our home. If we allow it to become an international flophouse and crash pad for any who want to come here, we will prove the unworthy heirs of those who died to make America the land of the free and the home of the brave. 19

SELECTION 7 QUESTIONS

Vocabulary

1. Explain what Buchanan means when he says that "her government lacked the fortitude" to help her. (paragraph 3)
2. Explain what Buchanan means when he says America's "melting pot is broken," that people are advocating "not assimilation but multiculturalism," and that "the integrationist ethos of the 1960s gives way to a separatist ethos." (paragraph 12)
3. Explain the implications of the phrase "La Reconquista in California." (paragraph 17)

Comprehension and Analysis

4. State Buchanan's thesis.
5. List and explain the four reasons Buchanan believes today's "immigration is radically different from the old."

6. Which ethnic group(s) from which country(ies) concerns Buchanan in this article? What do you think he believes about other immigrant groups? Please explain.

7. How does Buchanan feel about the United States assuming a military role in other countries around the world? Please explain.

8. What tone does Buchanan create with phrases like "avenue of invasion," "the armies of the night," and "illegal aliens breaking into our country"?

Reflect and Connect

9. How do you think Buchanan would react to Eldridge's recommendations such as placing a 10-year moratorium on all immigration and enacting harsh penalties on illegals? Please explain.

SELECTION 8 HE CROSSED BORDER FOR A BETTER LIFE

JIM SECKLER

Mr. Seckler is Staff Writer for Arizona's Kingman Daily Miner *newspaper where this article appeared January 10, 2003.*

AN IDEA TO THINK ABOUT

When you were 14 years old, what was your primary goal, and what did you have to do to accomplish it?

At 14, an age when many teenagers struggle to the next video game level, 1 Tomas Silva literally walked his way to a better life.

Silva, the Kingman Police Department's newest animal control officer, 2 made his way to Kingman from west-central Mexico in 1980, leaving his parents and his eight brothers and sisters behind.

"It was tough," he said. "It was scary. I was just a little kid. But I took a 3 chance."

Silva, now 37, said he knew he would be relegated to a life of working 4 long hours for little pay if he stayed in Mexico.

"I was looking for a better future," he said. 5

He and a friend hitchhiked most of the way to Nogales. Silva was caught 6 and deported eight times trying to cross the border near Nogales. On the ninth try, a Border Patrol officer stopped him, then ignored him to pursue other illegal immigrants.

Heading north, Silva walked for three days to Tucson, avoiding Border 7
Patrol officers and sleeping under railroad bridges.

Near a ranch, he used his shirt to strain mucky water from a stream. 8
Starving, he managed to kill a chicken with a rock and ate the bird raw.

"The things people do to survive is incredible," he said. 9

Near Tucson, he hitched a ride with an American who spoke Spanish. 10
When he asked where Silva was going, Silva shrugged and asked where the
driver was going, thinking they were headed to California.

But the driver said Kingman, a town Silva had never heard of. 11

In Kingman, the man offered the boy some clothes and a place to stay just 12
behind the Kingman Regional Medical Center. He also got Silva a job with a
Hispanic man who owned an upholstery shop.

For five years, Silva did not leave the shop for fear of being deported. 13
During that time he also did not speak any English. Finally, wanting to succeed,
he started watching movies and *Sesame Street* to learn the language. Within a
year, he learned enough to get his own place.

"It still wasn't enough," he said. "I committed myself to learn to read and 14
write, which I did."

He married a local woman who helped him take classes at Mohave Com- 15
munity College.

Through the years he got a work permit, then a red card, then a green 16
card. But he was still not satisfied. He wanted to vote and make a difference.
On March 4, 1994, he became an American citizen.

In 1999, he applied for a job with the city and was hired for the mainte- 17
nance department. Last September, he became an animal control officer.

"This is my career now," Silva said. "I learn something new every day 18
with this job. I enjoy being involved with people and I love animals. I want to
make sure people take care of their pets."

Silva still takes English and writing classes, partially because of the re- 19
ports animal control officers have to write.

"My goal is to continue to go to school," Silva said. "And to see my kids 20
grow up to be good people."

SELECTION 8 QUESTIONS

Comprehension and Analysis

1. Why did Silva take the "chance" and come to the United States?
2. List two examples of Silva's perseverance in reaching his goals.
3. In what ways do you think Silva's story is similar to and/or different than
   the stories of other illegal immigrants?
4. What do you think Seckler wanted to achieve with this story? Do you
   think Seckler was successful? Please explain.

Reflect and Connect

5. What do you think Buchanan would have to say about Silva's crossing the border into Arizona? What do you think he would have to say about Silva's life today?

SELECTION 9 RIP UP ILLEGALITIES BY THE REAL ROOTS

O. RICARDO PIMENTEL

Mr. Pimentel is a columnist with the Arizona Republic. *Before he joined the* Republic *in 1999, he was Executive Editor for* The San Bernardino County Sun *where he also wrote a weekly column. This column appeared in the* Arizona Republic *December 17, 2002.*

IDEAS TO THINK ABOUT

Should your professors be required to report students who are in the country illegally? If you knew the person sitting next to you in class was in the country illegally would you report him or her to the INS?

Virginia's attorney general has recommended that state colleges there not admit undocumented immigrants and that they report any now enrolled.   1

I know. This is where you expect outrage. But you know what? This is actually the seed of a great idea. The only flaw is that it is not expansive enough.   2

Why stop at singling out immigrants? Let's also root out those who, in their greed, depravity and ignorance, make it possible for these migrants to be here.   3

Here's what we could do.   4

Upset about all those day laborers congregating on street corners? Many of them are allegedly undocumented. Stake those corners out with cameras and post the photos of employers and their license plates on the Internet.   5

Once we find out who these people are, let's deny their children admittance to college. What use is a policy if it doesn't scorch a little earth?   6

Undocumented immigrants have allegedly overrun the construction trades. Your house was probably built with some measure of undocumented labor. Home builders and their subcontractors, of course, will say they don't knowingly hire undocumented immigrants.   7

Sorry. We've got to take a hard line here. If any undocumented immigrants are found in their employ, company assets should be seized. And as added punishment, the honchos' kids shouldn't be allowed to walk the hallowed halls of college.   8

But that still leaves your home. It was probably built with "illegal" labor. 9
Sorry, it should be sold at public auction. But rest assured that if you submit
the highest bid, the house is yours again. We shouldn't be heartless about this,
after all. Except with the kids. Barring them from college is just the right thing
to do.

Harsh, yes, but flipping hamburgers as a career isn't all that bad. There is 10
nobility in all work.

Restaurateurs and grocers who hire undocumented immigrants or use 11
food they've harvested? Close 'em down. Any food still in inventory goes to
the local food bank. And, yup, their kids will have to content themselves with
just finishing high school.

But let's not stop at making colleges root out those undocumented 12
people.

Doctors and nurses, you can perform a service and turn in your patients. 13
Public school teachers, your students. Mail carriers and cable television in-
stallers, you know who those people are. Turn them in. It's your duty.

Those college spots are for real American kids with real American par- 14
ents who pay real American taxes.

What? You say the parents of immigrant children also pay taxes that support 15
our institutions of higher learning? Just too bad, I guess. These kids simply should
have known better than to have allowed their parents to bring them here without
documents. They should have dug in their little heels just before crossing.

And if that didn't work, they should have reported their parents to the 16
INS or, at the very least, run away from home.

The more conspiracy-minded among you are likely jumping to the faulty 17
conclusion that the Virginia attorney general's recommendation might be part
of an overall effort to keep immigrants in their place—as a permanent underclass.

Poppycock. As my readers are fond of telling me, what part of illegal don't 18
you guys understand?

Anyway, we can't let enterprising immigrants who overcome, significant 19
hurdles compete with American kids in college. That just wouldn't be right.

I see that Virginia Gov. Mark Warner has pledged to form a task force to 20
see if Attorney General Jerry Kilgore's recommendation has merit.

This after many in Virginia's Latino community protested. And the gov- 21
ernor likely noticed that other states, including Arizona, don't penalize these
kids for college admission purposes. In Arizona, a student whose immigration
status is "undetermined" but who has lived in the state since he or she was a
young child doesn't even have to pay out-of-state tuition.

Or maybe Gov. Warner has noted pending congressional legislation that 22
would essentially give green cards to deserving immigrant students.

Seriously, let me suggest to Virginia's governor that he doesn't really need 23
a task force to tell him that punishing children for the sins of the parents is un-
American. It's probably even un-Virginian.

SELECTION 9 QUESTIONS

Vocabulary

1. What does Pimentel mean when he says the proposal "is not expansive enough"? (paragraph 2)
2. In paragraph 6, Pimentel says, "What use is a policy if it doesn't scorch a little earth?" What does he mean?

Comprehension and Analysis

3. Explain what Pimentel is suggesting. Does he mean for his suggestion to be taken literally? Please explain.
4. State Pimentel's thesis.

Reflect and Connect

5. How do you think Pimentel would describe "real American kids" and "real American parents"? How would those descriptions compare to descriptions Buchanan might give?

SELECTION 10   OPENING THE DOOR

THE ECONOMIST STAFF

Since it began in London in 1845, The Economist *has been written by a collection of staff journalists, freelance writers, and subject experts from across Europe and the United States. However, no matter how famous the author, no article in* The Economist *is signed. The main reason for anonymity is "a belief that what is written is more important than who writes it." This article appeared in the U. S. edition of* The Economist, *Nov. 2, 2002.*

AN IDEA TO THINK ABOUT

If the United States instituted a more "selective" immigration policy, what types of immigrants from what countries do you think we should allow to immigrate?

A possible conflict in Iraq; deteriorating economies in South America; famine in sub-Saharan Africa; turmoil in Indonesia; political instability in the Balkans. And in many developing countries, persistent crime, lousy education and a lack of opportunities for energetic people to prosper without graft and political connections. No wonder so many people want the chance of a better life in the stable, meritocratic economies of the rich world. No wonder they risk their life savings, or even their lives, to buy the hope of higher earnings, fairer treatment and better opportunities for their families.

This movement of humanity brings undoubted gains, and not just to the immigrants. The gap between earnings in the poor and rich worlds is vastly greater than the gap in the prices of traded goods. Our survey results indicate the potential economic benefits to the world of liberalising migration dwarf those from removing trade barriers. Where populations are aging and economies are sluggish, the benefits are especially great. Immigrants, unlike natives, move readily to areas where labour is in short supply, so easing bottlenecks. They bring a just-in-time supply of skills, too, which is why hospitals want to hire foreign doctors and nurses; farmers, spare hands to pick fruit and vegetables; and wealthy couples, nannies for their children. In many cases, immigrants also pay more in taxes than they cost in public spending. 2

But voters in rich countries often don't see things this way. Like other forces of globalisation, immigration is disruptive, and at the most intimate level. It changes the neighbourhood. People in the street speak odd languages; the neighbours' cooking smells strange. So immigration often meets passionate resistance. Even in countries built on immigration, like the United States, politicians hesitate to press for easier entry. America has refused to strike a deal with Mexico to let in more legal migrants. In Europe, hostility is deeper and can be more dangerous. In the past year, the far right has gained in elections in France, Denmark, Austria and the Netherlands. 3

The hostility may well increase. Immigration has boomed in the past decade partly because rich countries have created lots of jobs. If the economic slowdown persists, unemployment is sure to breed greater resentment. Another terrorist attack along the lines of September 11th 2001 would, rightly or wrongly, increase fears that immigrants threaten security. And, as HIV spreads in the poor world, rich countries will fret about the threat to their health services and the risk of AIDS. 4

How then to square the conflicting pressures of politics and economics? The first essential is to accept that the voters' right to a say about who and how many can enter must take precedence over the rights of those unlucky enough to be born in poorer parts of the world. The task of politicians—and of employers—is to persuade voters that immigration is not only inevitable but also in their long-term interests. 5

That will be possible only if migration is managed carefully. Voters resent illegal immigration, and not merely because illegals are particularly likely to undercut the pay of natives (and of other immigrants). Illegal migration, currently running at about 500,000 a year into both the United States and the European Union, indicates a breakdown of government control. However, tougher border controls are unlikely to help much. More important is a willingness to take stronger measures to force employers to check workers' credentials. 6

With legal migration, governments need to persuade voters that they are 7
accepting immigrants who will be good for the country, rather than simply
those who manage to find a way through the entry rules. Some legal routes
have become particularly prone to abuse. They include two that are especially
sensitive in liberal democracies: asylum claims and family reunion. In particular,
a United Nations convention (on refugees) more than half a century old is
surely no longer a strong enough basis for deciding whether to admit tens of
thousands of people each year.

BETTER WAYS

A workable policy would be more selective, not more restrictive. Countries 8
could, for instance, freely admit the citizens of any country with broadly the
same income per head as theirs, letting them work or stay as long as they liked.
It makes no sense for America to limit the working opportunities of young Aus-
tralians, or for EU countries to keep out Canadians.

In the case of migrants from the poor world, countries should give prefer- 9
ence to those who seem to integrate most readily. That would often mean
favouring not just the skilled (who already get preference everywhere) but
those from culturally similar backgrounds. It might mean insisting that migrants
learn the local language quickly; that they abide by local standards of tolerance
and good behaviour; that they are wary of demanding special treatment in matters of dress or religious observance. Race and religion must be a part of the
public discussion of migration. To pretend that they do not affect attitudes
makes policy more restrictive than it should be.

What about the unskilled? No country's entry policy welcomes them. 10
However, rich countries need them: to look after the old, to staff restaurant
kitchens, to pluck chickens or gut fish. Better, surely, to create legal ways for
some to enter—perhaps by an annual auction or lottery of places—than to
leave them only the option of the back of a truck.

Making immigration policy less restrictive brings a further benefit. Dra- 11
conian border controls discourage migrants from going home and facing a second dangerous and expensive trip when they next want to work abroad. Yet
inexpensive travel means that the natural pattern of movement now is more
one of circulation than of the one-way crossing of the emigrant ship. If immigration policy forces people to return, it will fail; if it facilitates and promotes
return, all will gain.

If voters see that immigration is managed for their benefit and not for that 12
of strangers, they may even learn to enjoy some of the changes it brings. It is
the mix of colours and cultures that gives such exuberance to New York and
London. Open the door, and let in new ideas, new foods, new businesses and a
new buzz along with those eager new faces.

SELECTION 10 QUESTIONS

Vocabulary

1. Explain the phrase "Draconian border controls." (paragraph 11)

Comprehension and Analysis

2. Why does the author believe people want to immigrate to countries like the United States?
3. Who gains from immigration according to the author? Please explain.
4. What are some reasons people dislike legal immigration? What are some reasons people resent illegal immigration?
5. State the author's thesis.
6. Explain how a "more selective, not more restrictive" immigration policy could work in America.
7. According to the author, what could happen when the "natives" see that immigration is managed for their benefit, not for that of the immigrants?

Reflect and Connect

8. The author says, "Some legal routes [of immigration] have become particularly prone to abuse . . . including family reunion." Compare this view with Eldridge's discussion of "chain immigration."

INVESTIGATING OTHER POINTS OF VIEW . . .

One way to investigate a variety of points of view on the complex issues surrounding immigration is through the resources of Research Navigator™. Once you log on to Research Navigator.com and enter your personal passcode (from inside the front cover of this text), you have access to three databases of credible and reliable source material: 1) EBSCO's Content Select Academic Journal Database with content from the leading academic journals, 2) *The New York Times* Search by Subject™ Archive with full-text articles from *The New York Times*, 3) Link Library providing editorially selected "best of the Web" sites. For more information about Research Navigator™ and how to use it efficiently, see "Introducing Research Navigator™" starting on page RN–1.

AFTER CONSIDERING SEVERAL POINTS OF VIEW . . .

A. It is generally agreed that illegal immigration is a problem that must be addressed. However, there is little agreement on how to go about it. Describe one approach to reducing illegal immigration that you think is workable. Include what group(s) would probably support your strategy and what group(s) might protest it.

B. According to one point of view, "We could reduce the number of immigrants to zero and still not stop terrorists from slipping into the country." Discuss your view of the relationship between immigration and terrorism. Describe strategies you believe would help us to better defend ourselves against terrorism.

C. Controversy has surrounded immigration throughout America's history. Many reasons have been given for limiting immigration, and many have been given for encouraging immigration. Discuss which idea(s) continues to have the most popular support today and which idea(s) are no longer considered valid.

THEME 4

BIOTECHNOLOGY

To scientists, "biotechnology is any commercial use or alteration of organisms, cells, or biological molecules to achieve specific practical goals" (Audesirk, Audesirk, and Byers, *Biology,* 2002). To consumers, biotechnology is a general term to describe a wide range of scientific techniques that can change living things. For example, we have used selected strains of yeast to make bread, cheese, and beer for millennia.

However, not all biotechnology practices are as accepted as those used to make bread and beer. For example, the foods developed with the tools of biotechnology during the last 10 years have brought controversy. According to the Food and Agriculture Organization of the United Nations, the "new biotechnologies, at once a collection of tools for research and new means of generating food and agricultural products, hold great promise—and some risk."

Advocates of genetically modified organisms (GMOs) say that only a major, revolutionary "technological leap" will enable the planet to feed all its people in the years to come. They strongly believe that GMOs could help to increase the supply, diversity, and quality of food products while reducing production and processing costs, pesticide use, and environmental degradation. Proponents see GMOs as the only answer to malnutrition. Others strongly disagree with that position and accuse major biotech companies of producing "Frankenstein food." They ask, "Who will monitor the changes in biodiversity that might result from unforeseen crossbreeding between GMOs and related wild species?" In addition, opponents of GMOs argue that most countries have food to eat and that malnutrition exists because the world's poor lack access to that food—a problem of unequal distribution. Those against GMOs plead for infrastructure changes, not gene changes.

Likewise, a firestorm of controversy surrounds human biotechnology experiments. For example, the May 2002 UNESCO essay, "The Ethics of Genetics—How Far Should We Let Scientists Go?" said,

Using human embryos as a source of spare body parts is an idea that both fascinates and terrifies. We are drawn by its promise. We are also frightened, because it has changed too quickly from science fiction to being real science and because we feel those involved in it have new and fearsome powers through their knowledge of how to alter living organisms.

The idea of beating an illness such as Parkinson's disease by replacing old or damaged cells with new and efficient ones taken from an embryo is by no means the only one that life sciences offer us these days. Other possibilities, on the contrary, are downright alarming. They include, for example, reproductive cloning of human beings, which some scientists and doctors say they are determined to press ahead with despite its prohibition by UNESCO's 1997 Universal Declaration on the Human Genome and Human Rights and the laws of many countries.

The ethical and emotional views on the variety of issues connected with biotechnology simultaneously frighten, comfort, horrify, and inspire society. The authors in this Theme present a sampling of the conflicting views.

The Theme opens with "Biotechnology," Chapter 13, from the introductory text, *Biology: Life on Earth,* sixth edition, by Audesirk, Audesirk, and Byers. They address questions such as these: "What is biotechnology?" "What are some applications of biotechnology?" and "What are some ethical implications of human biotechnology?"

The next four selections examine genetically altered food. In "Biotech for Better Health," the Council for Biotechnology Information advises that plant biotechnology is producing more food for a growing population and will provide researchers ways to develop healthier foods that can improve human health. However, in "Playing with Our Food," Charles Margulis asks that we "stop this massive food experiment, which poses unknown risks to human health and the global environment." Then cartoonist Clay Bennett takes us shopping for genetically altered food. Finally, in "Millions Served," Lynn J. Cook takes us to Africa to show us that "while the West debates the ethics of genetically modified food, Florence Wambugu is using it to feed her country."

Then four selections explore aspects of human biotechnology. Lee M. Silver suggests "How Reprogenetics Will Transform the American Family." Tom Schaefer shows us a "Cloning Scenario Getting Frighteningly Close to Reality." Editorial cartoonist Mike Thompson considers some possibilities of the human genome project. Finally, Alexandra Stikeman provides a view of the future with "Biomedicine."

Daniel E. Koshland closes the theme with "Ethical Decision Making in a Pluralistic Society." His article is from *Biotechnology: Science, Engineering, and Ethical Challenges for the 21st Century.*

As you read the selections in this Theme and other articles and essays on biotechnology, answer questions such as these as a matter of course:

1. Do I understand all the author's words and phrases?
2. What is the author's thesis (conclusion)?
3. What facts, opinions, and reasoned judgments does the author provide to support and develop the thesis?
4. Are the author's facts, opinions, and reasoned judgments derived from respected sources?
5. Are there factual errors or misleading interpretations?
6. Has significant information been omitted or arbitrarily discounted?
7. What new information does this author add to my understanding of the issue?

SELECTION 1   BIOTECHNOLOGY

TERRY AUDESIRK, GERRY AUDESIRK, AND BRUCE BYERS

Drs. Audesirk are Professors of Biology at the University of Colorado in Denver where they have taught introductory biology and neurobiology since 1982. In their research lab funded by the National Institutes of Health, they investigate the mechanisms by which neurons are harmed by low levels of environmental pollutants. Dr. Byers is Professor of Biology at the University of Massachusetts, Amherst, where he has taught introductory biology, ornithology, and animal behavior courses since 1993. His current research focuses on the behavioral ecology of birds. This is Chapter 13 from their introductory text, Biology: Life on Earth, *sixth edition.*

AN IDEA TO THINK ABOUT

What positive and negative connotations do the words and phrases "DNA," "genetic engineering," "cloning," and "genetically modified foods" create for you?

WORDS TO KNOW

Key Terms are in bold face type and are defined in the text.

Teaching an Old Grain New Tricks

Rice is the major food for about two-thirds of the humans on Earth. A bowl of rice provides a good supply of carbohydrates and some protein but is a poor source of most vitamins, including vitamin A. Unless people eat sufficient fruits and vegetables along with the rice to provide this essential vitamin, a condition called *vitamin A deficiency* results. Although uncommon in the U.S., each year this condition causes the deaths of more than a million children in Asia, Africa, and Latin America. In addition, more than 250,000 children in these developing nations become blind each year as a result of vitamin A deficiency. In 1999 biotechnology provided a simple possible cure: genetically engineered rice.

This new rice has a golden-yellow color because it contains elevated levels of beta-carotene, the vitamin A precursor that gives carrots their bright color. Eating approximately 10 ounces of the bioengineered rice each day (a typical amount in Asian diets) would prevent vitamin A deficiency.

How do scientists create genetically modified plants and animals? What are some potential risks and benefits of this technology? In this chapter, we explore these questions and discuss the increasing role that biotechnology plays in life on Earth.

WHAT IS BIOTECHNOLOGY?

In its broadest sense, **biotechnology** is any commercial use or alteration of organisms, cells, or biological molecules to achieve specific practical goals. By this definition, biotechnology is nearly as old as civilization itself. Archeological studies show that as long as 10,000 years ago, Neolithic cultures in Egypt and the Near East used yeast cells to produce beer and wine, much as we do today. Selective breeding of plants and animals in agriculture has a similarly lengthy history. Squash fragments preserved in a dry cave in Mexico were recently dated as 8000 to 10,000 years old. These squash have larger seeds and thicker rinds than those of wild varieties, providing evidence of selective breeding by humans—an early form of genetic manipulation. Prehistoric art and animal remains suggest that dogs, sheep, goats, pigs, and camels were also domesticated and selectively bred beginning about 10,000 years ago. 1

Selective breeding continues to be an important tool in biotechnology. However, modern biotechnology also commonly uses **genetic engineering,** the modification of genetic material to achieve specific goals. Genetically engineered cells or organisms may have genes deleted, added, or changed. Major goals of genetic engineering include: 2

1. to learn more about cellular processes, including inheritance and gene expression;

2. to provide better understanding and treatment of diseases, particularly genetic disorders; and

3. to generate economic and social benefits, including efficient production of valuable biological molecules and improved plants and animals for agriculture.

A key tool in genetic engineering is **recombinant DNA.** Recombi- 3 nant DNA contains genes or portions of genes from different organisms, often from different species. Large amounts of recombinant DNA can be grown in bacteria, viruses, or yeast and then transferred into other species, including animals and plants. These plants and animals, which express DNA that has been modified or derived from another species, are called **transgenic.** Since its development in the 1970s, recombinant DNA technology has grown explosively, providing new methods, applications, and possibilities for genetic engineering. Today most research labs involved in analysis of cell structure, genetics, molecular basis of disease, and evolution routinely use recombinant DNA technology in their experiments. Many genetically engineered products are used in preference to previously available ones, including human insulin and enzymes used for making cheese. However, also growing are concerns about the wisdom and safety of some of these methods and products.

HOW DOES DNA RECOMBINATION OCCUR IN NATURE?

Most of us tend to think of a species' genetic make-up as relatively stable and 4 static. However, many natural processes can transfer DNA from one organism—or even one species—to another. In fact, many recombinant DNA technologies used in the laboratory are based on these naturally occurring DNA recombination processes.

DNA Recombination Occurs Naturally Through Processes Such as Sexual Reproduction, Bacterial Transformation, and Viral Infection

Regardless of how it occurs, recombination changes the genetic makeup of or- 5 ganisms. DNA recombination within many species occurs during sexual reproduction: Crossing over during meiosis I exchanges DNA from each maternal chromosome with the homologous DNA from the paternal chromosome. Following recombination, the chromosomes contain new combinations of alleles, different from either parent. Thus, each egg and sperm produced by meiosis can be considered "recombinant."

Many people tend to consider recombination within a species during sexual reproduction as "natural" and therefore good but think of recombinations performed in the laboratory between different species as "unnatural" and therefore intrinsically bad. However, recombinations between species also occur in nature, as described next. 6

Transformation May Combine DNA from Different Bacterial Species Bacteria can undergo several types of recombination that allow gene transfer between unrelated species. A process called **transformation** enables bacteria to pick up free DNA from the environment. The free DNA may be part of the chromosome of another bacterium, including DNA from another bacterial species. Discovery of such chromosomal transformation was one of the first indications that DNA carries genes. Transformation may also occur when bacteria pick up tiny circular DNA molecules called **plasmids** (Fig. 4-1). Many types of bacteria contain plasmids, which can also be found in some fungi, algae, and protists. Plasmids range in size from about 1000 to 100,000 nucleotides long. For comparison, the *E. coli* chromosome is around 4,600,000 nucleotides long. A single bacterium may contain dozens or even hundreds of copies of a plasmid. When the bacterium dies, it releases these plasmids into the environment, where they can be picked up by bacteria of similar or different species. In addition, living bacteria can often pass a copy of their plasmid directly to other living bacteria. Passing of plasmids from living bacteria to living yeast has also been documented! 7

What use are plasmids? The bacterium's chromosome contains all the genes the cell normally needs for basic survival. However, genes carried by plasmids often allow the bacteria that carry them to grow in novel environments. Some plasmids contain genes that allow bacteria to metabolize novel energy sources, such as petroleum or other hydrocarbons. Other plasmids carry genes that cause disease symptoms, such as diarrhea, in the animal or other organism that the bacterium infects. (From the bacterium's point of view, diarrhea in the infected animal may be beneficial in that it enables the bacterium to spread and infect new hosts.) Still other plasmids carry genes that enable the bacterium to grow in the presence of an antibiotic, such as penicillin. In environments where antibiotic use is high, particularly hospitals, bacteria carrying these antibiotic-resistance plasmids can quickly spread among patients and health care workers, making antibiotic-resistant infections a serious problem. 8

Viruses May Transfer DNA Between Bacteria and Between Eukaryotic Species Viruses, which are little more than genetic material encased in a protein-containing coat, transfer their genetic material into cells during infection. Within the infected cell, viral genes replicate and direct the synthesis of viral proteins. The replicated genes and new viral proteins assemble inside the cell, forming new viruses that are released to infect 9

Biotechnology

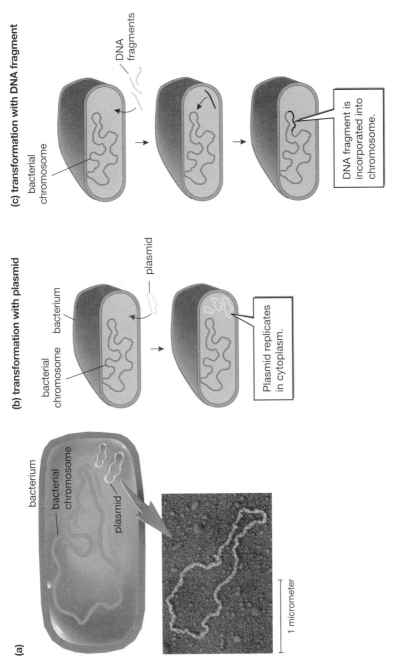

(c) transformation with DNA fragment

bacterial chromosome

DNA fragments

DNA fragment is incorporated into chromosome.

(b) transformation with plasmid

bacterial chromosome

bacterium

plasmid

Plasmid replicates in cytoplasm.

(a)

bacterium

bacterial chromosome

plasmid

1 micrometer

Figure 4–1 Recombination in bacteria (a) In addition to their large circular chromosome, bacteria commonly possess small rings of DNA called *plasmids*, which often carry additional useful genes. Bacterial transformation occurs when living bacteria take up **(b)** these plasmids or **(c)** fragments of chromosomes.

new cells (Fig. 4–2). Usually, a particular virus infects and replicates only in the cells of certain bacterial, animal, or plant species. For example, the canine distemper virus, which causes a frequently fatal disease in dogs, usually only infects dogs, raccoons, ferrets, otters, and related species. People who care for these sick animals are not at risk for contracting this viral disease.

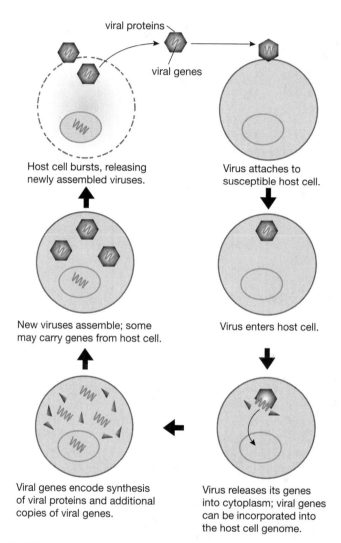

Figure 4–2 Viruses may transfer genes A virus infecting a eukaryotic cell uses its own genetic material and the host's cellular machinery to copy the virus. When copies are released from the cell, they can infect new host cells. Segments of the host DNA may be incorporated into the viral genome and transferred to hosts of other species.

During many viral infections, viral DNA sequences become incorpo- 10
rated into one of the host cell's chromosomes. The viral DNA can remain
there for days, months, or even years. The cell replicates the incorporated
viral DNA as well as the rest of its DNA every time the cell divides. When
new viruses are produced from the incorporated DNA, they can mistakenly
incorporate human genes into the virus genome, creating a recombinant
virus. When such viruses infect new cells, they also transfer a portion of the
previous host cell's DNA. Occasionally, viruses cross species barriers to infect
new species. For example, canine distemper, which usually doesn't infect cats,
has killed thousands of lions in the Serengeti plain of Africa. During such
cross-species infections, the new host may acquire genes that originally be-
longed to an unrelated species.

HOW DOES DNA RECOMBINATION OCCUR IN GENETIC ENGINEERING LABORATORIES?

The tools for creating and analyzing recombinant DNA molecules are con- 11
stantly being improved and simplified. What once could be done only in specialized university research labs is now routinely done in high school or even middle
school biology classes. Nevertheless, several key technologies continue to be
cornerstones of laboratory DNA recombination.

Restriction Enzymes Cut DNA at Specific Nucleotide Sequences

In the Case Study, you learned that hundreds of thousands of children go blind 12
each year because of insufficient vitamin A in their diets. Imagine that you
wanted to make a vitamin A-enriched rice plant that could provide the daily
requirement of vitamin A in one bowl of rice. How would you go about doing
this? One approach would be to find the genes needed to make vitamin A
from one organism and transfer these genes to the rice plant. How could you
find these genes? You would probably begin with an organism that naturally
made high levels of vitamin A. Daffodils are an example. But the daffodil
genome contains thousands and thousands of genes; which ones are the genes
you want?

An important tool for finding genes relies on the ability of **restriction** 13
enzymes to cut up large DNA molecules into smaller, more manageable
pieces. Many bacteria produce one or more restriction enzymes, which
cut through the DNA backbones wherever they encounter a particular
sequence of nucleotides. For example, the EcoRI restriction enzyme from
E. coli cuts through any DNA double helix wherever it encounters the following sequence:

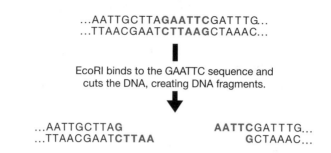

...AATTGCTTAGAATTCGATTTG...
...TTAACGAATCTTAAGCTAAAC...

EcoRI binds to the GAATTC sequence and
cuts the DNA, creating DNA fragments.

...AATTGCTTAG   AATTCGATTTG...
...TTAACGAATCTTAA   GCTAAAC...

Some enzymes (such as EcoRI) produce a staggered cut through the DNA double helix, leaving a small region of single-stranded DNA at the cut ends. Other enzymes produce blunt, double-stranded ends. In nature, restriction enzymes defend bacteria against viral infections by cutting apart invading viral DNA. The bacteria protect their own DNA by attaching methyl ($-CH_3$) groups to some of the DNA nucleotides. This modified DNA cannot be recognized by restriction enzymes. Researchers have isolated dozens of restriction enzymes and use them to cut DNA at specific sites, producing shorter DNA fragments. Incubating DNA with a restriction enzyme produces smaller DNA fragments with known sequences at their ends. Such fragments can be used to generate a collection of recombinant DNA called a "library."

Insertion of Foreign DNA into a Vector Can Produce a Recombinant DNA Library

To create a transgenic rice plant, we need large amounts of pure daffodil DNA 14 containing the genes we want. How can large amounts of DNA be produced? Scientists realized early on that they could harness plasmids and viruses to synthesize DNA. They added new features to the plasmids and viruses that made it easy to insert foreign DNA. Such specialized plasmids and viruses are called **vectors.** Biotechnology companies routinely develop and market new, improved vectors for research and other recombinant DNA uses. Researchers across the world also provide the vectors that they have developed to other researchers free of charge. When a recombinant plasmid is introduced into a bacterium, the bacterium replicates the recombinant plasmid whenever the bacterium divides. So, by simply growing the bacterium that contains the desired plasmid, the scientists can produce as much of the recombinant DNA as they need.

Inserting foreign DNA into a vector is simple (Fig. 4–3). For example, 15 DNA can be isolated from a daffodil, or any other organism, and cut with EcoRI, producing hundreds of thousands of small DNA fragments. Each daffodil DNA fragment has the same nucleotide sequence at its ends: TTAA on one end of each fragment, and AATT on the other end. The vector DNA is

         Biotechnology

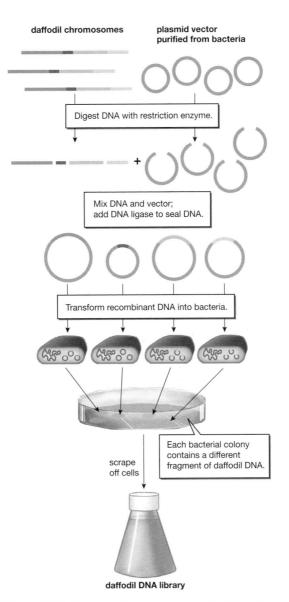

daffodil chromosomes

plasmid vector purified from bacteria

Digest DNA with restriction enzyme.

+

Mix DNA and vector; add DNA ligase to seal DNA.

Transform recombinant DNA into bacteria.

Each bacterial colony contains a different fragment of daffodil DNA.

scrape off cells

daffodil DNA library

Figure 4–3 Building a DNA library   Chromosomes, purified from the organism of interest, are cut with a restriction enzyme and mixed together with copies of a bacterial plasmid that has been cut with the same restriction enzyme. When the severed DNA molecules are mixed, each plasmid DNA joins with a piece of foreign DNA and the DNA backbones are joined together by DNA ligase, forming recombinant DNA molecules. The new recombinant DNA molecules are taken up into bacteria by transformation. The bacteria grow in dishes containing nutrients until they form colonies. Within each colony, each bacterial cell contains the same recombinant plasmid that carries the same fragment of foreign DNA. However, different colonies contain different recombinant plasmids with different pieces of foreign DNA. The bacterial cells are scraped up together into a test tube, creating a "DNA library."

Theme 4

also cut with EcoRI, so that the cut ends of the vector DNA are complementary to those of the daffodil DNA. Next, the vector DNA fragments are combined with the daffodil DNA fragments. DNA ligase, the enzyme used by cells during DNA replication to join DNA strands together, is added to the mixture. DNA ligase joins the vector DNA and daffodil DNA together, creating recombinant DNA molecules.

These daffodil/bacteria recombinant DNA molecules are then added to a   16
culture of bacteria. Via the process of transformation, each bacterium can take up a different recombinant DNA molecule. In this way, each bacterium contains a different portion of the daffodil genome carried in a vector. Growing a culture of these bacteria produces billions of copies of the various recombinant DNA molecules.

The entire process is analogous to taking a set of encyclopedias, cutting   17
the pages apart wherever you find the word *their* and then inserting the fragments into separate folders. Each folder contains just a small portion of the encyclopedia, but the collection of folders contains the entire encyclopedia. Similarly, each genetically modified bacterium contains just a small portion of the daffodil genome, but the collection of bacteria contains the entire daffodil genome. Such a collection is called a **DNA library.** This choice of name is unfortunate, since it brings to mind nicely organized and catalogued information. In contrast, a DNA library is typically a collection of billions of genetically modified bacteria in a single tiny test tube. Returning to the encyclopedia analogy, it's as if the folders were randomly stored in a box. To identify the daffodil genes needed to produce vitamin A, we would have to find the bacteria that have these genes and separate these bacteria from the millions of others that have other daffodil gene sequences. Isolation of a particular bacterial strain that carries a particular foreign gene from a DNA library is what scientists mean when they say that they have "cloned a gene."

HOW CAN RESEARCHERS IDENTIFY
SPECIFIC GENES?

As you may realize by now, creating recombinant DNA molecules is not a   18
major challenge for scientists. However, identifying the specific recombinant DNA molecules that contain the gene you are interested in can take years. The challenge of identifying a particular gene (that is, cloning the gene) is met in a variety of ways, three of which we describe next.

Restriction Fragment Length Polymorphisms
Can Be Used to Identify Genes

By the early 1980s libraries of human DNA had been created. Scientists   19
could use these libraries, together with restriction digestion and pedigrees, to identify specific genes using *restriction fragment length polymorphisms.*

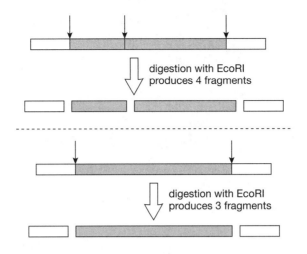

Recall that the DNA sequence of two individuals is very similar, but not identical. Some of these differences in DNA sequence create differences in the length of DNA fragments produced by digestion with a restriction enzyme. Two DNA double helices are depicted below. The location of each site recognized by EcoRI (GAATTC) is marked by an arrow. The DNA molecule in the bottom example has a single base pair difference that changes the middle GAATTC to CAATTC. This difference prevents EcoRI from cutting at that location.

Following digestion with EcoRI, the DNA molecule in the top example 20 will produce four smaller fragments; the one on the bottom will produce three smaller fragments. Differences in DNA sequence such as these that alter the size of restriction fragments are called **restriction fragment length polymorphisms,** or **RFLPs** for short.

RFLPs can be detected by separating restriction fragments via **gel elec-** 21 **trophoresis.** In this process, the mixture of DNA restriction fragments is loaded into an indented area, or well, in a slab of agar. Agar is a carbohydrate produced by seaweed that is also used to prepare various human foods. For example, the shiny "jelly" that surrounds a beautiful fruit torte is often made of agar. The agar slab is called a *gel.* When an electrical current is applied to the gel, the negatively charged DNA fragments move toward the positively charged electrode. The smaller fragments can slip through the spaces between the agar molecules more easily than the larger fragments. So, the smaller fragments move more rapidly, leaving larger fragments behind. Eventually the DNA fragments are separated by size, forming distinct bands on the gel.

How are restriction fragment length polymorphisms useful to re- 22 searchers? If an RFLP is inherited along with the gene for a particular trait, then the sequence of nucleotides in the RFLP must be close to the gene of in-

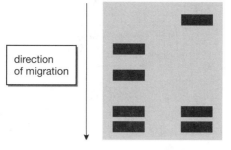

direction of migration

Larger fragments move more slowly; smaller fragments move more rapidly.

terest. The RFLP may even be within the gene! All we need to do is identify the bacteria in the DNA library that contain the RFLP DNA.

One way to identify bacteria carrying a specific gene or other DNA sequence takes advantage of DNA probes. A **DNA probe** is a short sequence of single-stranded DNA that can form base pairs with the DNA that we seek. The DNA probe has been modified, often by adding a radioactive atom, so that we can easily detect its presence. The bacteria that comprise our daffodil DNA library are spread out on solid growth medium and allowed to grow into separate colonies. Each colony is formed from a single cell that divided multiple times until it formed a mound of identical cells. By placing a filter paper on top of the colonies, we can transfer some of the cells from each colony onto the filter. (The plate with the remaining cells is stored so that bacterial colonies in which we are interested can be recovered later.) The cells on the filter are broken open so that the DNA probe can enter. After bathing these broken cells with the DNA probe and washing away excess, the probe will remain only in some of the cells. Specifically, the probe will be present only in cells containing daffodil DNA that can form base pairs with the DNA probe. We can detect cells that contain a radioactive DNA probe by laying a piece of X-ray film on top of the filter. The radioactivity in the DNA probe exposes the film, producing a dark spot on top of the bacterial colonies that we seek. We can then go back to the original plate and pick the colonies of interest, grow the cells, and analyze the DNA that they contain.

Genes from One Organism Can Be Identified Based on Similarity to Related Genes in Other Organisms

Once a gene has been cloned from any organism, it can be used to search for related genes in other organisms. Consider homeotic genes, which are extremely important for proper development of animal body structures. One of the first homeotic genes to be cloned was a fruit fly gene called *Antennapedia*. Mutations in this gene cause the antenna of fruit flies to develop abnormally. Instead of antenna, these flies develop legs! Much to the surprise of fruit fly researchers, the use of the *Antennapedia* gene as a probe identified a large class of related genes

Biotechnology

in other species, including humans. All of these genes share some sequence similarities, and most appear to serve as "master control switches" in early development. Thus, studying flies with legs growing where their antenna should be led to a much more complete understanding of early development in all animals.

Genes Can Be Identified Based on Their Protein Product

Some vectors are designed so that the inserted foreign gene is transcribed and translated in the transformed cell. If researchers wish to clone the gene encoding a particular enzyme, they can use the *protein's* activity to identify cells that contain that gene. For example, the gene encoding a key enzyme in cholesterol synthesis was cloned because yeast cells with high levels of this protein become resistant to a drug that inhibits the enzyme's activity. Only those cells with high levels of the enzyme (and consequently extra copies of the gene) can survive in the presence of the drug. 25

WHAT ARE SOME APPLICATIONS OF BIOTECHNOLOGY?

Once a gene has been cloned (isolated), it can be put to a variety of uses. Some applications of genes in biotechnology are described next. 26

Cloned Genes Provide Enough DNA for Gene Sequencing

After cloning, the exact nucleotide sequence of a gene can be determined. The most commonly used method relies on a variation of the polymerase chain reaction, a method that produces large quantities of specific segments of DNA in a test tube. This process, called the **polymerase chain reaction (PCR)** technique, does not require a living organism (Fig. 4–4). Developed in 1986 by Kary B. Mullis of the Cetus Corporation, PCR allows billions of copies of selected genes to be made faster and more cheaply than they can be grown in bacteria. PCR is so elegant and so crucial to continued advances in molecular biology that it earned Mullis a share in the Nobel Prize for Chemistry in 1993. 27

How Does the Polymerase Chain Reaction Provide Large Quantities of a Specific DNA Segment? The PCR technique is based on the activity of DNA polymerase, the enzyme that synthesizes new DNA strands. During DNA replication, enzymes unwind the double-stranded helix and each strand is used as a template to produce its complementary strand. DNA polymerase links up appropriate nucleotides to form each new single-stranded molecule of DNA. PCR requires three major components: DNA containing the nucleotide sequence that you want to synthesize, two short sequences of DNA called *primers,* and DNA polymerase. The primers form base pairs with the original DNA molecule, flanking the stretch of DNA to be synthesized: one 28

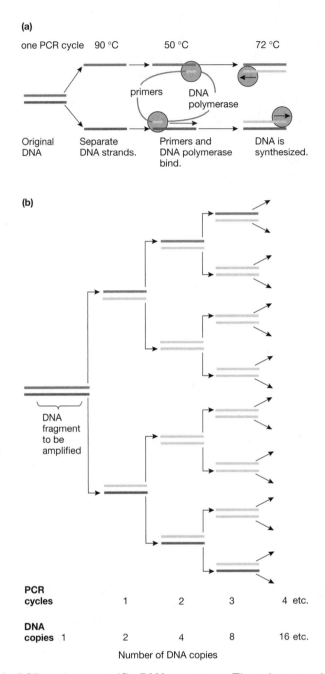

(a)

one PCR cycle   90 °C   50 °C   72 °C

primers   DNA
polymerase

| Original DNA | Separate DNA strands. | Primers and DNA polymerase bind. | DNA is synthesized. |

(b)

DNA fragment to be amplified

| PCR cycles | | 1 | 2 | 3 | 4 etc. |

| DNA copies | 1 | 2 | 4 | 8 | 16 etc. |

Number of DNA copies

Figure 4–4 PCR copies a specific DNA sequence The polymerase chain reaction consists of a series of 20 to 30 cycles. *(a)* During each cycle, ① the DNA strands are separated by heat, ② primers form base pairs with the target DNA that will be copied, and ③ complementary DNA molecules are synthesized by a heat resistant DNA polymerase enzyme. *(b)* After each cycle, the amount of the target DNA doubles.

234   **Biotechnology**

primer binds at the "beginning" of the DNA sequence to be synthesized, and the other primer binds to the "end" of the DNA sequence to be synthesized. DNA polymerase will synthesize the DNA that lies between the positions where the primers bind.

29 PCR involves the following basic steps, which are repeated for as many cycles as needed to generate sufficient copies of the DNA segment (usually about 30 cycles):

1. DNA is separated into single strands by heating to about 90°C.
2. When the temperature is lowered to about 50°C, the two primers form complementary base pairs with the original DNA strands.
3. Heat-resistant DNA polymerase (isolated from bacteria that thrive in hot springs or hot ocean vents) joins up nucleotides, synthesizing new DNA strands that are complementary to those in the original DNA.

30 With appropriate mixtures of primers, free nucleotides, and DNA polymerase, a PCR machine automatically runs heating and cooling cycles over and over again. Each cycle takes only a few minutes, so PCR can produce billions of copies of a gene or DNA segment in a single afternoon, starting, if necessary, from a single molecule of DNA (see Fig. 4–4). The DNA produced by PCR can then be examined for RFLPs, used to generate new recombinant DNA molecules, or used for many other purposes.

How Do Researchers Use the Polymerase Chain Reaction to Reveal 31
the Sequence of a Specific DNA Segment? A variation on the standard PCR reaction can be used to determine the nucleotide sequence of DNA. First, instead of using a pair of primers, only one primer is added to the PCR reaction mixture. This modification allows DNA polymerase to synthesize only one DNA strand, specifically the DNA strand that is complementary to the primer. Second, a fraction of each nucleotide added to the reaction is labeled with a fluorescent molecule, or tag. Each type of nucleotide (A, T, G, and C) is labeled with a different-colored tag. During PCR, DNA polymerase incorporates complementary nucleotides into the growing DNA strand as usual. If DNA polymerase adds an unlabeled nucleotide to the DNA strand that it is synthesizing, it continues along and adds the next complementary nucleotide to the growing chain. However, when DNA polymerase adds one of the fluorescently labeled nucleotides, it stops synthesis of the new DNA strand. As a result, this modified PCR reaction produces a series of single-stranded DNA fragments, each fragment one nucleotide longer than the next. Whether the terminal nucleotide is A, T, G, or C can be determined by its color. When the fragments are separated by gel electrophoresis, an automated sensor records the color of the nucleotide at the end of each increasingly longer DNA fragment. In this way, the nucleotide sequence complementary to the original DNA strand can be determined.

Why is knowing the nucleotide sequence of a gene useful? For one thing, 32 the nucleotide sequence determines the amino acid sequence of the encoded protein. Once the protein is known, its potential function in the cell can often be deduced. DNA sequences are also essential for diagnosing genetic diseases. For example, scientists determined the nucleotide sequence of one allele of the cystic fibrosis gene in 1989. Within a very short time, researchers had also determined the sequence of the alleles of this gene found in cystic fibrosis patients. Most of the patients had a defective allele that was missing three nucleotides. With this knowledge, researchers developed methods for rapidly determining whether an individual is a heterozygous carrier of this allele. Such genetic testing can also tell parents whether an unborn child has inherited two copies of the mutant cystic fibrosis allele and will thus develop the disease. Genetic tests are available for other inherited diseases, including sickle-cell anemia. In the U.S., state legislation mandates that all newborns be tested for several genetic diseases, including phenylketonuria and hypothyroidism. Most states also mandate testing for sickle-cell anemia and related hemoglobin defects. Our ability to diagnose infections ranging from tuberculosis to HIV also increasingly relies on genetic tests: these tests determine whether DNA from the disease-causing bacterium or virus is present in the patient.

In one of the most remarkable instances of cooperation and collaboration 33 in modern biology, scientists worldwide have essentially completed the ultimate DNA sequencing task—to sequence the entire human genome, described in more detail later in this chapter.

DNA Fingerprinting Facilitates Genetic Detection on Many Fronts

DNA fingerprinting is a type of RFLP analysis that has rapidly emerged as a 34 tool for genetic inquiry in many different contexts. Just as each person has a unique set of fingerprints, each person's DNA produces a unique set of restriction fragments. The pattern of these fragments creates a unique "DNA fingerprint" that can be used to identify an individual. DNA fingerprinting has proven extremely useful for establishing the innocence of suspected criminals, both before and after trials. For example, in the last ten years, DNA fingerprinting has shown that at least ten death row inmates were actually innocent of the crimes for which they had received the death penalty. In 2000, several bills were introduced in Congress proposing legislation to guarantee a convicted criminal's right to such DNA tests.

DNA fingerprinting also has dozens of other uses: it enables us to test po- 35 tential organ donors for compatibility with a particular patient, to monitor pedigree claims for livestock, to examine relationships among ancient human populations, and to determine whether endangered species laws are being complied with. For example, DNA fingerprinting of whale meat purchased in a Japanese market showed that some of the meat came from endangered whale species; the harvesting of these species was prohibited by international laws. DNA fingerprinting of a 5000-year-old frozen corpse found in the Alps in 1991 showed that this "Ice Man" was genetically related to people living today in northern Europe.

Genetic Engineering Is Revolutionizing Agriculture

Genetic engineering is rapidly replacing traditional breeding techniques to produce 36 improved strains of crops. Transgenic plants can be produced in several ways. One commonly used technique involves inserting recombinant DNA via a plasmid (called the *Ti* plasmid) found in a certain soil bacterium that infects plants. Alternately, genes can be directly inserted into plant cells using a "gene gun" that blasts DNA-coated particles directly into cells. The transgenic tobacco plant contains a firefly gene that encodes the enzyme luciferase. When this enzyme cleaves its substrate, it produces light. The plant's eerie glow clearly demonstrates that the firefly gene has been incorporated successfully into the plant genome.

Production of transgenic crops (or animals) requires approval by the U.S. 37 Department of Agriculture, the Environmental Protection Agency, and/or the Food and Drug Administration. These agencies also monitor compliance with

Table 4–1   Genetically Engineered Crops with USDA Approval

Genetically Engineered Trait	Potential Advantage	Examples of Bio-engineered Crops Receiving USDA Approval Between 1992 and 2000
Resistance to herbicide	Application of herbicide kills weeds, but not crop plants, producing higher crop yields.	beet, canola, corn, cotton, flax, potato, rice, soybean, tomato
Resistance to pests	Crop plants suffer less damage from insects, producing higher crop yields.	corn, cotton, potato
Resistance to disease	Plants are less prone to infection by viruses, bacteria, or fungi, producing higher crop yields.	papaya, potato, squash
Sterile	Transgenic plants cannot cross with wild varieties, making them safer for the environment and more economically productive for the seed companies that produce them.	chicory, corn
Altered oil content	Oils can be made healthier for human consumption or can be made similar to more expensive oils (such as palm or coconut).	canola, soybean
Altered ripening	Fruits can be more easily shipped with less damage, producing higher returns for farmer.	tomato

governmental regulation of transgenic organisms. As of November 2000, more than 5000 field trials of transgenic crops had taken place. Based on these tests, 73 applications for commercial production of transgenic crops had been examined by the USDA. Of these, 52 varieties have been deemed safe for commercial production: these crops can now be grown and crossed with no special government control or oversight. Transgenic crops currently approved for commercial growth are listed in Table 4-1.

Genetic Engineering Can Make Plants Resistant to Diseases, 38
Insects, and Weeds At present, the largest agricultural application of genetic engineering lies in producing crops that are more resistant to diseases, insects, and weeds. Scientists often incorporate genes into the crop's genome that allow crop plants to resist the effects of herbicides. Thus, herbicides can be applied to fields after the crop plants have sprouted to kill competing weeds. In January 2001 the U.S. Department of Agriculture estimated that 8% of the corn, 57% of the soybeans, and 46% of the cotton grown in the U.S. was an herbicide-resistant variety. To create resistance to insects, the most common strategy is to incorporate genes from a bacterium (*Bacillus thuringiensis,* or Bt) that code for the synthesis of a natural insecticide called Bt toxin. The Bt toxin gene has been introduced into more than 50 crop plants, including corn, soybeans, and potatoes. Genes that confer resistance to plant viruses have also been engineered into plants such as squash.

Genetic Engineering May Produce Plants with Therapeutic Benefits 39
In addition to producing plants that can resist herbicides and pests, some genetic engineers are trying to create plants that can serve as easy, cheap vaccines. Scientists have engineered potatoes that might be eaten raw, in small amounts, to produce resistance to hepatitis, type I diabetes, cholera, and a strain of *Escherichia coli* (*E. coli*) bacteria that causes serious diarrhea. Attempts are under way to use bananas instead of potatoes, since they are much tastier than raw potatoes and might be fed to infants. Such a banana vaccine against the dangerous *E. coli* strain would be particularly valuable in developing nations, where millions of infants and children die each year of diarrhea as a result of *E. coli* infections.

Genetic Engineering May Improve Domesticated Animals To create 40
transgenic animals, the cloned DNA is injected into a fertilized egg and, in the case of mammals, returned to a surrogate mother to allow it to develop. The resulting offspring are tested to see if they express the foreign gene, and those that do are bread with each other to produce animals homozygous for the foreign gene.

Progress in the genetic engineering of livestock has been much slower and 41
less successful than that in crop plants. For example, in an attempt to produce faster-growing, leaner hogs, researchers transferred human and cow growth-hormone genes into pigs. On a high-protein diet, the pigs grew faster, but they developed arthritis, ulcers, and sterility and died prematurely. Growth-hormone genes from rainbow trout have been introduced into salmon, carp, and catfish,

causing them to grow 40% faster than normal. These fish are not yet available for human consumption, and many question the value of such animals.

Will Biotechnology Create a Real 'Jurassic Park?'

Modern techniques for DNA analysis are yielding information long buried in 42 the DNA of extinct, even fossilized animals and plants. Indeed, DNA has been isolated from a 15-million-year-old magnolia leaf, a 20- to 40-million-year-old bee, and a 120-million-year-old weevil. Isolation and analysis of DNA from Neanderthal skeletons have demonstrated that they are unlikely to have contributed genetic information to modern humans.

Given all these amazing reports, might dinosaur DNA also be retrieved 43 and used to clone a dinosaur? To date, no one has succeeded in retrieving DNA from dinosaur remains. Even if dinosaur DNA were recovered, it is likely that the DNA would be too fragmented to allow us to reconstruct a complete set of dinosaur genes. Recent attempts to clone a wooly mammoth have captured headlines and imaginations through the world, but, as yet, no one has revived a long-extinct species using genetic engineering. In contrast, it appears that ancient microbes have actually been revived without the cloning steps. For example, fungi from grass lining the 5000-year-old shoes of the "Ice Man" appear to have been successfully isolated and cultured. Researchers have even reported that they have cultured bacteria that had been trapped for 250 million years within a salt crystal taken from a New Mexico salt mine!

WHAT ARE SOME MEDICAL USES OF BIOTECHNOLOGY?

Biotechnology applied to the human genome promises to have a profound and 44 growing impact on human health. One increasingly available application is the use of this technology to screen for genetic defects. Potential parents can learn if they are carriers of a genetic disorder: an embryo can be diagnosed early in a pregnancy. In the following sections we discuss some other important medical applications of biotechnology for today and tomorrow.

Knock-out Mice Provide Models of Human Genetic Diseases

Once a gene has been cloned, scientists can use the information to make 45 "knock-out" mice. Creation of knock-out mice combines recombinant DNA techniques, cell culturing, and manipulation of early-stage embryos, followed by selective breeding. The result is a mouse strain in which both alleles of a normal gene are replaced with nonfunctional copies. One important use of knock-out mice is to create animal models of human diseases, including cystic fibrosis, sickle-cell anemia, Huntington disease, cancers, Alzheimer's disease, and mad cow disease. These genetically engineered animals enable researchers to test the safety and value of new drugs or other treatments before they are used on human patients. Hundreds of different knock-out mice strains are currently available for research.

Genetic Engineering Allows Production of Therapeutic Proteins

Using giant vats of bacteria or yeast that carry and express human genes, 46 biotechnology firms generate large quantities of human proteins. The first human protein made by recombinant DNA technology was insulin. Prior to 1982, when recombinant human insulin was first licensed for use, diabetics used insulin extracted from the pancreas of cattle or pigs slaughtered for meat. Although these insulin proteins are very similar to human insulin, the slight differences caused an allergic reaction in about 5% of diabetics. This problem is avoided with the recombinant human insulin. Recombinant human growth hormone became available in 1985. Some of the other human proteins produced by recombinant DNA technology are listed in Table 4-2.

In addition to producing human proteins in bacteria and yeast, pharma- 47 ceutical companies also engineer cows, goats, pigs, rabbits, rats, and sheep to produce various therapeutic human proteins. For example, people who inherit a potentially fatal form of emphysema have a defective gene for the production of the protein alpha-1-antitrypsin (AAT), which they must take as a drug. The gene for the production of human AAT has now been introduced into sheep, who then secrete AAT into their milk—as much as 35 grams per liter (just over 1 ounce per quart). This protein may also help prevent lung damage in individuals with cystic fibrosis. In February 2000, clinical trials of this recombinant protein for treatment of patients with cystic fibrosis were under way.

Human Gene Therapy Is Just Beginning

More than 4000 diseases in humans, including cystic fibrosis, sickle-cell anemia, 48 and Huntington disease, result from defects in a single gene. Many more diseases, such as cancer, heart disease, arthritis, and asthma, involve impaired functioning of multiple genes. Gene therapy offers potential treatments for these diseases, as well as infections such as AIDS. Thus, the promise of human gene therapy is enormous. The challenges are equally large.

One major challenge to successful gene therapy is to deliver the func- 49 tional gene into a large number of the patient's cells. Several approaches for getting a patient's cells to take up DNA are used. Even if the challenge of getting large numbers of cells to incorporate the gene is solved, gene therapy faces another major challenge: The newly incorporated gene must be efficiently expressed so that the gene will produce enough of its protein to help the patient overcome the disease.

In the U.S., more than 418 clinical gene therapy trials involving more than 50 2000 patients were under way or had been completed by early 2001. Gene ther-

Table 4–2 Examples of Currently Used Products Produced by Recombinant DNA Methods

		Example		
Type of Product	*Purpose*	*Product*	*Year Approved*	*Genetic Engineering*	*Product Used as:*
Human hormones	Used in treatment of diabetes, growth deficiency	Humulin™ (human insulin)	1982	Human gene inserted into bacteria	Purified protein
Human cytokines (regulate immune system function)	Used in bone marrow transplants and to treat cancers and viral infections, including hepatitis and genital warts	Leukine™ (granulocyte-macrophage colony stimulating factor)	1991	Human gene inserted into yeast	Purified protein
Antibodies (immune system proteins)	Used to fight infections, cancers, diabetes, organ rejection, and multiple sclerosis	Herceptin™ (antibodies to HER2 protein, expressed at high levels in some breast cancer cells)	1998	Recombinant antibody genes inserted into cultured hamster cell line	Purified protein
Viral proteins	Used to generate vaccines against viral diseases and for diagnosing viral infections	Energiz-B™ (Hepatitis B vaccine)	1989	Viral gene inserted into yeast	Purified protein
Enzymes	Used in treatment of heart attacks, cystic fibrosis, and other diseases, and production of cheeses and detergents	Activase™ (tissue plasminogen activator)	1987	Human gene inserted into cultured hamster cell line	Purified enzyme

apy has been most successful for a few children with a rare genetic disorder called *SCID (severe combined immunodeficiency)*. Such children do not have a functional ADA gene, which encodes an enzyme called adenosine deaminase (ADA). Without this enzyme, individuals cannot develop a functioning immune system. Until the 1980s, children with SCID died in infancy or early childhood, unable to fight off infections. At that time, scientists developed an injectable version of the ADA enzyme prepared from cattle. Bone marrow transplants were also made available for treatment, provided a compatible donor could be found. In 1990 the first test of human gene therapy was performed on a SCID patient, 4-year-old Ashanti DeSilva. Some of her white blood cells were removed, genetically altered with a retrovirus containing a functional ADA gene, and then returned to her bloodstream. By late in 2000, at least 18 children in five countries had received similar gene therapy for SCID. French scientists are hopeful that two children have been permanently cured by this therapy. Other patients are not cured but continue to require injections of ADA.

The limited success of gene therapy has been disappointing. Even more 51 sobering, at least one individual has died as a direct result of his participation in a gene therapy trial. In September 1999 Jesse Gelsinger, an 18-year-old from Arizona, suffered a fatal immune reaction to the virus used in a gene therapy trial. This fatality has caused the National Institutes of Health to increase their scrutiny of all gene therapy trials currently under way. Nevertheless, most researchers in the field remain optimistic that gene therapy approaches to treating human diseases will eventually prove highly successful.

The Human Genome Project Has Completed a Working Draft of the Entire Human Genome

The Human Genome Project was launched in 1990 by the National Institutes 52 of Health (NIH) and the Department of Energy (DOE). The project has become an international effort to determine the sequence of nucleotides in each of the roughly 35,000 human genes. Initially, the time, effort, and cost (an estimated $3 billion) of sequencing the human genome seemed daunting. Technological improvements made this goal attainable, much more rapidly than researchers originally imagined possible. In February 2001 two groups of scientists involved in the Human Genome Project published independent working drafts of the human genome sequence. Data from the federally funded Human Genome Project is made available to all researchers, free of charge, via Web sites maintained by the National Center for Biotechnology Information. The technology and information resulting from the Human Genome Project is hastening completion of similar projects under way to determine the DNA sequence of chickens, dogs, cattle, corn, rice, swine, barley, and other organisms. This information will join the already completed sequences of baker's yeast, fruit flies, a roundworm, and about 30 different bacterial species. Such vast amounts of information allow novel approaches in biology that were undreamed of just several years ago.

WHAT ARE SOME ETHICAL IMPLICATIONS OF HUMAN BIOTECHNOLOGY?

As a direct or indirect result of the Human Genome Project, the ability to 53 screen for human diseases is increasing at an exponential rate. One company has developed a technology that can simultaneously analyze DNA from hundreds of patients, looking for mutations in several genes at once. Physicians will soon have access to dozens of easily administered tests that will reveal whether a patient carries a specific gene. These new powers demand a new set of decisions, both ethical and economic, by individuals, physicians, and society.

Genetic Tests for Cystic Fibrosis and Inherited Forms of Breast Cancer Illustrate Potential Problems

Cystic fibrosis (CF) is the most common fatal genetic disease in the U.S. Ap- 54 proximately 850 babies are born in the U.S. each year with cystic fibrosis, most to families with no known history of this disease. To reduce the number of these babies, a 1997 advisory panel of the National Institutes of Health recommended that testing for CF be offered to all couples who consider having a baby. If this policy is adopted, many couples who have never heard of CF will learn that they both carry a copy of the CF allele and that their chances are 1 in 4 of producing a child with CF. Will they get the medical information and counseling they need to deal with the results? They will need to be educated about the symptoms, treatments, and monetary and emotional costs, about the "genetic lottery" they are about to enter, and about their options. Should they remain childless or adopt? Should they conceive and then use prenatal genetic diagnosis to determine whether their child will develop CF? If tests are positive, then what? Is abortion acceptable to the couple? If not, they will give birth to a child who will struggle for breath and be hospitalized repeatedly for respiratory infections despite daily doses of antibiotics. The child will need to lie down and be pounded thoroughly on the chest and back twice a day to dislodge the thick buildup of mucus and will require a special diet fortified with digestive enzymes. Despite these treatments, their child will have a 50% chance of dying before he or she reaches age 30. The costs will be staggering. Should society bear these costs for a family who knowingly takes this risk? Are insurance companies justified in denying coverage for CF treatment to the children of parents who both knowingly carry the CF gene?

    Further dilemmas are posed by genetic tests that can indicate an individ- 55 ual has an elevated risk of developing Alzheimer's disease, breast cancer, or ovarian cancer. The presence of the gene does not condemn a woman to cancer, for example, but it does mean that her chances of developing cancer are very high. Some women find living with this "genetic time bomb," and the risk of passing it to their children, very distressing. Many have chosen not to have the test. Others, finding that they carry the gene, have made the painful decision to have both breasts and/or both ovaries surgically removed. Genetic counselors are concerned that women who find they have not inherited the defective gene might become lax about regular screening procedures: these women still have the same risks as others for non-inherited types of breast cancer. Many women who choose to be tested for the gene do so anonymously or under a false name to prevent the information from reaching their insurance companies.

The increasing availability and use of tests for genetic diseases raise major 56 concerns about genetic discrimination by insurance companies and employers. Many people worry that, under pressure to hold down rising costs, insurance companies will require information about genetic diseases and will use this information as a basis for denying or restricting the availability of life insurance or health insurance. Cases are on record in which companies terminated or denied health insurance based on required genetic tests, or family history of genetic diseases, such as Huntington disease. As more genetic information becomes available and treatments become more costly, this trend is sure to intensify. State and federal legislatures are devising new laws to address these issues. By April 1999 at least 24 states had passed laws prohibiting genetic discrimination. Thus far, no federal laws dealing with genetic information have been passed, although several have been introduced in the House of Representatives or the Senate.

Sickle-Cell Anemia and Tay-Sachs Disease Illustrate the Hazards and Benefits of Genetic Screening Programs

An example of the hazards of widespread genetic screening without adequate 57 education occurred in the 1970s when a major screening program for **sickle-cell anemia** was launched and, in some areas, even made mandatory. Although the intentions were good, the results were misused through ignorance and prejudice. Healthy carriers of the sickle-cell trait (most of whom are African American) were led to believe they were sick. Some African-American carriers were denied insurance; others were blocked from admission to the U.S. Air Force Academy or from jobs as flight attendants—on the inaccurate assumption that they were more likely to be affected by the lack of oxygen at high altitudes. Suggestions that carriers (who make up almost 7% of the African-American population) should avoid having children led to fears that the testing was intended as a means of reducing the numbers of this racial minority.

Testing for **Tay-Sachs disease,** which is prevalent among Jews of East- 58 ern European descent, is a contrasting success story. Tay-Sachs is a fatal degenerative disease in which an initially normal infant gradually loses mental and physical abilities, becomes blind and deaf, and dies in early childhood. This disease is recessive, like sickle-cell anemia, and results from deficiency of enzymes that regulate lipid breakdown in the brain. It is such a devastating illness that few people will knowingly give birth to such a child. Voluntary genetic testing for Tay-Sachs within the Jewish community, coupled with prenatal testing and careful genetic counseling, has dramatically reduced the incidence of this fatal disorder.

The Potential to Clone Humans Raises Further Ethical Issues

The cloning of Dolly the sheep from the nucleus of an adult cell introduced into 59 the cytoplasm of an egg led to a flurry of debate and proposed legislation regarding human cloning. There are no known technical barriers to the eventual development of human cloning. Are there ethical barriers that should restrict this technology to nonhuman species? One argument is that there is no valid reason to clone humans. Perhaps a small number of infertile couples would want to perpetuate their genes in this way, but there are already so many reproductive options (including sperm or egg donors) that cloning would not meet a pressing need. On the other hand, such technology might allow permanent correction of genetic defects in the couple's children. For some people, the possibility that cloning would be used by unscrupulous individuals in positions of power to perpetuate themselves or to create copies of certain people to fill specific functions raises the specter of a "Brave New World" type of society. Some argue that biological uniqueness is a fundamental human right and intrinsic to human dignity.

Countering these arguments are those who point out that identical twins 60 are more similar to one another than clones would ever be, because twins share not only the same genes, but also cytoplasmic factors from the same original egg cell, the same uterine environment, and the same home environment and upbringing. An individual trying to produce a self-copy might be sorely disappointed at the differences these environmental variables (not to mention growing up in a different generation) might produce.

Human cloning is illegal in England and Norway, but not in the U.S. How- 61 ever, at present, federally funded U.S. researchers are prohibited from using human embryos in research, a necessary step in human cloning. In contrast, privately funded research in the U.S. does not operate under these restrictions and has used human embryos discarded after in-vitro fertilization. These studies have succeeded in isolating embryonic stem cells, the precursors for all types of adult tissues. These embryonic stem cells might be used to clone humans, but they also might be used to regenerate adult tissues, such as bone marrow, hearts, and lungs. For example, recent success in using embryonic stem cells to regrow nerve cells offers hope of treating paralysis. Clearly, advances in our understanding and ability to manipulate the genes of humans and other species threaten to outpace the ability of society to understand and utilize the resulting technologies effectively. The next decade will see considerable upheaval as society struggles to come to grips with this new knowledge and the power that accompanies it.

Teaching an Old Grain New Tricks

Creating a rice strain with high levels of vitamin A precursors in their seeds was not a simple task. In fact, many scientists were skeptical that it could be done at all. However, Ingo Potrykus, a Swiss researcher, and Peter Beyer, a German researcher, teamed up and, with their students, inserted three genes into the rice genome. Two genes came from daffodils and one from a bacterium. Regulatory DNA sequences were included with the genes to control their expression, so that the inserted genes would be turned on in the rice seeds. The resulting genetically modified rice plants produce enough beta-carotene to prevent vitamin A deficiency if three bowls of the rice are eaten each day. The research to produce the golden rice was funded by non-profit organizations, including The Rockefeller Institute, the European Community Biotech Program, and the Swiss Federal Office for Education and Science. Seeds for the bioengineered rice are being supplied free of charge to agricultural research centers in developing countries. Local scientists or farmers can cross the bioengineered strain with their local rice strains to produce more nutritious rice that will grow well in local conditions.

Many people herald this golden rice as the first in a wave of bioengineered crops that will have higher nutritional values. Some even argue that these crops will help decrease the suspicion with which some consumers view biotechnology. Up till now, most bioengineering of crops has focused on meeting the needs of the farmer and farming industry. For example, pest-resistant potatoes indirectly benefit the consumer by allowing decreased amounts of pesticides to be used in farming. These same potatoes directly benefit the farmer, who obtains increased yields with less cost, and the biotech company that provides the seed potatoes for planting. Availability of a bioengineered crop that might prevent death and blindness in hundreds of thousands of impoverished children would seem more difficult for consumers to oppose.

Many consumers are skeptical of the safety of genetically modified animals and plants. Take a scientific approach to this issue: Make a list of the potential negative consequences of genetic engineering of crops and livestock. State each potential negative consequence as a hypothesis, for example, "The introduction of genes from another species may. . . ." Describe an experiment that would test that hypothesis. What evidence would disprove the hypothesis for each potential negative consequence on your list?

FOR MORE INFORMATION

Beardsley, T. "Vital Data," *Scientific American*, March 1996. Discusses the Human Genome Project and the problems and prospects of the tests for genetic diseases that are arising as a spin-off of this project.

Collins, F. S. and others. "New Goals for the U.S. Human Genome Project: 1998–2003." *Science,* October 1998. Explains goals of human genome project, including those involving bioethics.

Fackelmann. K. A. "DNA Dilemmas." *Science News,* December 17, 1994. Uses case histories to explore the ethical controversies surrounding human applications of genetic engineering.

Gibbs, N. "Baby. It's You! And You, and You . . ." *Time,* February 19, 2001. How close are we to cloning a human?

Gibbs, W. W. "Plantibodies." *Scientific American,* November 1997. Clinical trials using human antibodies engineered into corn began in 1998; the target was tooth decay!

Gura, T. "New Genes Boost Rice Nutrients." *Science,* August 1999. Explanation of how rice was genetically engineered to produce vitamin A precursors.

Karapelou, J. "Gene Therapy: Special Delivery." *Discover,* January 1996. Describes several methods on trial for delivering therapeutic genes into human cells.

Langridge, W. H. R. "Edible Vaccines." *Scientific American,* September 2000. Current state of attempts to develop plants that produce vaccines or treatments for diseases.

Lanza, R. P., Dresser, B. L., and Damiani, P. "Cloning Noah's Ark." *Scientific American,* November 2000. Using domestic animals as surrogate mothers for endangered species provides some hope for staving off extinction.

Marvier, M. "Ecology of Transgenic Crops." *American Scientist,* March/April 2001. A thoughtful article that weighs the benefits, risks, and uncertainties of bioengineered crops.

Miller, R. V. "Bacterial Gene Swapping in Nature." *Scientific American,* January 1998. How likely is it that genes introduced into bioengineered organisms might be inadvertently transferred to wild organisms?

Mirsky, S., and Rennie, J. "What Cloning Means for Gene Therapy." *Scientific American,* June 1997. Could human cloning technology help permanently repair genetic defects?

Roberts. L. "To Test or Not to Test." *Science,* January 1990. Should the entire childbearing population be screened for carriers of cystic fibrosis?

Ronald, P. C. "Making Rice Disease-Resistant." *Scientific American,* November 1997. Rice, a staple crop for millions of people, has finally been engineered for disease resistance.

Scientific American, June 1997. A special issue devoted to the prospects of human gene therapy.

Travis, J. "Cystic Fibrosis Controversy." *Science News,* May 10, 1997. Might gene therapy in the womb help CF patients?

SELECTION 1 QUESTIONS

Comprehension and Analysis

1. What is biotechnology?
2. What is genetic engineering? What are three major goals of genetic engineering?
3. What are three ways DNA recombination can occur in nature?
4. Can DNA be transformed/recombined in laboratories? Why is this important?
5. What are two major applications of biotechnology?
6. In the Case Study and Case Study Revisited, "Teaching an Old Grain New Tricks," the authors describe a new bioengineered crop—golden rice. They conclude that the availability of this crop "would seem more difficult for consumers to oppose" than previous biotech crops. Explain their reasoning. Do you agree with their reasoning? Can you think of any reason(s) why some people might still oppose the crop?

Reflect and Connect

7. What do you think are two of the potential benefits and two of the potential risks of biotechnology? Please give examples to illustrate your answer.

SELECTION 2   BIOTECH AND BETTER HEALTH

COUNCIL FOR BIOTECHNOLOGY INFORMATION

The Council for Biotechnology Information was launched in 2000 by several leading biotechnology companies and trade associations "to improve understanding and acceptance of biotechnology by collecting and communicating balanced, credible and science-based information about this new tool that promises to contribute so many benefits to people all over the world." This selection is posted on the Council's Web Site, http://www.whybiotech.com.

AN IDEA TO THINK ABOUT

Humanitarian groups estimate that there are 840 million chronically malnourished people in developing nations. There are also chronically hungry and malnourished people in America and other developed nations. What strategies can you envision to help reduce hunger and malnutrition around the world?

WORDS TO KNOW

***Bt* (¶7)**—designation that precedes the name of a crop (e.g., *Bt* cotton, *Bt* corn, *Bt* soybeans) to indicate that crop has been genetically modified with the bacterium *Bacillus thuringiensis* to create a resistance to insects

American Phytopathological Society (APS) (¶21)—APS is a nonprofit, professional, scientific organization dedicated to the study and control of plant diseases

Nobel Peace Prize Laureate Norman Borlaug says, "the first essential component of social justice is adequate food." Increasingly, he and many others say plant biotechnology is one of several tools that can be used to produce not only adequate food, but food that is better for you. 1

Plant biotechnology researchers are working to improve health in two important ways: 2

- By making more food available to meet basic dietary needs.
- By making better foods that are high in vitamins and have other healthy traits.

HOW PLANT BIOTECHNOLOGY CAN IMPROVE HUMAN HEALTH HAS A LOT TO DO WITH WHERE YOU LIVE

In the developing world, where 840 million are chronically malnourished, the challenge often is just getting people enough calories.[1] Experts in those countries say that biotech crop advances—hardier crops that can ward off insect pests and viruses—could go far in helping small subsistence farmers in southern Africa and Asia. 3

"Biotechnology is an essential tool for Africa to achieve food security," says Michael Mbwille, a Tanzanian pediatrician who's seen malnutrition—which affects one in three Africans—up close.[2] 4

Proponents of biotechnology for the developing world point out that several studies have documented the yield and income improvements that come with planting biotech seeds: 5

- In 2001 United States farmers grew an additional 4 billion pounds of food and fiber and generated an additional $1.5 billion in income by planting six biotech crops, according to a June 2002 study conducted by the National Center for Food and Agricultural Policy.[3] 6
- Between 1998 and 2001, global cotton farmers reaped an additional $1.7 billion in income by using *Bt* cotton, according to a December 2002 report from the International Service for the Acquisition of Agri-biotech 7

Applications.[4] Yield increases for *Bt* cotton ranged from 5 to 10 percent in China, 10 percent or more in the United States and Mexico, and 25 percent in South Africa. The report noted that the increased income allows families to spend more on food, which reduces hunger.

- In 2001–02, planting of *Bt* corn in Spain produced yield increases of between 10 and 15 percent—and an average income gain of 12.9 percent—in areas with high levels of insect infestations, according to a study funded by Agricultural Biotechnology in Europe.[5]   8

Noting the potential benefits—and the explosive population growth expected in many already underfed countries—the United Nations Human Development Report 2001 concluded plant biotechnology could be a "breakthrough technology for developing countries."[6]   9

HEALTHY INPUTS

As important as plant biotechnology is in producing more food for a growing population, researchers are also developing healthier foods than can improve human health. You need to look no further than America's recent history to discover how important food was to eliminating disease.   10

In the 1930s, immigrants to the United States living in big cities were unusually prone to rickets, a bone disease caused by a deficiency of vitamin D. Poor diet was one reason. Another was that the tall, tightly packed-in tenement buildings where many immigrants lived blocked most direct sunlight, another key source of vitamin D.   11

When food manufacturers began adding vitamin D to bread and milk shortly thereafter, rickets became very rare in the United States.   12

In a similar but much more precise and powerful way, scientists today can use biotechnology to improve a food by introducing health-enhancing traits it otherwise wouldn't have.   13

In Canada, for example, there are two varieties of biotech canola being grown that can produce cooking oils with a healthier balance of "good" and "bad" fats. By precisely modifying just a slice of canola's genetic structure, researchers created a low-cholesterol oil without affecting other qualities (like stability under high heat) that make canola oil good for cooking.[7]   14

Other biotech foods in testing will put new health benefits on the table: 15

Field tests are underway on a cancer-fighting tomato with three times more lycopene, an antioxidant, than conventional varieties. Lycopene protects human tissue and could help prevent breast and prostate cancers as well as heart disease. This was recently chosen by American consumers as 2002's top food biotechnology development.[8]   16

In India, mustard seeds have been enhanced so they contain more beta 17 carotene, which could help alleviate vitamin A deficiencies. Mustard seed oil is the second most commonly used oil in India.[9]

Several research teams are working to improve rice, a staple food for half 18 the world's population, by putting more nutrition into each grain. Enhanced "golden rice" may help reduce childhood blindness, while a new iron-rich rice could have a truly global impact—one in three people worldwide don't get enough of the nutrient.[10]

Researchers working with cassava, a staple food in many poorer parts of 19 the world, have boosted protein levels by 35 to 45 percent and increased the levels of essential amino acids, according to "Harvest on the Horizon," a report prepared by the Pew Initiative on Food and Biotechnology. [11]

Reducing Toxins and Allergens

Through biotechnology, foods will give us not only more of what we need but 20 also less of what we don't.

A paper from the American Phytopathological Society, for example, de- 21 scribes how one popular biotech corn variety, called *Bt* corn, has unusually low levels of mycotoxins, a cancer causing agent. Mycotoxins enter corn through holes chewed by insect pests like the European corn borer—pests that *Bt* corn, which releases a natural insecticide as it grows, is highly effective at repelling.[12]

For the 50 million people with food allergies, meanwhile, biotechnology 22 could mean fewer red eyes and runny noses and more choice at the dinner table.[13]

One team of researchers recently succeeded in disarming the P34 gene in 23 soybeans, an allergen that affects an estimated 6 to 8 percent of children and 1 to 2 percent of adults.[14] Steve Taylor, co-director of the University of Nebraska's Food Allergy Research Resources Program, predicts more of the same as scientists learn to switch off or dim the intensity of protein allergens.

"I think in the long term we will have foods that are less hazardous be- 24 cause biotechnology will have eliminated or diminished their allergenicity," Taylor says.[15] In Japan, researchers have successfully reduced the allergenicity of rice. Other teams are working on peanuts and wheat.

Health professionals like the members of the non-profit American Col- 25 lege of Nutrition are on record as supporting the use of biotechnology to "contribute to global food security," as well as to "enhance the safety and nutritional value of the food supply" by removing anti-nutrients and allergens.[16]

PLANT-BASED VACCINES

It's no secret that eating right is the way to stay healthy. But soon the blurry 26 line between foods and medicines may be erased altogether.

Research is underway to use staple foods to deliver inexpensive, effective 27
vaccines for specific illnesses—literally, "edible vaccines," which could save
some of the 15 million children who die each year from preventable diseases.[17]

For example, researchers are experimenting with building a vaccine for 28
hepatitis B, which attacks the liver, into bananas. When eaten, the vaccine is
absorbed through the intestine into the bloodstream, producing antibodies in
the same way as an injected vaccine. But the banana vaccine is expected to
cost about 2 cents a dose, rather than $125 for an injection. Plus, it could be
easily administered without the need for refrigeration or medical staff.[18]

These plant-based vaccines seem to respond directly to a challenge is- 29
sued centuries ago by Hippocrates, the Greek physician considered to be the
father of modern medicine.

He said, "Let food be your medicine and medicine be your food." 30

SEEDS FOR THE FUTURE

More research is required before many biotech products, particularly plant- 31
based vaccines, become widely available. But the potential benefits and the importance of this work are clear.

In October of 2002, *Nature Genetics* journal asked a group of internation- 32
ally renowned scientists to rank the top biotechnology applications that could
improve health in the developing world.

Using biotechnology to diagnosis diseases, to develop vaccines and to im- 33
prove diets are at the top of the list.[19]

NOTES

1. "Food in the 21st Century: Science to Sustainable Agriculture," Consulta-
   tive Group on International Agricultural Research, p. 18, www.worldbank
   .org/html/cgiar/publications/shahbook/shahbook.pdf.
2. "African Doctor Says Biotechnology Could Help Feed the Hungry," Council for Biotechnology Information.
3. "Plant Biotechnology: Current and Potential Impact for Improving Pest
   Management in U.S. Agriculture: An Analysis of 40 Case Studies," National Center for Food and Agricultural Policy, June 2002, www.ncfap
   .org/40CaseStudies.htm.
4. James, Clive. "Global Review of Commercialized Transgenic Crops: 2001.
   Feature: Cotton," International Service for the Acquisition of Agri-biotech
   Applications, Dec. 13, 2002, http://www.isaaa.org/kc/CBTNews/ISAAA_
   PR/briefs26_exeng.htm

5. Brookes, Graham. "The Farm Level Impact of Using *Bt* Maize in Spain," Sept. 16, 2002, http://www.europabio.org/upload/documents/gb_press_release/EuropaBio_btmaizeinspainreport_FINAL.pdf

6. "Although Controversial, GMOs Could Be Breakthrough Technology for Developing Countries," United Nations Development Programme, July 10, 2001, www.undp.org/hdr2001/pr2.pdf

7. Benefits of Biotechnology, Council for Biotechnology Information, Slide 27, and Phillips, Michael J., "The Future of Agricultural Biotechnology," 2001 D. W. Brooks Lecture, College of Agriculture and Environmental Science, University of Georgia, October 10, 2001, www.bio.org/foodag/weekly/lecture_100101.asp.

8. "Cancer-Fighting Tomato Tops America's 2002 Best in Biotech," Council for Biotechnology Information.

9. Mackey, Maureen, "The Application of Biotechnology to Nutrition: An Overview," *Journal of the American College of Nutrition*, Vol. 21, No. 3(S), www.jacn.org.

10. Lucca, Hurrell and Potrykus, "Fighting Iron Deficiency Anemia with Iron-Rich Rice," *Journal of the American College of Nutrition*, Vol. 21, No. 3(S), www.jacn.org.

11. "Harvest on the Horizon," Pew Initiative on Food and Biotechnology, September 2001, http://pewagbiotech.org/research/harvest/harvest.pdf.

12. "Threats to Health Reduced with *Bt* Corn Hybrids," The American Phytopathological Society, October 18, 1999, www.biotechknowledge.com.

13. Avery, Dennis T., "Amidst African Famine, Allergy Controversy Flares," Center for Global Food Issues, www.cgfi.org.

14. "Researchers Develop First Hypoallergenic Soybeans," USDA Agricultural Research magazine, September 2002, http://www.ars.usda.gov/is/AR/archive/sep02/soy0902.htm

15. Taylor, Steve, "Genetic Enhancement Guards Against Food Allergies," American Medical Association, www.ama-assn.org.

16. American College of Nutrition Statement on Crop Biotechnology, *Journal of the American College of Nutrition*, June 2002. Council for Biotechnology Information.

17. Chin, Mary Lee, "Food Biotechnology: Harvest on the Horizon," PowerPoint presentation.

18. "Edible Vaccines," Food & Ag Biotech, www.bio.org/food&ag/vaccine.html.

19. "Top 10 Biotechnologies for Improving Health in Developing Countries," Nature Genetics, October 2002, http://www.utoronto.ca/jcb/_genomics/top10ng.pdf

SELECTION 2 QUESTIONS

Vocabulary

1. Explain what Nobel Laureate Borlaug means when he says "the first essential component of social justice is adequate food." (paragraph 1)
2. Explain what the author means by "soon the blurry line between foods and medicines may be erased altogether." Include a definition of "edible vaccines."

Comprehension and Analysis

3. Describe two ways plant biotechnology researchers are working to improve health.
4. How did food manufacturers help to eliminate rickets in the 1930s? How could similar procedures be used today?
5. According to the author, what effect(s) will biotechnology have on food toxins and allergens?
6. What did scientists rank as the top three biotechnology applications that could improve health in the developing world?
7. State the author's thesis.

Reflect and Connect

8. In the Case Study, "Teaching an Old Grain New Tricks," in the Theme's opening text chapter, Audesirk, Audesirk, and Byers describe a new bio-engineered crop—golden rice. Discuss how this new golden rice crop supports or disputes the ideas in this article.

SELECTION 3   PLAYING WITH OUR FOOD: A MASSIVE FOOD EXPERIMENT ALREADY UNDERWAY

CHARLES MARGULIS

Mr. Margulis is a genetic engineering specialist with Greenpeace. He is a graduate of the University of California at Berkeley and a long-time professional baker. This selection is from the Earth Island Journal, *Winter 2002. The* Earth Island Journal *was first published in 1982 as a class project at Stanford University. Since 1987 it has been published as a quarterly magazine by the Earth Island Institute (EII), founded by veteran environmentalist David Brower to "foster the efforts of creative individuals by providing organizational support in developing projects for the conservation, preservation, and restoration of the global environment."*

AN IDEA TO THINK ABOUT

How many foods did you eat this week that contained genetically engineered (GE) ingredients?

Most Americans know little if anything about a massive food experiment already underway in our nation's fields and grocery stores. Already thousands of products, including many of the best-known brand name foods found in millions of households, contain ingredients from genetically engineered (GE) crops. Yet since none of these products are labeled as "genetically engineered," consumers don't even know about—and cannot avoid—these genetic experiments in their shopping cart. 1

Greenpeace is working to stop this massive food experiment, which poses unknown risks to human health and the global environment. We oppose any release of genetically engineered organisms, since these human-made life-forms can not be controlled or contained once they are let loose into nature. The companies producing genetically engineered crops today are among the worst polluters of the 20th century. Their chemical experiments have left a legacy of contamination that threatens nature and human health on a planetary scale. Now, with genetic engineering, these companies are introducing a new form of pollution: biological pollution, pollution that is a qualitatively different than any previous human intrusion on nature. 2

With this technology, we face the specter of pollution that is alive, that reproduces and moves through the environment. Doctors warn that genetically engineered foods could pose immediate and long-term risks to our health, while the biotech industry goes about contaminating the entire food supply with its genetic experiments. 3

YOUR RIGHT TO KNOW

Many GE crops have been approved for commercial sale in the US, and consumers are often confused about what foods in their stores might be gene-altered. Though many crops are in development, just four crops—soy, corn, canola and cotton—make up nearly all the genetically engineered crop acreage in the US. There are virtually no fresh foods sold in supermarkets grown from gene-altered seed (with the possible exception of papaya from Hawaii, where about half the crop is GE). 4

Yet estimates routinely note that 60–70 percent of the foods in supermarkets are made with gene-altered ingredients. This reflects the massive amount of processed foods that include ingredients from soy and corn. A look at processed food labels shows how ubiquitous ingredients like soy oil, lecithin, soy protein and corn syrup, cornstarch and other corn and soy ingredients have become. Canola and cottonseed oil are also widely used in processed foods. Avoiding just these four foods requires eliminating virtually all processed foods from our diets. 5

It is also important to know that just two gene-altered traits account for almost all of the US acreage of GE crops. GE crops are being grown either for insect resistance (including corn and cotton) or herbicide tolerance (including soy, corn, cotton and canola). While industry repeatedly touts biotech foods that will be more nutritious, better tasting, or healthier, neither of these varieties has any such benefits.

Herbicide tolerant crops make up about 70 percent of the acreage of GE crops in the US. These crops are engineered so toxic plant-killing pesticides can be sprayed directly on the crop. Previously, farmers using such herbicides had to carefully avoid the crop, which would also be killed by the chemical. Now, GE herbicide-tolerant varieties can be sprayed once, twice, even three times a season, without harming the crop. While industry promotes genetic engineering as reducing pesticide spraying, independent researchers have shown that farmers who grow Monsanto's "Roundup Ready"(RR) soy actually use two to five times more chemicals than farmers who grow natural soy. In fact, when its RR soy was in development, Monsanto successfully petitioned the Environmental Protection Agency (EPA) to raise the amount of its flagship chemical Roundup allowed on soybeans. Overnight the agency raised the tolerance of Roundup on this food from 6 ppm to 20 ppm.

The remaining biotech crop acreage in the US is in insect resistant crops. Also called Bt crops, these plants pose a tremendous threat to organic farming. Bt is a natural pest control, used in emergency situations by about half of America's organic farmers to control certain insects. The Bt sprays they use are derived from natural soil bacteria, and farmers (both conventional and organic) have used the sprays safely for over 30 years. Now the biotech industry has engineered plants so that the plant produces an altered form of Bt. Unlike natural Bt sprays, which naturally degrade in the environment in a matter of a few days, genetically engineered Bt plants produce an altered toxin throughout the entire growing season, at a very high dose. This scenario will surely lead to insect resistance to Bt, probably in just a few years. When such resistance develops, farmers who use pesticides and GE crops will simply move on to the next toxin, but organic farmers will have no options. This threat to organic farming led Greenpeace to bring together over 70 organic farmers and farming organizations in a lawsuit challenging EPA's registration of Bt crops.

Biotech industry proponents say that there is no evidence that GE foods cause any harm. In fact, there is already evidence of environmental problems from GE crops, and doctors around the world warn that these foods could harm human health. Lab evidence that Bt corn could harm monarchs and other endangered butterflies has been verified in the field. Despite a massive industry attempt to debunk this research, the scientific debate is still raging. In Canada, scientists have found that engineered canola has become a nearly uncontrollable weed. One scientist there said the crop is a classic "superweed." Other scientific studies show that GE crops can cause insecticides to build up in soils, cause food chain effects, transfer genes to wild relatives, and contaminate natural crops.

For consumers, the prospects are even more worrisome. *The New England* 10
Journal of Medicine warned in 1996 that the Food and Drug Administration's
(FDA's) policy on GE food left consumers at risk from potential new food allergies, yet the agency still has made no change (the policy has actually never been
finalized, leading a federal judge to rule that FDA has no rules regarding GE
foods). This is even more stunning after the StarLink incident, in which a gene-
altered corn that was never approved for human consumption contaminated
over 300 products sold in supermarkets and restaurants across the country. Scientists repeatedly told the government that the corn could trigger dangerous
food allergies, and hundreds of consumers reported allergic reactions. Even more
recently, Britain's leading scientific body, the Royal Society, suggested that consumers should be tracked for potential allergic responses to GE foods, noting that
infants and children could be especially at risk. Of course, since there is no labeling of GE foods in the US, such tracking here would be virtually impossible.

THE TRUE FOOD NETWORK:
ACTION FOR CHANGE

While the problems are daunting, we have seen amazing successes. When 11
Greenpeace tested Gerber baby food and found contamination from gene-
altered soy and corn, we were able to pressure the company to announce it
would eliminate all GE ingredients from its products. Gerber's announcement
forced Heinz, its main competitor, to follow suit.

Consumer pressure also lead McDonald's, Frito Lay and McCain Foods 12
(one of the world's largest potato processors) to reject *Bt* potatoes. Monsanto
has since been forced to shut its *Bt* potato development facility, and the crop is
off the US market. The FDA has approved genetically engineered rice and
sugar beet, but the biotech industry has been forced to shelve the crops, since
farmers know consumers don't want these GE foods. As more and more
Americans learn about GE foods, it becomes even harder for industry to bring
these genetic experiments into the market.

Yet the industry continues to fight labeling of GE food, so Greenpeace took 13
action, compiling the True Food Shopping List to support your right to know
what is in your food. Since the first launch of the List in October 2000, thousands of consumers have joined our free True Food Network to take action
against GE food. The Network connects consumers across the country in a
grassroots effort to force food companies to stop using GE food. Last year, the
Network won a major victory when a year-long campaign against the supermar-
ket chain Trader Joe's resulted in that company declaring it would eliminate GE
foods from its line of store brand products. Now the campaign is focusing on
other supermarkets, including the New England–based Shaw's stores and the national chain Safeway. In Europe, this kind of consumer action forced nearly the
entire food industry away from GE food. Together, we can do the same here.

SELECTION 3 QUESTIONS

Vocabulary

1. Explain what Margulis means when he says, "With this technology, we face the specter of pollution that is alive, that reproduces and moves through the environment." (paragraph 3)
2. Explain what Margulis means when he says, "While industry repeatedly touts biotech foods that will be more nutritious, better tasting, or healthier, neither of these varieties has any such benefits." (paragraph 6)
3. Explain what Margulis means when he says, "Despite a massive industry attempt to debunk this research, the scientific debate is still raging." (paragraph 9)

Comprehension and Analysis

4. List the four crops that make up nearly all the genetically engineered crop acreage in the United States. Why does Margulis believe the two gene-altered traits in those crops have more potential for harm than health?
5. How easy is it to avoid eating foods made with these genetically engineered crops? Please explain.
6. According to Margulis, what effect(s) will genetic engineering have on food allergens? Compare and contrast this view to the one presented in the article "Biotech and Better Health" by the Council for Biotechnology Information.
7. State Margulis's thesis.
8. Explain why Margulis thinks the EPA should ban the use of genetically engineered *RR* crops and *Bt* crops.
9. List two actions Margulis would like consumers to take. List one action he would like the EPA to take and one action he would like the FDA to take.

Reflect and Connect

10. In the Case Study, "Teaching an Old Grain New Tricks," in the Theme's opening text chapter, Audesirk, Audesirk, and Byers say, "Availability of a bioengineered crop [golden rice] that might prevent death and blindness in hundreds of thousands of impoverished children would seem more difficult for consumers to oppose." Do you think Margulis and other Greenpeace genetic engineering specialists would oppose the bioengineered golden rice? Please explain.

SELECTION 4   EDITORIAL CARTOON

CLAY BENNETT

Pulitzer Prize–winning Editorial Cartoonist Bennett has been with The Christian Science Monitor *since 1998. In addition to producing five full-color cartoons each week for* The Christian Science Monitor, *he produces fully animated editorial cartoons for the Internet and draws cartoons for distribution through King Features Syndicate.*

AN IDEA TO THINK ABOUT

How carefully do you read the labels of the food you buy?

SELECTION 4 QUESTIONS

1. Explain Bennett's message.
2. Describe how you think the authors of the three selection you have read so far—(1) Audesirk, Audesirk, and Byers, (2) the Council for Biotechnology Information, and (3) Margulis—would react to Bennett's cartoon.

SELECTION 5   MILLIONS SERVED

LYNN J. COOK

Ms. Cook is a frequent contributor to Forbes *magazine. This selection is from* Forbes, *December 23, 2002.*

AN IDEA TO THINK ABOUT

Assume you and your family are experiencing long-term chronic malnutrition. A humanitarian aid program offers you regular allotments of rice, sweet potatoes, and bananas that have been genetically modified to provide high levels of nutrients. No long-term studies have been conducted on any potential side effects. What do you do?

While the West debates the ethics of genetically modified food, Florence Wambugu is using it to feed her country.

Civil war in Angola and Sudan and drought in Eritrea mean that Africa is on the brink of another mass famine like the one that swept Ethiopia in the early 1980s. Florence Wambugu knows the kind of hunger that swells the stomach and dulls the eyes. She grew up with it. Now she has the makings of a cure. Wambugu was born in 1953, just a few kilometers away from Treetops, Kenya's famous game reserve. But proximity to the posh highlands resort didn't spare Wambugu and her nine brothers and sisters from going a day or two at a time without eating. When Kenya's colonial government crumbled in 1963, Wambugu's father was rounded up—like so many young men—and trucked off to work on a white settler's farm. That left her mother and ten children to scratch a life from the land. They stayed alive on sweet potatoes, a rich source of calories, vitamin A and beta carotene.

"The sweet potato is a woman's crop, a security crop," Wambugu says. "If we didn't have sweet potatoes, we had nothing." But pests love it. Growing underground, it is prone to infestation by the feathery mottle virus and worms. Africa's year-round tropical temperatures offer no winter to freeze off disease cycles, so each year nearly half the sweet potato crop fails. In Africa the sweet potato harvest averages two and a half tonnes an acre; the global average is more than twice that. Indeed, African yields rank dead last in every major crop harvested.

Today the dismal yields are improving, thanks to Wambugu's decade-long effort to genetically modify crops to withstand pests. Into the sweet potato she spliced a gene from the pyrethrum, a white flower whose ingredients are fatal to insects and the feathery mottle virus.

This shuffling of genes is a hit-or-miss, years-long affair. First Wambugu isolates the gene that codes for the production of insecticidal pyrethrins in the pyrethrum flower and extracts them. Next, tens of thousands of copies are made and mixed together with tungsten balls just one micron in diameter. Thousands of genes stick to each ball, and the combination is loaded into a "gene gun"—two small stainless-steel chambers and a vacuum pump—that uses compressed helium. The gun shoots the microscopic gene-bearing balls into sweet potato leaves. Some of the genes migrate from the tungsten into the nuclei of the leaves' cells and are absorbed into the DNA that defines the plant.

It was a breakthrough 25 years in the making. From the time Wambugu   6
entered the University of Nairobi's plant pathology program as an undergraduate in 1975 until she earned her Ph.D. in plant virology from the University of Bath in the U.K. in 1991, she tried various conventional hybridization techniques to outbreed the viruses that wipe out the otherwise drought-resistant and energy-rich tuber. Nothing worked, nor did her experiments in a decade at the Kenya Agricultural Research Institute. Then in 1992 the U.S. Department of Agriculture offered her a grant to study transgenetics in St. Louis, Missouri, in collaboration with Washington University and Monsanto, the agrochemical company. For three years Wambugu labored in Monsanto's labs, trying to splice genes for viral resistance into the sweet potato. It took another two years to test the transgenic tubers in greenhouses and yet another two years to obtain the necessary permits from Kenya to plant the crops for field testing. The results, halfway through field trials, are astonishing.

The sweet potato is sub-Saharan Africa's first genetically modified crop,   7
and its yields are double that of the regular plant. The modified potatoes are bigger and richer in color, with more nutritional value. Africa's population is growing faster than its food supply. Wambugu's modified sweet potato offers tangible hope. According to the World Bank, biotech crops could increase food production in the developing world by 25%.

Wambugu overcame long odds even to get the education she needed for   8
this venture. When she was 13, with food scarce and every child's hands needed to work the family plot, her mother sold the family cow to pay for Wambugu's boarding school 16 kilometers away. Her mother needed a dispensation from the village council to sell the animal; most thought that she was crazy to educate a daughter when it would be easier to marry her off instead.

Today Wambugu, who lives and works in Nairobi, faces a different sort   9
of obstacle. Groups that include Greenpeace and the Union of Concerned Scientists fret that Africa is being manipulated by multinational corporations, in effect serving as one big—potentially dangerous—genetic experiment. Some Africans are so fearful of plant technology that Zambia's government would rather have its citizens starve than accept donated food that includes genetically modified corn. Concerned with the misunderstanding about transgenic corn, Wambugu created A Harvest Biotech Foundation International to serve as a pan-African voice on the issue.

Wambugu concedes that genetically modified (GM) crops are experimen-   10
tal but insists the potential good far outweighs the risks. It's like penicillin, she says. Some people are allergic to it, but the medicine has cured far more people

than it has hurt. "This is not a question of export to Europe or America," she says. "If they don't want it, they don't have to have it. We have local demand. We're dying, so can we eat first?" Her former boss, Cyrus Ndiritu, a former director of the Kenya Agriculture Research Institution, agrees. "I'd like to make something clear. It is not multinationals that have a stranglehold on Africa. It is hunger, poverty and deprivation. If Africa is going to get out of that, it has to embrace GM technology."

If tissue-culture technology, a predecessor to genetically modifying organisms, is any indicator, the payoff for Africa could be huge. Wambugu won the World Bank award for global development in 2000 after introducing the tissue-culture banana to Kenya. In this process a piece of tissue is cut from a healthy plant and grown in a sterile environment into several plantlets that root in pasteurized soil before being transferred to the field. It turned what was once a subsistence crop into a major income earner for women farmers, more than doubling average banana harvests.

Wambugu's next challenge is to get the funding to help Kenyan farmers pay for the modified sweet potato and tissue-propagated banana plants.

She already has her next project in mind: to reforest areas that have been stripped by those in search of firewood.

SELECTION 5 QUESTIONS

Comprehension and Analysis

1. Historically, how have the agricultural yields in Africa compared to the global average? Why is the yield changing?
2. Why do you think Wambugu selected the sweet potato to modify? Why do you think she kept working on the project for 25 years instead of just giving up?
3. According to the field trials, what are the yield estimates and nutritional value of Wambugu's modified sweet potato?
4. To help express her point of view, Wambugu compares genetically modified crops to penicillin. Explain her comparison. Do you think it is a valid comparison?
5. Explain who is in favor of using Wambugu's modified sweet potato in Africa and why. Explain who is against using Wambugu's modified sweet potato in Africa and why.

Reflect and Connect

6. Margulis cautions us that "genetically engineered foods could pose immediate and long-term risks to our health." What do you think he would say to Wambugu about using her modified sweet potato in Africa? What do you think she would tell him?

SELECTION 6 HOW REPROGENETICS WILL TRANSFORM THE AMERICAN FAMILY

LEE M. SILVER

Dr. Silver is Professor in the Department of Molecular Biology at Princeton University and a member of the Program in Science, Technology & Environmental Policy, the Center for Health and Well-Being, and the Office of Population Research at the Woodrow Wilson School of Public and International Affairs. He is the author of Remaking Eden: How Genetic Engineering and Cloning Will Transform the American Family, *which has been published in 15 languages. He prepared this excerpt from his book for the* Hofstra Law Review.

AN IDEA TO THINK ABOUT

If you were considering having a child and had the option for the embryo to be given a no-risk genetic vaccine against AIDS or other serious diseases, would you take the option?

WORD TO KNOW

appellation (¶ 8)—name, label

INTRODUCTION

Incredible advances in reproductive technology continue to offer people new options for having babies that were inconceivable just a few short years ago.[1] Men once classified as sterile because they were unable to produce sperm can now become biological fathers with the use of nuclear injection into the unfertilized eggs of their partners.[2] Postmenopausal women of any age, unable to produce their own eggs, can use donor eggs and hormone treatment to become pregnant and give birth.[3]

    Even more exotic possibilities for reproduction have already been demonstrated in other mammalian species and will soon be applied to humans as well. These include protocols that allow two women to have a baby together by embryo fusion,[4] and somatic cell nuclear transfer techniques that will allow infertile couples and individuals to have monoparental biological children.[5] Indeed, our current understanding and technological prowess over the process of human reproduction is so extensive that it will soon be possible for any one or two people, of any sex or age, to have monoparental or biparental children. For reasons to be discussed below, these expanding reproductive horizons are scaring the daylights out of some people.

At the same time, as reproductive horizons are expanding, there has been   3
an explosion in the area of genetic research and technology. The Human Genome Project, with its goal of identifying each and every human gene, has been pried from the nonprofit government agencies, the National Institutes of Health and the Department of Energy, and sucked into the private sector where biotech companies are already in hot competition to profit handsomely from controlling this goldmine of information.[6] Identifying all 100,000 or so human genes, which is set to be accomplished by the year 2003, is actually only the first step in this massive effort. The second step, which is just as important, is to identify all of the major ways in which people differ at each of these genes, and how these genetic differences correlate with differences in critical personal characteristics, like resistance or susceptibility to every known infectious and inherited disease, and the efficacy of specific drugs or medical protocols in counteracting these diseases.[7] It is only a matter of time before connections are also made between genetic profiles and physical or mental attributes that we commonly refer to as innate talents.

Most scientists and other scholars are willing to accept the fact that   4
genes influence complex physical and mental attributes, but many believe that the pathways from genes to expressed traits are so complex that we will never be able to figure them out. The conclusion these people seem to draw is that misdiagnosis and the manipulation of complex genetic traits will always be beyond our reach.[8]

For better *and* worse, this conclusion is no longer valid. Advanced genetic   5
technologies merged with computer technology to yield new tools for analysis like deoxyribonucleic acid ("DNA") chips, which will make it possible to scan a person's entire genome cheaply and rapidly.[9] Companies will surely use this powerful tool to conduct large population studies. The results will allow correlations to be made between specific genetic profiles and the expression of specific complex traits, even as the path from gene to trait remains hidden within a black box. We do not have to understand how a gene works to know its ultimate impact on a human life.

I. REPROGENETICS AND EUGENICS

The new genetic technologies have implications for the practice of all forms of   6
medicine, but when they are combined with reproductive technologies in the form of reprogenetics, the implications are staggering. Prospective parents will soon be able to choose which of their genes to give to their children,[10] and whether to add in genes they do not even carry in order to provide them with increased chances for health, longevity, happiness, and success.[11]

Again, there are those who believe that it will not be possible to manipu-   7
late complex human attributes in the embryo.[12] However, if a complex disease

like diabetes can be controlled with the use of a single molecule (insulin) after birth, it and many other similarly complex traits will certainly be amenable to significant manipulation with the use of single, well-placed genes before pregnancy even begins. As another example, consider height—this complex trait is probably influenced by hundreds of genes, and yet, we already know that a single gene addition (growth hormone) could easily change this trait in a way that is desired.

When reproductive and genetic technologies are combined in this way, both their design and purpose are so different from that of either technology alone that the combination is deserving of a new appellation: reprogenetics. Reprogenetics is the use of genetic technologies in the course of reproduction to ensure or prevent the inheritance of particular genes in the child.[13]

To a limited degree, reprogenetics is already practiced and accepted by a major portion of society. Each time a woman decides to abort a fetus based on the results of amniocentesis, she is choosing against the presence of certain genes in her children. And each time an abortion is chosen because the resulting child would have been mentally retarded (without other medical problems), reprogenetics is being practiced for the sole purpose of increasing the intelligence of the child that is ultimately born as a result of a later pregnancy.

Why is there such a reluctance on the part of many in society to call a spade a spade in this context? One part of the answer is that the practice of reprogenetics sounds suspiciously like the discredited social theory of eugenics. Indeed, many social commentators confuse the two even though they are fundamentally different in both purveyors and goals.[14]

The stated purpose of eugenics was the improvement of the so-called "gene pool" of a society by state control over the breeding practices of its citizens.[15] In America, early twentieth century attempts to put this idea into practice brought about the forced sterilization of people deemed genetically inferior because of supposed reduced intelligence, minor physical disabilities, or possession of a supposed criminal character.[16] Further "protection of the American gene pool" was endeavored by congressional enactment of harsh immigration policies aimed at restricting the influx of people from Eastern and Southern Europe, which were seen as regions harboring populations with undesirable genes.[17] Two decades later, Nazi Germany used an even more drastic approach. It attempted to eliminate, in a single generation, those who carried undesirable genes.[18] In the aftermath of World War II, all of these misguided attempts to practice eugenics were rightly repudiated as discriminatory, murderous, and infringing upon the natural right of human beings to reproductive liberty.[19]

While eugenics is practiced at the level of a state, reprogenetics will be practiced at the level of individuals and couples. And while eugenics is concerned with the vague notion of a gene pool,[20] reprogenetics is concerned with the very real, but narrow, question of what genes a single child will receive. While the enaction of eugenics would lead to a restriction of reproductive freedom or worse, reprogenetics will do exactly the opposite. It will give people the opportunity to have children who will be healthy, happy, and loved.

If reprogenetics is used to increase happiness for all those involved in its 13 practice and outcome, what could possibly be wrong with it? Plenty, according to some people. But before discussing the fears it engenders, it is important to first build the case for why I am convinced this technology will actually be used.

II. GENETIC ENGINEERING

Over the last eighteen years, the technology of germline genetic engineering 14 was used with increasing efficiency to alter in very specific ways the embryonic genomes of a variety of mammalian species, including mice, pigs, and sheep.[21] Until recently, however, the possibility that this technology might be applied to human embryos was not given serious consideration by most scientists. There were three levels of technical problems that seemed insurmountable. First, the technology was extremely inefficient, with success rates typically less than fifty percent (in terms of the fraction of animals born with the intended modification).[22] Second, the application of the technology was associated with a high risk of newly induced mutations.[23] Finally, there was, and still is, a general sense that genetic engineering can never be performed on people because of the possibility that a particular modification might have unanticipated negative side effects. The existence of any one of these problems alone would be sufficient to categorize human germline genetic engineering as unethical and unallowable.

As we approached the new millennium, the technological landscape 15 changed and it seems likely that all three of these technical problems could be overcome. With the application of both cloning and new DNA screening technologies at the embryonic level, it becomes possible to pre-select only those genetically engineered embryos in which the desired genetic change is implemented, without any damage to the pre-existing genome. This technical advance would eliminate the first and second problems associated with genetic engineering. But what about the question of unintended side effects from the added genetic material?

The issue of unintended side effects can be eliminated if genetic engineer- 16 ing is applied specifically to provide children with genes that other members of the population receive naturally. As an example, approximately one percent of people with a Western European ancestry carry a gene that provides complete resistance to infection by HIV, the AIDS-causing virus.[24] The absence of any deleterious side effects of this specific gene on human beings can be demonstrated by examining large numbers of people who already carry it naturally. In a situation of this type, we must ask whether any rationale exists for a state authority to stop parents from using genetic engineering to place an AIDS resistance gene in their child. Is there any moral difference between a genetic vaccine given to an embryo and a protein-based polio vaccine given to an infant?

One difference is that the polio vaccine is made available to all children in 17 our society, irrespective of the affluence of their parents. Unfortunately, it seems unlikely to me that genetic engineering will ever be available in such an egalitarian fashion. Some might argue that this is the difference that is ethically significant.[25] But, if we look at the world population as a whole, there are places where vaccines against deadly diseases are not available to children who grow up with a real risk of dying from the disease. At this level of analysis, afterbirth vaccines given today are no different ethically from future genetic vaccines. In both cases, there are lines drawn between individuals or populations who are affluent enough to receive the vaccine and those who are not.

But beyond vaccines against disease, parents of the future will be able to 18 provide their children with many other genes that enhance physical or mental characteristics which other children inherit naturally. The first class of genes that comes to mind are ones that increase life span.[26] Beyond that will be genes that provide talents, like perfect musical pitch,[27] genes that attenuate personalities against both shyness and hyper-aggression,[28] and genes that provide particular mental skills, like an increased ability to learn multiple languages.[29]

Again, I want to emphasize that to avoid unintended consequences, it is 19 likely that in the near future, all of these so-called enhancements will be based on genes that occur naturally in a proportion of the population. In the long run, however, our knowledge of the human genome and the way in which it works is sure to advance to the point where enhancements beyond those present in any person alive today will become safe and efficient.

III. THE MEDICAL MODEL VERSUS THE MARKET MODEL

Some bioethicists are concerned that reprogenetic technologies will cater 20 only to "the basest drives of humanity," or that they will objectify human beings and place them on par with products to be modified and manipulated at will.[30] There is often the stated notion that these technologies will be used by unscrupulous governments or groups aiming to produce people for their special needs.[31] Many of these scenarios take their cue from Huxley's influential novel *Brave New World*, which describes a world in which the state exerts complete control over human reproduction and human nature as well. In this brave new world, the state uses fetal hatcheries to breed each child into a predetermined intellectual class that ranges from alpha at the top to epsilon at the bottom.

While Huxley guessed right about the power we would gain over the 21 process of reproduction, I think he was dead wrong when it came to predicting *who* would use the power and for what purposes. These technologies will be of no use to governments for the simple reason that they will not allow the birth of babies "to order" because human beings are much more than their genes.

Indeed, we are more than our genes and our environment combined. Alone among all species, human beings can consciously choose to go against genetically programmed instincts. And they can choose to go against cultural dictates as well. Thus any leaders who think they can create human beings predetermined to behave in a specified way will be greatly disappointed.

More importantly, however, what Huxley failed to understand, or refused to accept, was the driving force behind babymaking. Governments do not make babies, people do. It is individuals and couples—not governments—who want to reproduce themselves biologically in their own images. It is individuals and couples who want their children to be happy and successful. And it is individuals and couples who will seize control of these new technologies to reach otherwise unattainable reproductive goals, and to help their children achieve health, happiness, and success. That is the way it has always been since humans first walked the face of the earth. 22

I claim here that most people do not wish to overcome these powerful instinctive forces. It is the desire to have biological children, and the desire to provide one's children with all possible advantages in life, that will drive the use of reprogenetic technologies. The desire to have and raise a child is such a powerful instinctive force that many people who experience it have a hard time explaining where it comes from. The reason we cannot figure it out is because we have little control over it. It is programmed into our genes, and is second in power in most people only to the drive for self-preservation. Not surprisingly, infertility can have a devastating effect on people. Many say it is equivalent to the death of a loved one. It can cause serious depression and lead to the breakup of marriages. This is why many couples are willing to spend thousands of dollars in attempts to have a baby with the use of in vitro fertilization,[32] or the services of a surrogate mother. Of course, when parents do adopt children, they discover that they love them as much as any parent could love a child (because of a further instinct that we have for taking care of "children we find in our nest"). 23

The second driving force, the desire to provide our children with all possible chances for happiness and success in life, is universally expected in normal parents. Indeed, many normal parents do not simply want normal children, they want their children to be *better* than normal in some way. The drive to protect and advantage children extends across many other species besides human beings, including most mammals and birds. 24

I argue here that reproductive and reprogenetic technologies will be used exclusively by individuals and couples who are driven by these two primary forces. Advanced reproductive technologies will be used to provide infertile couples and individuals with the opportunity to have biological children in the context of loving families. Reprogenetic technologies will be used to provide children with increased chances of physical and mental health and increased longevity. If standard medical practice is followed, no technology will be applied until its safety and efficacy is demonstrated to the greatest degree possible in 25 both non-human model organisms and natural human populations. If standard medical practice is followed, the benefits will outweigh the risks.

There are those who will argue that parents do not have the right to control the characteristics of their children-to-be in the way described above.[33] American society, in particular, accepts the rights of parents to attempt to control every other aspect of their children's lives from the time they are born until they reach adulthood. If one accepts the parental prerogative after birth, it is hard to argue against it before birth, if the intention and expectation is to increase health and happiness.

Indeed, the problem with reprogenetic technologies is not that they are inherently bad, or that people will use them for harmful reasons. The problem, I believe, is that they are too good. The power of reprogenetics is so great that those families and groups *not* able to afford its use could become severely disadvantaged. Thus, I believe the real ethical concern with reprogenetics is one of fairness and equality of access, not harm.

This ethical problem is not a new one (expect perhaps in degree). It is inherently unfair for some people to have access to technologies that can provide advantages while others, less well-off, are forced to depend on chance alone. But in every democratic society, affluent parents are able to give their children very real advantages in life that less affluent parents are unable to afford. In American society, children of the affluent receive better health care and better education, and they are often raised in an environment that is more conducive to developing strategies for future success. If one accepts the right of affluent parents to provide their children with an expensive private school education, it becomes difficult to use "unfairness" as a reason for rejecting the use of reprogenetic technologies intended to accomplish the same goal of increasing chances for success and happiness.

In a society that places a high value on individual freedom, like that found in the United States, it is hard to find any legitimate basis for restricting the use of reprogenetics. Each individual use of the technology can be viewed in the light of personal reproductive choice with no ability to change society at large. But when taken together over many individuals and many generations, these new technologies could drastically affect the nature of human society. The ultimate, and perhaps inevitable outcome of a libertarian market-based society could be a genetic gap between classes, the GenRich and the Naturals,[34] that becomes wider and wider with each generation.

On March 14, 1996, John Maddox, the editor of the British journal *Nature* wrote an impassioned editorial saying in part:

> That the growing power of molecular genetics confronts us with future prospects of being able to change the nature of our species is a fact that seldom appears to be addressed in depth. Scientific knowledge may not yet permit detailed understanding, but the possibilities are clear enough. . . . [In the end] the agenda is set by mankind as a whole, not [simply] by the subset involved in the science.[35]

Unfortunately, I disagree with the editors of *Nature*. Scientists will not be [32] able to control the agenda even if they wanted to. They are simply not the ones with power in a market-based society. But, it is utterly naive to think that mankind as a whole, unable to reach consensus on so many other critical societal issues, will have any effect whatsoever. Instead, I believe that power will lie in the marketplace, and that the agenda will be set by individuals and couples who will act on behalf of themselves and their children. And my fear is that the marketplace could very well determine the evolution of humankind.

Is there an alternative? So long as sovereign states prevail, international [33] borders can do nothing to halt the passage of cells and genes lying deep within a woman's body. Only a single world state could control the use of reprogenetics, providing it in measured amounts to all its citizens. From our vantage point at the beginning of the third millennium, such a Huxley-like world seems much more securely in the realm of fiction than even the most fantastical scenarios imagined in this book. Nevertheless, the future of humankind is a thousand times longer than its past and is impossible to foresee.

I have no doubt that the growing use of reprogenetics is inevitable. For [34] better *and* worse, a new age is upon us—an age in which we as humans will gain the ability *to change the nature of our species.*

NOTES

1. *See generally* Lee M. Silver, *Remaking Eden: How Genetic Engineering and Cloning Will Transform the American Family* (1998) (discussing genetic and physiologic technologies in regard to human reproduction).

2. *See id.* at 160.

3. *See id.* at 225–26.

4. *See id.* at 206–22.

5. *See id.* at 137–41.

6. *See* J. Craig Venter et al., *Shotgun Sequencing of the Human Genome*, 280 SCI. 1540, 1540–41 (1998).

7. *See* Leonid Kruglyak, "The Use of a Genetic Map of Biallelic Markers in Linkage Studies," 17 *Nature Genetics* 21, 21–23 (1997).

8. *See* Dean Hamer & Peter Copeland, *Living with Our Genes: Why They Matter More Than You Think,* 307–09 (1998); *see also* Richard J. Tasca & Michael E. McClure, "The Emerging Technology and Application of Preimplantation Genetic Diagnosis," 26 J.L. *Med. & Ethics* 7, 11–14 (1998) (discussing the technical and inherent risks attributable to misdiagnosis).

9. *See* Hamer & Copeland, *supra* note 8, at 302–03.

10. *See* Silver, *supra* note 1, at 233–47.

11. *See id.* at 269–73.

12. *See* Hamer & Copeland, *supra* note 8, at 307–09.

13. *See* John A. Robertson, "Oocyte Cytoplasm Transfers and the Ethics of Germ-Line Intervention," 26 J.L. *Med. & Ethics* 211, 211 (1998).

14. *See* Silver, *supra* note 1, at 185–90 (discussing the policies and background of eugenics).

15. *See id.* at 254.

16. *See* Philip R. Reilly, *The Surgical Solution: A History of Involuntary Sterilization in the United States* 41 (1991). Between 1907 and 1963, more than 60,000 people were involuntarily sterilized. *See id.* at 94.

17. *See id.* at 22–24. All four of the Author's grandparents were from these regions.

18. *See id.* at 105–10. It has been reported that under the German sterilization program, the Nazis sterilized 3,500,000 people between 1933 and 1945, thereby far eclipsing similar American activities. *See id.* at 109–10.

19. *See generally* Stefan Köhl, *The Nazi Connection: Eugenics, American Racism, and German National Socialism* 100 (1994) ("After World War II, members of the American Eugenics Society sought to distance themselves from their former support for Nazi race policies. The elimination of millions of Jews, Gypsies, and handicapped people had completely discredited Nazi race policies."); Elizabeth S. Scott, *Sterilization of Mentally Retarded Persons: Reproductive Rights and Family Privacy*, 1986 Duke L.J. 806, 811 ("By the 1960's, involuntary sterilization was frequently characterized as an unjustified intrusion by the state on individual liberty and privacy.").

20. *See* Silver, *supra* note 1, at 258–59.

21. *See* Brigid Hogan Et Al., *Manipulating The Mouse Embryo: A Laboratory Manual* at v (2d ed. 1994).

22. *See* Sharon Begley, *Little Lamb, Who Made Thee?*, Newsweek, Mar. 10, 1997, at 53, 56.

23. *See id.* at 59.

24. *See* Rong Liu et al., "Homozygous Defect in HIV-1 Coreceptor Accounts for Resistance of Some Multiply-Exposed Individuals to HIV-1 Infection," 86 *Cell* 367, 373 (1996); *see also* Caroline Quillent et al., "HIV-1-Resistance Phenotype Conferred by Combination of Two Separate Inherited Mutations of CCR5 Gene," 351 *Lancet* 14 (1998) (describing CCR5, a gene that is associated with resistance to HIV-1 infection).

25. *See* Jeremy Rifkin, "Who Will Decide Between Defect and Perfect?", *Washington Post*, Apr. 19, 1998, at C4.

26. *See* Dan Seligman, "Outlawing DNA," *Forbes*, July 6, 1998, at 110.

27. *See* Joseph Profita & T. George Bidder, "Perfect Pitch," 29 *Am. J. Med. Genetics* 763, 766–69 (1988).

28. *See* Seligman, *supra* note 26, at 110.

29. *See* Hamer & Copeland, *supra* note 8, at 231–34.

30. *See* Leon R. Kass & James Q. Wilson, *The Ethics of Human Cloning* 38–39 (1998).

31. *See* Lawrence Wu, Note, "Family Planning Through Human Cloning: Is There a Fundamental Right?", 98 *Colum. L. Rev.* 1461, 1511 (1998).

32. *See* Peter J. Neumann et al., "The Cost of a Successful Delivery with In Vitro Fertilization," 331 *New Eng. J. Med.* 239–42 (1994).

33. *See* Kass & Wilson, *supra* note 30, at 42.

34. *See* Silver, *supra* note 1, at 4.

35. John Maddox, "Exploring Life as We Don't Yet Know It" 380 *Nature* 89 (1996).

SELECTION 6 QUESTIONS

Vocabulary

1. Define *reprogenetics*.
2. Define *eugenics*. Compare and contrast reprogenetics and eugenics.
3. Explain what Silver means in paragraph 17 when he says, "Unfortunately, it seems unlikely to me that genetic engineering will ever be available in such an egalitarian fashion."

Comprehension and Analysis

4. List what Silver sees as the two eventual outcomes of the Human Genome Project.
5. Explain why Silver believes that "any leaders who think they can create human beings predetermined to behave in a specified way will be greatly disappointed."
6. What does Silver believe is the real ethical concern about reprogenetics?
7. What does Silver forecast as the "ultimate, and perhaps inevitable outcome of a libertarian market-based society"?
8. What does Silver predict will drive the use of reprogenetic technologies?
9. State Silver's thesis.

Reflect and Connect

10. How do you think Silver would answer these questions posed by Audesirk, Audesirk, and Byers in "Applying the Concepts" at the end of the Theme's opening text chapter: "Do you think that using DNA technologies to change the composition of a human egg cell is ever justified? If so, what restrictions should be placed on such a use?" Compare and contrast what you think Silver would say to your answers.

SELECTION 7   CLONING SCENARIO GETTING FRIGHTENINGLY CLOSE TO REALITY

TOM SCHAEFER

Mr. Schaefer writes about religion and ethics for the Wichita Eagle *in Kansas in which this selection appeared January 15, 2003.*

AN IDEA TO THINK ABOUT

What mental, emotional, and physical characteristics do you think are most critical to a person's success?

It's several years into the 21st century. Sam and Chris have decided that Adam, their "perfect" 7-year-old son, needs a brother exactly like him—with a few modifications. The parents visit Dr. Seedy's Human Cloning Lab to place their order.   1

SAM: We've filled out all the forms, and we're ready to proceed.   2

CHRIS: We're so excited about getting a match for our son, Adam. We didn't want to take a chance that Mother Nature might misfire. She can be so unpredictable.   3

DR. SEEDY: Well, your paperwork seems in order. We just need to finalize some of the specifics. Under "Human Disorders to Be Deleted" you've checked gluttony, greed, sloth, envy and pride.   4

SAM: And if we're limited on the number of choices, we definitely want gluttony on the deletion list. The last thing we want is a kid looking like Estelle and Ed's. I'd be amazed if Chuckie's an ounce under 90 pounds.   5

CHRIS: And trying to keep an eye on Adam when he's with Chuckie wears me out. You never know when the snack-time alarm will go off in Chuckie's head and Ding Dongs suddenly appear out of nowhere.   6

DR. SEEDY: No problem. We can keep your child svelte into his 50s. It's just a matter of mixing the right ingredients in the petri dish.   7

CHRIS: Sweetheart, I thought we agreed that pride is an important quality for our child to have. You have it under the "delete" column on the form.   8

SAM: Honey, when I say pride, think of Larry and Darla's kid. Do you want our child acting as if he's God's gift to the human race?   9

CHRIS: I understand, dear, but we also don't want a child with a fragile ego like Felicia, Ted and Alice's 10-year-old. Even after she went to computer camp last summer, she still couldn't program her 486DX2-66. Ted and Alice were devastated—and so was Felicia.   10

SAM: But that's not a lack of pride, dearest, that's pure ignorance. And with my genes, our child will have plenty of gray matter.   11

CHRIS: I just hope he doesn't have your lack of self-control.   12

SAM: Now hold on. I may get overly excited at times, but I'm never out 13
of control.

CHRIS: Of course not, love of my life. The door to the china closet 14
simply shattered on its own yesterday when you slammed the back
door.

DR. SEEDY: Please, please. Can we stay focused on the matter at hand? 15
You've requested a healthy dose of self-reliance for your cloned child, but
you also want to include a smidgen of altruism.

SAM: Right. We don't want our child to forget the less fortunate of the 16
world.

DR. SEEDY: Hmmm. A mixture of two parts Ted Turner with one part 17
Mother Teresa should do the trick.

CHRIS: Just as long as he doesn't have a grating Southern drawl. 18

SAM: Or a compelling drive to live in the slums of India. 19

DR.SEEDY: I'll do my best. 20

CHRIS: Excuse me? You'll do your best? Your advertisement guarantees 21
results. We will be given what we've asked for, won't we?

DR.SEEDY: Well, yes, but . . . 22

SAM: There are no "buts" to this agreement, pal. That's why we came 23
to you: to ensure that we'll get a perfect child.

CHRIS: And I have your ad with me. It says right here: "If you're not 100 24
percent satisfied with your purchase, return the cloned product within a
10-year period for a complete refund. (Refund does not include expenses
incurred from day of delivery till day of return.)"

SAM: The fine print also says: "Product guaranteed to perform as re- 25
quested, though the purity of each quality requested may vary."

CHRIS: Hey, what's going on here? Is this some kind of bait-and-switch 26
scam? Do you attract hapless couples who think you'll give them just
what they want in a child and instead hand over a brat they could have
created on their own? Is that it?

DR.SEEDY: Now, look. There are no absolute guarantees in this world. I 27
can promise you a kid that you've asked for—blond hair, blue eyes, math
and business skills that lean toward a career in high finance, and the
propensity not to have such negative qualities as gluttony, envy, sloth and
anger—but you'll still encounter unforeseen factors that will affect your
child's development.

CHRIS: Unforeseen factors? That's why we're here—to factor out those 28
unforeseen factors!

DR.SEEDY: Listen. If you don't like the stipulations of the contract, you 29
can cancel it right now. I have plenty of other customers in the waiting
room.

SAM: This is unbelievable! You come in to a cloning lab, expecting to deal 30
with high-minded professionals, and instead you get the equivalent of a

shady used-car salesman. I have a mind to report you to the Federal
Ethics Commission for Reputable Cloning.

CHRIS: Let's get out of here, dear.   31

(Both leave the office.)

SAM: Thank goodness there are plenty of other labs in the area.   32

CHRIS: Yeah. And hopefully they don't have scientists who think they're 33
God Almighty.

SELECTION 7 QUESTIONS

Comprehension and Analysis

1. What words and phrases does Schaefer use in the first paragraph to set
   the tone and establish his point of view?
2. What do Sam and Chris want from Dr. Seedy?
3. Why isn't the negotiation successful?
4. State Schaefer's thesis.

Reflect and Connect

5. How do you think Schaefer would answer these questions posed by Audesirk, Audesirk, and Byers in the theme's opening text chapter: "Do you
   think that using DNA technologies to change the composition of a
   human egg cell is ever justified? If so, what restrictions should be placed
   on such a use?" Compare and contrast Schaefer's probable answers with
   what you predicted Silver would say.

SELECTION 8   EDITORIAL CARTOON

MIKE THOMPSON

Mr. Thompson is Editorial Cartoonist for the Detroit Free Press. *His work has
won numerous honors, including The 2002 Overseas Press Club Award for
cartooning, the national 2000 Society of Professional Journalists Sigma Delta
Chi Award, and the 2000 National Press Foundation Award. Thompson, who
also draws for* USA Today, *has had his work reprinted in publications such as*
Time, Newsweek, The New York Times, *and* The Wall Street Journal. *In addition, his cartoons have been featured on* CNN, C-SPAN, *the NBC "Today"
show, and the* Fox News Network.

AN IDEA TO THINK ABOUT

If you could change your physical attributes—for example, have perfect vision, be shorter or taller—do you think your behavior would change?

SELECTION 8 QUESTIONS

1. Explain Thompson's message.
2. Compare and contrast how you think Silver and Schaefer would respond to Thompson's cartoon.

SELECTION 9 BIOMEDICINE

ALEXANDRA STIKEMAN

Ms. Stikeman was Associate Editor of Technology Review *when she wrote this June 2002 article.* Technology Review *(Cambridge, MA.) has been MIT's magazine of innovation since 1899. Its goal is "to promote the understanding of emerging technologies and their impact on business and society."*

IDEAS TO THINK ABOUT

Are you allergic to any medicine? If so, how did you discover the allergy? How do you think most allergies are discovered?

Your dirt-biking expedition has ended painfully—a few ribs broken in a tumble on the trail—and the emergency-room doctor has sent you home with a bottle of codeine. It should be enough to tide you over until the bones heal, unless you're one of the 20 million Americans who have a mutated form of an enzyme called cyp2d6, which normally converts codeine into the morphine that soothes pain. If you are, the enzyme won't work, and the pills won't even take the edge off. Worse yet, neither you nor your physician will know that until you take the drug. 1

Such is the reality of medicine today. Physicians can prescribe a drug based on a patient's symptoms, but the hidden details of an individual's genetic or molecular makeup can make him or her the wrong patient for that drug. Medications work differently in different people. What's more, in the case of diseases like cancer or arthritis, a patient's symptoms alone don't always tell doctors exactly what's wrong; subtle molecular differences can underlie seemingly similar illnesses. So choosing the treatment most likely to fix the problem is a hit-or-miss proposition. But that one-drug-fits-all reality is beginning to give way to a new era of "personalized medicine," in which physicians can diagnose their patients with unprecedented accuracy and treat each of them with drugs tailored not only to the disease, but also to the patient's genetic or metabolic profile. 2

"It's going to totally transform medicine, there's no question about it" says Susan Lindquist, director of MIT's Whitehead Institute for Biomedical Research. And it's going to be happening soon. Mark Levin, CEO of Cambridge, MA-based Millennium pharmaceuticals, offers one vision of what personalized medicine might mean for a patient: "When we walk into the doctor's office 10 years from now, we'll have our genome on a chip." Using that chip, Levin says, a doctor will be able to determine what diseases a patient is predisposed to and what medicines will provide the most benefit with the fewest side effects. Even the way we think about disease will be different, says Jeffrey Augen, director of life sciences strategy at IBM, because doctors will make diagnoses based on genes and proteins rather than on symptoms or the subjective analysis of tissue samples under a microscope. "So instead of a person having chronic inflammation or cancer, he or she will have a cox-2 enzyme disorder or a specific set of genetic mutations," Augen predicted at a recent conference in Boston. 3

The change is possible due in large part to emerging technologies that enable researchers to identify and analyze genes and proteins with phenomenal speed—thereby pinpointing the exact nature of different diseases and predicting individuals' responses to drugs. Even using conventional DNA and protein analysis technologies, researchers have already taken some first steps toward 4 personalized medicine. A woman with breast cancer, for example, can take a gene- or protein-based test that reveals whether her cancer will respond to certain drugs. But the key to gathering the massive amounts of genetic and molecular information that will expand personalized medicine's reach—and make it a commonplace tool in the doctor's office—is the thumbnail-sized biochip. These chips can analyze thousands of genes, proteins and other molecules at once from a single drop of blood.

One of the first triumphs for biochips in uncovering the molecular differences between diseases was a study led by biologists Patrick Brown at Stanford University and Louis Staudt at the National Cancer Institute in 2000. Using DNA microarrays—glass wafers spotted with thousands of DNA strands—the researchers examined patterns of gene activity underlying a type of cancer called non-Hodgkin's lymphoma. After examining nearly 18,000 genes, they discovered that what was once thought to be one disease was in fact two distinct diseases. What's more, the chemotherapy regimen normally prescribed for non-Hodgkin's lymphoma patients was significantly less successful for patients with one of those two diseases—a clear indication that better knowledge of what's going on at the genetic level could help doctors make better decisions about treatment.

DNA chips might soon begin to inform physicians' decisions about how they prescribe some of the most commonly used pharmaceuticals. Santa Clara, CA-based Affymetrix and Basel, Switzerland-based Roche Diagnostics have teamed up to develop biochips that could help predict patients' responses to such drugs as antidepressants and blood pressure regulators. The devices will be able to screen for several different mutations in the gene for the cyp2d6 enzyme—which helps metabolize a number of drugs in addition to codeine—and in another key enzyme gene.

Even-more-sophisticated biochips might ultimately provide a quicker means of reading genetic fingerprints right in the doctor's office. One drawback of existing DNA chips, for example, is that researchers first have to modify the sample of DNA in order for the chip to detect it. But physicist Scott Manalis and his group at MIT's Media Laboratory are fabricating a silicon microchip that could potentially provide instant notification when it detects specific gene sequences in a sample of blood. In their device, micrometer-sized silicon cantilevers sense the molecular charges associated with biological molecules such as DNA and could produce a telltale electrical signal. "This opens up the possibility of making a simple biosensor for point-of-care diagnostics," says Manalis.

Sometimes, however, DNA doesn't tell the whole story. It's often the proteins encoded by the DNA that actually determine whether a person is sick or well, and whether a drug is beneficial or toxic. Biologist David Sabatini at the Whitehead Institute found a way to look at the real-life activity of proteins by building arrays of living cells on glass chips. Sabatini recently cofounded the biotech firm Akceli in Cambridge, MA, to commercialize his technology, which he hopes to start selling to drug companies in the near future. Drug researchers could, for instance, equip each cell on the chip with a different variant of the body's drug-metabolizing enzymes, and then expose the chip to a variety of drugs. By monitoring the cells' responses, researchers could determine if a drug is toxic across the board, only to people with a particular enzyme variant, or not at all. "You can essentially create drug side-effect profiles," says Sabatini. If a drug is toxic to some people but otherwise looks promising, a company may decide to pursue its development, targeting it to only those patients it benefits. Such a drug, developed specifically for people with not only a particular disease but a particular metabolic profile as well, would be the epitome of a personalized medication.

In the next decade, more and more such drugs, and the diagnostic tests   9 necessary to choose among them, will begin to hit the market. So in the future, when you go to pop a pill you haven't tried before, you won't have to wonder if it's really the right drug for you. You'll know.

SELECTION 9 QUESTIONS

Vocabulary

1. Explain the concept of "personalized medicine."
2. Explain "point-of-care diagnostics."

Comprehension and Analysis

3. Give an example of a medication that works differently in different people. Give an example of how seemingly similar illnesses can be very different and require different treatments. What does Stikeman see as a remedy to this problem?
4. How could biomedical advances help existing medicines to be more effective and aid the development of new medicines?
5. State Stikeman's thesis.

Reflect and Connect

6. How do you feel about the concept of "personalized medicine"? Describe what you see as one potential positive effect and one potential negative effect.

SELECTION 10 ETHICAL DECISION MAKING IN A PLURALISTIC SOCIETY

DANIEL E. KOSHLAND, JR.

Dr. Koshland is Professor Emeritus of molecular biology at the University of California, Berkeley, and was the long-time Editor-in-Chief of Science *magazine. He helped establish and was chairman of the Academy Forum, a committee of the National Academy of Sciences charged with developing policy on issues that pose dilemmas at the interface between science and societal problems. His awards include the National Medal of Science, the Pauling Award of the American Chemical Society, and election to the National Academy of Sciences. This article is from* Biotechnology: Science, Engineering, and Ethical Challenges for the 21st Century, *Frederick B. Rudolph and Larry W. McIntire (eds.), published by the National Academy of Sciences.*

IDEAS TO THINK ABOUT

What do you consider the "best" scientific discovery of the last 50 years? What do you consider to be the "worst" scientific discovery of the last 50 years?

WORDS TO KNOW

prescient (¶6)—foresighted, perceptive
actuarial (¶11)—the theories of probability and statistical calculations of life expectancy; mortality tables and probability tables dealing with events such as sickness and death are determined by an actuary. The rates for the various types of insurance are set on the basis of these tables. The basic assumption in actuarial science is that the frequency with which events occurred in the past may be used to predict or measure the probability with which they will occur in the future.

Ethics is largely a matter of each person's independent judgment, because morality is largely defined by religion. Many religions have similar standards, but nevertheless, we have a pluralistic society with many religions. Thus, it is going to be very difficult for society to decide what is absolutely morally right and wrong. It is even more difficult to preemptively judge new scientific discoveries. Science has never been more powerful than it is today, and in the future it is going to be able to do a lot more things than it is going to be allowed to do.

Many scientists today feel perplexed by, and indignant about, the criticism of science. They think they have never done more for society and for its standard of living. In 1878, life expectancy was 34 years; in 1900, 47 years; in 1953, 67 years; and in 1991, 76 years. Scientists have added not only to life expectancy, but also to our pleasures in life. We have television and radio, which add to people's enjoyment. We have diminished mental illness and infectious diseases. So, with all of these amazing benefits, many scientists are perplexed about being criticized for the supposedly terrible damage that science has done to society.

Part of the reason for this criticism is that in a democracy we do not want to have any group that is adored as superior beings. The essence of a democracy is that any barber or taxi driver thinks he could run the country better than the president of the United States. We do not want people adoring a Hitler or a Mussolini and yet we ask people to acquire knowledge in some of these areas of science before they come to judgments. I was once interviewed by a television reporter who thought that scientists all got together every year and decided (against the wishes of humanity) what discoveries we were going to make and what research we would do. As we all know, that is not the way it is done. We cannot decide in advance what should and should not be discovered.

All knowledge is an advance. Two of the most controversial areas of knowledge—genetic engineering and cloning of organisms—are areas in which the advance of knowledge has been spectacular and has added to the increase in the life expectancy. Yet, even I, a strong proponent of science, see that there are some areas that we perhaps should avoid. However, in almost every case, I believe these areas are easily handled by society's decisions. It is up to scientists to inform the public of what they have done or are capable of doing and to give them the information in the most clear and simple terms. The public, in an informed dialogue, must decide what discoveries should be applied. It will be very dangerous if we start saying that there are certain areas of science that should not even be investigated.

So why are scientists criticized? Why are scientists accused of polluting the atmosphere? Why are we accused of doing these bad experiments in genetic engineering? A great deal of it is due to our successes. If the automobile had not been as popular as it is, we would not have the problem of clogged highways and carbon dioxide in the atmosphere. If people had not been living as long and so able to procreate, we would not have the overpopulation problem. People who criticize science do not pause to consider that the benefits of science have been the reasons for the excesses.

There is more to the public's reaction. A prescient book called *Future Shock* stated the essence of the problem: The rate of change in society is too rapid for us to assimilate. When golf was invented, it was a threat to the church. Suddenly, men had an alternative on Sunday mornings instead of going with the family to church. It was a serious problem, but gradually people coped with that problem and churches responded. Then the automobile came along, which was not merely a form of transportation, but also a change in the morality of society. In Victorian days, young girls did not go out with a man unless there was a chaperone present, but the automobile changed that and changed the morality of society. It took years for society to adjust to this new world. Then came birth control pills, surrogate mothers, and genetic engineering, all in rapid succession and following each other ever more rapidly. Society reacts: "These scientists are changing our lives." Not just a little bit, by inventing a television set you can turn on and off, but by changing moral values as well. Scientists must learn to assume responsibility for describing the ramifications and society must decide how far we should go. We do not want to stop the knowledge, but we want to consider the applications and their effects.

THE HUMAN GENOME PROJECT: IS IT BENEFICIAL?

Let us consider problems related to the Human Genome Project. One result of the project might be that we could do preemptive medicine, preventing problems before they become too extensive. There are people who say that we should not even know about the Genome, that it is too much information and too predictive of the future. Long before the genome project, we knew about a disease called phenylketonuria, a genetic disease that could be predicted in a family if there were certain signs. This disease was likely to attack a young child, but if you eliminated phenylalanine from the child's diet in the early days of its life and controlled phenylalanine consumption later, that child was completely normal. If the child consumed the amount of phenylalanine that most babies usually consume, it would develop severe mental retardation and never become a fully functional adult. No one would seriously argue that you should deny the information to that family or that child. The Human Genome Project is really a big extension of this situation.   7

Another example is a disease called hypercholesterolemia. If you are homozygous for this disease, you produce cholesterol deficiencies such that you will get atherosclerosis at an early age and will probably be dead in your early teens. If you have a moderate version of the disease and are extraordinarily careful not to ingest any cholesterol, you could live to a reasonable age. There are many diseases that can be avoided by a change in lifestyle.   8

There can be positive aspects to knowing your genetic heritage. I happen to have been extraordinarily clever at picking my ancestors. I discovered recently that I can eat any amount of eggs Benedict and Hollandaise sauce without any damage to my arteries. I consider it terrible that I learned this just recently. If, because of the Human Genome Project, I had this information earlier, my life would have been much more enjoyable.   9

SOCIETAL PROBLEMS RELATING
TO THE HUMAN GENOME PROJECT

10

What are the disadvantages of the Genome project? Why would anybody say you should not know about the Genome? Suppose a director of a medical school has access to an applicant's DNA sequence and sees that the applicant's life expectancy is low. Another applicant is almost as qualified and is going to live to be 80. What is the benefit for society of accepting people who are not going to be using their medical knowledge for very long instead of people who could use it for a long time? Should we be faced with that? A corporation, you could argue, wants to train young executives, and the longevity problem arises again. I believe that is a fairly easy problem to handle. Society as a whole must decide whether we are going to do that. There is a certain inefficiency in training M.D.s who will not get a chance to practice very long, but the alternative—telling young people that they have no future—is too terrible for us to contemplate and we are not going to do it. So we come to an understanding that life expectancy is not a prerequisite for medical school or other jobs.

11

The insurance problem, which is frequently mentioned as a result of the genome project, seems to me no problem at all. The insurance companies now have two forms of insurance. One is group insurance, which is what they generally like to sell because they sell to a large number of people, all of whom are getting insurance. They know ahead of time that some of those people are going to die or have very serious illness very quickly, but they use actuarial principles to figure that a certain number are going to be healthy and pay the premiums and a certain number are going to get sick.

12

There is no reason why genetic information is going to affect that. Insurance companies can use the same actuarial principles. Knowledge of the genome and medical science will only make it better for the insurance companies, because a certain number of diseases will be cured and those people will live longer than expected from past data.

But what about individual insurance? Insurance companies now ask very intrusive questions, such as Do you smoke? When did your brothers and sisters die? When did your parents die? When did your grandparents die? Have you had a heart attack? Have you refused any operations? In other words, they compile a lot of information and provide coverage on the basis of actuarial principles. There is no reason why DNA sequence cannot be one part of this body of information along with the rest.

14

Is that too intrusive? Maybe so. Laws can make it illegal to have insurance companies get that information, but all it will change is the actuarial calculations. It is not either moral or immoral. It is society's decision that, in effect, fairly healthy people will pay a little higher rates to cover people who have less life expectancy. However, there is a reciprocal requirement. If the insurance company should not have that DNA information, individuals who want to be insured also should not have it. If you allowed people access to that information and they knew they were going to die soon, they could then buy millions of dollars of insurance and tilt the actuarial tables. So when people consider the morality of insurance, they must also consider the reciprocal obligations of all concerned.

The genome project is a blessing. It is going to save many lives. The information from the project is already enormously valuable. We have now found, for example, that an inheritable disease such as colorectal cancer is related to other cancers, such as kidney cancer and uterine cancer. They are all related by the same genes. That means if you have a family history of any of these cancers, you should have a colonoscopy. Colorectal cancer is a 100 percent curable disease if you are warned in time. If you do not have the genetic tendency, your statistics are lower and you can avoid the rather unpleasant colonoscopy. 15

That kind of information is going to be available with DNA sequencing, and I see very little reason not to go ahead with it. You can make various rules about using DNA information for jobs and insurance, but with insurance, you are just changing actuarial calculations. I was amused in the discussion on health care that some people were outraged that the insurance companies were actually turning people down because they already had a disease. Insurance was seen as sort of a civil right that you cannot be denied. In other words, after you have cancer you go and take out insurance, or after you become pregnant you take out insurance for health care for pregnant mothers. There is nothing moral in that. If you could be allowed to get insurance after you know you have the disease, it would be a wonderful system, but you would have to pay quite different premiums. The actuarial system depends on a number of healthy people carrying the load for people who are ill. 16

CLONING

What about cloning individuals? I am more hesitant here. My initial reaction was that nobody should be cloned. Then I thought of having eight people exactly like me and all of us on the Supreme Court. Then I began to think the Celtics would probably like five people just like Larry Bird and the Lakers five just like Magic Johnson. Would that be a good idea? You could get Secretariats produced in large numbers and horse races would become a thing of the past. So I think there is some limit on this. 17

However, there does not seem to be an absolute disadvantage to cloning. The initial reaction of most people is that you cannot use humans for experiments, but that is modified in ethical drug trials. The National Institutes of Health, for example, makes it difficult to change the germ line. That really is peculiar because we are changing the germ line all the time. Insulin is used to keep alive people with diabetes who formerly would have died very early in life. That is changing the germ line enormously. We are keeping very ill people 18 alive and are changing the germ line for the worse. Now, if someone wants to help a family who has had diabetes in its germ line for years and years by putting in a good gene so the next generations will not have that problem, is that a terrible thing?

I am defective person. My eyes are such that I was 20/200 when I was a 19 kid. I would not have seen a saber tooth tiger until it came up to lick my face, so my family and all of its descendants would have been done for. I wear glasses to correct that defect. We do not have fur so we live in air conditioned rooms and wear clothes. So the idea of keeping defective people alive is something society has been doing for a long time, but all of a sudden it is a bad thing to change the germ line. I am not sure that I understand this logic.

Genetic engineering can be abused. I do not want to understate this. 20 However, if a child has diabetes, you ask to correct the gene. Everybody would say that is fine. If a child has an IQ of 50, or the family has the gene for an IQ of 50, we would all probably agree that the gene should be corrected. What about a family that has a series of children who have IQs of 95 and they would like to have children with IQs of 120? The children would get into Harvard and do very well in some law school. Is that bad? You start worrying a little about that.

Once you invent something people are going to want to use it; I do not 21 want to pretend that a discovery in science will not be used in some bad ways. Consider again the cloning of humans. Suppose you could produce 20 identical people who could solve a very important problem by being part of an experiment on why violence exists. If these 20 identical cloned people were to grow up in 20 different environments with good homes, bad homes, ghettos, and very aggressive communities, how would that change their lives? Would it be a terrible thing to use cloning for that purpose?

EXPERIMENTING WITH HUMANS

We are already experimenting with humans in major ways without knowing it. 22 We pass laws that constrain our behavior, and we are not always sure that it is going to turn out correctly. So it seems to me that each of these decisions is going to have to be decided not on a moral or ethical basis, but on the basis of common sense. I think we all have sort of an ingrained sense of what is right and wrong, but sometimes in the modern world of television and instant slogans we get the wrong impression.

Several years ago I was asked to discuss the question of whether or not 23 we should work with microcephalic children. This is a "child" born without a brain. The brain essentially begins at the end of the stem, so the child really has no brain. In the old days it would have died very, very quickly, but now it can be kept alive on a life support system. I would not call this "a person" because the courts have decided that death occurs when the brain goes dead. So this organism, if you want to call it that, has no brain, yet it is functioning. Its heart is functioning so it can be kept alive. Some people were suggesting using its organs for organ transplants or using it for the study of development. My advice was that you might learn a lot of science, but it would be too ghoulish. People would react against scientists. Recently a federal judge ruled that a family who had a microcephalic baby and who wanted to end the life support system would not be allowed to do so because it violated the rights of that so-called child.

I think it is rather interesting that a group of scientists decided it was too 24 ghoulish to run experiments or keep children alive for organs that could be used later, and yet a judge sees it from a different point of view. He cites the rights of children and orders this family to do a very expensive procedure in a situation where this organism will never develop into what anyone would call a child.

The same situation arose in California recently where the growth hor- 25 mone made by recombinant DNA, which produces much more milk in cows by genetic engineering methods, has been declared a terrible thing. It is an amusing case because although the Food and Drug Administration (FDA) said that the product is not dangerous to people's health, it was pressured by dairy farmers to say use of the hormone would produce so much milk that the price of milk would drop, and therefore the hormone should be banned. The FDA finally came out for use of the growth hormone but did so with much hesitation. This was noted by the people who are against it and they waged a big campaign. Moreover, the California law is rather interesting. The law says supermarkets have to say that this milk is guaranteed not to have this hormone, which is a natural hormone. All the genetic engineering has done is to produce more of it in cows. So if this law is passed, it means that no milk can be sold in California because the milk contains natural hormone. California already is a nuclear-free zone. It is now also going to be a milk-free zone.

NEED FOR PUBLIC EDUCATION

There is great pressure on scientists to be perfect. However, for all future ex- 26 periments to be ethically correct requires a concomitant commitment on the part of the public, and in particular the media, to have a reasonable amount of scientific information so that they can make informed judgments about scientific matters. Scientists do not have to explain to the public the details of DNA or the structure of a protein before they can get an opinion on whether fertilizing eggs in a test tube for childless couples is approved, but society needs to make the decisions: Do we want to have this technology used? Do we want to use it under certain limited circumstances?

Scientists have a big advantage over other people in helping society 27 solve these problems because scientists have experience with complexity.

They are used to dealing with complicated issues that are not clear-cut. I happen to be in the pro-choice group on abortion, but I was not pleased with the people who argued that pro-choice was simply morally right and a woman had the right to her own body. Good slogan, but oversimplified. There were many devout Catholics who were also good friends of mine who really felt that it was morally wrong. That is an illustration of what I mentioned earlier. In a pluralistic society there are going to be people with deep religious convictions, so no one can say what is morally right for everyone. There have to be compromises. Each person has a choice on that issue. Some of the people who said a woman has control of her own body as an argument for abortion then reverted to the other side on surrogate motherhood, saying a woman should not be allowed to have a child for something as crass as money. If a woman has the right to her own body, she should have the right to create life as well as a right to destroy it.

Many of these issues are very complicated and will require a great deal of 28 common sense, but the decision making is going to be made easier by people who understand complexity. We need to sort things out in the very big mixture of things rather than just state a big moral principle and be stuck with this generalization.

Many of these subjects are not clear-cut morally or ethically. When re- 29 combinant DNA research began, nobody could have predicted the big biotechnology industry, how valuable it would be, how many lives it would save, how many jobs it would create. We now have an enormous capacity to solve a lot of problems. A good example of a benefit of the Human Genome Project is that it will be particularly useful for multigenic diseases, for example, mental illness. It has been estimated that 50 percent of the people who are homeless are mentally ill. So when the president of the United States says he is going to solve the homeless problem by retraining, somebody has not told him what the real problem is. If you can solve the problem of mental illness indirectly by a genome project, it seems to me that you have contributed an enormous amount to society.

We, scientists and nonscientists, are all going to have to work together. I 30 think that scientists who are in the ivory tower would much rather just solve scientific problems. Earlier in my life, I said that my job was to solve problems. Society could use the science it wanted and I should not be forced to get out of my laboratory and explain to other people what was going on. I now think that is impossible. Discoveries in science are now so powerful that we are affecting people's lives every day. We are going to have to explain the nature of these problems, the nature of discoveries, and the random nature of investigator-initiated research, which I think brought us to where we are today.

Some discoveries are going to be made that will have a big effect on soci- 31 ety, and society has a right to hear about these discoveries. It is going to be a lot of work for all of us, but that is the way that the ethical problems need to be solved.

SELECTION 10 QUESTIONS

Vocabulary

1. Explain what Koshland means in paragraph 1 when he says, "It is even more difficult to preemptively judge new scientific discoveries."

2. Koshland says that "for all future experiments to be ethically correct requires a concomitant commitment on the part of the public, and in particular the media. . . ." (paragraph 26) Explain the "concomitant commitment."

3. Explain what Koshland means in paragraph 30 by "the random nature of investigator-initiated research."

Comprehension and Analysis

4. Why does Koshland believe it is going to be very difficult for society to decide and agree on what is absolutely morally right and wrong?

5. Describe two examples Koshland uses to support his premise that the rate of change in society is too rapid for us to assimilate.

6. Describe one advantage and one of disadvantage of the Human Genome project. Does Koshland predict that overall there will be more advantages or disadvantages result from the project?

7. State Koshland's thesis.

Reflect and Connect

8. Silver, Thompson and Koshland all directly discuss the possibilities of the Human Genome project. Compare and contrast their views on the advantages and disadvantages of the project's results.

INVESTIGATING OTHER POINTS OF VIEW . . .

One way to investigate a variety of points of view on the many issues connected with biotechnology is through the resources of Research Navigator™. Once you log on to Research Navigator.com and enter your personal passcode, (from inside the front cover of this text) you have access to three databases of credible and reliable source material: 1) EBSCO's Content Select Academic Journal Database with content from the leading academic journals, 2) *The New York Times* Search by Subject™ Archive with full-text articles from *The New York Times*, 3) Link Library providing editorially selected "best of the Web" sites. For more information about Research Navigator™ and how to use it efficiently, see "Introducing Research Navigator™" starting on page RN–1.

AFTER CONSIDERING SEVERAL POINTS OF VIEW . . .

A. Genetically modified (GM) seeds could significantly increase the per-acre yield of crops such as corn, sweet potatoes, rice, and cotton while significantly reducing pesticide use. However, GM seeds could be potentially harmful to human health and the environment. Select one crop and discuss what you see as the advantages and/or disadvantages of using GM seeds. In addition, address the issue of whether the world should standardize any restrictions on planting GM seeds or whether each country should decide independently.

B. Most of the Human Genome Project and related biotechnical research focuses on how the new technologies can be used in industrialized nations. There is, however, considerable information that many of these technologies could be focused to help improve health in developing countries, such as, creating tests to accurately diagnose the early stages of infectious diseases and developing vaccines against infectious diseases. Discuss the advantages and disadvantages of focusing our biotechnical research on global health issues.

C. Much hope has been placed in the work of genetic scientists, but accompanying the potential miracles are serious ethical questions. For example, allowing prospective parents to choose which genes to give to their children to provide them increased chances for health, longevity, happiness, and success sounds miraculous. However, the ethical questions surrounding the procedure abound. Select one example of human genetic engineering and discuss what you see as the immediate and long-term advantages and disadvantages of the procedure.

THEME 5

RESPONSIBILITY

Enron executives. A famous ImClone shareholder. Politicians. Sports, movie, and music stars. Arthur Andersen accountants. It seems that the list of folks who attempt to evade or at least reduce their responsibility for their behavior gets longer every day. In fact, a 2002 survey of college students by Students in Free Enterprise found that 84 percent believe the United States is having a business crisis, and 77 percent think CEOs should be held personally responsible for it.

It doesn't appear, however, that responsibility for personal behavior and developing ethical guidelines to live by are problems of just the rich and famous. When the same students were asked about their own ethics, they had a different view: Almost 60 percent admitted cheating on a test (66 percent of men, 54 percent of women), and only 19 percent said they would report a classmate who cheated.

Are Americans experiencing a crisis in ethics? Do we have a tendency to slither out of taking responsibility for our behavior? Have we become a nation of blamers and excuse-makers: "Other people do it"; "My boss told me to do it"; "My actions didn't hurt anybody"; "It was an unfair situation"; "No one knew"?

Consider these situations:

The cashier at the grocery store gives you too much change—a $10 bill instead of a $1 bill. What do you do?

The questions on today's biology test are more difficult than the professor predicted and you are having a tough time. You notice that the person on your right is cheating. You could see those answers if you moved just a bit.

At work, your project team has a major proposal due tomorrow. In your final meeting today, one of the members tells of a personal tragedy that makes it impossible for him to complete his share of the tasks. The other members of the team plead with you to work overtime with them and complete the project. If you work, you'll miss a much-anticipated date; if you don't work, the proposal will never get done.

What do you do? How do you make "responsible" choices? Ethicists say the first step is to acknowledge that acting responsibly is a first-person activity: It doesn't matter if other people see us or know about the behavior because the person that matters the most—our self—knows our intentions and motivations. W. H. Ferry, in a Center for the Study of Democratic Institutions paper, says responsibility always has to do with behavior—action rather than thought; what an individual does, not what he or she considers doing.

However, scientists disagree on just how much control we have over our decisions and actions. At one end of the continuum, we have the often-accepted view that individual responsibility is a myth because a person does not have autonomous control of his or her behavior. According to psychologist B. F. Skinner, "A scientific analysis of behavior must, I believe, assume that a person's behavior is controlled by his genetic and environmental histories rather than by the person himself as an initiating, creative agent." At the other end of the continuum, we have the also accepted view that a person is an independent individual free to weigh the consequences of his or her behavior, take action, and accept the consequences.

Additional questions spin around whether society should have special compassion for those who grow up in dysfunctional families, live in troublesome surroundings, or are members of oppressed groups. "American life is increasingly characterized by the plaintive insistence: I am a victim," says author Charles J. Sykes. "From the drug addicts of the ghettos to the self-help groups of the suburbs, the mantra is the same: I am not responsible; it's not my fault." "We've gotten to the point," says Chicago attorney Newton Minow, "where everybody's got a right and nobody's got a responsibility."

The authors in this Theme provide a variety of insights into how we make our choices and accept responsibility for them.

To place the topic in context, the Theme opens with "Self-Justification and the Need to Maintain Self-Esteem," Chapter 6 of Aronson, Wilson, and Akert's *Social Psychology* text. Topics include the need to justify our actions and self-justification versus self-maintenance.

Next, Antonio Machado y Ruiz, one of the most important and popular Spanish poets of his generation, creates a word picture of how we move through life as a "Traveler/Caminante."

Yale Law School Professor Stephen L. Carter, in an excerpt from his book *Integrity*, sets forth the case for how Americans who "are full of fine talk about how we need more integrity, but when push comes to shove would rather be winners," can work toward "Becoming People of Integrity." In "I Think You

Should Be Responsible; Me, I'm not So Sure" educator-writer Gordon D. Marino wonders whether we've considered the potentially disturbing consequences of the commandment to "take responsibility for ourselves."

Seth Godin then recalls how "I Was Almost Killed on My Way to Work Today" and wonders if people behave the same way with friends as when they are anonymous.

Cartoonist Clay Bennett asks, "How important are ethics in today's society?"

In "Why Pay When It's 'Free'?" Noel C. Paul says the decision whether to accept free Internet, cable, and satellite TV hookups seems as simple as Ethics 101. So, he has to wonder about the new industries that have sprung up to facilitate what many experts label the practice of "justified" theft. Then Martha Beck relates how we all face the question of whether to accept blame or not to accept blame in "It Ain't Me, Babe."

The Asian myth, "Otter's Children," provides our final insight into the complicated nature of life and the concept of individual responsibility.

As you read the selections in this Theme and other articles and essays on responsibility, answer questions such as these as a matter of course:

1. Do I understand all the author's words and phrases?
2. What is the author's thesis (conclusion)?
3. What facts, opinions, and reasoned judgments does the author provide to support and develop the thesis?
4. Are the author's facts, opinions, and reasoned judgments derived from respected sources?
5. Are there factual errors or misleading interpretations?
6. Has significant information been omitted or arbitrarily discounted?
7. What new information does this author add to my understanding of the issue?

SELECTION 1   SELF-JUSTIFICATION AND THE NEED TO MAINTAIN SELF-ESTEEM

ELLIOT ARONSON, TIM WILSON, AND ROBIN AKERT

Dr. Aronson has done pioneering work in the areas of social influence, persuasion, and prejudice reduction. He has written or edited numerous books, and is the only person in the history of the American Psychological Associa-

tion to have earned all three of its major academic awards for *Distinguished Teaching, Distinguished Research,* and *Distinguished Writing.* He is currently Professor Emeritus at the University of California Santa Cruz and a Visiting Professor at Stanford University.

Dr. Wilson has been Professor of Psychology at the University of Virginia for more than 20 years. He has written extensively in the areas of introspection, attitude change, and self-knowledge. He is active in numerous professional organizations, and his research has received the support of the National Science Foundation and the National Institute for Mental Health.

Dr. Akert is Professor of Psychology at Wellesley College, where she was awarded the Pinanski Prize for Excellence in Teaching. She publishes primarily in the area of nonverbal communication.

AN IDEA TO THINK ABOUT

Most of us see ourselves as reasonable, moral, and smart. How do you react when someone or something challenges how you view yourself?

WORDS TO KNOW

Key terms are in bold face type and are defined in context.

On March 26, 1997, thirty-nine people were found dead at a luxury estate in Rancho Santa Fe, California—participants in a mass suicide. They were all members of an obscure cult called Heaven's Gate founded by Marshall Herff Applewhite, a former college professor. Each body was laid out neatly, feet clad in brand-new black Nikes, face covered with a purple shroud. The cult members died willingly and peacefully—and didn't really consider it suicide. They left behind detailed videotapes describing their beliefs and intentions: They believed the Hale-Bopp Comet, at the time clearly visible in the western sky, was their ticket to a new life in paradise. They were convinced that Hale-Bopp's wake was a gigantic spaceship whose mission was to carry them off to a new incarnation. To be picked up by the spaceship, they first needed to rid themselves of their current "containers." That is, they needed to leave their own bodies by ending their lives. Alas, no spaceship ever came.

Several weeks before the mass suicide, when Hale-Bopp was still too distant to be seen with the naked eye, some members of the cult walked into a specialty store and purchased a very expensive high-powered telescope. They wanted to get a clearer view of the comet and the spaceship they believed was traveling behind it. A few days later, they made their way back to the store, returned the telescope, and politely asked for their money back. When the store manager asked them if they had problems with the scope, they replied, "Well, gosh, we found the comet, but we can't find anything following it" (Ferris, 1997). Although the store manager tried to convince them that there was nothing wrong with the telescope and that there was nothing following the comet, they remained unconvinced. Their attitude was clear, and given their premise, their logic was impeccable: (1) We know an alien spaceship is following behind the Hale-Bopp Comet, and (2) if an expensive telescope failed to reveal that spaceship, then (3) there must be something wrong with the telescope.

Their logic might strike you as strange, irrational, or stupid. But generally speaking, the members of the Heaven's Gate cult were not stupid or irrational or crazy. How do we know this? For one thing, neighbors who knew them considered them pleasant, smart, reasonable people. Moreover, they were expert at using computers and the Internet and earned their living by setting up highly innovative Web pages. Clients who worked closely with them were impressed, describing them as unusually bright, talented, and creative. What is the process by which intelligent, sane people can succumb to such fantastic thinking and self-destructive behavior? We will attempt to explain their actions near the end of this chapter. For now, we will simply state that their behavior is not unfathomable—it is simply an extreme example of a normal human tendency: the tendency to justify our actions.

*   *   *

THE NEED TO JUSTIFY OUR ACTIONS

During the past half-century, social psychologists have discovered that one of the most powerful determinants of human behavior stems from our need to preserve a stable, positive self-concept. In other words, we humans strive to maintain a relatively favorable view of ourselves, particularly when we encounter evidence that contradicts our typically rosy self-image (Aronson, 1969, 1992a, 1998; Baumeister, 1993; Cooper, 1998; Devine, 1998; Harmon-Jones, 1998; Leippe & Eisenstadt, 1998; Wicklund & Brehm, 1998). Most of us want to believe that we are reasonable, decent folks who make wise decisions, do not behave immorally, and have integrity. In short, we want to believe that we do not do stupid, cruel, or absurd things. But maintaining this belief is not always easy. As we go through life, we encounter a great many challenges to this belief. The topic of this chapter is how human beings deal with those challenges.

The Theory of Cognitive Dissonance

Most of us have a need to see ourselves as reasonable, moral, and smart.
When we are confronted with information implying that we may have behaved in ways that are irrational, immoral, or stupid we experience a good deal of discomfort. This feeling of discomfort caused by performing an action that runs counter to one's customary (typically positive) conception of oneself is referred to as **cognitive dissonance.** A half-century of research has demonstrated that cognitive dissonance is a major motivator of human thought and behavior. Leon Festinger (1957) was the first to investigate the precise workings of this powerful phenomenon and elaborated his findings into what is arguably social psychology's most important and most provocative theory, the theory of cognitive dissonance. Initially, social psychologists believed that cognitive dissonance could be caused by *any* two discrepant cognitions (Brehm & Cohen, 1962; Festinger, 1957; Festinger & Aronson, 1960; Wicklund & Brehm, 1976). But subsequent research made it clear that not all cognitive inconsistencies are equally upsetting. Rather it was discovered that dissonance is most powerful and most upsetting when people behave in ways that threaten their image of themselves. This is upsetting precisely because it forces us to confront the discrepancy between who we think we are and how we have behaved (Aronson, 1968, 1969, 1992a, 1998; Aronson, Chase, Helmreich, & Ruhnke, 1974; Greenwald & Ronis, 1978; Harmon-Jones & Mills, 1998; Thibodeau & Aronson, 1992).

Cognitive dissonance always produces discomfort and therefore motivates a person to try to reduce the discomfort, in much the same way as hunger and thirst produce discomfort that motivates a person to eat or drink. But unlike satisfying hunger or thirst by eating or drinking, the ways of reducing dissonance are not simple; rather, they often lead to fascinating changes in the way we think about the world and the way we behave. As you will see, many of these behaviors are powerful and nonobvious. How can we reduce dissonance? There are three basic ways:

- By changing our behavior to bring it in line with the dissonant cognition
- By attempting to justify our behavior through changing one of the dissonant cognitions
- By attempting to justify our behavior by adding new cognitions.

To illustrate, let's look at a behavior that millions of people engage in several times a day—smoking cigarettes. If you are a smoker, you are likely to experience dissonance because you know you are engaging in behavior that stands a good chance of producing a painful, early death. How can you reduce this dissonance? The most direct way is to change your behavior—to give up smoking. Your behavior would then be consistent with your knowledge of the link between smoking and cancer. Though many people have succeeded in doing just that, it's not easy—many have tried to quit and failed. What do these people do? It would be erroneous to assume that they simply swallow hard and prepare to die. They don't. Rick Gibbons and his colleagues (Gibbons, Eggleston, & Benthin, 1997) studied the behavior and attitudes of heavy smokers who attended a smoking cessation clinic and succeeded in quitting smoking for a while but then relapsed into heavy smoking again. What do you suppose the researchers discovered? Heavy smokers who tried to quit and failed actually succeeded in lowering their perception of the dangers of smoking. In this way, they could continue to smoke without feeling terrible about it.

Smokers can come up with some pretty creative ways to justify their smoking. Some succeed in convincing themselves that the data linking cigarette smoking to cancer are inconclusive. Others try to add new cognitions—for example, the erroneous belief that filters trap most of the harmful chemicals and thus reduce the threat of cancer. Some add a cognition that allows them to focus on the vivid exception: "Look at old Sam Carruthers—he's 97 years old and he's been smoking a pack a day since he was 12. That proves it's not always bad for you." Still others add the cognition that smoking is an extremely enjoyable activity, one for which it is worth risking cancer. Others even succeed in convincing themselves that all things considered, smoking is worthwhile because it relaxes them, reduces nervous tension, and so on.

These justifications may sound silly to the nonsmoker. That is precisely our point. As the smokers' rationales we have presented show, people experiencing dissonance will often go to extreme lengths to reduce it. Similar justifications have been generated by people who try and fail to lose weight, who refuse to practice safer sex, or who receive unwelcome information about their general health (Aronson, 1997b; Croyle & Jemmott, 1990; Goleman, 1982; Kassarjian & Cohen, 1965; Leishman, 1988). To escape from dissonance, people will engage in quite extraordinary rationalizing. Occasionally, these illusions can be helpful; for example, Shelley Taylor and her colleagues have demonstrated that those who harbor unrealistically positive illusions about surviving a terminal illness like AIDS live longer than those who are more "realistic" (Taylor, 1989; Taylor & Armour, 1996; Taylor & Brown, 1988; Taylor & Gollwitzer, 1995). Far more often (as in the case of smoking) these illusions are destructive.

Rational Behavior versus Rationalizing Behavior

Most people think of themselves as rational beings, and generally speaking, that is accurate: We are certainly capable of rational thought. But as our examples illustrate, the need to maintain our self-esteem produces thinking that is not always rational; rather, it is *rationalizing*. People who are in the midst of reducing dissonance are so involved with convincing themselves that they are right that they frequently end up behaving irrationally and maladaptively. In the case of cigarette smoking, the end result could be tragic.

To demonstrate the irrationality of dissonance-reducing behavior, Edward Jones and Rika Kohler (1959) performed a simple experiment. Their experiment was conducted in a southern town in the late 1950s, when segregation was still widespread. First, they selected individuals who were deeply committed to a position on the issue of racial segregation—some of the participants were in favor of segregation, and others were opposed to it. Next the researchers presented these individuals with a series of arguments on both sides of the issue. Some of the arguments, on each side, were plausible, and others, on each side, were rather silly. The question was, which of the arguments would people remember best?

If Jones and Kohler's (1959) participants were behaving in a purely rational manner, we would expect them to remember the plausible arguments best and the implausible arguments least, regardless of which side they were on. After all, why would anyone want to remember implausible arguments? What does dissonance theory predict? A silly argument in favor of one's own position arouses some dissonance because it raises doubts about the wisdom of that position or the intelligence of the people who agree with it. Likewise, a sensible argument on the other side of the issue also arouses some dissonance because it raises the possibility that the other side might be closer to the truth than the person had thought. Because these arguments arouse dissonance, one tries not to think about them; that is, one might not learn them very well, or one might simply forget about them. This is exactly what Jones and Kohler found. The participants in their experiment did not remember in a rational or functional manner. They tended to remember the plausible arguments agreeing with their own position and the implausible arguments agreeing with the opposing position. Subsequent research has yielded similar results on a wide variety of issues, from whether or not the death penalty deters people from committing murder to the risks of contracting AIDS through heterosexual contact (e.g., Biek, Wood, & Chaiken, 1996; Edwards & Smith, 1996; Lord, Ross, & Lepper, 1979; Vallone, Ross, & Lepper, 1985). All of this research indicates that we human beings do not process information in an unbiased manner. Rather, we distort it in a way that fits our preconceived notions. The major results of the Jones and Kohler experiment are presented in Figure 5–1.

This process probably accounts for the fact that on issues like politics and religion, people who are deeply committed to a view different from our own will almost never come to see things our way (the proper way!), no matter how powerful and balanced our arguments might be.

Decisions, Decisions, Decisions

Every time we make a decision, we experience dissonance. How come? Let's take a close look at the process. Suppose you are about to buy a new car. After looking around, you are torn between a van and a subcompact. There are various advantages and disadvantages to each: The van would be convenient; you can haul things in it, you can sleep in it during long trips, and it has plenty of power, but it gets poor mileage and is not easy to park. The subcompact is a lot less roomy, and you are concerned about its safety, but it is less expensive to buy and operate, is a lot zippier to drive, and has a pretty good repair record.

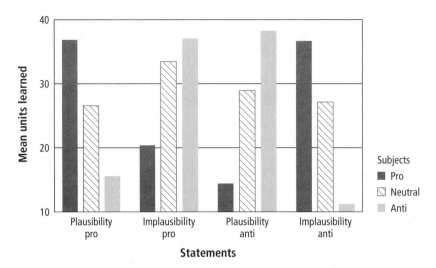

Figure 5–1 The effects of plausibility on the learning of controversial statements.
People tend to remember plausible arguments that support their position and implausible arguments that support the opposing position. To remember either implausible arguments that support your position or plausible arguments that support the opposing position would arouse dissonance. (Adapted from Jones & Kohler, 1959)

Before you make the decision, you will probably seek as much information as you can. Chances are you will read *Consumer Reports* to find out what this expert, unbiased source has to say. Perhaps you'll confer with friends who own a van or a subcompact. You'll probably visit automobile dealers to test-drive the vehicles to see how each one feels. All of this predecision behavior is perfectly rational. Let us assume you make a decision—you buy the subcompact.

What happens after the decision? We predict that your behavior will 12 change in a specific way: You will begin to think more and more about the number of miles to the gallon as though it were the most important thing in the world. Simultaneously, you will almost certainly downplay the importance of the fact that you can't sleep in your subcompact. Similarly, your mind will skim lightly over the fact that driving your new car can be particularly hazardous in a collision. How does this happen?

Distorting Our Likes and Dislikes In any decision, whether it is be- 13 tween two cars, two colleges, or two potential lovers, the chosen alternative is seldom entirely positive, and the rejected alternative is seldom entirely negative. So while making the decision, you have your doubts. After the decision, your cognition that you are a smart person is dissonant with all of the negative things about the car, college, or lover you chose; that cognition is also dissonant with all of the positive aspects of the car, college, or lover you rejected. We call this **postdecision dissonance** (Brehm, 1956; Wilson, 1997). Cognitive disso-

Responsibility

nance theory predicts that to help yourself feel better about the decision, you will do some mental work to try to reduce the dissonance. What kind of work? An early experiment by Jack Brehm (1956) is illustrative. Brehm posed as a representative of a consumer testing service and asked women to rate the attractiveness and desirability of several kinds of appliances, such as toasters and electric coffeemakers. Each woman was told that as a reward for having participated in the survey, she could have one of the appliances as a gift. She was given a choice between two of the products she had rated as being equally attractive. After she made her decision, her appliance was wrapped up and given to her. Twenty minutes later, each woman was asked to rerate all the products. Brehm found that after receiving the appliance of their choice, the women rated its attractiveness somewhat higher than they had the first time. Not only that, but they drastically lowered their rating of the appliance they might have chosen but decided to reject.

In other words, following a decision, to reduce dissonance we change the way we feel about the chosen and unchosen alternatives—cognitively spreading them apart in our own minds in order to make ourselves feel better about the choice we made.

The Permanence of the Decision It stands to reason that the more important the decision, the greater the dissonance. Deciding which car to buy is clearly more important than deciding between a toaster and a coffeemaker; deciding which person to marry is clearly more important than deciding which car to buy. Decisions also vary in terms of how permanent they are—that is, how difficult they are to revoke. It is usually a lot easier to go back to the car dealership and trade in your new car for another one than it is to extricate yourself from an unhappy marriage. The more permanent and less revocable the decision, the greater the need to reduce dissonance. 14

An excellent place to investigate the significance of irrevocability is the racetrack. Experienced bettors typically spend a great deal of time poring over the "dope sheets," trying to decide which horse to put their money on. When they make a decision, they head for the betting windows. While they are standing in line, they have already made their decision, but we would hypothesize that because it is still revocable, they have no urge to reduce dissonance. However, once they get to the window and place their bet—even if it's for only $2—it is absolutely irrevocable. Thirty seconds later, one cannot go back and tell the nice person behind the window that one has had a change of mind. Therefore, if irrevocability is an important factor, one would expect greater dissonance reduction among bettors a few minutes after placing the bet than a few minutes before placing the bet. 15

In a simple but clever experiment, Knox and Inkster (1968) intercepted people who were on their way to place $2 bets and asked them how certain they were their horses would win. The investigators also intercepted other bet- 16 tors just as they were leaving the $2 window, after having placed their bets, and asked them the same question. Almost invariably, people who had already placed their bets gave their horses a much better chance of winning than did those who had yet to place their bets. Since only a few minutes separated one group from another, nothing real had occurred to increase the probability of winning; the only thing that had changed was the finality of the decision—and thus the dissonance it produced.

Lowballing: The Illusion of Irrevocability   The irrevocability of a de-   17
cision always increases dissonance and the motivation to reduce it. Because of this, unscrupulous salespeople have developed techniques for creating the illusion that irrevocability exists. One such technique is called **lowballing** (Cialdini, Cacioppo, Basset, & Miller, 1978; Weyant, 1996). Robert Cialdini, a distinguished social psychologist, temporarily joined the sales force of an automobile dealership to observe this technique closely. Here's how it works: You enter an automobile showroom intent on buying a particular car. Having already priced it at several dealerships, you know you can purchase it for about $18,000. You are approached by a personable, middle-aged man who tells you he can sell you one for $17,679. Excited by the bargain, you agree to the deal and, at the salesperson's request, write out a check for the down payment so that he can take it to the sales manager as proof you are a serious customer.

Meanwhile, you rub your hands in glee as you imagine yourself driving   18
home in your shiny new bargain. But alas, ten minutes later the salesperson returns, looking forlorn. He tells you that in his zeal to give you a good deal, he made an error in calculation and the sales manager caught it. The price of the car actually comes to $18,178. You are disappointed. Moreover, you are pretty sure you can get it a bit cheaper elsewhere. The decision to buy is not irrevocable. And yet in this situation, research by Cialdini and his colleagues (1978) suggests that far more people will go ahead with the deal than if the original asking price had been $18,178, even though the reason for purchasing the car from this particular dealer—the bargain price—no longer exists. How come?

There are at least three reasons why lowballing works. First, while the   19
customer's decision to buy is certainly reversible, a commitment of sorts does exist, due to the act of signing a check for a down payment. This creates the illusion of irrevocability, even though, if the car buyer really thought about it, he or she would quickly realize it is a nonbinding contract. However, in the razzle-dazzle world of high-pressure sales, even temporary illusion can have powerful consequences. Second, this commitment triggered the anticipation of an exciting event: driving out with a new car. To have had the anticipated event thwarted (by not going ahead with the deal) would have produced dissonance and disappointment. Third, although the final price is substantially higher than the customer thought it would be, it is probably only slightly higher than the price at another dealership. Under these circumstances, the customer in effect says, "Oh, what the heck. I'm already here, I've already filled out the forms,

I've already written out the check—why wait?" Thus by using dissonance reduction and the illusion of irrevocability, high-pressure salespeople increase the probability that you will decide to buy their product at their price.

The Decision to Behave Immorally   Needless to say, life is made up of 20 more than just decisions about cars, appliances, and racehorses. Often our decisions involve moral and ethical issues. When is it permissible to lie to a friend, and when is it not? When is an act stealing, and when is it borrowing? Resolving moral dilemmas is a particularly interesting area in which to study dissonance because of the powerful implications for one's self-esteem. Even more interesting is the fact that dissonance reduction following a difficult moral decision can cause people to behave either more or less ethically in the future.

Take the issue of cheating on an exam. Suppose you are a college sopho- 21 more taking the final exam in a physics course. Ever since you can remember, you have wanted to be a surgeon, and you know that your admission to medical school will depend heavily on how well you do in this physics course. The key question on the exam involves some material you know fairly well, but because so much is riding on this exam, you experience acute anxiety and draw a blank. The minutes tick away. You become increasingly anxious. You simply cannot think. You look up and notice that you happen to be sitting behind the smartest person in the class. You glance at her paper and discover that she is just completing her answer to the crucial question. You know you could easily read her answer if you chose to. Time is running out. What do you do? Your conscience tells you it's wrong to cheat—and yet if you don't cheat, you are certain to get a poor grade. And if you get a poor grade, there goes medical school. You wrestle with your conscience.

Regardless of whether or not you decide to cheat, you are doomed to ex- 22 perience the kind of threat to your self-esteem that arouses dissonance. If you cheat, your cognition "I am a decent, moral person" is dissonant with your cognition "I have just committed an immoral act." If you decide to resist temptation, your cognition "I want to become a surgeon" is dissonant with your cognition "I could have acted in such a way that would have ensured a good grade and admission to medical school, but I chose not to. Wow, was that stupid!"

In this situation, some students would decide to cheat; others would decide 23 not to cheat. What happens to the students' attitudes about cheating after their decision? Suppose that after a difficult struggle, you decide to cheat. How do you reduce the dissonance? According to dissonance theory, it is likely that you would try to justify the action by finding a way to minimize the negative aspects of the action you chose. In this instance, an efficient path of dissonance reduction would entail a change in your attitude about cheating. In short, you will adopt a more lenient attitude toward cheating, convincing yourself that it is a victimless crime that doesn't hurt anybody, that everybody does it, and so it's not really that bad.

Suppose, by contrast, that after a difficult struggle you decide not to 24 cheat. How would you reduce your dissonance? Once again, you could change your attitude about the morality of the act—but this time in the opposite direction. That is, to justify giving up a good grade, you must convince yourself that cheating is a heinous sin, that it's one of the lowest things a person can do, and that cheaters should be rooted out and severely punished.

How Dissonance Affects Personal Values What has come about is 25 not merely a rationalization of your own behavior but an actual change in your system of values; individuals facing this kind of choice will undergo either a softening or a hardening of their attitudes toward cheating on exams, depending on whether or not they decided to cheat. The interesting and important thing to remember is that two people acting in the two different ways could have started out with almost identical attitudes toward cheating. Their decisions might have been a hair's breadth apart—one came within an inch of cheating but decided to resist, while the other came within an inch of resisting but decided to cheat. Once they made their decisions, however, their attitudes toward cheating will diverge sharply as a consequence of their actions.

These speculations were put to the test by Judson Mills (1958) in an ex- 26 periment he performed in an elementary school. Mills first measured the attitudes of sixth graders toward cheating. He then had them participate in a competitive exam, with prizes being offered to the winners. The situation was arranged so that it was almost impossible to win without cheating. Mills made it easy for the children to cheat and created the illusion that they could not be detected. Under these conditions, as one might expect, some of the students cheated and others did not. The next day, the sixth graders were again asked to indicate how they felt about cheating. Those children who had cheated became more lenient toward cheating, and those who had resisted the temptation to cheat adopted a harsher attitude toward cheating.

Classic experiments conducted in the laboratory often inspire contempo- 27 rary research in the real world. A case in point: While conducting research among mid-level business executives in India, Chockalingam Visweswaran and Satish Deshpande (1996) came up with some interesting data pertinent to Mills's results. These investigators reasoned that executives who were in the process of making a decision about whether or not to behave ethically were in a vulnerable state: On the one hand, they wanted to behave ethically; on the other hand, they were undoubtedly concerned lest they might need to behave unethically in order to succeed. The investigators found that executives who had substantial reason to believe that managerial success could only be achieved through unethical behavior experienced far greater dissonance (in the form of job dissatisfaction) than those who were given no reason to believe this. Our guess is that if the investigators had returned a year or two later, they would have found a reduction in dissonance in this group; that is, as with Mills's subjects, most of those who behaved unethically would have found a way to justify that behavior after the fact.

The Justification of Effort

Most people are willing to put out a lot of effort to get something they really 28
want. For example, if there's a particular job you want, you are likely to go the
extra mile to get it. This might involve shopping for appropriate clothing, studying extra hard to meet entrance requirements, passing a battery of difficult
exams, or putting up with a series of stressful interviews.

Let's turn that proposition inside out. Suppose you expend a great deal of 29
effort to get into a particular club and it turns out to be a totally worthless organization, consisting of boring, pompous people engaged in trivial activities.
You would feel pretty foolish, wouldn't you? A sensible person doesn't work
hard to gain something worthless. Such a circumstance would produce a significant amount of dissonance; your cognition that you are a sensible, adept
human being is dissonant with your cognition that you worked hard to get into
a dismal club. How would you reduce this dissonance? How would you justify
your behavior? You might start by finding a way to convince yourself that the
club and the people in it are nicer, more interesting, and more worthwhile than
they appeared to be at first glance. How can one turn boring people into interesting people and a trivial club into a worthwhile one? Easy. Even the most
boring people and trivial clubs have some redeeming qualities. Activities and
behaviors are open to a variety of interpretations; if we are motivated to see
the best in people and things, we will tend to interpret these ambiguities in a
positive manner. We call this the **justification of effort**—the tendency for individuals to increase their liking for something they have worked hard to attain.

In a classic experiment, Elliot Aronson and Judson Mills (1959) explored 30
the link between effort and dissonance reduction. In their experiment, college
students volunteered to join a group that would be meeting regularly to discuss
various aspects of the psychology of sex. To be admitted to the group, they volunteered to go through a screening procedure. For one-third of the participants, the procedure was an extremely effortful and unpleasant one; for
one-third, it was only mildly unpleasant; and one-third were admitted to the
group without undergoing any screening procedure.

Each participant was then allowed to listen in on a discussion being con- 31
ducted by the members of the group they would be joining. Although they
were led to believe that the discussion was a live, ongoing one, what they actually heard was a prerecorded tape. The taped discussion was arranged so that it
was as dull and bombastic as possible. After the discussion was over, each participant was asked to rate it in terms of how much they liked it, how interesting
it was, how intelligent the participants were, and so forth. The major findings
are shown in Figure 5–2.

The results supported the predictions: Participants who underwent little 32
or no effort to get into the group did not enjoy the discussion very much. They
were able to see it for what it was—a dull and boring waste of time. They re-
gretted that they had agreed to participate. Participants who went through a

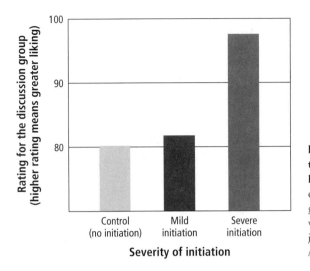

Figure 5-2 The tougher the initiation, the more we like the group. The more effort we put into gaining group membership, the more we like the group we have just joined. *(Adapted from Aronson & Mills, 1959)*

severe initiation, however, succeeded in convincing themselves that the same discussion, though not as scintillating as they had hoped, was dotted with interesting and provocative tidbits and was therefore, in the main, a worthwhile experience. In short, they justified their effortful initiation process by interpreting all the ambiguous aspects of the group discussion in the most positive manner possible. Similar results have been obtained by other researchers (e.g., Cooper, 1980; Gerard & Mathewson, 1966).

It should be clear that we are not suggesting that most people enjoy effortful, unpleasant experiences—they do not. Nor are we suggesting that people enjoy things that are merely associated with unpleasant experiences—they do not. What we are asserting is that if a person agrees to go through a difficult or an unpleasant experience in order to attain some goal or object, that goal or object becomes more attractive. Thus if you were walking to the discussion group and a passing car splashed mud all over you, you would not like that group any better. However, if you volunteered to jump into a mud puddle in order to be admitted to a group that turned out to be trivial and boring, you *would* like the group better.

The Psychology of Insufficient Justification

When we were little, we were taught never to tell a lie. Indeed, our elementary school history courses were full of mythical stories (disguised as truths) like that of George Washington and the cherry tree, apparently aimed at convincing us that we had better be truthful if we aspired to the presidency. Alas, the world is a complicated place. There may be some people in the world who have never told a lie, but most of us have yet to meet one. At times, most of us feel that, for good reason, we need to be less than perfectly truthful. One such reason in-

Responsibility

volves something else that we were taught—to be kind to one another. Occasionally, in order to be kind to someone, we find it necessary to tell a lie.

Suppose you walk into your friend Sam's house and notice an atrocious painting on the wall. You look at it, and it's so bad that you think it's a joke. You are about to burst into raucous laughter when Sam says, with considerable pleasure and excitement, "Do you like it? It cost a great deal. It's by a relatively unknown local artist named Carol Smear; I think she's very talented, so I went into hock to buy it from her. Don't you think it's beautiful?"

How do you respond? You hesitate. Chances are you go through something like the following thought process: "Sam seems so happy and excited. Why should I rain on his parade? If I were to tell him my true feelings, I would almost certainly cause him distress. He obviously likes the painting and paid a great deal for it. Telling him my honest opinion might make him annoyed with me or might make him feel he made a terrible mistake. Either way, it will be unpleasant. Even if I end up convincing Sam that it's a piece of garbage, he can't take it back. What's the sense in telling him the truth?"

So you tell Sam that you like the painting very much. Do you experience much dissonance? We doubt it. There are a great many thoughts that are consonant with having told this lie, as outlined in your reasoning in the preceding paragraph. In effect, your cognition that it is important not to cause pain to people you like provides ample **external justification** for having told a harmless lie.

Counterattitudinal Advocacy   What happens if you say something you don't really believe and there is no ample external justification for doing so? That is, what if your friend Sam was fabulously wealthy and bought paintings constantly? What if he sincerely needed to know your opinion of this purchase? What if in the past you'd told him he'd bought a veritable eyesore and your friendship survived? Now the external justifications for lying to Sam about the painting are minimal. If you still refrain from giving your true opinion (saying instead, "Gee, Sam, it's, uh, interesting"), you will experience dissonance. When you can't find external justification for your behavior, you will attempt to find **internal justification**—you will try to reduce dissonance by changing something about yourself (e.g., your attitude or behavior). How can you do this? You might begin looking for positive aspects of the painting—some evidence of creativity or sophistication that might have escaped you previously. If you look hard enough, you will probably find something. Within a short time, your attitude toward the painting will have moved in the direction of the statement you made—and that is how saying becomes believing. This phenomenon is generally referred to as **counterattitudinal advocacy,** a process that occurs when a person states an opinion or attitude that runs counter to his or her private belief or attitude. When this is accomplished with a minimum of external justification, it results in a change in the individual's private attitude in the direction of the public statement.

This proposition was first tested in a groundbreaking experiment by Leon Festinger and J. Merrill Carlsmith (1959). In this experiment, college students were induced to spend an hour performing a series of excruciatingly boring and repetitive tasks. The experimenter then told them that the purpose of the study was to determine whether or not people would perform better if they had been informed in advance that the tasks were interesting. They were each informed that they had been randomly assigned to the control condition—that is, they had not been told anything in advance. However, he explained, the next participant, a young woman who was just arriving in the anteroom, was going to be in the experimental condition. The researcher said that he needed to convince her that the task was going to be interesting and enjoyable. Since it was much more convincing if a fellow student rather than the experimenter delivered this message, would the participant do so? Thus with his request the experimenter induced the participants to lie about the task to another student.

Half of the students were offered $20 for telling the lie (a large external 40 justification), while the others were offered only $1 for telling the lie (a very small external justification). After the experiment was over, an interviewer asked the lie-tellers how much they had enjoyed the tasks they had performed earlier in the experiment. The results validated the hypothesis: The students who had been paid $20 for lying—that is, for saying the tasks had been enjoyable—rated the activities as the dull and boring experiences they were. But those who were paid only $1 for saying the task was enjoyable rated the task as significantly more enjoyable. In other words, people who had received an abundance of external justification for lying told the lie but didn't believe it, whereas those who told the lie without a great deal of external justification succeeded in convincing themselves that what they said was closer to the truth.

One might ask whether this phenomenon works when important atti- 41 tudes are involved. Can you induce a person to change an attitude about things that matter? Subsequent research has shown that the Festinger-Carlsmith paradigm has wide ramifications in areas of great significance. Consider an experiment by Arthur R. Cohen (1962), for example. Cohen was a social psychologist at Yale University during a turbulent period when the city police were often descending on the campus to control the behavior of Yale students. Occasionally, the police reacted with excessive force. After one such altercation, Cohen visited a Yale dormitory, indicating he worked for a well-known research institute. He told the students that there were two sides to every issue and that the institute was interested in looking at both sides of the police-student issue. He then asked the students to write forceful essays supporting the behavior of the police. Moreover, he told them he was able to offer them an incentive for writing the essay. Depending on the condition to which the students were assigned, he offered them 50 cents, $1, $5, or $10. (None of the students was aware of what the others were being offered.) After the students wrote their essays, Cohen assessed their real attitude toward the actions of the city police.

The results were clear: The smaller the incentive, the more favorable 42 people became toward the city police. In other words, when the students were given a great deal of external justification for writing the essay, they did not need to convince themselves that they really believed what they had written. However, when they faced the fact that they had written positive things about the police for 50 cents or $1, they needed to convince themselves that there may have been some truth in what they had written.

In a similar experiment, Elizabeth Nel, Robert Helmreich, and Elliot 43 Aronson (1969) approached college students who initially believed that marijuana was harmful and induced them to compose and recite a videotaped speech favoring its use and legalization. Some were offered large incentives; others were offered small incentives. Again, the findings were clear: The smaller the incentive, the greater the softening of the attitude toward the use and legalization of marijuana.

In many of these experiments, people behaved without integrity (told a lie) 44 in a manner that also might have harmed another person. For example, if you believe that marijuana is dangerous and you tell someone that it is not, you might be doing that person a great deal of harm. Accordingly, it is reasonable to raise the following question: Is lying enough? Is harming another person a necessary condition for dissonance, or is dissonance produced simply by behaving without integrity—even if no harm results? An experiment by Eddie Harmon-Jones and his colleagues (1996) makes it clear that behaving without integrity, in and of itself, produces dissonance. In their experiment, people who drank an awful-tasting beverage and then volunteered to say that it tasted good actually came to believe that it tasted good (compared to the rating of a control group). The way they "said" it tasted good was to write their false opinion down on a small slip of paper, which they then immediately crumpled up and threw away. Thus although their lie could not possibly harm anyone, the act of lying produced changes in belief aimed at softening the dissonance and restoring a sense of integrity.

Counterattitudinal Advocacy and Race Relations

How might the 45 laboratory experiments on counterattitudinal advocacy be applied directly to important social problems? Let's look at race relations and racial prejudice, surely one of our nation's most important and enduring problems. Would it be possible to get people to endorse a policy favoring a minority group and then see if their attitudes become more favorable toward that group? You bet! In an important set of experiments, Mike Leippe and Donna Eisenstadt (1994, 1998) induced white college students to write a counterattitudinal essay publicly endorsing a controversial proposal at their university to double the amount of funds available for academic scholarships for African American students. Because the total amount of funds was limited, this meant cutting by half the amount of scholarship funds available to white students. As you might imagine, this was a highly dissonant situation. How might the students reduce dissonance? The best way would be to convince themselves that they really believed deeply in that policy. Moreover, it is reasonable to suggest that dissonance reduction might generalize beyond the specific policy—that is, the theory would predict that their general attitude toward African Americans would become more favorable and more supportive. And that is exactly what Leippe and Eisenstadt found.

Hypocrisy and AIDS Prevention In the past decade, this aspect of 46 dissonance theory has also been applied to another important social issue—the prevention of the spread of AIDS. As you know, since it first made its presence known in the early 1980s, AIDS has become an epidemic of epic proportions throughout the world. The U.S. government has spent millions of dollars on AIDS information and prevention campaigns in the mass media. Although these campaigns have been moderately effective in conveying information, they have not been nearly so successful in preventing people from engaging in risky sexual behavior. For example, although college students are aware of AIDS as a serious problem, a surprisingly small percentage use condoms every time they have sex. The reason seems to be that condoms are inconvenient and unromantic, and they remind people of disease—the last thing they want to be thinking about when getting ready to make love. Rather, as researchers have consistently discovered, people have a strong tendency to experience denial where sexual behavior is involved—in this case, to believe that while AIDS is a problem for most people, they themselves are not at risk. If the mass media have been ineffective, is there anything else that can be done?

In the past several years, Elliot Aronson and his students (Aronson, Fried, 47 & Stone, 1991; Stone, Aronson, Crain, Winslow, & Fried, 1994) have had considerable success at convincing people to use condoms by employing a variation of the counterattitudinal advocacy paradigm. They asked college students to compose a speech describing the dangers of AIDS and advocating the use of condoms every time a person has sex. In one condition, the students merely composed the arguments. In another condition, the students composed the arguments and then recited them in front of a video camera after being informed that the resulting videotape would be played to an audience of high school students. In addition, half the students in each condition were made mindful of their own failure to use condoms by making a list of the circumstances in which they had found it particularly difficult, awkward, or impossible to use them.

Essentially, then, the participants in one condition—those who made a 48 video for high school students after having been made mindful of their own failure to use condoms—were in a state of high dissonance. This was caused by their being made aware of their own hypocrisy; they were fully aware of the fact that they were preaching behavior to high school students that they themselves were not practicing. In order to remove the hypocrisy and maintain their self-esteem, they would need to start practicing what they were preaching. And that is exactly what Aronson and his colleagues found: Each student was given the opportunity to purchase condoms very cheaply. The results demonstrated that the students in the hypocrisy condition were far more likely to buy condoms than students in any of the other conditions. Figure 5–3 illustrates the results of this experiment. A follow-up telephone interview several months

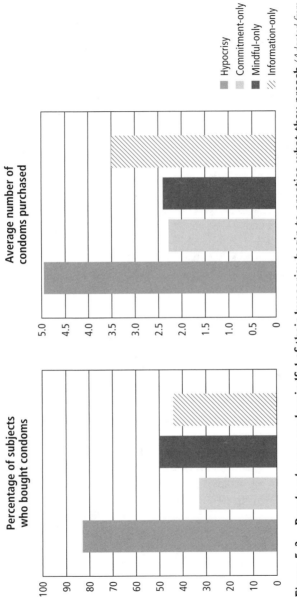

Figure 5–3 People who are made mindful of their hypocrisy begin to practice what they preach (*Adapted from Stone, Aronson, Crain, Winslow, & Fried, 1994*)

after the experiment demonstrated that the effects were long-lasting: People in the hypocrisy condition reported far greater use of condoms than those in the control conditions.

Insufficient Punishment Another form of insufficient justification is in- 49 sufficient punishment. Complex societies run, in part, on punishment or the threat of punishment. As members of society, we constantly find ourselves in situations where those who are charged with the duty of maintaining law and order are threatening to punish us if we do not comply with their rules and regulations. For example, while cruising down the highway at 75 miles an hour, we know that if we get caught, we will end up paying a substantial fine. If it happens often, we will lose our license. So we learn to obey the speed limit when patrol cars are in the vicinity. By the same token, youngsters in school know that if they cheat on an exam and get caught, they could be humiliated by the teacher and severely punished. So they learn not to cheat while the teacher is in the room watching them. But does harsh punishment teach adults to *want* to obey the speed limit? Does it teach youngsters to value honest behavior? We don't think so. Rather, we believe that all it teaches is to try to avoid getting caught.

Let's look at bullying behavior. It is extremely difficult to persuade chil- 50 dren that it's not right or enjoyable to beat up smaller children. But theoretically, it is conceivable that under certain conditions they will persuade themselves that such behavior is unenjoyable. Imagine that you are the parent of a 6-year-old boy who often beats up his 4-year-old brother. You've tried to reason with him, to no avail. In an attempt to make him a nicer person (and to preserve the health and welfare of his little brother), you begin to punish him for his aggressiveness. As a parent, you have at your disposal a number of possible punishments, ranging from the extremely mild (a stern look) to the extremely severe (a hard spanking, forcing the child to stand in the corner for two hours, depriving him of TV privileges for a month). The more severe the threat, the greater the likelihood the youngster will cease and desist—while you are watching him. But he may very well hit his brother again as soon as you are out of sight. In short, just as most drivers learn to be vigilant of the Highway Patrol while speeding, your 6-year-old has not lost his enjoyment of bullying his little brother; he has merely learned not to do it while you are around to punish him. Suppose that you threaten him with a mild punishment. In either case—under threat of severe punishment or of mild punishment—the child experiences dissonance. He is aware that he is not beating up his little brother, and he is also aware that he would like to beat him up. When he has the urge to hit his brother and doesn't, he implicitly asks himself, "How come I'm not beating up my little brother?" Under severe threat, he has a convincing answer in the form of a sufficient external justification: "I'm not beating him up because if I do, my parents are going to really punish me." This serves to reduce the dissonance.

The child in the mild threat situation experiences dissonance too. But 51 when he asks himself, "How come I'm not beating up my little brother?" he doesn't have a very convincing answer because the threat is so mild that it does not provide a superabundance of justification. In short, this is **insufficient punishment.** The child is refraining from doing something he wants to do, and while he does have a modicum of justification for not doing it, he lacks complete justification. In this situation, he continues to experience dissonance. Therefore, the child must find another way to justify the fact that he is not aggressing against his kid brother.

The less severe you make the threat, the less external justification there is; the less external justification, the greater the need for internal justification. The child can reduce his dissonance by convincing himself that he doesn't really want to beat up his brother. In time, he can go further in his quest for internal justification and decide that beating up little kids is not fun. Allowing children the leeway to construct their own internal justification enables them to develop a permanent set of values.

Thus far, this has all been speculative. Will threats of mild punishment for performing any behavior diminish the attractiveness of that behavior to a greater extent than severe threats will? This proposition was first investigated by Elliot Aronson and J. Merrill Carlsmith (1963) in an experiment with preschoolers.

In this experiment, because the researchers were dealing with very young children, ethical concerns precluded their trying to affect important values, like those concerning aggressive behavior. Instead, they attempted to change something that was of no great importance to society but was of great importance to the children—their preference for different kinds of toys. The experimenter first asked each child to rate the attractiveness of several toys. He then pointed to a toy that the child considered among the most attractive and told the child that he or she was not allowed to play with it. Half the children were threatened with mild punishment if they disobeyed; the other half were threatened with severe punishment. The experimenter then left the room for several minutes to provide the children with the time and opportunity to play with the other toys and to resist the temptation of playing with the forbidden toy. None of the children played with the forbidden toy.

The experimenter returned to the room and asked each child to rate how much he or she liked each of the toys. Initially, all of the children had wanted to play with the forbidden toy. During the temptation period, all of them had refrained from playing with it. Clearly, this disparity means that dissonance was aroused in the children. How did they respond? The children who had received a severe threat had ample justification for their restraint. They knew why they hadn't played with the attractive toy, and hence they had no reason to change their attitude about the toy. These children continued to rate the forbidden toy as highly desirable; indeed, some even found it more desirable than they had before the threat.

But what about the others? Lacking an abundance of external justification for refraining from playing with the toy, the children in the mild threat condition needed an internal justification to reduce their dissonance. They succeeded in convincing themselves that the reason they hadn't played with the toy was that they didn't really like it. They rated the forbidden toy as less attractive than they had at the beginning of the experiment. What we have here is a clear example of self-justification leading to self-persuasion in the behavior of very young children. The implications for child rearing are fascinating.

The Permanence of Self-Persuasion

Let's say you've attended a lecture on the evils of cheating. It might have a temporary effect on your attitudes toward cheating. But if a week or two later you found yourself in a highly tempting situation, your recent change in attitude would probably lack the staying power to act as a deterrent. Social psychologists know that mere lectures do not usually result in permanent or long-lasting attitude change. In contrast, suppose you went through the kind of situation experienced by the children in Judson Mills's (1958) experiment on cheating, discussed earlier in this chapter. Here we would expect the attitude change to be far more deepseated and permanent. The children who were tempted to cheat but resisted came to believe that cheating is a dastardly thing to do not because someone told them so but through **self-persuasion**—they persuaded themselves of this belief as a means of justifying the fact that by not cheating, they had given up an attractive prize.

The long-lasting effects of attitudes generated by self-justification have been clearly demonstrated in a number of contexts. To take one dramatic example, Jonathan Freedman (1965) performed a replication of Aronson and Carlsmith's (1963) forbidden toy experiment. Several weeks later, a young woman came to the school, ostensibly to administer some paper-and-pencil tests to the children. In actuality, she was working for Freedman; however, the children were totally unaware that her presence was in any way related to Freedman, the toys, or the threats that had occurred several weeks earlier. Coincidentally, she was administering her tests in the same room Freedman had used for his experiment—the room where the same toys were casually scattered about. After administering the test, she asked the children to wait for her while she went to the next room to score the test. She then casually suggested that the scoring might take a while and that—how lucky!—someone had left some toys around and the children could play with any of them they wanted to.

The results were striking: The overwhelming majority of the children whom Freedman had mildly threatened several weeks earlier decided, on their own, not to play with the forbidden toy. By contrast, the great majority of the children who had been severely threatened did in fact play with the forbidden toy. Thus a single mild threat was still very effective several weeks later, whereas a severe threat was not.

Again, the power of this phenomenon rests on the fact that the reason the children didn't play with the toy was not that some adult told them the toy was undesirable; such admonitions would not have persisted for very long after

Responsibility

the admonishing adult had left the premises. The reason the mild threat persisted for at least several weeks was that the children were motivated to convince themselves the toy was undesirable. The results of Freedman's experiment are presented in Figure 5–4.

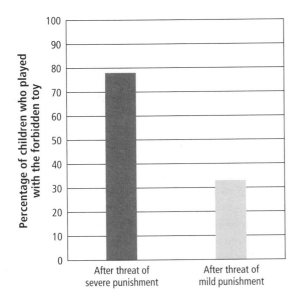

Figure 5–4 Several weeks afterward, children who had received a threat of mild punishment were far less likely to play with the forbidden toy than children who had received a threat of severe punishment. Those given a mild threat had to provide their own justification by devaluing the attractiveness of the toy.
(Adapted from Freedman, 1965)

What Do We Mean by "Insufficient Justification"? The term *ins-* 61
ufficient external justification needs clarification. In one sense, the justification is sufficient—sufficient to produce the behavior. For example, the students in Festinger and Carlsmith's (1959) experiment did agree to lie about how interesting it was to perform the boring job. The experimenter's request was just sufficient to get them to do the behavior, but it wasn't sufficient, later, for them to explain to themselves how they could have done such a mean thing to another student. After all, nobody had held a gun to their heads; they agreed, of their own free will, to lie—at least, that's how these participants saw it.

In fact, this situation, like many others in life, is characterized by the "illu- 62
sion of freedom." We think we're free to choose our response, but powerful social norms and rules often dictate what we will actually do. How could these participants say no to a politely worded, fairly innocuous request from an authority figure? The cards were stacked—indeed, close to 100 percent of participants in these types of studies agree to the experimenter's request; basically, no one says no. So how much real choice could there be? Yet the participants don't perceive the inherent restraints on their ability to truly choose between saying yes or no to the request. Later, when thinking about why they lied to an innocent person, they don't blame it on the experimenter and his or her request; they see it as their personal choice. The best way to maintain their self-

esteem is to decide that the task was sort of fun and interesting after all; hence it wasn't such a lie.

So even though we like to think of ourselves as fully rational creatures, 63 we frequently find ourselves doing things without entirely thinking them through—saying yes when we wanted to say no. Indeed, the irony is that precisely because we like to believe that we are rational, sensible, and moral creatures, we are vulnerable to dissonance-induced self-persuasion.

Not Just Rewards or Punishments   As we have seen, a sizable re- 64 ward or a severe punishment is an effective way of providing external justification for an action. Accordingly, if you want a person to do something or to refrain from doing something only once, the best strategy would be to promise a large reward or threaten a severe punishment. But if you want a person to develop a deep-seated attitude, the smaller the reward or punishment that will induce momentary compliance, the greater will be the eventual attitude change and therefore the more permanent the effect. Large rewards and severe punishments, because they are strong external justifications, are consonant with compliance and thus prevent attitude change.

We should note that this phenomenon is not limited to tangible rewards 65 and punishments; justifications can come in more subtle packages as well. Take friendship, for example. We like our friends; we trust our friends; we do favors for our friends. Suppose you are at a formal dinner party at the home of a close friend. Your friend is passing around a rather strange-looking appetizer. It's not quite a potato chip, but it looks like it's been fried. "What is it?" you ask warily. "Oh, it's a fried grasshopper; I'd really like you to try it," your friend answers. Because she's a good friend and you don't want to cause her any discomfort or embarrassment in front of the other guests, you gingerly pick one out of the bowl, place it in your mouth, chew it up, and swallow it. How much do you think you will like this new snack food?

Keep that in mind for a moment as we expand the example. Suppose you 66 are a dinner guest at the home of a person you don't like very much, and he hands you, as an appetizer, a fried grasshopper and tells you that he'd really like you to try it. In much the same way, you put it in your mouth, chew it up, and swallow it.

Now the crucial question: In which of these two situations will you like 67 the taste of the grasshopper better? Common sense might suggest that the grasshopper would taste better when recommended by a friend. But think about it for a moment; which condition involves less external justification? Common sense notwithstanding, dissonance theory makes the opposite prediction. In the first case, when you ask yourself, "How come I ate that disgusting insect?" you have ample justification: You are it because your good friend asked you to. In the second case, you lack this kind of justification for having eaten the grasshopper. Therefore, you must add some justification of your own; namely, you must convince yourself that it was tastier than you would have imagined, that as a matter of fact, it was quite good—"I'm thinking of laying in a supply myself."

While this may seem a rather bizarre example of dissonance-reducing be- 68
havior, it's not as far-fetched as you might think. Indeed, Philip Zimbardo and his colleagues conducted an experiment directly analogous to our example (Zimbardo, Weisenberg, Firestone, & Levy, 1965). In this experiment, army reservists were asked to eat fried grasshoppers as part of a research project on survival foods. Reservists who ate grasshoppers at the request of a stern, unpleasant officer increased their liking for grasshoppers far more than those who ate grasshoppers at the request of a well-liked, pleasant officer. Those who complied with the unfriendly officer's request had little external justification for their actions. As a result, they adopted more positive attitudes toward eating grasshoppers in order to justify their otherwise strange and dissonance-arousing behavior.

The Aftermath of Good and Bad Deeds

Whenever we act either kindly or cruelly toward a person, we never quite feel 69
the same way about that person again.

The Ben Franklin Effect It is obvious that when we like people, we 70
tend to treat them well, speak kindly to them, do them favors, and smile at them with warmth and joy. If we don't like them, we treat them less kindly, avoid them, say bad things about them, and perhaps even go out of our way to snub them. But what happens when we do a person a favor? In particular, what happens when we are subtly induced to do a favor for a person we do not like—will we like them more? Or less? Dissonance theory predicts that we will like that person more after doing the favor. Think about it. Can you see why? You might want to jot down your answer in the margin.

This phenomenon was not discovered by dissonance theorists; in fact, it 71
has been a part of folk wisdom in several cultures for a very long time. For example, the great Russian novelist Leo Tolstoy wrote about it in 1869: "We do not love people so much for the good they have done us as for the good we have done them." And more than a century before Tolstoy's observation, Benjamin Franklin confessed to having used this bit of folk wisdom as a political strategy. While serving as a member of the Pennsylvania state legislature, Franklin was disturbed by the political opposition and apparent animosity of a fellow legislator. So he set out to win him over.

> I did not . . . aim at gaining his favour by paying any servile respect to him 72
> but, after some time, took this other method. Having heard that he had in his library a certain very scarce and curious book I wrote a note to him expressing my desire of perusing that book and requesting he would do me the favour of lending it to me for a few days. He sent it immediately and I returned it in about a week with another note expressing strongly my sense

of the favour. When we next met in the House he spoke to me (which he had never done before), and with great civility; and he ever after manifested a readiness to serve me on all occasions, so that we became great friends and our friendship continued to his death. This is another instance of the truth of an old maxim I had learned, which says, "He that has once done you a kindness will be more ready to do you another than he whom you yourself have obliged." (Franklin, 1868/1900. pp. 216–217)

Benjamin Franklin was clearly pleased with the success of his blatantly 73 manipulative strategy. But as striking as this anecdote might be, as rigorous scientists, we should not be fully convinced by it. There is no way to be certain whether Franklin's success was due to this particular gambit or simply to his general, all-around charm. To be certain, it is important to design and conduct an experiment that controls for such things as charm. Such a study was conducted by Jon Jecker and David Landy (1969) more than 240 years after Franklin's more casual experiment. In the Jecker and Landy experiment, students participated in an intellectual contest that enabled them to win a substantial sum of money. After the experiment was over, one-third of the participants were approached by the experimenter, who explained that he was using his own funds for the experiment and was running short, which meant he might be forced to close down the experiment prematurely. He asked, "As a special favor to me, would you mind returning the money you won?" The same request was made to a different group of subjects, except this time not by the experimenter but by the departmental secretary, who asked them if they would return the money as a special favor to the (impersonal) psychology department's research fund, which was running low. The remaining participants were not asked to return their winnings at all. Finally, all of the participants were asked to fill out a questionnaire that included an opportunity to rate the experimenter. Participants who had been cajoled into doing a special favor for the experimenter found him the most attractive; that is, after they did him a favor, they convinced themselves he was a wonderful, deserving fellow. The others thought he was a pretty nice guy but not anywhere near as wonderful as the people who had been asked to do him a favor. Figure 5–5 shows the results of this experiment.

Recall the experiment by Mike Leippe and Donna Eisenstadt in which 74 white students became more favorable in their general attitudes toward African Americans after having made a public commitment favoring preferential treatment for African American students. Can you see how the "Ben Franklin effect" might apply here—how this act of helping might have contributed to their change in attitudes?

Suppose you find yourself in a situation where you have an opportunity 75 to lend a helping hand to an acquaintance but because you are in a hurry or because it is inconvenient, you decline to help that person. How do you think this act of omission might affect your feelings for this person? This is precisely the kind of situation investigated by Gail Williamson and her colleagues

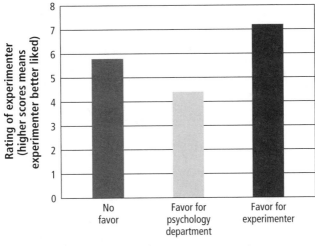

Who was the recipient of the favor?

Figure 5–5 **If we have done someone a favor, we are more likely to feel more positively toward that person.** *(Adapted from Jecker & Landy, 1969)*

(Williamson, Clark, Pegalis, & Behan, 1996). As you might expect, this refusal led to a decline in the attractiveness of the acquaintance. This was an act of omission. But suppose you actually did harm to another person. What do you suppose might happen then? We will discuss that in the following section.

How We Come to Hate Our Victims   During the height of the war in Vietnam, Elliot Aronson hired a young man to help paint his house. 76

77

> The painter was a gentle and sweet-natured person who had graduated from high school, joined the army, and fought in Vietnam. After leaving the army, he took up housepainting and was a good and reliable craftsman and an honest businessman. I enjoyed working with him. One day while we were taking a coffee break, we began to discuss the war and the intense opposition to it, especially at the local university. It soon became apparent that he and I were in sharp disagreement on this issue. He felt that the American intervention was reasonable and just and would "make the world safe for democracy." I argued that it was a terribly dirty war, that we were killing, maiming, and napalming thousands of innocent people—old people, women, children—people who had no interest in war or politics. He looked at me for a long time; then he smiled sweetly and said, "Hell, Doc, those aren't people; those are Vietnamese! They're gooks." He said it matter-of-factly, without obvious rancor or vehemence. I was astonished and chilled by his response. I wondered how it could be that this apparently good-natured, sane, and gentle young man could develop that kind of attitude. How could he dismiss an entire national group from the human race?

Over the next several days, as we continued our dialogue, I got to know more about him. It turned out that during the war he had participated in actions in which Vietnamese civilians had been killed. What gradually emerged was that initially he had been racked by guilt—and it dawned on me that he might have developed this attitude toward the Vietnamese people as a way of assuaging his guilt. That is, if he could convince himself that the Vietnamese were not fully human, it would make him feel less awful about having hurt them, and it would reduce the dissonance between his actions and his self-concept as a decent person.

It goes without saying that these speculations about the causes of the housepainter's attitude are far from conclusive. While it is conceivable that he derogated the Vietnamese people as a way of reducing dissonance, the situation is complex; for example, he might always have had a negative and prejudiced attitude toward the Vietnamese, and this might have made it easier for him to behave brutally toward them. To be certain that the justification of cruelty can occur in such situations, it is essential for the social psychologist to temporarily step back from the helter-skelter of the real world and test the proposition in the more controlled setting of the experimental laboratory.

Ideally, if we want to measure attitude change as a result of dissonant cognitions, we should know what the attitudes were before the dissonance-arousing behavior occurred. Such a situation was produced in an early experiment performed by Keith Davis and Edward Jones (1960). Each student's participation consisted of watching a young man being interviewed and then, on the basis of this observation, providing him with an analysis of his shortcomings as a human being. Specifically, the participants were told to tell the young man (a confederate) that they believed him to be a shallow, untrustworthy, boring person. The participants succeeded in convincing themselves they didn't like the victim of their cruelty—after the fact. In short, after saying things they knew were certain to hurt him, they convinced themselves that he deserved to be hurt. They found him less attractive than they had prior to saying the hurtful things to him.

Let us return to our housepainter example. Suppose for a moment that all the people he killed and injured in Vietnam had been fully armed enemy soldiers, instead of a sizable number of noncombatants. Do you think he would have experienced as much dissonance? We think it is unlikely. When engaged in combat with an enemy soldier, it is a "you or me" situation; if the housepainter had not killed the enemy soldier, the enemy soldier might have killed him. So even though hurting or killing another person is probably never taken lightly, it is not nearly so heavy a burden as it would be if the victim were an unarmed civilian—a child, a woman, an old person.

These speculations are supported by the results of an experiment by Ellen Berscheid and her colleagues (Berscheid, Boye, & Walster, 1968). In this study, college students volunteered for an experiment in which each of them administered a (supposedly) painful electric shock to a fellow student. As one might expect, these students derogated their victim as a result of having admin-

78

79

80

81

82

istered the shock. However, half of the students were told there would be a turnabout: The other student would be given the opportunity to retaliate against them at a later time. Those who were led to believe their victim would be able to retaliate later did not derogate the victim. In short, because the victim was going to be able to even the score, there was very little dissonance, and therefore the harm-doers had no need to belittle their victim in order to convince themselves that he or she deserved it.

The results of these laboratory experiments lend credence to our specu- 83 lations about the behavior of the housepainter; the results suggest that during a war, military personnel have a greater need to derogate civilian victims (because these individuals can't retaliate) than military victims. Moreover, several years after Aronson's encounter with the housepainter, a similar set of events emerged during the court-martial of Lieutenant William Calley for his role in the slaughter of innocent civilians at My Lai in Vietnam. In a long and detailed testimony, Lieutenant Calley's psychiatrist made it clear that the lieutenant had come to regard the Vietnamese people as less than human.

As we have seen, systematic research in this area demonstrates that peo- 84 ple do not perform acts of cruelty and come out unscathed. We can never be completely certain of how the housepainter, Lieutenant Calley, and thousands of other American military personnel came to regard the Vietnamese as subhuman, but it seems reasonable to assume that when people are engaged in a war where a great number of innocent people are being killed, they might try to derogate the victims in order to justify their complicity. They might poke fun at them, refer to them as "gooks," and dehumanize them. Ironically, success at dehumanizing the victim virtually guarantees a continuation or even an escalation of the cruelty. It becomes easier to hurt and kill subhumans than to hurt and kill fellow human beings. Reducing dissonance in this way therefore has sobering future consequences: It increases the likelihood that the atrocities people are willing to commit will become greater and greater through an endless chain of violence followed by self-justification (in the form of dehumanizing the victim), followed by greater violence and still more intense dehumanization. In this manner, unbelievable acts of human cruelty—such as the Nazi "Final Solution" that led to the murder of 6 million European Jews—can occur. Unfortunately, atrocities are not a thing of the past but are as recent as today's newspaper.

The Evidence for Motivational Arousal

The theory of cognitive dissonance is largely a motivational theory; in other 85 words, the theorists maintain that discomfort and arousal are what motivate the individual to change beliefs or behavior. How do we know that this is in fact the case? Is there any independent evidence indicating that people who experience cognitive dissonance are in a state of discomfort or arousal? Patricia Devine and her colleagues developed a paper-and-pencil instrument designed to measure this kind of arousal directly (Devine, 1998; Elliot & Devine, 1994). She finds that when people are put in a dissonance-arousing situation, they do indeed report feeling more agitated and more uncomfortable than people in the control condition.

Some striking behavioral evidence for the motivating qualities of disso- 86 nance has been provided by several investigators, including Zanna and Cooper (1974) and Fried and Aronson (1995). In the Zanna and Cooper study, participants were given a placebo pill. Some were told that the pill would arouse them and make them feel tense. Others were told that the pill would make them feel calm and relaxed. Participants in the control condition were told that the pill would not affect them in any way. After ingesting the pill, each person was induced to write a counterattitudinal essay, thus creating dissonance.

As you know, dissonance theory predicts that such participants will 87 change their attitudes, bringing them in line with their essays in order to reduce their uncomfortable arousal state, only if they actually feel aroused. However, if some of the participants think the arousal they are experiencing is due to the pill, they won't need to alter their attitudes to feel better about themselves. At the opposite end of the spectrum, if some of the participants think they should be feeling relaxed due to the pill, any arousal they experience should be very salient to them, and they should change their attitudes a great deal. Thus the theory predicts that attitude change will come or go across conditions, depending on whether the arousal due to dissonance is masked by an alternative explanation ("Oh, right—I took a pill that's supposed to make me feel tense; that's why I'm feeling this way") or magnified by an alternative explanation ("Oh, no—I took a pill that's supposed to make me feel relaxed and I feel tense").

And that is exactly what Zanna and Cooper (1974) found. Participants in 88 the control condition underwent considerable attitude change, as would be expected in a typical dissonance experiment. Participants in the aroused condition, however, did not change their attitudes—they attributed their discomfort to the pill, not their counterattitudinal essay. Finally, participants in the relaxed condition changed their attitudes even more than the control participants did. They inferred that writing the counterattitudinal essay had made them very tense, since they were feeling aroused despite administration of a relaxing drug. Thus they inferred that their behavior was very inconsistent with their perception of themselves as decent and reasonable people, and they changed their attitude to bring it into line with their essay contents. These data are illustrated in Figure 5–6.

NEW DIRECTIONS OF RESEARCH
ON SELF-JUSTIFICATION

Throughout this chapter, we've indicated that human beings generally have a 89 need to see themselves as intelligent, sensible, and decent folks who behave with integrity. Indeed, what triggers the behavior change and cognitive distortion that occurs in the process of dissonance reduction is precisely the need people have to maintain this picture of themselves. At first glance, much of the

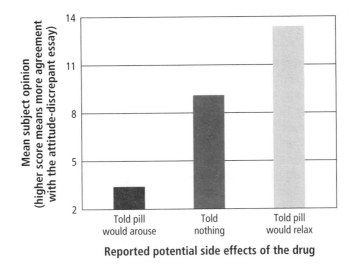

Reported potential side effects of the drug

Figure 5–6 If subjects can misattribute the arousal associated with the dissonance, they do not show the typical attitude change following a counterattitudinal essay. This is strong support for the notion that dissonance causes physiological arousal.
(Adapted from Zanna & Cooper, 1974)

behavior described in this chapter may seem startling—people coming to dislike others more after doing them harm; people liking others more after doing them a favor; people believing a lie they've told only if there is little or no reward for telling it. These behaviors would be difficult for us to understand if it weren't for the insights provided by the theory of cognitive dissonance.

In recent years, social psychologists have continued to explore this basic 90 premise in greater depth and in new contexts. On the following pages, we will review the most prominent of these more recent approaches.

Self-Discrepancy Theory

As we have seen, most of the classic dissonance experiments have involved be- 91 havior that in some way falls short of people's standards of competence or morality, such as working hard for something of questionable value or lying to someone for no good reason. Tory Higgins and his colleagues (Higgins, 1987, 1989b, 1996b, 1999; Higgins, Klein, & Strauman, 1987) have delved deeply into this issue, taking a close look at the precise nature of the emotional distress that occurs when we perceive ourselves as not measuring up to our ideals and standards. They call this **self-discrepancy theory.**

Self-discrepancy theory holds that people become distressed when their 92 sense of who they truly are—their actual self—is discrepant from their personal standards or desired self-conceptions. For Higgins and his colleagues, these standards are reflected most clearly in the various beliefs we hold about the type of person we aspire to be—our *ideal* self—and the type of person we believe we should be—our *ought* self. Comparing our actual self with our ideal and ought selves provides us with an important means of self-evaluation. We make judgments about our abilities, our personal attributes, our behavior, and the extent to which we are adhering to our goals.

What happens when we become aware that we have failed to measure 93 up to our standards? Like dissonance theory, self-discrepancy theory predicts that this blow to our self-esteem will generate psychological distress, along with the motivation to reduce the inconsistency associated with the self-discrepancy. Engaging in various forms of self-justification allows us to narrow the gap that sometimes exists between who we are, as implied by our self-discrepant actions, and who we aspire to be.

To illustrate, consider the predicament of Ana, a first-year college stu- 94 dent who has always had very high academic standards. In terms of self-discrepancy theory, academic competence is a central component of her ideal self. Moreover, she's become accustomed to living up to these high standards over the years: With only a modest level of effort, it was pretty much a breeze in high school to earn A's in most subjects and B's in the others. In her first semester at a competitive, prestigious college, however, Ana has discovered those A's much harder to come by. It seems that the courses she has enrolled in are far more rigorous and demanding than she had anticipated. As a matter of fact, in her introductory chemistry course—a prerequisite for her major—she barely managed to earn a C. Given this scenario, how is Ana likely to experience this discrepancy between her ideal and actual selves?

To begin with, we might imagine that the threat to her self-concept as a 95 high achiever would almost certainly generate fairly strong levels of emotional discomfort—for example, disappointment in herself and perhaps an unaccustomed sense of uncertainty regarding her abilities. Self-discrepancy research supports this view. In a series of studies, Higgins and his colleagues (Higgins, 1989; Higgins, Bond, Klein, & Strauman, 1988) have found that when people are made mindful of a discrepancy between their actual and ideal selves, they tend to experience a pattern of feelings involving dejection, sadness, dissatisfaction, and other depression-related emotions.

Now consider if Ana had encountered a self-discrepancy involving her 96 ought self—not the ideal self she aspired to but the "should" self she felt obligated to uphold. Imagine that being a top-notch student was not enormously significant to Ana as a means of satisfying her own ideal self-aspirations. Instead, suppose that her parents had always held this standard as highly important and that Ana, out of respect for them, was very responsive to their expectations regarding academic excellence. How, then, would Ana experience this discrepancy between her actual and ought selves in the face of a mediocre performance in her first semester at college? Higgins and his colleagues have found that a different pattern of emotions would tend to occur than in the case of actual-ideal self-discrepancy. Specifically, their research indicates that Ana would be likely to experience fear, worry, tension, and other anxiety-related emotions.

How might Ana attempt to cope with the dissonance arousal and nega- 97 tive feelings generated by either of these two forms of self-discrepancy? According to the theory, self-discrepancies not only produce emotional discomfort but also provoke strivings to minimize the gap between the actual and the ideal or ought selves. As discussed throughout this chapter, self-justifying thoughts and behaviors provide a ready means of restoring a positive self-concept when it has been threatened by a self-discrepant experience. For example, recall the predicament of subjects in Festinger and Carlsmith's (1959) classic study who, for a paltry $1, told a "fellow student" that a tedious experimental task was actually quite fascinating. We could well imagine that the ideal or ought selves of these subjects included the notion of behaving with honesty and integrity. As a result, the act of lying would have produced a discrepancy between their actual selves and their standards. How did they reduce the dissonance associated with this self-discrepancy? By minimizing the extent of their dishonesty—that is, by expressing greater liking for the boring task.

In Ana's case, reducing dissonance might involve construing her lackluster 98 academic performance in a manner that protects her long-standing belief in herself as an excellent student. In fact, in several experiments, undergraduate students who received a failing grade on an exam reacted in precisely this way: Failing students blamed their poor performance on the alleged unfairness of the test, rather than attributing it to personal factors such as poor ability or insufficient effort. In other words, when confronted with a discrepancy between their actual and desired selves, they reduced the discrepancy by eschewing personal responsibility for their dismal performance (Arkin & Maruyama, 1979; Davis & Stephan, 1980). Similarly, Ana might convince herself that the grading was unfair or that her chemistry instructor was totally inept or in some other way interpret her mediocre performance in the most positive light possible. Of course, as we've noted repeatedly in this chapter, self-justification, though a self-protective strategy in the short run, might not be the most adaptive approach Ana could adopt in coming to terms with dissonance arousal. Rather, she would undoubtedly benefit far more from reassessing her situation—concluding, perhaps, that maintaining her high academic standards might require greater effort than she was accustomed to exerting in the past, when her courses were less challenging.

Self-Completion Theory

Self-completion theory suggests that when people experience a threat to a 99 valued aspect of their self-concept, or identity, they become highly motivated to seek some sort of social recognition of that identity. Once achieved, this acknowledgment allows people to restore their valued self-conceptions, thereby serving as a means of reducing dissonance and maintaining the self (Brunstein & Gollwitzer, 1996; Gollwitzer & Wicklund, 1985; Wicklund & Gollwitzer, 1982).

Imagine, for example, that you are an aspiring poet. You think your work has a good deal of promise, and one of your poems has already been published in a small, regional poetry journal. Bolstered by this success, you have recently sent out a new batch of poems to a more prestigious journal with a larger circulation. You are also committed to developing your talents further, and so you sign up for a writing course offered by an up-and-coming poet whose work you greatly admire. As you're leaving the house on your way to the first class, you stop off at your mailbox to pick up the mail. Sorting through it, you discover a letter from the poetry journal to which you've submitted your work. With great excitement, you rip open the letter. To your dismay, however, you find an impersonal form letter from the editor informing you that your poems have been deemed unacceptable for publication in the journal. Disappointed and annoyed, you tear up the letter, get into your car, and proceed to your writing class. After the classroom has filled, the instructor asks everyone to take out the samples of their work they had been asked to bring to the first meeting. She then announces that most of the class time will be spent listening to student poetry but that given the unexpectedly large size of the group, only a few students will have the opportunity to read at the first meeting. She then asks for volunteers to read their work to the class.

Given the recent blow to your cherished identity as a poet, how do you think you would react to the instructor's request? Would you shrink back into your chair and let the others grab for the spotlight? Probably not. Rather, research on self-completion theory strongly suggests that even before the instructor had finished her sentence, your hand would have shot up into the air, vigorously vying for an opportunity to have your poems heard by the rest of the class. Why would this be the case? According to Wicklund and Gollwitzer (1982), when we experience a threat to an identity to which we are committed, we become highly motivated to restore that aspect of our self-concept through social recognition. We tend to look for ways to signal to others that we do in fact have a credible, legitimate claim to a particular identity that has been challenged. Thus in the present example, by reading poems to a group of strangers, we are able to reduce the dissonance stemming from the threat to our valued notions of self.

In an experiment very similar to this hypothetical scenario, subjects who were committed to their identities as promising dancers wrote essays about their training in dance (Gollwitzer, 1986). Half the subjects were asked to describe the worst dance instructor they had ever trained with; the other half wrote essays about their most gifted instructor. In the former condition, then, subjects were made uncomfortably aware of an aspect of their training that undermined their identities as dancers (having a poor instructor), whereas in the latter condition subjects were asked to recall an aspect of their background that supported their identities as dancers (having a great instructor). Later, in an entirely different setting, all of the subjects were invited to participate in a dance concert and were given an opportunity to select a date for their performance.

As self-completion theory predicts, dancers whose identities had been threatened—those who had recently been asked to recall an inadequate aspect of their training—expressed the desire to perform in public nearly two weeks earlier than subjects whose self-concepts as dancers had not been challenged. Similar results have been found in research involving medical students whose identities as aspiring physicians were threatened (Gollwitzer, 1986), as well as individuals who were made to feel inadequate about their identities as athletes (Gollwitzer & Wicklund, 1985). Compared to subjects whose self-concepts had not been called into questions, threatened subjects were especially eager to engage in self-symbolizing activities that bolstered their claim to an identity that had recently been challenged.

Self-Evaluation Maintenance Theory

Most dissonance research concerns how our self-image is threatened by our 103 own behavior, such as acting contrary to our attitudes or making a difficult decision. Abraham Tesser and his colleagues have explored how other people's behavior can threaten our self-concept in ways that have important implications for our interpersonal relationships (Beach, Tesser, Mendolia, & Anderson, 1996; Tesser, 1988; Tesser, Martin, & Mendolia, 1995).

Suppose you consider yourself to be a good cook—in fact, the best cook of 104 all your friends and acquaintances. You love nothing better than playing with a recipe, adding your own creative touches, until—*voilá*—you have a delectable new creation. Then you move to another town, make new friends, and alas, your favorite new friend turns out to be a superb cook, far better than you. How does that make you feel? We suspect that you might feel more than a little uneasy about the fact that your friend outdoes you in your area of expertise.

Now consider a slightly different scenario. Suppose your new best friend 105 is, instead of a superb cook, a very talented artist. Are you likely to experience any discomfort in this situation? Undoubtedly not; in fact, you are likely to bask in the reflected glory of your friend's success. "Guess what?" you will probably tell everyone. "My new friend has sold some of her paintings in the most exclusive New York galleries."

The difference between these two scenarios is that in the first one, your 106 friend is superior at an attribute that is important to you and may even be a central part of how you define yourself. We all have abilities and traits that we treasure—we are especially proud of being good cooks, talented artists, gifted musicians, or inventive scientists. Whatever our most treasured ability, if we encounter someone who is better at it than we are, there is likely to be trouble—trouble of the dissonance variety. It is difficult to be proud of our ability to cook if our closest friend is a far better chef than we are.

This is the basic premise of Tesser's (1988) **self-evaluation mainte-** 107 **nance theory:** One's self-concept can be threatened by another individual's behavior; the level of the threat is determined by both the closeness of the other individual and the personal relevance of the behavior. There is no problem if a close friend outperforms us on a task that is not particularly relevant to us. In fact, we feel even better about ourselves. Dissonance occurs when a close friend outperforms us on a task that is relevant to our self-definition.

The Reduction of Dissonance   We can try to change any one of the 108 three components that produced this dissonance. First, we can distance ourselves from the person who outperforms us, deciding that he or she is not such a close friend after all. Pleban and Tesser (1981) tested this possibility by having college students compete against another student, who was actually an accomplice of the experimenter, on general knowledge questions. They rigged it so that in some conditions, the questions were on topics that were highly relevant to people's self-definitions and the accomplice got many more of the questions correct. Just as predicted, this was the condition in which people distanced themselves the most from the accomplice, saying they would not want to work with him again. It is too dissonance-producing to be close to someone who is better than we in our treasured areas of expertise (Wegner, 1986).

A second way to reduce such threats to our self-esteem is to change how 109 relevant the task is to our self-definition. If our new friend is a far better cook than we are, we might lose interest in cooking and decide that auto mechanics is really our thing. To test this prediction, Tesser and Paulus (1983) gave people feedback about how well they and another student had done on a test of a newly discovered ability, cognitive-perceptual integration. When people learned that the other student was similar to them (scored high in closeness) and had done better on the test, they were especially likely to say that this ability was not very important to them—just as the theory predicts.

Finally, people can deal with self-esteem threats by changing the third 110 component in the equation—their performance relative to the other person's. If our new best friend is a superb cook, we can reduce the dissonance by trying to make ourselves an even better cook. This won't work, however, if we are already performing to the best of our abilities. If so, we can take a more diabolic route, wherein we try to undermine our friend's performance so that it is not as good as ours. If our friend asks for a recipe, we might leave out a crucial ingredient so that the resulting *saumon en brioche* is not nearly as good as ours.

Why Might We Help a Stranger More than a Friend?   Are people 111 really so mean-spirited that they try to sabotage their friends' performances? Surely not always; there are many examples of times when we are extremely generous and helpful toward our friends. If our self-esteem is on the line, however, there is evidence that we are not as helpful as we would like to think. Tesser and Smith (1980) asked students to play a game of Password, wherein one person gives clues to help another guess a word, and to do so paired with both a friend and a stranger. The students could choose to give clues that were helpful, making it easy for the other player to guess the word, or obscure, making it hard for the other player to guess the word. The researchers set it up so that people first performed rather poorly themselves and then had the opportunity to help the other players by giving them easy or difficult clues. The question was, who would they help more, the strangers or their friends?

By now, you can probably see what self-evaluation maintenance theory 112 predicts. If the task is not self-relevant to people, they should want their friends to do especially well so that they can bask in the reflected glory. If the task is self-relevant, however, it would be threatening to people's self-esteem to have their friends outperform them. So they might make it difficult for their friends, by giving them especially hard clues. This is exactly what Tesser and Smith found. They made the task self-relevant for some participants by telling them that performance on the game was highly correlated with their intelligence and leadership skills. Under these conditions, people gave more difficult clues to their friends than to the strangers because they did not want their friends to shine on a task that was highly important to them. When the task was not self-relevant, people gave more difficult clues to the strangers than to their friends (see Figure 5–7).

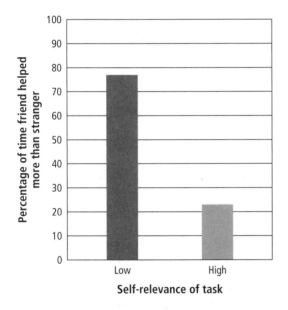

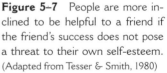

Figure 5–7 People are more inclined to be helpful to a friend if the friend's success does not pose a threat to their own self-esteem. (Adapted from Tesser & Smith, 1980)

In sum, research on self-evaluation maintenance theory has shown that 113 threats to our self-concept have fascinating implications for our interpersonal relationships. Though much of the research has been with college students in laboratory settings, the theory has been confirmed in field and archival studies as well. For example, Tesser (1980) examined biographies of male scientists, noting how close these scientists were to their fathers. As the theory predicts, when the scientists' field of expertise was the same as their fathers', they had a more distant and strained relationship with their fathers. Similarly, the greatest amount of friction between siblings was found to occur when the siblings were close in age and one sibling was significantly better on key dimensions, such as popularity or intelligence. When performance and relevance are high, it can be difficult to avoid conflicts with family members. Consider how the novelist Norman Maclean (1983) describes his relationship with his brother in *A River Runs through It:* "One of the earliest things brothers try to find out is how they differ from each other. . . . Undoubtedly, our differences would not have seemed so great if we had not been such a close family."

Self-Affirmation Theory

As we have seen, people will go to great lengths to maintain a good image of 114 themselves, by changing their attitudes, their behavior, or their relationships with other people. In each case, people try to restore a sense of integrity by warding off a specific threat to their self-concept. If we smoke cigarettes, we try to deal with the specific threat to our health by quitting or by convincing ourselves that smoking is not really bad for us. Sometimes, however, threats to our self-concept can be so strong and difficult to avoid that the normal means of reducing dissonance do not work. It can be difficult to stop smoking, as millions of people have discovered. It is also difficult to ignore all the evidence indicating that smoking is bad for us and might even kill us. So what can we do? Are smokers doomed to wallow in a constant state of dissonance? **Self-affirmation theory** suggests that people will reduce the impact of a dissonance-arousing threat to their self-concept by focusing on and affirming their competence on some dimension unrelated to the threat.

Research has revealed how self-affirmation comes about (Aronson, 115 Cohen, & Nail, 1999; Steele, 1988). "Yes, it's true that I smoke," you might say, "but I am a great cook" (a terrific poet, a wonderful friend, a promising scientist). Self-affirmation occurs when our self-esteem is threatened; if possible, we will attempt to reduce the dissonance by reminding ourselves of some irrelevant aspect of our self-concept that we cherish as a way of feeling good about ourselves in spite of some stupid or immoral action we have just committed.

In a series of clever experiments, Claude Steele and his colleagues 116 demonstrated that if you provide people with an opportunity for self-affirmation prior to the onset of dissonance, they will often grab it (Steele, 1988; Steele, Hoppe, & Gonzales, 1986; Steele & Liu, 1981). For example, Steele, Hoppe, and Gonzales (1986) performed a replication of Jack Brehm's (1956) classic experiment on postdecision dissonance reduction. They asked students to rank ten record albums, ostensibly as part of a marketing survey. As a reward, the students were then told that they could keep either their fifth- or sixth-ranked album. Ten minutes after making their choice, they were asked to rate the albums again. You will recall that in Brehm's experiment, after selecting a kitchen appliance, the participants spread apart their ratings of the appliances, rating the one they had chosen much higher than the one they had rejected. In this manner, they convinced themselves that they had made a smart decision. And that is exactly what the students did in this experiment as well.

But Steele and his colleagues built an additional set of conditions into their experiment. Half of the students were science majors, and half were business majors. Half of the science majors and half of the business majors were asked to put on a white lab coat while participating in the experiment. Why the lab coat? A lab coat is associated with the idea of science. Steele and his colleagues suspected that the lab coat would serve a "self-affirmation function" for the science majors but not for the business majors. The results supported their predictions. Whether or not they were wearing a lab coat, business majors reduced dissonance just as the people in Brehm's experiment did: After their choice, they increased their evaluation of the chosen album and decreased their evaluation of the one they had rejected. Similarly, in the absence of a lab coat, science majors reduced their dissonance in the same way. However, science majors who were wearing the lab coat resisted the temptation to distort their perceptions; Steele suggests that the lab coat reminded these students that they were promising scientists and thereby short-circuited the need to reduce dissonance by changing their attitudes toward the albums. In effect, they said, "I might have made a dumb choice in record albums, but I can live with that because I have other things going for me; at least I'm a promising scientist!" A simplified version of these findings is presented in Figure 5–8.

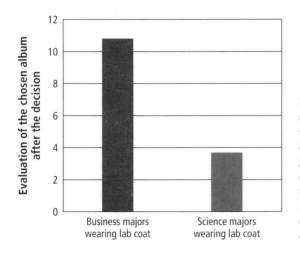

Figure 5–8 Dissonance and self-affirmation People who were allowed the opportunity to affirm their values (science majors wearing lab coats) were able to avoid the pressures to reduce dissonance by increasing the attractiveness of the chosen album. *(Adapted from Steele, Hoppe, & Gonzales, 1986)*

As you can see, self-affirmation is a rather indirect way of reducing dissonance in the sense that the individual does not deal directly with the cause of the dissonance. We would argue that because self-affirmation is less direct, it is also less complete and less efficient than dealing directly with the dissonant cognitions. That is, instead of changing our behavior to bring it in line with our beliefs or changing our beliefs in order to bring them in line with our behavior, as dissonance theory predicts, we are simply adding a positive cognition about ourselves that makes us feel a bit better but doesn't really deal with the source of the dissonance. In short, although we have comforted ourselves, the fact still remains that we may have done a stupid or immoral thing.

Here's something to think about. Suppose you committed a stupid or im- 119 moral act. Let's say that you betrayed a friend by blabbing about something private that he had confided to you. What do you think you might do? Suppose that after the fact, you were given the opportunity either to change your behavior in a way that dealt directly with the action you had taken or to affirm some unrelated aspect of your self-concept. Which path do you think you would follow?

In a series of experiments, Jeff Stone and his colleagues asked that very 120 question. They placed students in a situation where they were experiencing dissonance and had clear options; they could have gone in either direction. Their results showed that when given their choice, the overwhelming majority of participants chose the more direct and clearer path—they changed their behavior (Stone, Wiegand, Cooper, & Aronson, 1997).

SELF-JUSTIFICATION VERSUS SELF-MAINTENANCE: THE ROLE OF NEGATIVE SELF-BELIEFS

We have said repeatedly that people will typically experience dissonance when- 121 ever their self-concepts are threatened. The astute reader may have noticed that this prediction becomes tricky when applied to people who have a poor opinion of themselves. To illustrate, let's reconsider our example of smokers who continue to smoke, knowing full well that smoking is a great danger to their health. As we've noted, smokers are likely to experience high levels of dissonance because knowingly jeopardizing one's health is inconsistent with maintaining a positive self-concept. Note, however, that this conclusion rests on an important premise: It assumes that the smoker in question has a favorable self-image, one that would be inconsistent with foolish behavior. But what if we're dealing with smokers who have negative self-concepts, who already think of themselves as fairly incompetent and thus thoroughly capable of engaging in an absurdly self-destructive habit? In this case, dissonance reduction would not be required as a means of self-maintenance, since there is no need to reestablish a positive sense of self that is not present to begin with. While such individuals would almost certainly experience a blow to their self-esteem, the stability of their self-concepts would not be threatened by smoking, as would be the case for smokers who think highly of themselves.

It turns out that the vast majority of dissonance experiments have been 122 conducted among college student populations who are known to have fairly high levels of self-esteem. For such individuals, acting in a foolish, immoral, or absurd manner not only is threatening to their self-esteem but also calls into question the stability of their self-conceptions. As a result, self-justification works in the service of self-maintenance: By reducing dissonance, people with favorable self-images are able to restore a positive sense of self as well as a consistent and stable sense of self.

Research that has taken self-esteem into account reveals that in some instances, individuals with negative self-concepts do not engage in the kinds of self-justifying behaviors that are typical of people with relatively high-self-esteem. For example, an experiment by David Glass (1964) involved subjects who were induced to deliver what they believed to be painful electric shocks to an innocent "fellow student," who was actually a confederate of the experimenter. Before doing so, however, subjects were given bogus feedback on a personality test, designed to temporarily lower or raise their self-esteem. In one condition, the test results were esteem-enhancing, depicting subjects as compassionate, mature, and otherwise virtuous individuals. For other subjects, however, the feedback described them as fairly self-centered, insensitive to others' feelings, and so forth. Glass found that, after "shocking" the confederate, the two groups of subjects did not react in the same way to this potentially dissonance-arousing situation. Specifically, subjects in the high-self-esteem condition reduced dissonance by justifying their immoral behavior. They rated the "fellow student," whom they believed they had injured, as less attractive, less likable, and so forth. In contrast, subjects whose self-esteem had been temporarily lowered did not show this tendency to derogate the "victim." Why was this the case? For low-self-esteem subjects, acting immorally was apparently consistent with their self-concepts. As a result, they had no need to derogate the "fellow student" as a means of restoring their self-concepts. Instead, they maintained their unfavorable self-concepts. High-self-esteem subjects, by contrast, engaged in self-justification in order to protect their threatened self-concepts as good and decent people.

Self-Verification versus Self-Enhancement

William Swann and his colleagues have explored this tendency we have to pre- 124 serve our customary self-beliefs, even when those beliefs are unfavorable (Giesler, Josephs, & Swann, 1996; Swann, 1990, 1996; Swann & Hill, 1982; Swann & Pelham, 1988; Swann & Schroeder, 1995). Swann calls this **self-verification theory,** suggesting that people have a need to seek confirmation of their self-concept whether the self-concept is positive or negative; in some circumstances, this tendency can conflict with the desire to uphold a favorable view of oneself. For example, consider Patrick, who has always thought of himself as a lousy writer with poor verbal skills. One day he is working on a term paper with a friend, who remarks that she thinks his paper is skillfully crafted, beautifully written, and superbly articulate. How will Patrick feel? He should feel pleased and gratified, we might predict, because the friend's praise gives Patrick's self-esteem a boost.

On the other hand, Patrick's friend has given him feedback that challenges 125 a long-standing view of himself as a poor writer, and he might be motivated to maintain this negative view. Why? For two reasons. First, like dissonance theory, self-verification theory also rests on the basic premise that it is unsettling and confusing to have our views of ourselves disconfirmed; if we changed our self-concept every time we encountered someone with a different opinion of us, it would be impossible to maintain a coherent, consistent self-concept. Second, self-verification theory holds that interacting with people who view us differently from the way we view ourselves can be embarrassing. People who don't know us might have unrealistic expectations, and we might be embarrassed when they find out that we are not as smart or as artistic or as creative as they think we are. Better to let them know our faults at the outset.

In short, when people with negative self-views receive positive feedback, 126 opposing needs go head to head—the desire to feel good about themselves by believing the positive feedback (self-enhancement needs) versus the desire to maintain a consistent, coherent picture of themselves and avoid the embarrassment of being found out (self-verification needs). Which needs win out?

Throughout this chapter, we have been telling you that human beings 127 have a powerful need to feel good about themselves—in short, that the need for **self-justification** is a major determinant of our attitudes and behaviors. We now have to qualify this statement. Along with the Glass (1964) experiment, several studies suggest that when the two motives are in conflict, our need to maintain a stable self-concept under certain conditions overpowers our compelling desire to view ourselves in a positive light (Aronson & Carlsmith, 1962; Brock, Edelman, Edwards, & Schuck, 1965; Maracek & Mettee, 1972; Swann, 1990). For example, Swann and his colleagues have found that people prefer to remain in close relationships with friends, roommates, and romantic partners whose evaluations of their abilities are consistent with their own (sometimes negative) self-evaluations (Swann, Hixon, & De La Ronde, 1992; Swann & Pelham, 1988). In other words, people prefer to be close to people whose evaluations of them are not more positive than their own self-concept. In a close relationship, most people find it better to be known than to be overrated.

The need to self-verify, however, appears to dominate our behavior only 128 under a limited set of circumstances. First, people generally strive to uphold their negative self-beliefs only when they are highly certain of those beliefs (Maracek & Mettee, 1972; Swann & Ely, 1984; Swann & Pelham, 1988). Thus if Patrick had been less thoroughly convinced of his poor talents as a writer, he almost certainly would have been more receptive to his friend's praise. Second, if the consequences of being improperly evaluated are not too great—for example, if our contact with these individuals is rare so that it is unlikely they will discover we are not who we appear to be—then even people with negative views prefer positive feedback (Aronson, 1992a). Finally, if people feel there is nothing they can do to improve their abilities, they generally prefer positive feedback to accurate feedback. Why remind ourselves that we are terrible if there is nothing we can do about it? If, however, people feel that a negative self-attribute can be changed with a little work, they prefer accurate feedback, because this information can help them figure out what they need to do to get better (Steele, Spencer, & Josephs, 1992).

Dissonance Reduction and Culture

Dissonance effects have been shown to exist in almost every part of the world 129 (e.g., Beauvois & Joule, 1996, 1998; Sakai, 1999). But it does not always take the same form. Harry Triandis (1995) has argued that in less individualistic societies than ours, dissonance-reducing behavior might be less prevalent—at least on the surface—than behavior that promotes group harmony rather than individual consistency. In a similar vein, Gui-Young Hong (1992) argues that dissonance-reducing behavior may be less extreme in Japan than it is in the Western world because the Japanese culture considers an individual's acceptance of inconsistency to be a sign of maturity and broad-mindedness. This reasoning received some support from an experiment by Steven Heine and Darrin Lehman (1997b), who found that Japanese were less likely to engage in self-justification following a decision than Canadians.

Conversely, it may be that self-justification takes place in less individualis- 130 tic societies but is triggered in more communal ways. In a striking set of experiments, Japanese social psychologist Haruki Sakai (1999) investigated dissonance-reducing behavior in Japan by combining his interest in dissonance with his expert knowledge of Japanese community orientation. In a nutshell, what Sakai found was that in Japan, not only does a person reduce dissonance after saying that a boring task is interesting and enjoyable (as in the classic Festinger and Carlsmith experiment), but in addition, if a person merely observes someone he knows and likes saying that a boring task is interesting and enjoyable, that will cause *the observer* to experience dissonance. Consequently, in that situation, the observers' attitudes change. In short, the observers bring their evaluation more in line with the lie their friend has told!

Why is dissonance painful? The fact that people seem to experience and 131 reduce dissonance in every culture in which it has been investigated suggests strongly that dissonance may be a universal or near-universal experience. If so, what might be the underlying mechanism? One of the most interesting possibilities rests in the fact that we humans are almost certainly the only organisms who are fully aware of our own mortality. This awareness usually manifests itself in the fear of death. Although the fear of death constantly haunts us, most people are fairly adept at keeping that in the background—most of the time. According to Jeff Greenberg, Sheldon Solomon, Tom Pyszczynski, and their colleagues (1997, 1999, 2001), people can manage this constant fear of death by focusing on experiences that help us to feel good about ourselves. But when we are confronted with threats to our self image, the underlying terror of death comes to the fore, causing us discomfort. In a series of experiments, these investigators showed people graphic scenes of death aimed at building anxiety about their own death. Prior to witnessing these scenes, half of the participants had been given positive feedback aimed at boosting their self esteem. That experience made those people much more adept at managing their fear. Their high self-esteem apparently served as a buffer; compared to the participants in the control situation, they showed less anxiety and less defensiveness in the face of those graphic scenes of death.

Avoiding the Rationalization Trap

Dissonance-reducing behavior can be useful because it provides us with a feeling of stability and allows us to maintain our self-esteem. And as we have seen, it can help us manage the ultimate terror: the fear of death. But as you have discovered, dissonance-reducing behavior can be dangerous as well. The tendency to justify our past behavior can lead us into an escalation of rationalizations that can be disastrous. We call this the **rationalization trap:** the potential for dissonance reduction to produce a succession of self-justifications that ultimately result in a chain of stupid or irrational actions. The irony, of course, is that to avoid thinking of ourselves as stupid or immoral, we set the stage for increasing our acts of stupidity or immorality.

Learning from Our Mistakes

If we human beings were to spend all of our time and energy defending our egos, we would never learn from our mistakes. Instead, we would sweep our mistakes under the rug or, worse still, try to turn them into virtues. If we did not learn from our mistakes, we would get stuck within the confines of our narrow minds and never grow or change. As we have seen throughout this chapter, the process of dissonance reduction perpetuates error and can lead to tragedy. For example, people who hurt others can derogate their victims to the point where the perpetrators' actions seem not only justified but even heroic in their eyes. Similarly, we have seen how people, who say something they don't really believe will come to believe the statement—and some of those beliefs might be tragically erroneous. The memoirs of some of our most beleaguered former presidents are full of the kind of self-serving, self-justifying statements that can best be summarized as "If I had it all to do over again, I would not change anything important" (Johnson, 1971; Nixon, 1990; Reagan, 1990).

An interesting and more complex example of this phenomenon can be found in the memoirs of Robert McNamara (1995), who was secretary of defense and one of President Lyndon Johnson's principal military advisers during the Vietnam War. In a painful revelation, McNamara admits he came to the realization that the war was unwinnable in 1967—several years prior to our eventual withdrawal. But he chose to remain silent on this issue after leaving office while the war raged on, wasting several thousand additional American lives as well as countless Vietnamese lives. Most knowledgeable analysts believe that to have been a tragic and catastrophic error, arguing that if he had spoken out publicly, it could have shortened the war and saved thousands of people. In his book, McNamara makes a spirited but unconvincing attempt to justify his public silence out of some sort of personal and professional loyalty to his commander in chief.

In order to learn from our mistakes, it would be helpful to learn to toler- 135 ate dissonance long enough to examine the situation critically and dispassionately. We then stand a chance of breaking out of the cycle of action, followed by self-justification, followed by more intense action. For example, suppose that Mary has acted unkindly toward a fellow student. In order to learn from that experience, she must be able to resist the need to derogate her victim. Ideally, it would be effective if she were able to stay with the dissonance long enough to say, "OK, I blew it; I did a cruel thing. But that doesn't necessarily make me a cruel person. Let me think about why I did what I did."

This is easier said than done. But a clue as to how such behavior might 136 come about is contained in some of the research on self-affirmation we discussed previously (Steele, 1988). Suppose that immediately after Mary acted cruelly but before she had an opportunity to derogate her victim, she was reminded of the fact that she had recently donated several pints of blood to the Red Cross to be used by earthquake victims or that she had recently gotten a high score on her physics exam. This self-affirmation would be likely to provide her with the ability to resist engaging in typical dissonance-reducing behavior. In effect, Mary might be able to say, "It's true—I just did a cruel thing. But I am also capable of some really fine, intelligent, and generous behavior. I can do better."

Indeed, self-affirmation can serve as a cognitive buffer, protecting a per- 137 son from caving in to temptation and committing a cruel or immoral act. This was demonstrated in an early experiment on cheating (Aronson & Mettee, 1968). In this experiment, college students were first given a personality test and then given false feedback that was either positive (aimed at temporarily raising self-esteem) or negative (aimed at temporarily lowering self-esteem), or they received no information at all. Immediately afterward, they played a game of cards in which, to win a large pot, they could easily cheat without getting caught. The results were striking. Students in the high-self-esteem condition were able to resist the temptation to cheat to a far greater extent than the students in the other conditions were. In short, a temporary boost in self-esteem served to inoculate these students against cheating because the anticipation of doing something immoral was more dissonant than it would have been otherwise. Thus when they were put in a tempting situation, they were able to say to themselves, "Terrific people like me don't cheat." And they didn't (see also Spencer, Josephs, & Steele, 1993; Steele, Spencer, & Lynch, 1993). We find these results encouraging. They suggest a viable way of reversing the rationalization trap.

*   *   *

HEAVEN'S GATE REVISITED

At the beginning of this chapter, we raised a vital question regarding the followers of Marshall Herff Applewhite of Heaven's Gate. How could intelligent people allow themselves to be led into what to the overwhelming majority of us is obviously senseless and tragic behavior, resulting in mass suicide? Needless to say, the situation is complex; there were many factors operating, including the charismatic, persuasive power of the leader, the existence of a great deal of social support for the views of the group (from other members of the group), and the relative isolation of the group from dissenting views, producing a closed system—a little like living in a roomful of mirrors.

In addition to these factors, we are convinced that one of the single most powerful forces in these types of groups is the existence of a high degree of cognitive dissonance within the minds of each of the participants. After immersing yourself in this chapter, you now realize that when individuals make an important decision and invest heavily in that decision (in terms of time, effort, sacrifice, and commitment), this results in a strong need to justify those actions and that investment. The more they give up and the harder they work, the greater will be the need to convince themselves that their views are correct; indeed, they may even begin to feel sorry for others who do not share their beliefs. The members of the Heaven's Gate cult sacrificed a great deal for their beliefs: They abandoned their friends and families, turned their backs on their professions, relinquished their money and possessions, moved to another part of the world, and worked hard and long for the particular cause they believed in—all increasing their commitment to the belief. Those of us who have studied the theory of cognitive dissonance were not surprised to learn that the Heaven's Gate people, having bought a telescope that failed to reveal a spaceship that wasn't there, concluded that the telescope was faulty. To have believed otherwise would have created too much dissonance to bear. That they went on to abandon their "containers," believing that they were moving on to a higher incarnation, although tragic and bizarre, is not unfathomable. It is simply an extreme manifestation of a process that we have seen in operation over and over again throughout this chapter.

IF YOU ARE INTERESTED

Aronson, E. (1992). "The Return of the Repressed: Dissonance Theory Makes a Comeback." *Psychological Inquiry, 3*, 303–311. A brief but penetrating discussion of the conceptual linkage between the theory of cognitive dissonance and recent developments in cognitive psychology.

Aronson, E. (1997). "The Theory of Cognitive Dissonance: The Evolution and Vicissitudes of an Idea." In C. McGarty & S. A. Haslam (Eds.). *The Message of Social Psychology: Perspectives on Mind in Society* (pp. 20–35). Oxford: Blackwell. A readable account, tracing the development and evolution of the theory in the context of general social psychology.

Aronson, E. (1998). "Dissonance, Hypocrisy, and the Self-Concept." In E. Harmon-Jones & J. S. Mills (Eds.), *Cognitive Dissonance Theory: Revival with Revisions and Controversies* (pp. 103–106). Washington, DC: American Psychological Association. Bringing Festinger's original theory up to date, with special reference to the roles of self-esteem and the self-concept.

Festinger, L. (1957). *A Theory of Cognitive Dissonance.* Evanston, IL: Row & Peterson. The original presentation of dissonance theory. A classic in social psychology—clear, concise, and engagingly written.

Harmon-Jones, E., & Mills, J. S. (Eds.) (1998). *Cognitive Dissonance Theory: Revival with Revisions and Controversies.* Washington, DC: American Psychological Association.

Remains of the Day (1993). Adapted from Kazuo Ishiguro's classic novel, this stunning film explores self-justification from the perspective of a proper British butler, played by Anthony Hopkins. Shying away from friendship and romance, the butler rationalizes his lonely lifestyle by reasserting his belief that such intimacy is improper for a man in his position—and is worthwhile because of the worthiness of the gentleman in whose service he is employed.

Swann, W. B., Jr., & Schroeder, D. G. (1995). "The Search for Beauty and Truth: A Framework for Understanding Reactions to Evaluations." *Personality and Social Psychology Bulletin, 21,* 1307–1318.

Wicklund, R. A., & Brehm, J. W. (1976). *Perspectives on Cognitive Dissonance.* Hillsdale, NJ: Erlbaum. A scholarly, readable presentation of dissonance theory written two decades after its inception. Contains a description of much of the early research as well as some of the more important conceptual modifications of the theory.

SELECTION I QUESTIONS

Comprehension and Analysis

1. Why do we need to justify our actions?
2. Briefly explain cognitive dissonance theory.
3. People experiencing dissonance often go to extreme lengths to reduce it. List a positive and a negative example of such behavior.
4. Why do we often experience postdecision dissonance?
5. Explain how "dissonance reduction following a difficult moral decision can cause people to behave either more or less ethically in the future."
6. What is the problem with reducing dissonance in ways that make us feel better about ourselves? How can we avoid this trap?

Reflect and Connect

7. Why are the results of Jones and Kohler's (1959) experiment and similar subsequent research studies important for critical readers?

SELECTION 2   TRAVELER/*CAMINANTE*

ANTONIO MACHADO Y RUIZ

Machado y Ruiz is one of the most important and popular Spanish poets of his generation, the famous "Generation of 1898." He was born in Seville, Spain, in 1875. He published Solitudes, the first of many books of poetry, in 1903. His poems reflect the sober and simple expression of deep human emotions symbolic of the Generation of '98. His work, which often includes personal references, uses symbols such as the road, rivers, and the solitary traveler.

AN IDEA TO THINK ABOUT

Picture yourself running along a beach where the waves are coming in just behind you, walking up a desert sand dune with the wind blowing at your back, skating across the ice just ahead of the zamboni, or tramping down your street during a snow storm. With each step forward you leave a mark or make a footprint. But when you look back at your trail, what do you see?

Traveler	**Caminante**
Traveler, your footprints are	*Caminante, son tus huellas*
the road and nothing more.	*el camino, y nada mas;*
Traveler, there is no road;	*Caminante, no hay camino;*
the road is made as you travel.	*se hace el camino al andar.*
Traveling, the road is made,	*Al andar se hace camino*
and as you turn to look back	*Y al volver la vista atras*
you can see the path that	*se ve la senda que nunca*
shall not be walked on again.	*se ha de volver a pisar.*
Traveler, there is no road,	*Caminante, no hay camino,*
only a trail in the sea.	*si no estelas en la mar.*

SELECTION 2 QUESTIONS

Comprehension and Analysis

1. Explain what Machado means when he says "there is no road; the road is made as you travel."
2. Explain what Machado means when he says that the path "shall not be walked on again."
3. What is Machado's thesis?

4. *Caminante* was written a century ago. What effect, if any, does that time have on its message and on your evaluation of the message?

Reflect and Connect

5. In the text chapter that opens this Theme, Aronson, Wilson, and Akert explain that once we make a difficult decision—to cheat or not cheat on an exam, for example—our attitudes and values are changed. Do you think Machado would agree? Please explain.

SELECTION 3 BECOMING PEOPLE OF INTEGRITY

STEPHEN L. CARTER

Dr. Carter is Law Professor at Yale University. He frequently appears as an expert commentator on Nightline *and* Face the Nation, *and his work regularly appears in the popular press and legal journals. He is the author of the best-selling* The Emperor of Ocean Park. *His widely praised nonfiction books include* The Culture of Disbelief, Reflections of an Affirmative Action Baby, *and the trilogy of books on the most important elements of the character of a good citizen,* Integrity, The Culture of Disbelief, *and* Civility. *This selection is excerpted from* Integrity.

IDEAS TO THINK ABOUT

Think about two or three people you would describe as "having integrity." What characteristics do they have and what behaviors do they exhibit that you associate with integrity? Do you, and those you know, think these are important characteristics and behaviors? Write your definition of *integrity*.

WORDS TO KNOW

opprobrium (¶ 3)—disgrace, shame
add a bit of verisimilitude (¶ 5)—to give more of an appearance of being true
blatant (¶ 8)—obvious
described, in a loose and colloquial way (¶ 8)—in common, ordinary language
neoromantic image (¶ 11)—idealized image
slinks cravenly from office having been lambasted by the press (¶ 13)—leaves office like a coward after the press uncovers problems
discerning what is right (¶ 14)—figuring out what is right
neologism (¶ 28)—new word

My first lesson in integrity came the hard way. It was 1960 or thereabouts and I   1
was a first-grader at P.S. 129 in Harlem. The teacher had us all sitting in a circle,
playing a game in which each child would take a turn donning a blindfold and
then trying to identify objects by touch alone as she handed them to us. If you
guessed right, you stayed in until the next round. If you guessed wrong, you
were out. I survived almost to the end, amazing the entire class with my abilities. Then, to my dismay, the teacher realized what I had known and relied
upon from the start: my blindfold was tied imperfectly and a sliver of bright reality leaked in from outside. By holding the unknown object in my lap instead of
out in front of me, as most of the other children did, I could see at least a corner
or a side and sometimes more—but always enough to figure out what it was.
So my remarkable success was due only to my ability to break the rules.

Fortunately for my own moral development, I was caught. And as a re-   2
sult of being caught, I suffered, in front of my classmates, a humiliating re-
minder of right and wrong: I had cheated at the game. Cheating was wrong. It
was that simple.

I do not remember many of the details of the public lecture that I received   3
from my teacher. I do remember that I was made to feel terribly ashamed; and it
is good that I was made to feel that way, for I had something to be ashamed of.
The moral opprobrium that accompanied that shame was sufficiently intense
that it has stayed with me ever since, which is exactly how shame is supposed to
work. And as I grew older, whenever I was even tempted to cheat—at a game,
on homework—I would remember my teacher's stern face and the humiliation
of sitting before my classmates, revealed to the world as a cheater.

That was then, this is now. Browsing recently in my local bookstore, I   4
came across a book that boldly proclaimed on its cover that it contained in-
structions on how to cheat—the very word occurred in the title—at a variety
of video games. My instincts tell me that this cleverly chosen title is helping the
book to sell very well. For it captures precisely what is wrong with America
today: we care far more about winning than about playing by the rules.

Consider just a handful of examples, drawn from headlines of the mid-   5
1990s: the winner of the Miss Virginia pageant is stripped of her title after officials determine that her educational credentials are false; a television network
is forced to apologize for using explosives to add a bit of verisimilitude to a tape
purporting to show that a particular truck is unsafe; and the authors of a popular book on management are accused of using bulk purchases at key stores to
manipulate *The New York Times* best-seller list. Go back a few more years and
we can add in everything from a slew of Wall Street titans imprisoned for violating a bewildering variety of laws in their frantic effort to get ahead, to the
women's Boston Marathon winner branded a cheater for spending part of the
race on the subway. But cheating is evidently no big deal: some 70 percent of
college students admit to having done it at least once.

That, in a nutshell, is America's integrity dilemma: we are all full of fine   6
talk about how desperately our society needs it, but, when push comes to

shove, we would just as soon be on the winning side. A couple of years ago as I sat watching a football game with my children, trying to explain to them what was going on, I was struck by an event I had often noticed but on which I had never reflected. A player who failed to catch a ball thrown his way hit the ground, rolled over, and then jumped up, celebrating as though he had caught the pass after all. The referee was standing in a position that did not give him a good view of what had happened, was fooled by the player's pretense, and so moved the ball down the field. The player rushed back to the huddle so that his team could run another play before the officials had a chance to review the tape. (Until 1993, National Football League officials could watch a television replay and change their call, as long as the next play had not been run.) But viewers at home did have the benefit of the replay, and we saw what the referee missed: the ball lying on the ground instead of snug in the receiver's hands. The only comment from the broadcasters: "What a heads-up play!" Meaning: "Wow, what a great liar this kid is! Well done!"

Let's be very clear: that is exactly what they meant. The player set out to 7 mislead the referee and succeeded; he helped his team to obtain an advantage in the game that it had not earned. It could not have been accidental. He knew he did not catch the ball. By jumping up and celebrating, he was trying to convey a false impression. He was trying to convince the officials that he had caught the ball. And the officials believed him. So, in any ordinary understanding of the word, he lied. And that, too, is what happens to integrity in American life: if we happen to do something wrong, we would just as soon have nobody point it out.

Now, suppose that the player had instead gone to the referee and said, 8 "I'm sorry, sir, but I did not make the catch. Your call is wrong." Probably his coach and teammates and most of his team's fans would have been furious: he would not have been a good team player. The good team player lies to the referee, and does so in a manner that is at once blatant (because millions of viewers see it) and virtually impossible for the referee to detect. Having pulled off this trickery, the player is congratulated: he is told that he has made a heads-up play. Thus, the ethic of the game turns out to be an ethic that rewards cheating. (But I still love football.) Perhaps I should have been shocked. Yet, thinking through the implications of our celebration of a national sport that rewards cheating, I could not help recognizing that we as a nation too often lack integrity, which might be described, in a loose and colloquial way, as the courage of one's convictions.

We, the people of the United States, who a little over 200 years ago or- 9 dained and established the Constitution, have a serious problem: too many of us nowadays neither mean what we say nor say what we mean. Moreover, we hardly expect anybody else to mean what they say either.

A couple of years ago I began a university commencement address by 10 telling the audience that I was going to talk about integrity. The crowd broke into applause just because they had heard the word integrity—that's how starved for it they were. They had no idea how I was using the word, or what I was going to say about it, or, indeed, whether I was for it or against it. But they knew they liked the idea of simply talking about it. Indeed, this celebration of integrity is intriguing: we seem to carry on a passionate love affair with a word that we scarcely pause to define.

The Supreme Court likes to use such phrases as the "Constitution's structural integrity" when it strikes down actions that violate the separation of powers in the federal government. Critics demand a similar form of integrity when they argue that our age has seen the corruption of language or of particular religious traditions or of the moral sense generally. Indeed, when parents demand a form of education that will help their children grow into people of integrity, the cry carries a neoromantic image of their children becoming adults who will remain uncorrupted by the forces (whatever they are) that seem to rob so many grown-ups of . . . well, of integrity.

Very well, let us consider this word integrity. Integrity is like the weather: everybody talks about it but nobody knows what to do about it. Integrity is that stuff we always say we want more of. We want our elected representatives to have it, and political challengers always insist that their opponents lack it. We want it in our spouses, our children, our friends. We want it in our schools and our houses of worship. And in our corporations and the products they manufacture: early in 1995, one automobile company widely advertised a new car as "the first concept car with integrity." Such leadership gurus as Warren Bennis insist that integrity is of first importance. And we want it in the federal government, too, where officials all too frequently find themselves under investigation by special prosecutors. So perhaps we should say that integrity is like good weather, because everybody is in favor of it.

Scarcely a politician kicks off a campaign without promising to bring integrity to government; a few years later, more often than is healthy for our democracy, the politician slinks cravenly from office, having been lambasted by the press for lacking integrity; and then the press, in turn, is skewered for holding public figures to a measure of integrity that its own reporters, editors, producers and, most particularly, owners could not possibly meet. And for refusing to turn that critical eye inward, the press is mocked for—what else? a lack of integrity.

Everybody agrees that the nation needs more of it. Some say we need to return to the good old days when we had a lot more of it. Others say we as a nation have never really had enough of it. And hardly any of us stop to explain exactly what we mean by it—or how we know it is even a good thing—or why everybody needs to have the same amount of it. Indeed, the only trouble with integrity is that everybody who uses the word seems to mean something slightly different. So in an essay about integrity, the place to start is surely with a definition.

When I refer to integrity, I have something very simple and very specific in mind. Integrity requires three steps: 1) discerning what is right and what is wrong; 2) acting on what you have discerned, even at personal cost; and

3) saying openly that you are acting on your understanding of right from wrong. The first criterion captures the idea of integrity as requiring a degree of moral reflectiveness. The second brings in the ideal of an integral person as steadfast. The third reminds us that a person of integrity can be trusted, which includes the sense of keeping his or her commitments.

The word *integrity* comes from the same Latin root as integer and histori- 16 cally has been understood to carry much the same sense, the sense of *wholeness:* a person of integrity, like a whole number, is a whole person, a person somehow undivided. The word conveys not so much the idea of single-mindedness as of completeness—not the frenzy of a fanatic who wants to remake all the world in a single mold but the serenity of a person who is confident in the knowledge that he or she is living rightly. The person of integrity need not be a Gandhi but also cannot be a person who blows up buildings to make a point. A person of integrity lurks somewhere inside each of us: a person we feel we can trust to do right, to play by the rules, to keep commitments. Perhaps it is because we all sense the capacity for integrity within ourselves that we are able to notice and admire it even in people with whom, on many issues, we sharply disagree.

Indeed, one reason to focus on integrity as perhaps the first among the 17 virtues that make for good character is that it is in some sense prior to everything else: the rest of what we think matters very little if we lack essential integrity, the courage of our convictions, the willingness to act and speak in behalf of what we know to be right. In an era when the American people are crying out for open discussion of morality—of right and wrong—the ideal of integrity seems a good place to begin. No matter what our politics, no matter what causes we may support, would anybody really want to be led or followed or assisted by people who lack integrity? People whose word we could not trust, whose motives we didn't respect, who might at any moment toss aside everything we thought we had in common and march off in some other direction?

The answer, of course, is no: we would not want leaders of that kind, 18 even though we too often get them. The question is not only what integrity is and why it is valuable, but how we move our institutions, and our very lives, closer to exemplifying it. . . .

Integrity is not the same as honesty, although honesty obviously is a de- 19 sirable element of good character as well. From our definition, it is clear that one cannot have integrity without also displaying a measure of honesty. But one can be honest without being integral, for integrity, as I define it, demands a difficult process of discerning one's deepest understanding of right and wrong, and then further requires action consistent with what one has learned. It is possible to be honest without ever taking a hard look inside one's soul, to say nothing of taking any action based on what one finds. For example, a woman who believes abortion is murder may state honestly that this is what she thinks, but she does not fulfill the integrity criteria unless she also works to change abortion law. A man who believes in our national obligation to aid the homeless cannot claim to be fulfilling the criteria unless he works to obtain the aid he believes is deserved—and perhaps provides some assistance personally.

All too many of us fall down on step one: we do not take the time to discern right from wrong. Indeed, I suspect that few of us really know just what we believe—what we value—and, often, we do not really want to know. Discernment is hard work; it takes time and emotional energy. And it is so much easier to follow the crowd. We too often look the other way when we see wrongdoing around us, quite famously in the widely unwitnessed yet very unprivate murder of Kitty Genovese 30 years ago. We refuse to think in terms of right and wrong when we elect or reject political candidates based on what they will do for our own pocketbooks. On the campuses, too many students and not a few professors find it easier to go along with the latest trends than to risk the opprobrium of others by registering an objection. Indeed, social psychologists say that this all too human phenomenon of refusing to think independently is what leads to mob violence. But a public-spirited citizen must do a bit of soul-searching—must decide what he or she most truly and deeply believes to be right and good—before it is possible to live with integrity.

The second step is also a tough one. It is far easier to know what one believes—to know, in effect, right from wrong—than it is to do something about it. For example one may believe that the homeless deserve charity, but never dispense it; or one may think that they are bums who should not be given a dime, yet always dig into one's pockets when confronted. We Americans have a remarkable capacity to say one thing and do another, not always out of true hypocrisy but often out of a lack of self-assurance. . . . The late legal scholar Robert Cover illustrated the point quite powerfully when he examined the puzzling question of how avowedly antislavery judges in the early 19th century could hand down obviously proslavery decisions. Equally puzzling to many political activists is their inability to recruit support from people they know to be committed to their causes, who frequently explain that they simply do not want to get involved.

But in order to live with integrity, it is sometimes necessary to take that difficult step—to get involved—to fight openly for what one believes to be true and right and good, even when there is risk to oneself. I would not go so far as to insist that morally committed citizens living integral lives must fight their way through life, strident activists in behalf of all their beliefs; but I worry deeply about the number of us who seem happy to drift through life, activists in behalf of none of our beliefs.

This leads to the third step, which seems deceptively simple but is often the hardest of all: the person truly living an integral life must be willing to say that he or she is acting consistently with what he or she has decided is right. When the statements of a person of integrity are the result of discernment, of hard thought, we treat them as reliable, even when they are indicators of the future—"You've got the job" or "Till death do us part." But forthrightness also matters because people of integrity are willing to tell us why they are doing what they are doing. It does not promote integrity for one to cheat on taxes out of greed but to claim to be doing it as a protest; indeed, it does not promote integrity to do it as a protest unless one says openly (and to the Internal Revenue Service) that that is what one is doing. It does not promote integrity to ignore or cover up wrongdoing by a co-worker or family member. And it does not promote integrity to claim to be doing the will of God when one is actually doing what one's political agenda demands.

This third step—saying publicly that we are doing what we think is right, 24 even when others disagree—is made particularly difficult by our national desire to conform. Most of us want to fit in, to be accepted—and admitting to (or proudly proclaiming) an unpopular belief is rarely the way to gain acceptance. But if moral dissenters are unwilling to follow the example of the civil rights movement and make a proud public show of their convictions, we as a nation will never have the opportunity to be inspired by their integrity to rethink our own ideas.

This last point bears emphasis. Integrity does not always require following 25 the rules. Sometimes—as in the civil rights movement—integrity requires breaking the rules. But it also requires that one be open and public about both the fact of one's dissent and the reasons for it. A person who lives an integral life may sometimes reach moral conclusions that differ from those of the major-ity; displaying those conclusions publicly is a crucial aspect of the wholeness in which integrity consists.

Instead of a nation of public dissenters, we have become a nation experi- 26 enced in misdirection—in beguiling the audience into looking in one direction while we are busy somewhere else. The media culture unfortunately rewards this, not only because a misleading sound bite is more attractive (that is, mar-ketable) than a principled argument, but also because the media seem far more interested in tracking down hypocrisy than in reporting episodes of integrity.

If integrity has an opposite, perhaps it is corruption—getting away with 27 things we know to be wrong. We say that we are a nation that demands in-tegrity, but are we really? We call ourselves a nation of laws, but millions of us cheat on our taxes. We seem not to believe in the integrity of our commitments, with half of marriages ending in divorce. We say we want integrity in our politics, and our politicians promise it endlessly. (Try searching the Nexis database for uses of the word integrity by politicians and commentators, and you will be inun-dated.) But we reward innuendo and smear and barefaced lies with our votes.

Corruption is corrosive. We believe we can do it just a little, but I wonder 28 whether we can. Nearly all of us break small laws—I do it all the time—laws governing everything from the speed at which we may drive to when and how we may cross the street. Few of us will stop on the highway to retrieve the paper bag that the wind whips out the window of our moving car; we may not have thrown it out intentionally, but it still came from our car and it's still litter-ing. These I shall refer to as acts of unintegrity, not an attractive neologism, but one way of avoiding the repeated use of the word corruption which might be misleading. And one who engages in repeated acts of unintegrity may be said to be living an unintegral life.

Some of these acts of unintegrity can be cured by simple calls upon the 29
virtue of consistency. It is both amusing and sad to hear liberals who have
fought against the portrayal of vicious racial stereotypes in the media now saying that portrayals of sex and family life in the media affect nobody's behavior;
it is just as amusing, and just as sad, to see conservatives bash the president of
the United States for criticizing hateful speech on the nation's airwaves and
then turn around and bash Hollywood for speech the right happens to hate.
But inconsistency is the easiest example of unintegrity to spot.

I shared the story about the cheating football player with a few of my col- 30
leagues over lunch in the wood-paneled faculty dining room at the Yale Law
School. Like me, they are lawyers, so none could be too outraged: our task in
life, after all, is sometimes to defend the indefensible. They offered a bewildering array of fascinating and sophisticated arguments on why the receiver who
pretended to catch the ball was doing nothing wrong. One in particular stuck in
my mind. "You don't know if he was breaking the rules," one of the best and
brightest of my colleagues explained, "until you know what the rules are about
following the rules."

On reflection, I think my colleague was exactly right. What are our rules 31
about when we follow the rules? What are our rules about when we break them?
Until we can answer those two questions, we will not know how much integrity
we really want in our public and private lives, to say nothing of how to get it.

SELECTION 3 QUESTIONS

Vocabulary

1. Where does the word *integrity* come from and what has it meant historically?

Comprehension and Analysis

2. What does Carter think is America's integrity dilemma?
3. Does Carter believe integrity and honesty are the same thing? If not,
   does he think you can have integrity without honesty? Honesty without
   integrity? Explain his reasoning.
4. According to Carter, what are the three steps integrity requires? Why is
   each one so difficult?
5. According to Carter, does a person of integrity always follow the rules? If
   not, what are the "requirements" for breaking the rules?
6. What does Carter believe is the opposite of integrity?
7. State Carter's thesis.
8. Review the examples, facts, opinions, and reasoned judgments Carter
   uses to develop his thesis. List two that you think help to most logically

develop and support his thesis and two that you think are irrelevant to or detract from his thesis.

9. Review your answers to Question 8. Can you detect any personal bias in the information you identified as "logical" or "irrelevant?" (Think about Jones and Kohler's [1959] research findings from the opening text chapter. Did you label ideas or details that agreed with your prior belief as "logical" and classify statements opposite to your opinion as irrelevant or distracting?) Explain your answer.

Reflect and Connect

10. Carter says "in order to live with integrity, it is sometimes necessary to take that difficult step—to get involved—to fight openly for what one believes to be true and right and good, even when there is risk to oneself." From personal experience or recent media stories, describe an example that you believe supports Carter's statement or an example that counters his view.

SELECTION 4   I THINK YOU SHOULD BE RESPONSIBLE; ME, I'M NOT SO SURE

GORDON D. MARINO

Dr. Marino is Associate Professor of Philosophy and Curator of the Hong/Kierkegaard Library at St. Olaf College in Minnesota. He is the author of Kierkegaard in the Present Age *and co-author of* The Cambridge Companion to Kierkegaard. *His essays have appeared in* The Atlantic Monthly, The Christian Century, The New York Times Magazine, *and many other periodicals. This essay is from* Commonweal.

IDEAS TO THINK ABOUT

You walk by a homeless person on the street. On the bus, you sit next to a person who is seriously overweight or underweight. You see a person driving a new red convertible down your street. What do you think: Are they controlling their own behavior or are they controlled by their heredity and environment? How much control do you think we have over our own lives?

WORDS TO KNOW

abjure (¶ 1)—reject, stay away from
coda (¶ 1)—concluding remarks meant to reinforce the message
frequently iterated (¶ 2)—repeated often

homily (¶ 2)—serious moral talk
ukase (¶ 2)—arbitrary decree, having the force of a law
virtuosi (¶ 2)—experts
assent (¶ 4)—allow, consent to
historical epoch (¶ 4)—period of time in history
creedal assumption (¶ 5)—fundamental belief
palpable (¶ 6)—easily felt, obvious
dogma (¶ 7)—long-term belief
ethos (¶ 8)—attitude
impecunious (¶ 8)—poor
meliorism (¶ 9)—belief that the world tends to get better when people help each other
palaver (¶ 9)—talk
gaffe (¶ 10)—embarrassing mistake

Not long ago I was wheeling around the radio dial when I happened to catch a New Age evangelist sermonizing on the importance of eating only organically-grown foods. Given the epidemic cancer rate in this country, this seemed like sound advice so I decided to listen for a few minutes to what turned out to be the benediction of a weekly program of mass therapy. Having offered specific dietary counsel, the speaker went on to more general issues. In a softly hypnotic voice she exhorted her flock, "it takes great courage to be healthy." How so, I puzzled? Is it because many of our unhealthy habits, like overeating, alcohol and drug abuse are attempts to stave off anxiety; hence, the pursuit of health requires a willingness to abjure from unhealthy defenses against anxiety? That wasn't exactly her drift. The coda continued, "if you want to be healthy, the first and foremost thing is to be willing to take responsibility for yourself." In other words, the pursuit of health requires the courage to proceed as though the lives we live are nothing more nor less than the lives we have chosen. 1

    The commandment to take responsibility for ourselves is, these days, frequently iterated. Indeed, on a recent Sunday I heard almost the same homily that I had caught on the radio delivered from the pulpit of a local church. Though depressive shades of mind can certainly obscure the fact, we do have more control over our lives than some of us would care to admit. Amongst those with a full belly and a therapist, and, I suppose, amongst those without a full belly and a therapist, much suffering is self-wrought. People neglect their bodies and then moan about their fate on the way to the emergency room. Parents who could not put their ambitions aside for a moment when their children were growing up feel embittered when they begin to comprehend that their now grown Jack and Jill abhor the idea of spending time with them. As the Danish philosopher, Søren Kierkegaard, was fond of pointing out, we often create unpleasant states of mind and/or affairs which once set in motion acquire their own momentum and so spin beyond our control. If the truth be told, we are not always as passive in our suffering as our suffering would make us think; which is, 2 in part, to concede that the ukase to take responsibility for oneself has its proper applications. If, however, Freud, Foucault and other virtuosi of suspicion have taught us anything it is about the necessity of reading our thoughts for their connotations and submerged interests. With this kind of an ear cocked, the rhetoric of responsibility carries some potentially disturbing undertones.

There is a relationship between the way we talk to ourselves and the way   3 we talk to others. People who are always snarling at themselves are either always snarling at others or always trying to refrain from snarling. Though most of us are thankfully much less than absolutely consistent, the individual who imagines herself to be the pure product of her own choices is likely to think the same about her neighbor, be that neighbor someone whose most pressing problem is trying to decide whether or not to dip into her principal, or a single mother struggling to find a job, take care of a handicapped son, and come up with the rent on a rat-infested apartment. Whether or not the fanatics of freedom intend the letter of their sermons is open to question, but the claim that we ought to take absolute responsibility for the kind of people we are suggests that we enjoy complete control over our lives. Guess what? We do not.

Depending upon your situation in life, some claims are much easier to as-   4 sent to than to believe, and yet surely everyone must agree with the essayist Joseph Epstein who writes, "We do not choose to be born. We do not choose our parents. We do not choose our historical epoch, the country of our birth, or the immediate circumstances of our upbringing" (*Ambition: The Secret Passion*, Dutton, 1980). And one could go on and on and on. All the clucking about owning one's choices notwithstanding, our lives are shaped by many contingencies. It will, of course, be gainsaid that while we may not be able to control what comes our way, we can at least control our response to it. Put another way, while we cannot choose the circumstances of our lives we cannot help but choose what kind of people we are going to be. Where character is concerned, there are no contingencies. I am both the author and the book; or, to put it in Epstein's terms:

> We do choose how we shall live: courageously or in cowardice, honorably or dishonorably, with purpose or drift. We decide that what makes us significant is either what we do or what we refuse to do. But no matter how indifferent the universe may be to our choices and decisions, these choices and decisions are ours to make. We decide. We choose. And as we decide and choose so are our lives formed.

Interpretation: no matter how horrid our situation, be it Auschwitz or   5 Cambodia, we are still left with choices (e.g., whether or not to live courageous, loving, honest lives) and it is in responding to these choices that we decide what kind of people we are going to be. Despite the nearly unanimous conviction that human beings are nothing if not corruptible, the creedal assumption is that nothing can rob us of our freedom.

Yet the conceptual pressures carried by such an assumption are palpable.   6 That is why we do not want our armed robbers walking free, even though they might plead that they grew up in violent circumstances; nor do we want our friends to lie to us, only to explain that they can't help it because mutual deception was a way of life for their parents. And yet the outer does cast its shadow on the inner.

The circumstances of our lives can render it more or less impossible to make certain movements of the will. Yesterday I read of a farmer who lost his wife and three children to dehydration brought on by a water shortage caused by a long and typically ridiculous civil war. This man could not control the fate of his family but as the old dogma would have it, he can control how he is going to respond to his loss. It is, for instance, up to him whether or not he will become embittered. Or is it? What client of Club Med could chastise such a Job for cursing the day he was born? Those of us in the pink of life have, I think, a responsibility to acknowledge that people who have had the rug, floor, and foundation pulled out from under them are up against a slightly different beast than the rest of us.

For people born into a family with a garden, the tend-to-your-own-garden ethos carries the possible implication that we bear no responsibility toward people who don't have any gardens. The church in which I heard the "take responsibility for yourself" sermon was a wealthy congregation, with considerable resources for helping their neighbors up and down the road. Naturally, the last thing this flock wanted to hear about was rich folk, salvation, and eyes of needles. The next-to-last thing was that as winners in the lottery of material life they ought to stop groaning about low interest rates and spend some of the money they were going to use for that much-needed third vacation to help the horde of people whom life has placed against the wall. Not surprisingly, the first and last thing they did hear was exactly what they wanted to hear, namely, that we all need to take responsibility for ourselves. Though I am not sure that he would want to take responsibility for his moral, the pastor explained that what our impecunious neighbors really need are not Good Samaritans, but rather to take charge of their own lives.

In order to give life to his invocation, the minister discussed the death of Len Bias, a college basketball superstar and high N.B.A. draft choice who died from a drug overdose before he was ever able to take a single jump shot as a pro. Understandably many sports writers blamed this young man's death on the fact that he grew up under crushing circumstances. The shepherd of my flock would, however, have none of this meliorism. He insisted that if anything outside of Len Bias's will were responsible for Len Bias's death it was the acceptance of just this kind of palaver about individuals not being responsible for themselves. The truth, as he intoned it, was that Len Bias was solely to blame for Len Bias's death. Different circumstances would not have made a bit of difference. Had Len Bias played his high school ball at Phillips Exeter, summered on Martha's Vineyard, had a therapist to help him work through his self-destructive impulses, the result still would have been the same, or so this narrative goes. I am not so sure. While I would hate to encourage anyone to think that they cannot control themselves, it is a mistake to pretend that the nurturing environment which we all struggle to provide for our children is actually of no moral or characterological consequence. Just as the well-to-do will find it infinitely more difficult to adopt certain spiritual postures than someone less (but, as faith might have it, more) fortunate, so will the downtrodden find it more difficult than others to will themselves into certain states of mind (e.g., confidence about the future, or a conviction that it is a just world and that hard work will be rewarded). Poverty, no less than riches, but in a different way, can severely diminish the sway we have over ourselves.

Some years ago President Ronald Reagan was being pressured about the 10 exponentially increasing number of people without roofs over their heads. At one of these pressure points, he burbled that it wouldn't do any good to sacrifice public funds for the homeless because most of the folks who were sleeping on grates were doing so out of their own free will. Most of us who caught this gaffe thought the president was hyperextending the concept of free choice in order to beg out of his social obligations. The rhetoric of responsibility is, I think, often put to the same self-excusing purpose and as such it is capable of undermining our sense of social responsibility. The moralists who preach that those without boots ought to pull themselves up by the bootstraps ought at least to recognize that of all possible messages, this moral is, strangely enough, the one which taxes them the least.

SELECTION 4 QUESTIONS

Vocabulary

1. Explain what Marino means by "much suffering is self-wrought." (paragraph 2)
2. Explain what Marino means when he says "our lives are shaped by many contingencies." (paragraph 4)
3. In the last sentence of paragraph 9, Marino says, "Poverty, no less than riches, but in a different way, can severely diminish the sway we have over ourselves." Explain what he means.

Comprehension and Analysis

4. According to the New Age evangelist Marino quotes in his opening paragraph, what's the first thing a person must do if he or she wants to be healthy?
5. In paragraph 2, Marino classifies people as those "with a full belly and a therapist," and those "without a full belly and a therapist." What other words could you use to describe those two categories of people?
6. Does the essayist Joseph Epstein believe we have a choice in how we live? What reasons does he give for that belief?

the viewpoint of the minister Marino paraphrases in para-
8–9? Why did the minister discuss the death of basketball star
Bias?

what is Marino's thesis?

Review the essay with special attention to the language Marino uses. For example, in paragraph 1: "weekly program of mass therapy . . . in a softly hypnotic voice she exhorted her flock." Does his language and the connotative meanings of his words and phrases affect the way you view his message? Please explain.

10. What is one of Marino's primary concerns about commanding people to "take responsibility for yourself?" Did he present enough facts, opinions, and reasoned judgments to convince you his concerns are valid? Please explain.

Reflect and Connect

11. Describe how you think Marino would respond to Carter's premise that "in order to live with integrity, it is sometimes necessary to take that diffi-cult step—to get involved—to fight openly for what one believes to be true and right and good, even when there is risk to oneself."

SELECTION 5 I WAS ALMOST KILLED ON MY WAY TO WORK TODAY

SETH GODIN

Mr. Godin is a best-selling author, a contributing editor at Fast Company, *a renowned speaker, and an entrepreneur. His best-selling books include* Permission Marketing, The Big Red Fez, Unleashing the Ideavirus—*the most popular ebook ever written—and his latest book,* Survival Is not Enough. *He has been called "the Ultimate Entrepreneur for the Information Age" by* Business Week *and was recently chosen as one of 21 Speakers for the Next Century. This article is from* Fast Company.

AN IDEA TO THINK ABOUT

Imagine working or going to class with people who wear masks and disguises every day. You never know their names or anything about them—they are to-tally anonymous. How do you think being anonymous might change peoples' behavior?

People who know me realize that my brushes with death are fairly common, but this one was instructive. As I was driving down the road, a Verizon repair truck burst out of a driveway, narrowly missed my bumper, and tore across two lanes of traffic. The driver sped off, but not too fast for me to get her license-plate number. 1

Cell phone in hand, I was ready to call her supervisor. This wasn't just a matter of annoying suburban commuters—it was truly reckless driving. Alas, I couldn't call: There was no "Don't like my driving?" bumper sticker. No phone number to call. 2

Determined to follow through (Think of the innocent school-children!), I called information, tracked down the number for the corporate offices of Verizon, and was connected with an anonymous operator who couldn't have cared less about the anonymous truck driver. I hit a dead end, and the driver-perp went on her merry way. 3

My conclusion: Big companies and the Internet are sucking the civility out of society. 4

Have you ever noticed that people you know are far less likely to cut you off in traffic, curse at you, or steal your parking space than total strangers seem to be? There's a reason: Anonymity is the enemy of civility. 5

In a town of 200 people, you can't get away with bad behavior. Sooner or later, even bullies need the help of those around them—and even bullies know that their bad behavior will keep them from getting help. 6

Given total privacy and a cloak of invisibility, many people become coarse. They do selfish things—things that they would never do if a friend (or a video camera) were watching. Pornographic online chat rooms would be empty if users had to type in their real names to register. Polluting the Hudson River would be a lot harder to do if you had to meet with neighbors and explain that it was your decision. 7

Here's the problem: Orwell-obsessed critics complain that we're entering the era of Big Brother, where there are no secrets, where marketers know everything there is to know about us. I say that we're entering an era of anonymity. 8

Big companies are one culprit. A big company can do things that a neighbor would never dream of doing—because big companies can hide behind voice mail and "policy." When we get truly angry at a company for bad service (think about United canceling its flights last year) or for repeated promise breaking (think about getting your DSL installed), it's largely because anonymous strangers have made our lives miserable, without our getting the satisfaction of looking them in the eye. 9

A year ago, I did a friend a favor and agreed to interview a candidate for a job opening that he had. The person he sent me came from a big telephone company. I glanced at her resume and said, "Wow, you must know the person responsible for the DSL debacle. I can't believe what a horrible job your old company did with my line—and the line of every person I know." 10

Her face turned bright red, and she admitted that, in fact, she had been the person responsible.

What a moment. She had a rare chance to meet someone from whom 11
her company had stolen hours of time. And I had a once-in-a-lifetime opportunity to see an actual face behind big-company greed. (By the way, she didn't get the job.)

The other force working against personal responsibility is the Internet. I 12
don't know who was responsible for making the Internet an anonymous place, but it was a truly dumb idea.

Who benefits from the dark alleys and the lack of accountability that 13
comes from online anonymity? Let's take a look:

- Online auction services such as eBay work poorly in an anonymous environment, and, as we've seen, despite their best efforts, anonymity can lead to theft and fraudulent bidding.
- Email is falling apart, largely as a result of spam. The torrent of anonymous messages that clog our inboxes would disappear in a day if all email messages could be traced to the individuals who had sent them—with a bill then sent to those people for the costs incurred.
- Information exchange is becoming crippled as a result of anonymous rumors. Everything from online stock tips to news becomes specious when we're unable to figure out who said what.
- News groups are being rendered useless because individuals are able to show up, yell, scream, and otherwise disrupt a useful conversation—and there's not a thing we can do about it, because we don't know who anyone is and can't lock people out if they change their user name and then come back.

Stop for a minute, and consider how well the real-world analogs for these 14
services work, and how much better they'd work in an online environment with no anonymity.

Could you imagine a work place where everyone came in wearing a 15
mask? People would sit wherever they wanted to, take anything that interested them, say whatever they felt like saying—and then they'd disappear, possibly forever. Nothing would get done.

Here's a humble suggestion: Let's build a parallel Internet, a Net where 16
no one is welcome unless they have a verifiable identity. Let's require everyone to take responsibility for their actions if they want to participate in our new online society.

Will privacy go out the window in a world with no anonymity? 17

Well, in the old days we had far less anonymity and far more privacy. As 18
the Internet and the shields of large corporations have increased anonymity, it doesn't seem as if privacy is increasing. And by the way, is privacy necessarily such a good thing?

I recently did some work with a moderately well-known author. He ex- 19
plained to me the steps that he takes to avoid being contacted. He has no email
address, he said. If you want to contact him, you need to send a note to a
friend of his, who screens his messages. He has no business card, no mailing address, and no phone in his office. He has never bought anything online, and
when he flies, he buys his tickets with cash. After considering that this was sort
of bizarre behavior (he's a little bit of a bizarre personality to begin with), I felt
sad for him. In order to save himself 20 or 30 minutes a day screening email
messages from folks he doesn't know, he's decided to remove himself from the
world. As a result, as an anonymous, private person, he's under a lot less pressure to be civil and to be a productive member of our society.

What if there were no privacy? What if everyone knew how much 20
money you made, what you paid in taxes, what you gave to charity, and how
many dogs you had? And let's add just two more assumptions to the mix:

One, the government doesn't get overthrown and replaced with blue- 21
helmeted thought-controlling soldiers enforcing a new world order. And two,
we're all equally exposed. You have no anonymity and no privacy—but no one
else gets any either.

What would happen? I'm not proposing that I want a world like that—but 22
I do think that the idea is worth discussing. Somewhere along the way, we seem
to have come to the conclusion that rampant chaos, aided and abetted by tiny
circles of privacy, is the best way to ensure our future as a civil society. I think
that if I had my choice, I'd vote for the village where everyone knew my name.

At least we'd all drive better. 23

SELECTION 5 QUESTIONS

Vocabulary

1. Explain the reference to and meaning of "Orwell-obsessed critics" and
   "era of Big Brother." (paragraph 8)
2. Godin says, "Big companies and the Internet are sucking the civility out
   of society." (paragraph 4) What do you think he would list as some elements of "civility" that we are losing?

Comprehension and Analysis

3. State Godin's thesis.
4. What two major forces does Godin say are working against personal responsibility? Briefly describe how those forces foster a lack of personal
   responsibility.
5. Why does Godin propose creating a "parallel Internet"? How would it
   work?

Reflect and Connect

6. Godin says he'd prefer to live in a village where everyone knows his name. How about you? Compare and contrast your reasoning with Godin's.

SELECTION 6   EDITORIAL CARTOON

CLAY BENNETT

Pulitzer Prize–winning Editorial Cartoonist Bennett has been with The Christian Science Monitor *since 1998. In addition to producing five full-color cartoons each week for* The Christian Science Monitor, *he produces fully animated editorial cartoons for the Internet and draws cartoons for distribution through King Features Syndicate.*

AN IDEA TO THINK ABOUT

How important are ethics in today's society?

Comprehension and Analysis

1. How does Bennett answer the question, "How important are ethics in today's society?" Please explain.

Reflect and Connect

2. In what way(s) does Bennett's cartoon support or contradict Carter's premise that America is facing an integrity dilemma? Please explain.

SELECTION 7   WHY PAY WHEN IT'S "FREE"?

NOEL C. PAUL

Mr. Paul is a staff writer of The Christian Science Monitor.

IDEAS TO THINK ABOUT

Let's assume you often buy a cup of coffee at the cafeteria. Each day after you've paid for the drink, you have added sugar and milk and taken a stir stick and a couple of napkins from the condiments station. But today is different: On the condiments station there is a sign posted by a self-pay coin box asking you to pay a dime for each item you take. What do you do? Do you take your usual condiments and put 50 cents in the box? Do you not take any condiments? Do you take your usual items with the promise to pay next time? Is it even fair to ask you to pay for something you have traditionally gotten for free?

WORD TO KNOW

abet (¶ 17)—assist, promote

Consumers disgruntled by a fee increase for certain services will often switch to a competitor or cancel. 1

Many, however, are turning to another option: stealing. A host of businesses that facilitate consumer theft have sprung up in recent years, say experts, largely in an effort to attract consumers infuriated by what they perceive to be unfair prices. 2

The businesses primarily sell products that allow consumers to circumvent monthly bills for services such as cable and satellite television. Others offer information on how to avoid paying for home utilities and telephone bills. 3

Combined with consumers' widespread practice of distributing copyrighted music and movies over the Internet, the growing prominence of these "fraud services" has given rise to an increasingly pressing question: Are consumers growing more comfortable with committing theft? 4

Several experts believe the answer is yes, even though one result is an increase in fees for consumers who do pay their bills. "Many people, particularly young adults, don't see it as right or wrong anymore, but in terms of what is most convenient for them," says Paul Witt, a communications professor at the University of Texas at Arlington. 5

The evolution of technology that often gives its users a veil of anonymity is largely responsible for changing consumers' standards, say experts. 6

But people are not committing fraud simply because technology has made it possible. Their acts, say observers, are partly a defense of long-held expectations. For more than 50 years, Americans have been conditioned to expect entertainment services, in particular, that are cheap or free. 7

Many believe that services are now priced so unfairly that theft has become a justifiable form of civil disobedience. 8

"People have gotten so used to getting things for free [that] they probably should be out there paying for, they've come to believe that that's the way it should be," says Bob Kruger, vice president of enforcement for the Washington-based Business Software Alliance (BSA). 9

Theft of cable and other mainstream services is not new, but the degree to which ordinary consumers are stealing appears to be growing, according to observers within several industries. 10

"These are people who wouldn't necessarily try to do this on [a regular basis]," says Ellen Silver, product manager of CyberSource, a financial transaction consultancy in Mountain View, Calif. "This is not their regular lifestyle." 11

The number of consumers stealing satellite TV service, for example, is expected to grow from 400,000 in 2000 to 5.4 million in 2009, says the Carmel Group, an electronics research group in Carmel, Calif. 12

The utilities, software, and telecommunications industries all report rising incidents of theft. In each of the latter two, the theft results in losses of $10 billion a year. 13

MASKING INTENT?

Each of these industries blames the surge, in part, on businesses, primarily Internet-based, that instruct an audience of lay thieves in the art of stealing a particular service, or sell products that help accomplish the task. 14

Cable-descrambler boxes that are engineered to pick up every cable 15
channel available in a given region are widely available online for about $300.
Other sites sell similar software for satellite services for $150.

These businesses protect themselves against prosecution by posting dis- 16
claimers on their websites that say customers must report the use of these
products to the local cable or satellite company to avoid breaking the law.

But the intent of the sites, many experts maintain, is clearly to sell prod- 17
ucts that abet consumer theft.

"You could theoretically buy a black box to enhance an old TV, but no 18
one still uses them for that," says Marc Smith, spokesperson for the National
Cable & Telecommunications Association in Washington.

People who would not normally consider stealing are doing so now partly 19
because technology makes it so easy—and makes it seem so harmless.

Many end up stealing largely because of their instinct to get as much as they 20
can out of technology. But increasingly, that causes them to run afoul of ethics.

One example: networks that give consumers wireless Internet in their 21
home. Such "Wi-Fi" networks are so expansive they can sometimes be shared
with a neighbor—saving him the cost of broadband Web access—without significantly slowing connections speeds.

Many people, particularly young adults, often assume that firms would 22
not allow technology to accomplish a task if it weren't an acceptable use. "The
technology is moving fast, and the legal system and educational system are not
keeping up with it," says Mr. Kruger.

That is one reason the BSA—an organization known for doggedly pursu- 23
ing prosecution of those who illegally distribute copyrighted software—recently launched a softer agenda: publishing piracy-education material in
"Weekly Reader" school magazines.

But studies show that even adults minimize the significance of stealing 24
services as opposed to tangible products.

In several surveys over the past decade, University of Mississippi market- 25
ing professor Scott Vitell found that half of all consumers believe that it is OK
to steal a service that can be replicated elsewhere—like cable programming or
digital music. Yet nearly all of those people said stealing a can of soda, for example, was wrong. "There's some notion that if the original is still available, you
haven't done anything wrong [by copying it]," says Mr. Vitell.

Consumers' failure to recognize the value of intellectual property, as op- 26
posed to a tangible product, is rooted in historical precedent.

"For most of the 20th century . . . consumers grew accustomed to re- 27
ceiving [TV and radio] broadcasts for free, once having made the initial investment in the receiver," says Michael Rappa, a professor of technology
management at North Carolina State University.

The same model was strengthened in the minds of younger consumers 28
when most businesses on the Internet chose not to charge for access to their
Websites.

Consumers have also been given broad rights to save entertainment for 29
future viewing. The most important case: Sony versus Universal City Studios,
a 1984 decision that allowed consumers to record TV programming onto VHS
cassettes without paying an added fee.

Because of this model for access, efforts by companies to charge a fee for 30
entertainment have consistently been met with stiff resistance by many people.

Consumer psychologists call this response "psychological reactance." 31
Whenever consumers' freedoms are challenged, the theory goes, they will go
to great lengths to overcome the loss.

A "RIGHT" TO FREE SERVICES

"It is particularly true of Americans that whenever you try to take something 32
away from them, they will do whatever they can to restore that freedom," says
Larry Compeau, director of the Society for Consumer Psychology.

"When you begin to feel it's your right that [these services] should be 33
free, if they start charging, maybe you don't feel any guilt in trying to evade
that," says Vitell, the marketing professor.

The cable industry, for example, loses about $6.8 billion to consumer 34
theft each year. Many experts cite rate increases as a key reason. Cable rates
nationwide have jumped 45 percent in the past six years, according to Consumers Union.

Rather than sue their own customers, businesses must adapt their own 35
practices so they better fit consumer psychology, experts suggest. "Folks who
sell intellectual property have to adopt models that make accessing entertainment feel virtually free," says Michael Carroll, a law professor at Villanova
University.

One example: Charging customers a one-time subscription fee of $5 36
to download digital music. Under that scenario, music distributors will be
more able to replicate the feeling people expect of unlimited access, without
penalties.

SELECTION 7 QUESTIONS

Vocabulary

1. Explain what Paul means when he says "theft has become a justifiable
   form of civil disobedience." (paragraph 8) Does he think it is acceptable
   behavior?

Comprehension and Analysis

2. Explain what "fraud services" are and what they promote. Give two
   examples.

3. Why do some experts believe consumers are growing more comfortable with theft?
4. What do some experts believe is largely responsible for changing consumers' standards? Would Godin agree? Please explain.
5. Explain the role of "long-held expectations" in our behavior. How does this concept relate to what a person might choose to do in the "Ideas to Think About" scenario for this article?
6. What appears to be making it easier to steal cable and other services?
7. How is stealing a can of soda from the corner market the same as or different from installing a piece of software on your computer that you didn't buy?
8. State Paul's thesis.

Reflect and Connect

9. In the text chapter that opens this Theme, Aronson, Wilson, and Akert explain how a "dissonance-reducing behavior" can be useful because it provides us a feeling of stability and allows us to maintain our self-esteem. They also discuss how our tendency to justify our past behavior can lead to an escalation of rationalizations that can be disastrous. Discuss how the behaviors Paul describes relate to these concepts.

SELECTION 8 IT AIN'T ME, BABE: TO ACCEPT BLAME OR NOT TO ACCEPT BLAME, THAT IS THE QUESTION

MARTHA BECK

Dr. Beck is an innovator in life design and a monthly columnist for O: The Oprah Magazine, *where this article first appeared. NPR calls her "the best-known life coach in America," and her clients have ranged from those just beginning their careers to corporate executives from Fortune 500 companies. She has taught career development at the American Graduate School of International Management and performed research at Harvard Business School. The author of* Expecting Adam: A True Story of Birth, Rebirth *and* Everyday Magic *among other books, she lives in Phoenix, Arizona.*

IDEAS TO THINK ABOUT

Think about the last couple of times people have apologized to you for mistakes they made. Were they honest about it from the beginning, or did you have to point out the problem before they acknowledged the error? Did you take responsibility the last time you made a mistake?

It's a scene we've watched a hundred times: A public figure glares into the camera with an expression of outraged innocence and declares, "I am not a crook!" or "It was dehydration, not a drug overdose!" or "I have never had an affair!" Most of us in the viewing audience used to give these folks the benefit of the doubt, but not anymore. We've grown jaded watching a succession of well-known people make bold disclaimers that later proved to be flat-out falsehoods. I think the cover-ups bother us more than the original misdeeds. "Oh, come on!" I want to shout as I watch yet another notable person do the Weasel Dance. "We can forgive you for the toad-licking habit! We can even sort of see why you'd stalk Charo—but please, just admit it!"

Of course, this always makes me conscious of my own weaselish tendencies. It's so easy to commit the occasional sin of omission, to tell the little white lie that conveniently precludes taking the blame for my mistakes. But even when I'm doing this, I know it's a short-term solution with disastrous long-term effects. Avoiding responsibility for our actions is the single most effective way to get stuck—or stay stuck—in a life that doesn't work. It turns all the energy we might use for problem solving into keeping us insulated from the very experiences and information we most need to learn and grow.

First off, recognize when it's not your fault.

While some folks avoid blame, others apologize for everything, from their allergies to global warming to the Spanish Inquisition. Accepting blame for things over which we have no control is just as counterproductive as dodging the blame we deserve.

It's not surprising that many people take the blame when it doesn't belong to them. We females, in particular, are often socialized to hold ourselves responsible for other people's feelings and behavior, thinking that if we don't take care of them physically and emotionally, their bad moods or reprehensible actions are our fault.

I'll never forget the day a middle-school teacher gave me a royal tongue-lashing because my daughter Katie was handing in wrinkled homework papers. It was my responsibility as a parent, said the teacher, to make this kid tidy up her act. That evening I ordered Katie to iron every piece of paper in her backpack. While she did this, I paced around the ironing board, threatening to enlist her in the army, where she'd have to keep her things neat. Katie thought for a moment, pushed the steam button, and said blandly, "Two words: dishonorable discharge."

At that instant I saw that nobody—not me, not a middle-school teacher, not the U.S. military—could completely control Katie's behavior except for Katie. On the other hand, it was my responsibility to decide my own actions— for instance, the way I would react to the lecture from the teacher. I could choose to obsess, feel guilty, and run myself ragged trying to control this woman's opinion of my mothering skills, or I could just do my parental best and let it go. As the philosopher Lao Tzu once wrote, "Care about people's approval and you will be their prisoner."

Watch your language. If, like yours truly you sometimes get confused 8
about what is or is not your responsibility, you might want to use a very simple
and effective method of differentiating between things you can't control and
things you can. All you have to do is pay close attention to the way you
talk–specifically, the way you use the phrases "I have to" and "I can't." Pretend
you're wearing a shock collar and you get zapped every time you use these
phrases when they aren't literally, physically true.

"I have to finish this report." Zap! No, you don't. Take it from me: If you 9
really put your mind to it, you can go a long, long time without finishing anything. The truth is that you're choosing to finish the report because that will
create positive consequences.

"I can't say no." Zap! You just said it, so we know you have the physical 10
ability to pronounce the word. What you mean is that you're reluctant to say
no because you're afraid how other people might react.

"I can't make it to the meeting; I have to go to the dentist." Zap! Zap! The 11
dentist isn't abducting you at gunpoint. You could cancel the appointment and
attend the meeting if you really wanted to—but you don't, and that's okay.

Being this ridiculously literal may seem like splitting hairs, but these 12
weasel words can be deadly when used without awareness. When you sound
like a passive victim of circumstance, you come to act and think the way victims do. The power to determine your own thoughts and actions goes out the
window—and with it, your chance at a fulfilling life.

Try this verbal discipline for a week or so. Instead of saying "I can't," 13
substitute more accurate phrases like "I choose not to" or "I don't want to."
Rather than "I have to," say "I choose to" or "I've decided to" or simply "I'm
going to." Suddenly, you'll see a wide range of choices and options available
to you in situations where you once felt powerless. This isn't always comfortable, but it is incredibly liberating. Instead of a nice, fuzzy cheesecloth of
excuses, you'll be staring at some hard realities: Sometimes you make mistakes. Sometimes you make choices you later realize were just plain stupid.
Sometimes you know a choice is stupid right from the get-go and you make it
anyway. Ouch.

Taking the blame stings, like most disinfectants. But the longer you wait 14
to deal with your mistake, the more miserable the process is going to be. Better
to accept responsibility the way you'd clean a wound: quickly, thoroughly, with
no nonsense whatsoever. This means fully admitting a mistake, apologizing to
anyone you may have harmed by your actions, and making any amends you
possibly can, without wallowing in shame or acting pathetic in a bid for le-
niency.

If you take the blame this way, the results will be far more positive than 15
you'd expect. That's what I discovered when, for the purposes of this article, I
vowed to fess up to every bad choice and thickheaded mistake I made for a
whole month. Clearing up a problem with my bank records, I pointed out to my
banker that I could have prevented the whole mix-up by keeping better

records. During a medical checkup, I admitted to my doctor that I was phobically avoiding the baseline mammogram he had authorized six months before. I showed some of my writing to an intelligent friend and made no excuses when she pointed out what was wrong with it.

In these cases and many more, I found that my willingness to accept the blame seemed to defuse the other person's desire to blame me. Instead of the punishment I had expected, each of them actually gave me a very valuable gift, consisting of exactly the things I needed most: the precise information and support necessary to help me break through the "stuck" places in various aspects of my life. 16

When I mentioned my disorganized financial records to my banker, he showed me a filing system that worked brilliantly. My doctor noted my mammogram phobia on my medical records, so that the personnel at the radiology clinic saw me through the procedure with incredible kindness. The advice my friend gave me about my writing helped me push through a major block far more quickly than I could have without her input. 17

After these incidents and dozens of similar ones, I've almost begun to look forward to taking the blame, and I've become acutely aware of how much easier life is when I'm getting useful feedback, instead of pouring my energy into excuses and cover-ups. Compared to facing new challenges and learning effective ways to shape your own life, the Weasel Dance is boring and repetitive. What's more, everyone looks terrible doing it. I've wasted way too much time on it myself—and make no mistake about it, I have only myself to blame. 18

SELECTION 8 QUESTIONS

Vocabulary

1. Explain what Beck means when she says, "We've grown jaded watching a succession of well-known people make bold disclaimers that later proved to be flat-out falsehoods." (paragraph 1)
2. What is a "Weasel Dance"? Give an example.

Comprehension and Analysis

3. What happens when we avoid taking responsibility for our actions?
4. Why do we sometimes accept blame for things that are not our fault? Is it a good thing to do?
5. What did Beck come to realize about behavior as Katie was ironing the paper from her backpack?
6. Why does Beck advise "accepting responsibility the way you'd clean a wound"?

7. State Beck's thesis.

Reflect and Connect

8. Marino said, "While we cannot choose the circumstances of our lives we cannot help but choose what kind of people we are going to be." Discuss how you think Beck would respond to Marino's premise. How do you respond?

SELECTION 9   OTTER'S CHILDREN

"Otter's Children" is an Asian myth. Similar to folktales such as "Cinderella," myths are fictional, traditional stories set in the timeless past. They tell us about the culture of the peoples who developed them. Typically, myths focus the reader's attention on serious social concerns and reveal or illustrate the culture's philosophical beliefs.

Skipping Stones advice columnist "Dear Hanna" used the myth to illustrate her answer about staying out of trouble. Skipping Stones is a nonprofit children's magazine that encourages cooperation, creativity, and the celebration of cultural and environmental richness.

AN IDEA TO THINK ABOUT

Think about a time when you believed someone had jumped to a conclusion or rushed to judgment. What did you think needed to happen if the person wanted to reach a valid conclusion?

INTRODUCTION

Dear Hanna: When I get into trouble in school, my folks say, "If you don't break any rules, you can't get into trouble." It's a lot more complicated than that, but no one listens to the way I see it.—J. J.

Dear J. J.: You and I are in agreement. Life is vastly more complicated; it is not simply a system of rules. The following Asian myth clearly brings this message home.

Otter rushed before the King, crying: "You said you have established a Kingdom where peace reigns! Peace does not reign! Weasel is responsible for the death of my children. I dove into the water to hunt food for my children, leaving them in the care of Weasel. When I returned, they were dead!"

The King confronted Weasel, who explained: "Alas, I am responsible for the death of Otter's children through a terrible accident. When Woodpecker sounded the War Alarm, I rushed to my Defense Post, and accidentally trampled Otter's children in my haste."

The King summoned Woodpecker, who recounted the events: "I began the War Alarm instantly when I spied Scorpion sharpening his dagger. You know that is a designated Act of War."

In defense, Scorpion told the King: "I readied my dagger the instant I saw Lobster swinging its javelin!"

When Lobster appeared before the King, she explained: "Indeed, I frantically swung my javelin, when I saw Otter swimming straight toward my children, ready to devour them."

Turning to Otter, King said slowly, sadly, quietly: "Weasel is not guilty. Your own deed brought about the death of your children!"

FINAL NOTE

Thank you, J. J.! You helped us all stop and look at a point often ignored. To achieve true justice, one must always look at the whole picture. Each person must be listened to fully. Speedy judgments based on isolated broken rules may be quick and easy but often do not lead to lasting, satisfying peace.

SELECTION 9 QUESTIONS

Comprehension and Analysis

1. Which animal's children were killed?
2. Which animal physically killed the children?
3. Which animal does the judge say is responsible for the children's death?
4. What is (are) the message(s) or lesson(s) behind the myth?
5. Explain what Hanna means when she says, "Speedy judgments based on isolated broken rules may be quick and easy but often do not lead to lasting, satisfying peace."

Reflect and Connect

6. What would you say to the Otter if you were King? Why?

INVESTIGATING OTHER POINTS OF VIEW . . .

One way to investigate a variety of points of view on how we make our choices and accept responsibility for them is through the resources of Research Navigator™. Once you log on to www.ResearchNavigator.com and enter your personal passcode, (from inside the front cover of this text) you have access to three databases of credible and reliable : EBSCO's Content Select Academic Journal Database with leading academic journals, 2) *The New York Times* Search by with full-text articles from *The New York Times*, 3) Link Libra rially selected "best of the Web" sites. For more informati Navigator™ and how to use it efficiently, see "Introducing tor™" starting on page RN–1.

AFTER CONSIDERING SEVERAL POINTS OF VIEW . . .

A. There is a continuum of opinion about how much control we have over our behavior and our life. Discuss an individual's ability to control his or her behavior and life. Include factors that you believe individuals can control and cannot control and the effects.

B. Some writers and philosophers believe "blaming" people to shape ethically acceptable behavior has unfortunate results while others believe not "blaming" people for their actions has unfortunate results. Examine the similarities and differences you see between "blaming" someone for his or her behavior and having a person accept responsibility for his or her behavior. Discuss the positive and negative results of assigning blame and or responsibility with specific examples from today's society.

C. In a speech in 1941, John D. Rockefeller, Jr., said, "I believe that every right implies a responsibility; every opportunity, an obligation; every possession, a duty." Use Rockefeller's statement as the basis of a discussion on individual responsibility. Include whether you believe the concept of integrity impacts an individual's behavior and how it does so.

GLOSSARY

advocate   a supporter or defender of a particular position or point of view; advocates attempt to prove their view or position is right

analyze   examining a topic by separating it into its basic parts or elements; separating the parts—thesis and evidence—and seeing how they fit together

annotate, annotation   an active strategy for interacting with and marking readings; a way to highlight and organize main ideas and details by writing brief, useful information in the margins

argument, argumentation   the descriptive term for an essay or article that has the intent of persuading readers to believe or act in a certain way; an argument consists of a writer's thesis (also called *position, proposition,* or *conclusion*) and the reasons (also called *premises*; the emotional appeals and logical evidence) used to support it

assumption   an idea we believe to be true; something we take for granted

authority   an individual cited as an expert; one with special skill, knowledge, or mastery of a particular subject

bias, biases   a personal and sometimes unreasoned judgment; prejudice

cause and effect   reasoning that assumes one event, action, or condition can bring about another

clarify   to make clear; to explain

cliché   an expression or idea that has been so overused it no longer has any meaning

compare   looking at two or more objects, places, events, people, or ideas to see how they are similar; the similarities or degree of similarity between things of comparable nature

conclusion   a position or opinion on an issue; the part of the argument supported by the evidence/premises

connotation   the meaning suggested by a word apart from the thing it explicitly names or describes; the implied meaning of a word triggered by the feelings and emotions it creates; these positive and negative meanings evolve over time and may be different for different individuals because of background, environment, and attitudes

contrast   looking at two or more objects, places, events, people, or ideas to see how they are different; the differences or degree of difference between things of comparable nature

credibility   the reader's belief that the writer is trustworthy

critical reader   one who comprehends, questions, clarifies, and analyzes in order to reach objective, reasoned judgments; being willing and able to objectively evaluate what one reads; reaching reasoned judgments on the basis of the evidence presented rather than accepting or rejecting information based on emotion and anecdote.

cyberspace   the online world of computer networks

deductive reasoning   a form of reasoning by which we establish that a conclusion must be true because the statements on which it is based are true; starting with general knowledge and predicting a specific observation

denotation   the meaning of a word or phrase; a word's literal, dictionary meaning

evidence   any information a writer uses, such as details, facts, examples, opinions, and reasoned judgments, to support and develop a thesis or argument

expert   an authority, a specialist; experts work to uncover the accuracy and exactness of a view or position

exposition, expository   writing that explains, sets forth, or makes clear facts, events, or ideas; a more or less neutral reporting of information

evaluate   judge the merit of the parts and the whole

euphemism   a pleasant word or phrase used in place of a more direct, but harsh word; used to soften the impact; a "nice" way of saying something

fact   objective information that can be verified by observation or experimentation; a fact can change over time as new discoveries are made; also called *empirical evidence* because the interpretation does not change because of the view of the interpreter

fallacy   an error in reasoning because of faulty evidence or an incorrect inference

figurative language   words used in an imaginative way to help the reader comprehend the message more clearly by creating a mental image, or picture, of what the writer is talking about; figurative expressions often compare something the writer thinks the reader knows about to what he or she wants the reader to understand

generalize   arrive at a sensible, rational inference based on a limited sample; reach a statement about what is not known or has not happened on the basis of what is known or has happened

graphic organizer   a graphic, such as an informal outline or information map, that you create to show the basic structure of a reading selection

imply   often confused with "infer," the two words are not interchangeable; *imply* means to suggest or hint; *infer* means to reach a reasoned conclusion based on the information given; writers imply, and readers infer

inductive reasoning   a form of reasoning by which we review facts and make inferences about probable conclusions; reasoning from particular experiences to general truths

inference, infer   a reasonable statement about what is not directly stated, based on what is stated; the best reasoned conclusion based on the information given

information map   a type of graphic organizer for main ideas and details that uses different size circles or boxes and different size writing to create a picture of the relationships among ideas

irrelevant   information that does not relate to an issue; ideas or evidence that detracts from the thesis or argument

jargon   a unique language developed and understood by a specific group, such as football fans or computer users; when used outside its specific group, jargon is usually meaningless or confusing

main idea   the umbrella idea that unifies, or holds together, all the sentences of one paragraph; the primary thought the writer wants you to understand in a paragraph

methods of development   the organizational structure a writer uses to develop and support the thesis or argument; six common development structures are example, comparison and/or contrast, division or classification, cause and effect, process/sequence, and definition

objectively analyze   impartially examine the writer's ideas and information, separate from the reader's personal biases

opinion   subjective information that cannot be proved true or false; is not inherently good or bad or right or wrong but, depending on the amount and type of evidence the writer examined before forming the opinion, it can be considered valid or invalid

outline   a type of graphic organizer for main ideas and details that uses differing amounts of indentation to create a picture of the relationships among ideas

paraphrase   an active strategy that requires you to think about and understand what the author is saying and express it in your own words; a *substantially* different sentence structure and vocabulary than the original—one that is typical of your writing style; paraphrase when you need a total, accurate restatement of short segments, such as a thesis or main idea

persuasion writing that intends to influence the reader by engaging his or her emotions or by presenting logical arguments to believe a certain way or take a particular action

point of view fundamental attitude, position, or opinion about the topic/issue

prejudice a preconceived judgment or opinion; a negative opinion that is formed without evidence or before sufficient knowledge is gathered

premise the parts of an argument that support and develop the thesis

preview to read key structural organizers, like titles and subtitles, that give you a view of the content

reasoned judgments thoughtful, coherent evaluations that informed individuals make from the available evidence; my label for critical thinkers' opinions

relevant statement that has a clear supportive connection to the thesis

reliable can be counted on to give a fair analysis of the issue; does not respond to undue influence from others; trustworthy and accurate

stance point of view; a writer's or reader's position or opinion on the topic or issue

strategy the tools and techniques selected to accomplish a particular task

style the individual approach a writer uses to express his or her ideas; a writer's personality on paper

subjective based on one's personal perceptions

summary, summarize a condensed version of the original; begins with a paraphrase of the thesis and includes the main ideas in the same order and with the same emphasis as the original; summarize when you need the essence or gist of long segments, such as a complete essay

thesis the umbrella idea that unifies, or holds together, all the ideas of a multiparagraph selection such as an essay or text chapter together

tone the emotional feeling or attitude created with words; the writer's attitude toward the reader and the topic determines the tone

topic the who or what of the essay or article; part of the thesis

valid reasoning and inferences that are relevant, meaningful, and logically correct

CREDITS

INDEX

Introducing Research Navigator™

Chapter 1

An Overview of Sources

What Are Sources?

When instructors speak of sources, they're usually referring to "outside" sources--materials outside your own knowledge or thinking that contain someone else's ideas. Sources provide information; they let you learn something you did not know before. Examples of legitimate sources include credible information from the Internet, library collections, and the spoken words of experts. They can be in the form of books, newspaper articles, interviews, television and radio programs, websites, maps, online databases, magazines, computer and video images, audiotapes, and academic journals. Sources add authority to what you write and nearly all college research assignments require their use.

Using sources well is the hallmark of sound nonfiction writing. Most research writing involves a combination of print and online sources. Although this guide will focus on online resources, the advice on evaluating sources--determining whether a website offers credible information that meets the standards of academic research--almost always applies to other sources as well.

Later chapters will help you use sources effectively in your writing. Chapter 2 will help you find online sources, use databases and search engines, and evaluate such sources for credibility. While the Internet is a nearly bottomless well of useful and enlightening information, it is also host to websites created by bigots, conspiracy theorists, and extremists--not to mention those who are well-intentioned but misinformed. Chapter 2 will help you sort the academically nutritious wheat from the Internet junk-food chaff.

Chapter 3 will help you avoid plagiarism, a cardinal sin. It will also acquaint you with paraphrasing and summarizing, and how to cite and document sources. Chapter 4 will introduce you to Research Navigator, a new online academic research service, and Chapters 5, 6, 7, and 8 will show you how to use the service's four major databases.

Primary and Secondary Sources

Primary sources are firsthand evidence, based on your own or someone else's original work or direct observation. They can be documents, records, letters, diaries, novels, poems, short stories, autobiographies, interviews, and journals. This original quality adds to a source's reliability and impact on the reader.

Here is playwright Endesha Ida Mae Holland in her memoir, "From the Mississippi Delta" (1997):

> I was born into the double shotgun house at 114 East Gibb Street. Mama rented both sides of the clapboard house, which stood on raised posts. A confused patch of petunias hugged the ground at the end of the front porch. Inside, the crudely painted walls were peeling and patched with newspaper. The ceiling was so low that I could read "Little Lulu" on the funny pages pasted there. (pp. 19-20)

Holland goes on to describe the cracks in the linoleum floor that offered a view of the earth under the house and the patched roof that let in daylight and rain. Her brief account does more than describe a house: it tells us, indirectly but powerfully, about the poverty she was born into.

Secondary sources report, describe, comment on, or analyze the experiences or work of others. In college, most textbooks are secondary sources. As a piece of evidence, a secondary source is at least once removed from the primary source. It reports on the original work, the direct observation, or the firsthand experience. But it can have great value and impact as a source if the reporter or writer is reliable, either as a result of special experience (a journalist who spent years observing and reporting on the civil rights movement) or special training (a tooth-decay expert with a dental degree).

Newspapers are typical secondary sources. In a three-part series the *New York Times* published in January, 2003, reporters who examined the safety record of an Alabama-based pipe-making company concluded that it was "one of the most dangerous businesses in America." They based their conclusion on primary sources: company and government records and interviews with current and former employees, including plant managers, safety directors, and environmental engineers.

Here is a quote from the story:

> "The people, they're nothing," said Robert S. Rester, a former McWane plant manager who spoke at length about his 24 years with the company. "They're just numbers. You move them in and out. I mean, if they don't do the job, you fire them. If they get hurt, complain about safety, you put a bull's-eye on them." (Barstow & Bergman, Jan. 9, 2003, p. A1)

The *Times*, and most newspapers and magazines, are generally reliable secondary sources--although even highly-regarded publications make errors under the pressure of deadlines or competition. That's why sound research requires more than one source to back up a disputable claim.

Types of Sources

Print Sources

Newspapers, magazines, academic journals, documents, reference works, and personal papers are all print sources, although more and more of them exist in an online form as well.

For college research, the main tool for locating print sources that are not online is still the library. Many times you'll need to use electronic resources, especially the library catalog, to locate the print materials that you need to pull from the library's shelves. One major advantage of libraries: they come equipped with librarians. Reference-desk staffers can help you home in on the topic you need to research, come up with a research strategy, and determine the best tools to use in your research. The "Using Your Library" section of Research Navigator can also help you use a library's vast resources more efficiently.

Online and Database Sources

The Internet offers unlimited opportunities for research. Many print sources-- newspapers, magazines, reference works, academic journals--are available online as well. One advantage of accessing print sources online, of course, is that you have millions of pages originating from across the globe at your fingertips. Another is that you can download and print a copy of an article for your files. Finally, many online-print sources are *searchable*: you can type a keyword into an archive or database to pull up the page you need. (Databases collect and organize content online so that users can find particular information. When did the "The Wizard of Oz" debut, and how many Oscars did it win? The Internet Movie Database, www.imdb.com, will tell you. Searching online databases is a skill of its own that will be covered in the next chapter.)

Online content that is *not* print-based is even more varied. The most useful sites for research usually are informational and have URL addresses that end in **.edu** or **.gov**. "Edu" websites are sponsored by educational institutions, and they may include research results, reference works, subject indexes, and databases useful in many disciplines. "Gov" sites, sponsored by government agencies, offer a trove of primary sources: census information, federal codes and regulations, licensing records, property data, and health statistics. Sites that end in **.org** are sponsored by a nonprofit organization, such as Planned Parenthood, the National Rifle Association, or Mothers Against Drunk Driving. Some "org" sites offer reliable, usable information--but remember that they are usually sponsored by a group or individual that seeks to influence public opinion.

Although most commercial sites (those with **.com** URLs) exist to sell merchandise, some do offer information useful to students and researchers at low or no cost. News sites are an example (www.nytimes.com, www.newsweek.com, www.washingtonpost.com). Most offer free access to at least the previous week's content. Unfortunately, more and more publications are charging for access to their archives--which contain the information most useful for research. Many college departments, however, buy a subscription to fee-charging online publications like the *Wall Street Journal* or news databases like LexisNexus. You will need to get a sign-on and password from your instructor or department office. (The online Research Navigator, www.researchnavigator.com, free with the purchase of any Prentice Hall college textbook, allows one-year access to the *New York Times*, along with searchable databases of academic and general interest publications and World Wide Web sites.)

Chapter 2

How to Find and Evaluate Online Sources

Finding Online Sources

Yes, there is a wealth of information on the Internet. In fact no one knows how many World Wide Web pages exist, because new ones are being created constantly--they number in the millions, certainly, and some say billions. But how do you find the information you need? And how do you make sure it is credible? Anyone with a few technical skills and access to a computer can publish on the Internet. Some sites offer information from experts; many sites are run by amateurs. Some sites are updated frequently; others, not at all.

To search the Web efficiently, it helps to be familiar with several different strategies and use the one that works best for your research topic. The two main vehicles for accessing information through the Internet are **subject directories** and **search engines**, which will be discussed in more detail in this chapter. If you try out several examples of both types, you will quickly find the search method you favor. Also, search engines and subject directories are not uniform in the techniques users must employ to narrow or broaden a search. So if you are comfortable with several methods of searching--using Boolean operators, truncation (or wild cards), and implied operators, also explained in this chapter-- you will be able to switch more easily from one search engine or subject directory to another.

Strategies for Searching the Web

Tailor your search to the scope of the information you are seeking. To do this, you will need to understand **search engines**, **subject directories**, and **specialized databases**. A subject directory will take you through a sequence of Internet subjects. You might start with "history," move to "military history," then to "Civil War history," "Civil War battles," and arrive finally at the Battle of Gettysburg, your goal. Internet search engines locate specific Internet sites devoted to your topic (such as Military History Online's "Battle of Gettysburg" site). They often feature both subject directories and keyword searches. Specialized databases, which usually search a targeted topic or aspect of a topic, are sometimes hard to find with search engines, but there are websites that specialize in collecting links to them. All three of these types of searching tools are explained in greater detail later in this chapter.

The two most popular organizers of Web content are probably Yahoo! (www.yahoo.com) and Google (www.google.com). Google is known mainly for its search engine, admired by many for the way it produces highly relevant results. Google does offer other services (discussion forums, a subject directory, and news sources) and is regularly adding new ones. Yahoo!, which is older, is known more as a Web **portal**, or a site that offers a range of resources and services, including e-mail, on-line shopping, games, and chat forums. As an information resource, Yahoo! was once identified with its subject directory, in contrast to Google's search engine. But in recent years, Yahoo! has added a search engine. In 2002, Yahoo!'s search engine--and others--began using Google's database in response to Google's popularity, as well as to criticism that Yahoo! search results could be influenced by advertisers who paid for inclusion in its database. Both Google and Yahoo! now accept commercial listings, but they are identified as "sponsored links" or "sponsored matches" and grouped separately, usually at the top of the first results page. Use caution when considering using any information from a site seeking to sell a product (see "Evaluating Online Sources," later in this chapter).

Subject Directories

For general, research-oriented queries, for browsing, and to view sites recommended by experts, use a subject directory. There are two basic types: academic and professional directories, which are most useful to researchers, and commercial portals that cater to the general public.

Here are some commercial portals:

- **About.com**   www.about.com
- **Go.network**   www.go.com
- **Lycos**   www.lycos.com
- **Yahoo!**   www.yahoo.com

For example, in early 2003, Yahoo!'s homepage featured 14 major categories as links to further information. Clicking on "Health" would take you to another page, with dozens more subcategories. Clicking on the subcategory "Teen Health" resulted in links to 60 websites on the subject. They ranged from a government site aimed at helping girls become "fit for life" to a men's magazine site that emphasized selling products as much as offering advice. Yahoo! and other commercial sites do not evaluate user-submitted content when adding Web pages to a database; they leave the evaluation up to the user.

Academic directories, on the other hand, are often annotated by experts and are usually the result of much thought and care. To get started on finding such directories, try the University of Albany list of Internet Subject Directories (http://library.albany.edu/internet/subject.html). Other suggestions:

- **The Librarians' Index to the Internet** (www.lii.org). Sometimes called "the thinking person's Yahoo!."
- **The WWW Virtual Library** (www.vlib.org). One of the oldest and most respected subject directories on the Web. Many of the individual subject collections are maintained at universities.
- **INFOMINE** (infomine.ucr.edu). Compiled by the University of California at Riverside.

Search Engines

For targeted and complex queries, use a search engine. A search engine does not search the entire Internet; it searches **databases,** or collections of logically-related information, that are developed by the company hosting the search engine. That's why different search engines will produce different results. There are at least two ways for a page to be recorded in the search engine's database: the page's publisher can register it with the engine, or the search engine can use software called "spiders" to search the Internet and gather information that is then recorded in the engine's database.

Search engines may offer both subject directories and keyword searches. With most search engines, you enter your search terms and click on a "go" button or hit your return key. Then the engine generates a page with links to resources containing all or some of your terms. The resources are usually ranked by term: that is, one will rank higher if your search term appears many times, near the beginning of the document, in the title, and so forth.

A fairly recent development is a "second-generation" search engine, such as Google, which ranks Web pages according to the number of pages that link to them. This strategy adds an element of human judgment---in essence, it ranks a site by how popular it is--to computer technology. Many users start with Google, even for general queries, because it does such an excellent job of finding relevant documents.

Some popular search engines are:

- **AltaVista**   www.altavista.com/
- **Excite**   www.excite.com
- **Google**   www.google.com/
- **Hotbot**   www.hotbot.com
- **Webcrawler**   www.webcrawler.com

Your choice of keywords to launch the search is just as important as your choice of search engine. Use the words you would like to find in the title, description, or text of an Internet site. Searching for a common or general word, such as "Clinton," will provide a massive search of every document that contains this term. (The lowercase **clinton** will find both upper- and lower-case instances of the term.) In fact, **clinton** generated 6.9 million results from Google, ranging from Hillary Clinton's official Senate Web page, to a biography of President

Clinton, to a Clinton County, Mich., government site--all on the first results page. You'll get more usable results by narrowing your query. Do you want a biography of President Clinton? Clinton's stand on a particular issue? A chronology of Clinton's impeachment trial? Using more than one keyword will narrow your results and make them more relevant to your needs; even with thousands of results, most search engines will put the most relevant pages at the top of the results list.

It's also possible to conduct too narrow a search. If you combine keywords for something like "Ulysses S. Grant's military strategy at Gettysburg," you may produce few or no results. Try dropping one or more keywords until you get a usable list of links.

A **metasearch engine**, instead of creating its own database of information, searches the databases of several search engines. For example, when you enter a query at the Mamma.com website, the engine simultaneously queries about ten of the major search engines, such as Yahoo!, Webcrawler, and Magellan. It then provides you with a short, relevant list of results. **President Clinton impeachment** generated 62 results from Mamma.com, from search engines Teoma, Ask Jeeves, MSN.com, and others. Results included primary sources such as government documents and secondary sources such as press coverage--a mixture that might be useful in writing a college paper.

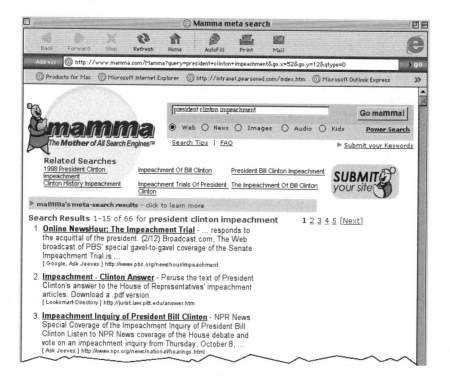

Ixquick is particularly helpful if your topic is obscure or if you want to retrieve results from several search engines without generating an enormous list. Ixquick returns only the top ten relevancy-ranked results from the source search services.

Some popular metasearch engines:

- **Ixquick**   www.ixquick.com
- **ProFusion**   www.profusion.com
- **Dogpile**   www.dogpile.com
- **Mamma.com**   www.mamma.com
- **Metacrawler.com** www.metacrawler.com

Using Boolean Terms and Other Search Limiters

When you use a search engine, you increase your chances of getting good results by formulating a precise query. Sometimes one word (or keyword) is sufficient, if it is distinctive enough.

Many times you can click on an advanced search option that will bring up a template to prompt you through the process. But sometimes it is helpful to know Boolean logic in order to narrow your search for manageable results.

Boolean logic comes from the ideas of British mathematician George Boole (1815-1864). From his writings come the Boolean operators: AND, OR, and NOT, used to link words and phrases for more precise queries for search engines and directories.

Increasingly, search engines are simplifying their search protocols by making "and" the default logic. If you type **president clinton impeachment** in most search engines, you will get results for the equivalent of **president** AND **clinton** AND **impeachment**.

Be sure to capitalize Boolean operators; some, but not all, search engines, will assume lowercase "and" or "or" to be part of a phrase and consider them "stop" words to be ignored. (Stop words are prepositions, articles, conjunctions, and other common words like **I, an, the, for**.) Most sites offer a link to a page that explains their defaults and other search protocols. From Google's homepage, for example, click on "Advanced Search" and then "Advanced Search Tips" to find this page:

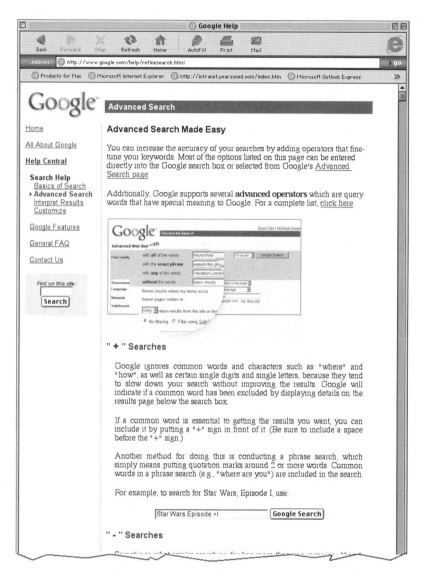

Boolean AND, OR, and NOT

The Boolean AND narrows your search by retrieving only documents that contain every one of the keywords you enter. The more terms you enter, the narrower your search becomes. Examples:

- gene AND therapy
- gene AND therapy AND risks

An Altavista search of **gene AND therapy** turned up more than 339,000 results; **gene AND therapy AND risks** generated 48,000.

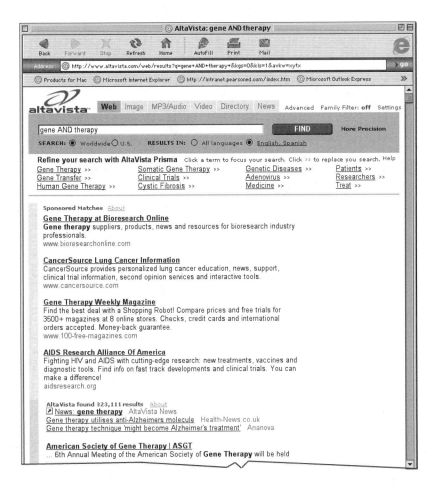

The Boolean OR expands your search by returning documents in which either or both keywords appear. Since the OR operator is usually used for keywords that are similar or synonymous, the more keywords you enter, the more documents you will retrieve. If you do a Google search of two keywords using OR and AND, you will see how OR broadens your search while AND narrows it:

- sea lions OR walruses (192,000 results)
- sea lions AND walruses (6,250 results)

The Boolean NOT or AND NOT limits your search by returning documents with only your first keyword but not the second, even if the first word appears in that document, too. For example, if you type in **seals** as a keyword, you'll get many results about Easter Seals. But if you wanted information on the animal, you could type:

- seals NOT Easter
- seals AND NOT Easter

Many search engines convert formal Boolean operators into more user-friendly template terminology when you enter their advanced search pages. The Google advanced search template gives you these options:

In the template above, "all the words" is equivalent to the Boolean AND; "at least one of the words," the Boolean OR; and "without the words," the Boolean NOT. "Exact phrase" means that if you type in **President Clinton,** you will get pages where **Clinton** is always preceded by **President**; if you use the "all the words" option and type **President Clinton**, you'll get pages with **President** and **Clinton**, but not necessarily together as a phrase.

Implied and Other Non-Boolean Limiters

While full Boolean operators are accepted in the advanced search option of some search engines, "implied" Boolean operators--or what some call "search engine math"--are accepted in the basic search options of an increasing number of search engines.

Implied Boolean operators use the plus (+) symbol for AND:

- gene +therapy +risks

The implied Boolean operator for NOT is a minus (-) symbol. Typing a (+) or (-) sign in front of a word will force the inclusion or exclusion of that word in the search statement.

- pinnipeds -walruses
- Star Wars Episode +I

Search engines have different rules about spacing before and after plus or minus signs. Google specifies a space before the symbol and no space after.

The "plus" technique is helpful when a key part of your search term is normally a stop word that a search engine would ignore. For example, typing **Star Wars Episode I** into Google will return results about all Star Wars episodes because Google will eliminate the "I" as a common word. Adding "+I" will return results only about Episode I.

Implied Boolean operators have no symbol for OR. A few search engines default to OR when two terms are searched (**war battle**), but most default to AND.

Quotation Marks

In most search engines, you can use quotation marks around two or more words to make them one unit (although proper names usually do not need quotation marks).

- "gene therapy risks"
- "SUV gas mileage"

Other Limiters

Proximity, or positional, operators--ADJ, for adjacent, or NEAR--are not really part of Boolean logic, but they serve a similar function in formulating search statements. Not all search engines accept proximity operators, but a few accept NEAR in their advanced search option. The NEAR operator allows you to search for terms situated within a specified distance of each other in any order. The closer they are, the higher the document appears in the results list. Using NEAR, when possible, in place of the Boolean AND usually returns more relevant results.

- sea lions NEAR pinnipeds
- Cheney NEAR Bush

With some search engines, you can truncate the word: use its root, followed by an asterisk, to retrieve variants of the word. For example, if you can't remember whether the organization is called Feminine Majority or Feminist Majority, you can enter **femini*** to find the site you want. This is also referred to as using a wild card or "stemming." Yahoo! supports wild card searches, but Google does not; if you don't get the results you want with one form of the word in Google, try the other (**walrus OR walruses**).

Another useful technique with some search engines is **field limiting,** which limits searches to a specified part of a page: title, URL, link, host, domain, image, or text, for example. Type in the field followed by a colon. If you wanted to make sure "multiple sclerosis" was in the title of a page in order to call up only sites devoted to the topic, you'd search for **title: multiple sclerosis**. Google uses "allintitle" for a title search, so a search for **allintitle: multiple sclerosis** would yield these results:

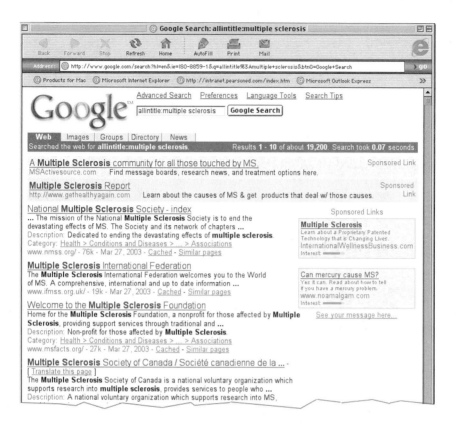

Online Databases

Much of the World Wide Web is not directly searchable from most search engines--the information is so specialized or constantly changing that it is "invisible" to the software that search engines use to access databases. These databases are often referred to as the "invisible Web" or "deep Web." Yet information stored in these databases is accessible if you know how to find it.

Some search engines and portals help by offering separate search options for the kinds of dynamically changing information, such as job listings and news, that search engines normally can't find. Yahoo's HotJobs (hotjobs.yahoo.com) and Google's news site (news.google.com) are examples of specialized search functions separate from the company's main search engine. Some sites also offer search options for multimedia and image files (Google's Image Search), and files created in non-standard file types such as Portable Document Format (PDF).

There are websites that specialize in collecting links to databases available on the Web.

Address: http://www.profusion.com/

Pro Fusion

home　alerts　options　feedback　help　sign in

Home　　　　　　　　　　　　　　　　　　　　Enabling Smarter Decisions

Enter your query terms to search Web Search Engines .

Search: [　　　　　　　　　　　　]　go　Advanced Search

Target your search by drilling into one of these vertical search groups:

My Search Groups	Create a new group
Arts and Humanities	Art, Architecture, Archaeology, Book Reviews...
Business	Business News, Small Business, Company Profiles, Business Publications...
Career	Jobs, Career Tips, High-Tech Jobs, Resumes...
Developer Toolbox	Developer Resources, HTML, ASP, Design Trends...
Discussions	Business Discussions, Finance Discussions, Product Reviews, Discussion Archives...
Downloads	MP3, Linux, Shareware and Freeware, Audio and Video...
Education	Educator Resources, K12 Resources, Bilingual Education, College Resources...
Entertainment	Movie Reviews, Television, Celebrities, Book Reviews...
Finance	Financial Tips, Ticker Symbol Lookup, Mutual Funds, Finance News...
Government	Federal Government, State and Local Government, Tax Forms, Agriculture...
Health	Health Tips, Drugs, Alternative Medicine, Medical Terms...
International	Australia, France, Latin America, United Kingdom...
Legal	Legal Tips, Legal Forms, Patents, Legal Directories...
Living	Food and Beverage, Genealogy, Consumer Tips, How-To Guides...
News	Headline News, Business News, Tech News, Sports News...
Reference	Biographies, Encyclopedias, PDF, Computer Terms...
Science	Biology, Agriculture, Astronomy

Such sites that collect links to Web databases include:

- **Resource Discovery Network**　www.rdn.ac.uk
- **ProFusion**　www.profusion.com
- **Complete Planet**　www.completeplanet.com
- **Geniusfind**　geniusfind.com

Strategies for Searching Online Databases

Google and other search engines can locate searchable databases by searching a subject term and the word "database." For example, type **aviation accidents database** in Google, and you will get thousands of results, including a federal government database with information from 1962 and later about civil aviation accidents in the United States.

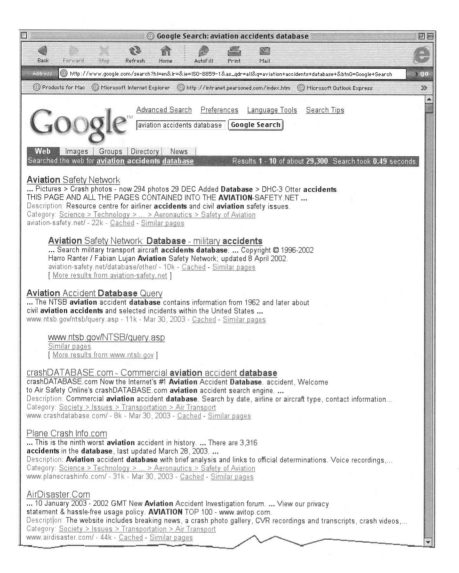

The word **database** is also helpful in searching a topic in Yahoo!, because Yahoo! uses the term to describe searchable databases in its listings. Examples:

- U.S. presidential election results database
- languages database
- toxic chemicals database

Such databases, especially if they are sponsored by government sites (identified by the **.gov** at the end of the URL), can be extremely useful as primary sources.

Planning a Search Strategy

The University of California at Berkeley has come up with a checklist (http://www.lib.berkeley.edu/TeachingLib/Guides/Internet/Strategies.html) to help you plan your search strategy. The first step is to analyze your topic to decide where to begin. Then you pick the right starting point depending on your analysis:

- If it has a distinctive word or phrase ("Battle of Gettysburg"), enclose the phrase in double quotation marks and test-run it in Google. Or search the broader concept in a subject directory.

- If it has *no* distinctive words or phrases, use more than one term or a phrase in double quotes to get fewer results from a search engine. Or try to find distinctive terms in subject directories.

- If you want an overview ("energy conservation"), look for a specialized subject directory on your topic.

- If you're seeking a narrow aspect of a broad or common topic (the role of governors in death-row pardons), try AltaVista's advanced search (www.altavista.com) or look for a directory focused on the broad subject (capital punishment).

- If your topic has synonyms (sea lion or pinniped), equivalent terms (energy conservation or fuel conservation), variant spellings (Thelonious Monk or Thelonius Monk), or endings that need to be included, choose engines with Boolean logic or truncation.

- If you don't even know where to start--you're confused and need more information--look for a gateway page or subject guide (Research Navigator's Link Library, www.researchnavigator.com), try an encyclopedia in a virtual library (the Internet Public Library, www.ipl.org), or ask at a library reference desk.

Then, stay flexible: learn as you go and vary your approach with what you learn. Don't get bogged down in a strategy that doesn't work. Switch from search engines to directories and vice versa. Find specialized directories on your topic and possible databases.

Evaluating Online Sources

In your career as a student and eventually as a professional, you will spend a great deal of time using the Internet to communicate and find information. But can you trust the information you find?

Suppose you come across two arguments regarding the greenhouse gas effect and global warming. Here are the views of a scientist who believes there is little or no greenhouse gas effect:

Although thermometers located at Earth's surface indicate that the planet's average temperature is higher today by about 1°F than it was 140 years ago, satellite measurements of the temperature of the atmosphere thousands of feet above the surface indicate little or no warming since 1979. The difference between temperatures aloft and at the surface is not predicted by computer climate models. Therefore these models cannot be relied upon to project future warming, and the surface warming itself may be an artifact caused by urban heat islands rather than a true global warming trend.

Here is the response of an environmental organization that believes global warming is human-caused and a real threat to the environment:

The method of translation of the satellite data into temperatures has been revised several times as errors were found and it is still not clear that these data provide a reliable means to determine long term trends. At higher altitudes, temperatures fluctuate more than at the surface due to natural climate influences like sunlight-reflecting particles from volcanoes. This variability or noise in the satellite record obscures the warming trend due to the buildup of the greenhouse gases, which is apparent in the global surface temperature data.

Which is more credible, the dissident scientist or the environmental organization? The organization also cites scientific research to back up its arguments. Because experts disagree, we need to consider the source.

Criteria for Evaluating Online Sources

How do you know which authorities and online sources to trust? When you look for information, you need to know the basis of the author's authority. Here are some questions you can ask to answer the question: How dependable is the source?

- Is the authority well-known and well-regarded?

- What are the authority's credentials (position, institutional affiliation)? You can check the Web page for a biography, check links to other documents, or check the author's homepage.

- Was the authority in a position to have access to pertinent facts? Someone who was a firsthand observer of the events in question is usually (but not always) more reliable. In general, primary sources are more impressive than secondary sources.

- Has the authority been screened by some organization? For example, articles in academic journals are evaluated by peers--experts in the field--to help determine if they should be accepted for publication.

- What are the likely biases? Factors that can influence how evidence is reported are personal needs, prior expectations, general beliefs, attitudes, values, theories, and ideologies. Few experts are without bias, but some have less bias than others. We can try to determine that bias by seeking information about the authority's personal interest in the topic of discussion. We need to be especially wary if an authority stands to benefit financially from the actions he or she advocates.

- How scholarly and fair has the author been? Does the author show knowledge of related sources, with appropriate citations? If claims need empirical support, does the author provide research evidence? If the topic is controversial, does the author acknowledge this and present several sides of the issue, or is the presentation one-sided? Does the document include a full biography, with references to high-quality sources, including primary sources and recent scholarly reviews? Is the information recent and up-to- date?

- Is the information timely and up-to-date? When was it produced and last updated?

Differences Among Sources of Information on the Web

The motives and purposes of those who put up websites vary greatly, and those differences affect the quality of the information. To determine the likely motives of website sponsors, you need to know who the sponsors are. Try to determine the following about any site you are using for information:

- The name of the organization or individual responsible.
- Links to additional information about the organization or individual.
- A clear statement of the site's goals.
- A clear indication of any financial sponsors and whether they are profit or nonprofit.

Your next question is: What are the likely motives of the source? Some possibilities:

- **To inform**. Many websites exist simply to present information on a topic. URL addresses that end in **.edu** or **.gov** tend to be informational because they are sponsored by educational institutions or by government agencies. Some examples: Library of Congress (lcweb.loc.gov), U.S. Environmental Protection Agency (www.epa.gov), the Internet Encyclopedia of Philosophy (www.utm.edu/research/iep/) and the U.S. Department of Commerce (www.commerce.gov).

- **To advocate.** The purpose of an advocacy page is to persuade you. Such pages reflect strong biases, which you need to identify in judging the quality of the information. URL addresses often end in **.org** if they are sponsored by a nonprofit organization. If a site's authors and sponsors seek financial donations, promote a cause, try to recruit members to an organization or provide ways for like-mind people to pursue further contact, it is an advocacy page. Organizations like Planned Parenthood, the National Rifle Association, the National Organization for Women, the Christian Coalition, and the ACLU sponsor advocacy sites.

- **To sell.** The primary purpose of many websites is to promote or sell products or services; you need to be especially alert to biases in information from such sites. URL addresses whose purpose is to sell often end in **.com**. Examples: Amazon.com, Ebay, the Gap, and Circuit City.

- **To provide news.** Many of these sites are postings of news from traditional print sources such as *The New York Times, USA Today, Newsweek,* and *Time.* Some news sites (Slate.com and Salon.com, for example) gather information from and link to multiple news sites as well as providing their own content.

- **To express individual opinions.** Many websites are created by individuals who want to express themselves. They may take the form of online journals, art galleries, or poetry sites. Web logs, called "blogs," whose authors comment on issues and link to news sites or like-minded Web authors, are increasingly popular. Personal opinion Web pages are very diverse and often very biased. Find out as much as you can about the person behind the site to decide how much credence to give his or her opinions.

- **Mixed motives.** Websites often reflect multiple motives. Be especially alert to sites that suggest one motive (information) but actually reflect other important motives (such as selling). An example is the "teen health" site listed on Yahoo! that is sponsored by a men's magazine--it blankets the site with advertising for health products. Another common practice is to make a website look as though it is informing when it is also advocating. If you are writing a paper on gun control, you may want to review sites sponsored by both pro- and anti-gun groups, but keep in mind their biases before you use any information from them.

Omitted Information

The information that you find at any particular site is selective. There are limitations imposed by time and space. Readers have limited attention spans and the communicator's knowledge is always incomplete. Sometimes, an author means to deceive: advertisers omit information that reflects badly on their products, and experts sometimes leave out information that would weaken their arguments. Finally, people have different values, beliefs, and attitudes. An individual's perspective may prevent him from noting information presented by those with different perspectives.

To get a fair picture of an issue or make a sound judgment on a research question, you need to pursue the omitted information. As you read a document, ask yourself questions to help you fill in what is missing:

- **Counterarguments**. What reasons would someone who disagrees offer? Are there research studies that contradict the studies presented? Are there missing examples that support the other side of the argument?

- **Definitions**. How would the arguments differ if key terms were defined in other ways?

- **Value preferences or perspectives**. From what other set of values might one approach this issue?

- **Origins of "facts" alluded to in the argument**. Are the factual claims supported by well-done research or by reliable sources?

- **Process used for gathering facts**. Was a survey conducted scientifically? How were respondents chosen and how were questions worded?

- **Figures, graphs, and data**. Would statistical results look different if they included evidence from different years? Have figures been selected to make a stronger case?

- **Effects of what is advocated or opposed**. What are the proposal's impacts, positive and negative, short- and long-term? Could there be unintended consequences? Which segments of society would gain and which would lose? What about other impacts: political, economic, biological, spiritual, health, interpersonal, or environmental?

- **Benefits accruing to the author.** Will the author benefit financially if we adopt his or her proposal?

Of course, reasoning is always incomplete. You could never form an opinion if you believed you had to find every possible piece of information on the subject first. But you can improve your arguments and your writing by gathering the most reliable and current information possible, given your limitations of time and space.

Chapter 3

Avoiding Plagiarism and Using Sources Ethically

What Is Plagiarism?

It is plagiarism to present another person's words or ideas as if they were your own. A kind of theft, plagarism can result in failing a course or even in expulsion from college. While blatant, intentional plagiarism is not the campus norm, many students fail to fully understand what constitutes plagiarism. Internet research in particular poses pitfalls: information can be copied from the Web with the click of a mouse, and too many students wrongly believe that anything on the Internet is in the public domain (see the section "Using Copyrighted Materials" at the end of this chapter). Others believe that they can escape detection because a professor couldn't read all the possible sources on a topic; however, instructors can now access websites that scan documents and search the Internet to identify plagiarized material.

The most flagrant forms of plagiarism are the use of another student's work, the purchase of a "canned" research paper, or knowingly copying passages into a research paper without documentation. Sometimes students unintentionally plagiarize through carelessness--by leaving off quotation marks or failing to document sources properly. Also, too many students believe that merely changing sentence order or a few words in a passage avoids plagiarism.

How to Avoid Plagiarism

Always credit the source for any ideas and words not your own. That said, a fear of plagiarism should not force you to document the obvious. You do not have to document common knowledge--information that most educated people know. (For example, that George W. Bush did not win the popular vote in the 2000 presidential election is common knowledge; a newspaper citation would be unnecessary.) You also do not have to document your own thinking, including points or conclusions that you have reached through the course of your research.

Paraphrasing

When you paraphrase, you restate *in your own words* a passage written or spoken by another person--and no more. Your writing should reflect the original passage's emphasis in your own phrasing and sentence structure. Compare the following passages. Here's the original, from a Stanford University website on South Africa:

> With the enactment of apartheid laws in 1948, racial discrimination was institutionalized. Race laws touched every aspect of social life, including a prohibition of marriage between non-whites and whites, and the sanctioning of "white-only" jobs. In 1950, the Population Registration Act required that all South Africans be racially classified into one of three categories, white, black (African) or colored (of mixed descent). The colored category included major subgroups of Indians and Asians. Classification into these categories was based on appearance, social acceptance and descent. For example, a white person was defined as "in appearance obviously a white person or generally accepted as a white person." A person could not be considered white if one of his or her parents were non-white. The determination that a person was "obviously white" would take into account "his habits, education and speech, and deportment and demeanor" (Chokshi, Carter, Gupta, Martin, & Allen, 1991).

Unacceptable Paraphrase (underlined words are plagiarized):

> According to Chokshi et al. (1991), racial discrimination was institutionalized with passage of the apartheid laws in 1948. Race laws touched every aspect of social life, including banning marriage between races, and the sanctioning of "white-only" jobs. The 1950 Population Registration Act required that all South Africans be racially classified as white, black (African) or colored (of mixed descent, Indian or Asian). Classification was based on appearance, social acceptance and descent. A white person, for example, was "in appearance obviously a white person or generally accepted as a white person." A person could not be considered white if one of his parents were non-white. According to the act, determining that a person was "obviously white" would take into account "his habits, education and speech, and deportment and demeanor.

In the above example, citing the authors (Chokshi et al., meaning "Chokshi and others") at the beginning does not legitimize using the authors' exact wording--nor does changing a few words and the order of phrases.

Acceptable Paraphrase:

> The 1948 apartheid laws made racial discrimination official. The wide-ranging laws allowed "white-only" jobs and banned marriage between races. Two years later, the Population Registration Act classified all South Africans into one of three racial categories: white, black

(African) or colored. "Colored" South Africans were of mixed descent or were Indians or Asians. According to Chokshi et al. (1991), the categories were determined by "appearance, social acceptance and descent." An officially "white" person, then, had been judged to look like a white person or was accepted as one. A white person could not have a non-white parent. The act posited that "habits, education and speech, and deportment and demeanor" would help determine the classification.

Here, the writer has borrowed two phrases from the original, but enclosed them in quotes or attributed them properly--to Chokshi et al. and the Population Registration Act.

Summarizing

A summary condenses the essentials of someone else's thought into a few statements. A summary is shorter than a paraphrase and provides only the main point from the original source. Keep it short; a summary should reduce the original by at least half. As with a paraphrase, keep your own ideas and opinions separate; you may want to note them to yourself and use them elsewhere in your paper, however.

Here is how the above quotation could be summarized:

The 1948 apartheid laws institutionalized racial discrimination in South Africa, affecting all aspects of social life. The 1950 Population Registration Act set up three categories of races, determined by such factors as appearance and descent (Chokshi, Carter, Gupta, Martin & Allen, 1991).

How to Include Reference Citations in Your Text

As you take notes, keep meticulous track of your sources. You may want to print a hard copy of each Web article used in order to save the author or authors, organization, title, date and URL for later reference--especially since Web pages are created and taken down constantly. Find out which documentation standard your instructor is using. The major styles used are MLA (Modern Language Association), APA (American Psychological Association), CMS (Chicago Manual of Style), or CBE (Council of Biology Editors, now the Council of Science Editors). All of these styles may be found on the Research Navigator homepage (www.researchnavigator.com) at the "End Notes & Bibliography" tab.

Here's how the entry on your "Works Cited" page would look for the apartheid quote using APA style:

Monal Chokshi, Cale Carter, Deepak Gupta, Tove Martin & Robert Allen (1991). Computers and the apartheid regime in South Africa. *South Africa. Guide to Internet Resources. Stanford University.* Retrieved Dec. 12, 2002, from the World Wide Web: http://www-cs-students.stanford.edu/~cale/cs201

In the example above, the authors' names are followed by the year the paper was written, the paper's title, and the name of the website (in italics). The date it was retrieved is followed by the URL. If the source is from a journal, you'll need to include the title of the periodical or electronic text, volume number, and pages.

The process for citing a Web source within text is similar to citing a print source. Within your text, you will need to provide enough information to identify a source with a name or website. If the site includes page numbers or paragraph numbers, use those as well. (In subsequent references to the same authority, the author's last name is usually sufficient.) Keep citations brief; you will fully document each source on the "Works Cited" page. If no author is listed, use the article title or website information for your in-text citation:

South Africa's minority government used technology--especially computer hardware and software--as a tool of repression (*Computers and the Apartheid Regime in South Africa*, 1991).

Quoting Sources

Direct quotations from online material follow the same rules as non-Internet material. Enclose within quotations marks all quoted materials--a phrase, a sentence, a paragraph. (Some documentation styles specify that if you are quoting more than a sentence or two, the quote should be indented instead and set off typographically.)

Don't load a paper with quotations; if more than a quarter of your essay consists of quotations, you are letting others speak for you and giving the impression that you have not synthesized the material. When drawing from an authority, rely mostly on paraphrase and summary. *Do* use a quotation, however, when it fits your message and its language is particularly on point or if the idea is hard to paraphrase accurately.

Diane Sollee (1996), the founder and director of the Coalition for Marriage, Family and Couples Education, said, "The number one predictor of divorce is the habitual avoidance of conflict."

Quote exactly; if you drop a quoted phrase within a sentence, make sure the grammar meshes with your own. If you eliminate a sentence or words within the quote, use ellipses according to the appropriate documentation style.

Halberstam (2001) described "… a dramatically changed America, one which has been challenged by the cruelest kind of terrorism, and which is in a kind of suspended state between war and peace …and where so much of our normal agenda has been brushed aside."

Using Copyrighted Materials

Just as a patent protects an inventor's rights to exploit a new product, a copyright signifies original creation and ownership of written words, music, or images. As a student, you may use copyrighted material in your research paper under the doctrine of fair use, which allows the use of others' words for such informational purposes as criticism, comment, news reporting, teaching, scholarship, or research. Academic integrity requires documenting such use in the manner covered in this chapter.

Copyright law is not intended to halt the flow of ideas and facts; it is meant to protect the literary, musical, or visual form that an author or artist uses to express his concepts. For example, there is a popular poem called "Warning" by Jenny Joseph (1961) that begins, "When I am an old woman I shall wear purple/ With a red hat which doesn't go and doesn't suit me." Several websites publish a shorter, adapted version of the poem, but anyone who wants a full version is directed to buy products from a company that has bought publishing rights to the poem. If anyone could sell products displaying Joseph's poem, its value to Joseph and the authorized publisher would be greatly diminished. Few artworks are as commercial as this, but a literary critic who published, without permission, all seven lines of a seven-line poem in her review would be violating copyright law as well. In either case, it *is* permissible to describe the ideas and facts contained in a work or quote brief passages; what is *not* permissible is to copy or reprint large portions of the work in its original literary, musical, or visual format without permission.

If you use substantial blocks of material, or you want to download images for your paper, you should seek permission from the author or website. When in doubt, consult your instructor or e-mail the author or another contact for the Internet site.

Chapter 4

Introducing Research Navigator™

What Is Research Navigator and How Can It Help with Research?

Research Navigator is an online academic research service that combines four major databases with practical research assistance--all in one place on the Web. It can help you understand the steps in the research process while also providing in-depth information on conducting library research.

Research Navigator offers these databases of credible and reliable source material: EBSCO's ContentSelect Academic Journal and Abstract Database, The *New York Times* Search by Subject Archive, *Financial Times* Article Archive and Company Financials, and "Best of the Web" Link Library. It also guides students step-by-step through the writing of a research paper. Access to Research Navigator is free with the purchase of any Pearson Education college textbook.

To begin using Research Navigator, register with the personal access code found in this *Guide to Online Research*. Once you register, you have access to all the resources in Research Navigator for six or twelve months, depending on your text.

What's in Research Navigator?

From the homepage, you can gain access to all of the site's main features, including the four databases--for academic journals and general interest publications (EBSCO's ContentSelect), newspaper articles (The *New York Times* Search by Subject Archive and *Financial Times* Article Archive), financial data (the *Financial Times* Company Financials), and World Wide Web sites ("Best of the Web" Link Library)--that will be discussed in greater detail later. If you are new to the research process, you may want to start by browsing "The Research Process," located in the upper right-hand section of the homepage. Here you will find help on all aspects of conducting research, from finding a topic to creating effective notes, research paper paradigms, and avoiding plagiarism.

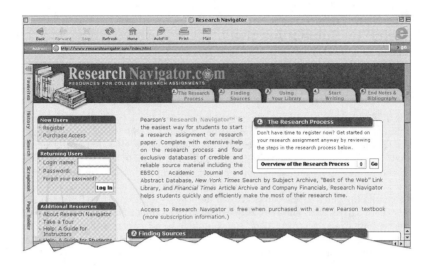

ContentSelect

EBSCO's ContentSelect Research Database gives you instant access to thousands of academic journals and periodicals from any computer with an Internet connection.

When you need the most authoritative take on a subject, especially one that is complex or very specialized, you will turn to academic journals. Academic journals are aimed at a professional audience--researchers, instructors, and experts, usually affiliated with colleges and universities. Academic-journal articles have been peer-reviewed before publication; that is, they have been checked for balance, methodology, and significance by other experts in the field. An article that doesn't meet the profession's standards will not be published in an academic journal. Examples of academic journals are *Science, Nature, American Ethnologist, Journal of Chemical Education*, and *Canadian Journal of Sociology.*

When you do a search, your list will include some results in full-text format. The full article may be in HTML, the common language used to write Web documents, or it may be in a PDF format. PDF is a file format that creates high-resolution documents; to read such documents, however, you need to first download a free viewer, Adobe Acrobat Reader.

Many ContentSelect results will be in a citation format; when you click on those results, you will get a biblographic reference with author, subject, and journal source. A citation will usually contain an abstract, or brief summary of the article, that will help you determine whether you want to find the full article. You then find the full article through the journal's online archive, or in a print or electronic version through your college library's catalog.

To use ContentSelect, select a database to search and then enter a keyword. For more detailed information, see Chapter 7.

The *New York Times*
Search by Subject Archive

Among daily newspapers, the *New York Times* is the gold standard. It is widely considered the nation's newspaper of record because it is comprehensive and staffed by reporters and editors who are experienced and well-regarded. It has substantial resources and a tradition of excellence.

The *Times*, however, like other newspapers, is aimed at a general audience and is limited by daily deadlines, competitive pressures, and space, so individual articles may not be suitable sources for a complex or very specialized research topic. But for day-to-day coverage of events and popular issues, and general, accessible background information on a wide range of topics, it is first rate.

Research Navigator gives you access to a one-year archive of articles from the *New York Times*. The archives are searchable by subject and by keyword. For tips on how to use the *New York Times* archive, see Chapter 5. Articles can be printed or saved for later use in your research assignment. Be sure to review the rules for citing a newspaper article in endnotes or a bibliography.

Link Library

Link Library is a collection of links to websites, organized by academic subject and key terms. To use this database, select a subject from the drop-down list. You will be taken to a list of key terms; find the key term for your subject and see a list of five or more editorially reviewed websites that offer educationally relevant and credible content. The Web links in Link Library are monitored and updated each week, reducing your chances of encountering dead links.

Financial Times Article Archive and Company Financials

There may be instances when your research assignment calls for business-related information and data. Through an exclusive agreement with the *Financial Times*, a leading daily newspaper covering national and international business, you can search a one-year archive of news stories affecting companies, industries, and economies.

Also use this database to access five-year financials for the 500 largest U.S. companies (by gross revenue), as well as over 200 Special Reports produced annually by the *Financial Times*.

Other Resources within Research Navigator

Using Your Library

Despite the Internet revolution, a visit to a bricks-and-mortar library continues to be an important part of the research process. Use the drop-down list on the Research Navigator homepage "Using Your Library" tab to select a "Library Guide" for your subject. The guide will list Library of Congress and Dewey call numbers, major print and online journals, organizations and associations, discussion lists, and Internet resources. Print it out and take it with you to help you navigate a library's vast resources more efficiently.

"Using Your Library" also discusses types of libraries, their resources, how to choose which ones to use, and the research process and how to develop a timeframe for it.

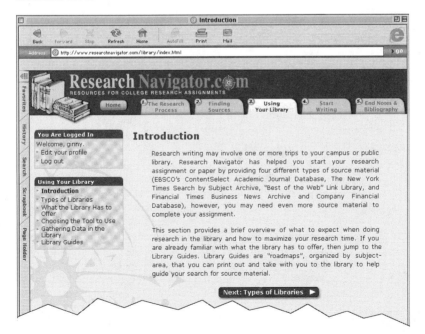

Start Writing

Once you have become acquainted with the steps in the research process and gathered source materials from Research Navigator™ and your school library, it is time to begin writing your assignment. Content found in this tab will help you do just that, beginning with a discussion on how to draft a research paper in an academic style. Other areas addressed include:

- Blending reference material into your writing
- Writing the introduction, body, and conclusion
- Revising, proofreading, and formatting the rough draft

This is also the tab where you will find sample research papers for your reference. Use them as a guide to writing your own assignment.

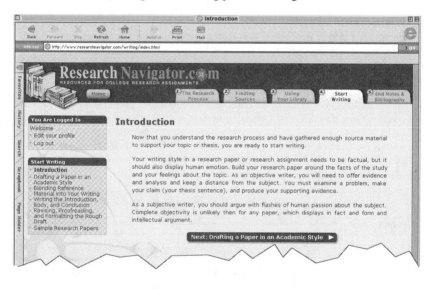

Endnotes & Bibliography

The final step in a research assignment is to create endnotes and a bibliography. In an era dubbed "The Information Age," knowledge and words are taking on more significance than ever. Laws requiring writers to document or give credit to the sources of information, while evolving, must be followed.

Various organizations have developed style manuals detailing how to document sources in their particular disciplines. For writing in the humanities and social sciences, the Modern Language Association (MLA) and American Psychological Association (APA) guidelines are the most commonly used, but others, such as those in *The Chicago Manual of Style* (CMS), are also required. The purpose of this Research Navigator™ tab is to help you properly cite your research sources. It contains detailed information on MLA, APA, CMS, and

CBE styles. You will also find guidance on how to cite the material you have gathered right from this Research Navigator™ site!

Chapter 5

Using the *New York Times* Search by Subject Archive

About the *New York Times*

Newspapers, also known as periodicals because they are issued in periodic installments (e.g. daily, weekly, or monthly), provide contemporary information. Although they don't have the scholarly authority of academic journals, newspapers are often the best source of the latest information on popular and controversial topics. Political struggles, economic debates, election campaigns and issues, scientific advances, the arts and contemporary social trends are all extensively covered by periodicals.

Research Navigator gives you access to a search-by-subject archive of articles from one of the world's leading newspapers: the *New York Times*. Since its founding in 1851, the *New York Times* has become the nation's newspaper of record--the publication that other media look to as a guide for coverage and responsible news judgment. The *Times* is still the leader among news organizations in winning Pulitzer Prizes, journalism's top award, with 108 prizes through 2002. It employs more than 1,000 editors, reporters, photographers, artists, and designers in its news department. Its reach is truly global: in 2001, the *Times* had 30 reporters in Washington, D.C.; 30 reporters in U.S. bureaus outside Washington and New York; and 40 staff correspondents and contributors in 26 news bureaus around the world.

Using the criteria we established in Chapter 2 for the dependability of sources, the *Times*:

- is well-known and well-regarded.
- has impressive credentials (Pulitzer Prizes, experienced reporters and editors).
- has access to pertinent facts (numerous correspondents provide firsthand accounts worldwide).

On the other hand, *Times* content is not peer-reviewed in the way that an academic journal is. Its content *is* screened informally by media observers and critics who are quick to pounce on any perceived errors or biases. In recent years, questions have been raised about the *Times*' coverage of a cancer "breakthrough," an Asian-American scientist suspected of being a spy, and attendance at anti-Iraq-war rallies. When *Times* editors have been convinced that criticisms have merit, they have published follow-up stories or editor's notes acknowledging errors of fact or emphasis. When smaller factual errors come to light, the *Times*, like most leading newspapers, prints timely corrections; some online archives, such as LexisNexis, append the corrections to the story.

So, while the *Times* is an excellent source for information on current topics, keep in mind that it has daily deadlines, competitive pressures, and fallible editors and reporters--like all newspapers. You need to apply the same skepticism toward the information it provides as you would with any other source. Check factual claims with other sources and be alert for signs of bias and omitted information.

What's in the Archive?

Research Navigator's *New York Times* archive organizes articles published in the past year by more than 138 academic subjects, from accounting to zoology. It only includes articles deemed relevant and timely for research; you will not find recipes or wedding announcements. The *Times* archive contents are updated every day.

The *Times*' regular website, www.nytimes.com, contains the full content of the print edition as well as additional articles and images. The newspaper's own archive includes articles from as far back as January 1, 1996, but at the time this guide was written, the *Times* charged a fee to access articles--except for art, book, and entertainment reviews--that were more than seven days old.

When and How to Use *New York Times* Articles

If you want to know the latest on an issue or breaking news story, check Research Navigator's *New York Times* archive. Want to know the status of congressional action regarding offshore income-tax shelters? What are the most recent developments with charter schools? What are the two major political parties' stands on affirmative action? Go to the relevant subject directory, or do a keyword search, or both.

But if you are researching existential philosophers, European colonialism in the Congo, or the photography of Walker Evans, for example, a newspaper archive is not the place to start. For non-contemporary subjects, especially complex academic topics, you should consider academic journals, subject directories, and search engines for finding online sources. Research Navigator's ContentSelect and Link Library, which are explained in the next two chapters, will help you find directories and search engines more suited to your topic.

Searching the Archive

Search by Subject

Searching the *New York Times* archive by subject is not only easy, it's also more suited to browsing than to finding a specific topic. The "constitutional law" grouping had 166 articles when this was written, and the "American government" heading had over 4,000. To search multiple subjects, hold down the Alt or Command key. Articles can be printed or saved for later use. Be sure to review the citation rules for how to cite a newspaper article in endnotes or a bibliography.

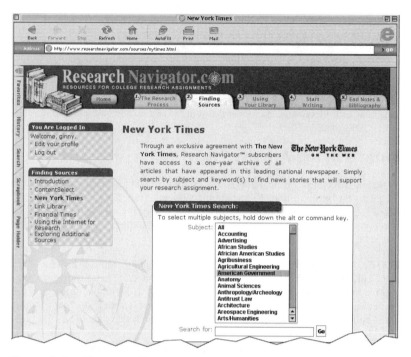

Search by Keyword

"And" Behavior

By default, the search engine only returns pages that match all of the keywords entered in a search query. The more keywords you use, the more refined the search becomes. There is no need to type the word "**and**" between keywords, as this is done automatically by the search engine.

Case Sensitivity

The Search engine does not differentiate between upper and lower case. A search for dna, DNA, or dNa will all return pages containing the keyword "DNA".

Searching Within Results

Often a first attempt at searching produces too many search results. To narrow the results, you may want to perform a new search that searches only within the results returned by the too-broad search query. This is often called "narrowing a search" or "searching within the current search results." To narrow a search, all you need to do is add more words to the end of your query. This give you a new query that will return a subset of the pages returned by the too-broad query.

Sorting by Date

The *New York Times* Search by Subject Archive sorts article results by relevance, with the most relevant appearing first. To view the most recently published articles first, use the "Sort by" pull down menu located just above the search results.

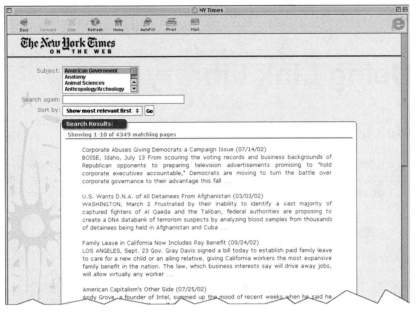

"Most Relevant" format

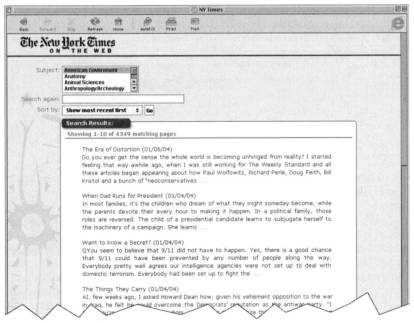

"Most Recent" format

Chapter 6

Using Link Library

Link Library and the Web

Link Library is a collection of Web links, organized into 34 academic subjects, which are in turn divided into subcategories and lists of individual sites. The sites are editorially reviewed, which means that they have been selected because they offer credible and reliable information.

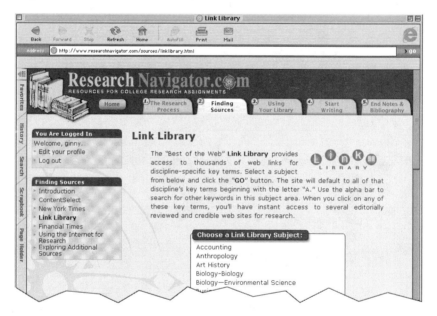

For example, if you were to select the "pollution" subcategory from the **Biology--Environmental Science** subject category, you would get a list of a dozen links. The site topics range from different types of pollution--air, noise, water--to the status of environmental legislation. How dependable are the sources? All are well-known and well-regarded government or educational institutions: the Environmental Protection Agency, NASA Ames Research Center, the University of California at Irvine. Some may quarrel with policies and enforcement efforts of government agencies, but the federal government has a long-established role in collecting data and disseminating information. The government websites listed here cover straightforward, non-controversial subjects: a definition of water pollution, how stratospheric ozone is being depleted, the latest city-by-city air pollution data, etc.

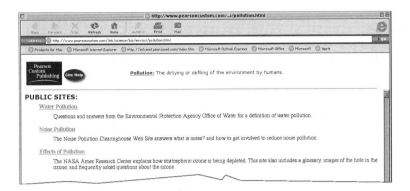

Suppose you look for the same information from websites listed by Yahoo! It turns out that many sites listed under "pollution" are from government and educational agencies. But you will also come across sites like one in which the author describes herself as "devoted to addressing the aspects of the environmental crisis left unacknowledged or inadequately addressed by the vast majority of existing environmental groups." The site is attractive, it doesn't solicit contributions, and it collects articles from generally well-regarded secondary sources, like the Associated Press. But its focus is on opinion, and lists topic headings such as "prophecy" and "prayer." It contains little of scholarly interest and no discernible research evidence. The site's author, while enthusiastic and well-intentioned, is not well-known or well-regarded.

In addition, the Web links in Research Navigator's Link Library are monitored and updated each week to reduce the chance of encountering "dead" links.

What's in Link Library?

Link Library echoes the variety of the World Wide Web. It offers images, text, government and academic documents and research, databases, and search engines. As with any subject directory, you need to narrow your search to the most useful category. You can find links to websites about AIDS, for example, in a half-dozen subject categories: biology, criminal justice, U.S. and world history, philosophy-ethics, and sociology. When you have selected a subject area and found the topic you are seeking, you will find a list of sites. The character of the site you choose to consult will often depend on your topic. The sites in Link Library can be:

- **Scholarly.** If you are researching photosynthesis and you go to the **Biology** subject area, you will find such sites as "What Is Photosynthesis?" and "Photosynthesis Research," maintained by Arizona State University. "Virtual Chloroplast," by the University of Illinois at Urbana-Champaign, contains an image of a chloroplast that lets you click on certain regions for more information.

- **Straightforward.** What if you want information on the 2000 presidential election but don't want to be flooded with opinion pieces about the disputed Florida results? Go to **Political Science – American Government > Presidential Elections**. It has sites such as "Atlas of U.S. Presidential Elections," with voting results for elections dating back to 1860; "U.S. Electoral College," the homepage for the National Archives and Records Administration Guide to the Electoral College; and "Elections," which provides graphs on electoral and popular votes for all U.S. presidential elections to date.

- **Controversial.** You're researching a topic that has heated arguments on both--or many--sides, and you want to summarize the range of public opinion. Link Library subject directories on such topics will lead you to a balanced variety of voices. Under **Philosophy–Ethics**, for example, you will find a list of "partial-birth abortion" links that include a pro-choice site, the text of the *Roe vs. Wade* decision, the National Right to Life Committee homepage, a site that attempts to provide all views of the issue, and a Planned Parenthood site that describes medical procedures performed at various stages of pregnancy.

- **Practical.** Want some help in finding sources on the Web? Go to the **Information Technology** subject directory. The "search engine" heading offers tips for effective Internet searching, common questions about how search engines work, and a chart to help you choose the best search engine for a task.

Finding Information with Link Library

To use this database, you choose a subject from the drop-down list, and, using the alphabetical directory, find the key term for the topic you are searching. Click on the key term and see a list of editorially reviewed websites.

Some topics with wide-ranging aspects appear under more than one subject heading. For example, a list of websites about alcoholism and alcohol abuse can be found under Criminal Justice, U.S. History, General Psychology, and Sociology.

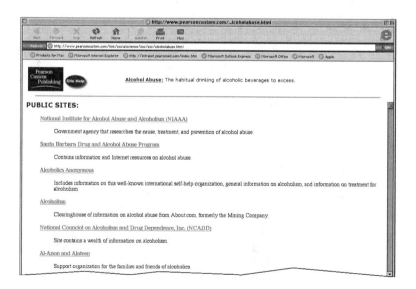

Chapter 7

Using ContentSelect

About ContentSelect

EBSCO's ContentSelect Academic Journal Database is an archive of scholarly peer-reviewed journals and general interest periodicals. Thousands of articles and citations from general interest publications and prestigious academic journals can be instantly accessed in several ways using ContentSelect's search engine. Titles are chosen to reflect multiple perspectives in a range of topics, under 30 broad subject headings in the sciences, humanities, and social sciences.

Of course, ContentSelect is not a substitute for evaluation. Careful research studies sometimes contradict one another, and even authorities disagree. However, while many sources on the Internet may present questionable data or rely on dubious authorities to draw conclusions, ContentSelect provides a wealth of professionally-reviewed information that you can search and evaluate with confidence.

What's in ContentSelect?

ContentSelect offers searchable databases of academic journals and general interest publications. Academic journals are peer-reviewed; general interest publications are not.

Academic Journals

Rather than having a staff of writers who write something on assignment, journals accept submissions from academic researchers all over the country and the world. The journal editor then relies on "peer reviewers," or experts in the author's field, to evaluate the papers submitted to help determine if they should be published. The result is that the content of journal articles meets a higher standard than that of popular magazines, newspaper articles or Web pages. Journals provide specialized knowledge and information about a research topic and adhere to strict professional guidelines for methodology and theoretical grounding.

Scholarly journals are published several times per year. All the issues published in one calendar year constitute a volume. For example, the *American Sociological Review*, the journal of the American Sociological Association, published Volume 65 in the year 2000. That year's volume was made up of six individual issues, numbered Vol. 65 No. 1 and so on.

Additionally, journal issues may contain letters to the editor, book reviews, and comments from authors.

General Interest Publications
In addition to scholarly journals, subject databases--particularly the General Interest database--in ContentSelect include periodicals that are not peer reviewed. Some examples are *Commentary, Washington Monthly, Newsweek, USA Today Magazine*, and the *Christian Science Monitor*. These publications are included because they have articles that are generally credible and reliable. If your topic is timely or controversial, general interest publications may offer more appropriate coverage than academic journals.

Sometimes it's not easy to know at first glance which category a publication fits. For example, you find an article in *Science News*. Is that an academic journal, as the journal *Science* is? Once you've conducted a search in your subject database, click on the "publications" tab at the top of your results page. You can scroll down to *Science News* or use the "browse" button to find it. When you click on *Science News*, you'll get an information box that describes the subjects it covers plus a characterization of its content: "presents articles of interest to scientists and others ..." The "and others" is a clue; then, when you check the "peer reviewed" section, it has an "N" for "no." So *Science News* is a general interest publication, not an academic journal. Still, any article in *Science News* is probably reliable, subject to the evaluation you conduct for all sources (see Chapter 2).

Searching ContentSelect

Select a Database

ContentSelect's homepage features a list of databases. To search within a single database, click the name of the database. To search in more than one database, hold down the alt or command key while clicking on the name of the database.

Basic Search

After selecting one or more databases, you must enter a keyword or keywords, then click on "go." This will take you to the basic search window. If you've selected a precise and distinctive keyword, your search may be done. But if you have too many results--which is often the case--you need to narrow your search.

Standard Search (Boolean)

- **And** combines search terms so that each result contains all of the terms. For example, search **SUV and conservation** to find only articles that contain both terms.

- **Or** combines search terms so that each result contains at least one of the terms. For example, search **SUV or conservation** to find results that contain either term.

- **Not** excludes terms so that each result does not contain the term that follows the "not" operator. For example, search **SUV not conservation** to find results that contain the term **SUV** but not the term **conservation.**

Using the above examples, suppose you were writing a paper about sport utility vehicles and energy conservation, in light of growing criticism of their low gasoline mileage. If you selected the "General Interest" database from ContentSelect and used the Boolean "or," at the time this was written, you would get 800 results for **SUV or conservation**. If you used the Boolean "and" option, (**SUV and conservation**) you would get only two results:

But suppose you decided to write about SUVs and didn't want articles that mentioned the energy conservation issue. If you searched for **SUV not conservation**, you would get 194 results:

Search by Article Number

Each and every article in the EBSCO ContentSelect Academic Journal and Abstract Database is assigned its own unique article number. In some cases, you may know the exact article number for the journal article you would like to retrieve. Perhaps you noted it during a prior research session on Research Navigator. Such article numbers might also be found on a companion website for your text, or in the text itself.

To retrieve a specific article, type the article number in the "Search by Article Number" field and click the **GO** button.

Advanced Search

On the tabbed tool bar, click **Advanced Search**. The advanced search window appears. Enter your search terms in the **Find** field. Your search terms can be keywords or selections from search history. Boolean operators (AND, OR, NOT) can also be included in your search.

You can also use **field codes** with your search terms. Fields refer to searchable aspects of an article or Web page; in the case of ContentSelect, they include author, title, subject, abstract, and journal name. Click **Field Codes** to display a list of field codes available with the databases you are using. Type the field code before your search terms to limit those words to the field you entered. For example, **AU Naughton** will find records that contain Naughton in the author field.

To **print**, **e-mail**, **or save** several search results, click on the folder next to the result; then print, e-mail, or save from the folder at the top of the results field. (You can still print, e-mail, or save individual results from the open article or citation.)

You can remove specific results, or clear the entire folder and collect new results, during your session. If you end your session, or it times out due to inactivity, the folder is automatically cleared.

Full Text Results

Some ContentSelect results will be available in full text--that is, if you click on the full text logo at the bottom of an entry, you will be able to call up the entire journal or magazine article. If you want to limit your search to results available in full text, click on the "search options" tab, and then on "full text." Then renew your search.

Abstract and Citation Results

Many ContentSelect results are in the form of citations containing abstracts. A **citation** is a bibliographic reference to an article or document, with basic information such as ISSN (International Standard Serial Number, the standard method for identifying publications) and publisher that will help you locate it. An **abstract** is a brief description of an article, usually written by the author. An abstract will help you decide whether you want to locate the work--either in an electronic database or a print version--through your college library.

A handy tip: once you have found an article that meets your research needs, you can search fields easily from the article citation to turn up similar articles. For example, suppose the *Christian Science Monitor* article "Gas-guzzling SUVs muster up a makeover" (Evarts, July 6, 2000) suits your paper perfectly. Go to the citation and click on the subject field to find similar articles. Or, if you want to see what else the author has written, click on the author field to produce a list of articles he has written.

EBSCO Research
HOST Databases

Basic   Advanced   Choose
Search   Search   Databases

Sign In to My EBSCOhost

Keyword   Publications

New Search | ⊡ View Folder | Preferences | Help | Exit

PEARSON EDUCATION

◄ 1 of 1 ► Result List | Refine Search   ⊞ Print ⊠ E-mail ⊟ Save ⊟ Add to folder   ⊟ Folder is empty.

Formats: ⊟ Citation ⊟ HTML Full Text

Title:	*Gas-guzzling SUVs muster* up a makeover.
Author(s):	Evarts, Eric C.
Source:	Christian Science Monitor; 7/6/2000, Vol. 92 Issue 157, p18, 0p, 1c
Document Type:	Article
Subject(s):	AUTOMOBILE industry & trade -- Environmental aspects
	SPORT utility vehicles -- Environmental aspects
Geographic Term(s):	UNITED States
Abstract:	Reports on the attempts by United States automobile makers to make sport utility vehicles (*SUV*) more efficient and less-polluting vehicles. INSET: Psst! Next year's model over here.
Full Text Word Count:	1297
ISSN:	0882-7729
Accession Number:	3290060
Persistent link to this record:	http://search.epnet.com/direct.asp?an=3290060&db=yih
Database:	ContentSelect General Interest

★ ★ ★

Section: ideas

GAS-GUZZLING SUVS MUSTER UP A MAKEOVER

Bad boys of the open road scrub their image as automakers toy with the idea of cleaner hybrids

In many cases you can search the full text of articles using electronic databases and then read the entire article online. Typically, in order to use these databases you need to have a library card number or special password provided by the library. But sometimes when you use an electronic database you will find that the text of an article won't be accessible online, so you'll have to go to the library's shelves to find the magazine or newspaper in which the article originally appeared.

For more information, explore the "Using Your Library" tab on the Research Navigator homepage.

Appendix

Documenting Your Electronic Sources

Copyright laws came into effect when people started realizing that income could be made by selling their words. In an era dubbed "The Age of Information," knowledge and words are taking on more significance than ever. Laws requiring writers to document or give credit to the sources of their information, while evolving, are still in effect.

Various organizations have developed style manuals detailing, among other style matters, how to document sources in their particular disciplines. For writing in English composition and literature, Modern Language Association (MLA) and American Psychological Association (APA) guidelines are the most commonly used, but others, such as those in *The Chicago Manual of Style* (CMS), are available. Always find out from your instructor what style to use in a specific assignment so that you can follow the appropriate guidelines.

For general information on MLA and APA citations, the best print sources are:

Gibaldi, Joseph. MLA Handbook for Writers of Research Papers. 5th ed. NY: MLA, 1999.

American Psychological Association. (2001). *Publication Manual of the American Psychological Association* (5th ed.). Washington: APA.

Because the methods of obtaining electronic information are developing so rapidly, printed style manuals have had difficulty in keeping up with the changes and in developing documentation styles for electronic sources. As a result, the most up-to-date information from the MLA and the APA about documenting online sources with URLs can be found on these organizations' websites. This Appendix shows you how to credit your electronic sources based on the information there.

When you cite electronic sources, it is vital to type every letter, number, symbol, and space accurately. Any error makes it impossible to retrieve your source. Since electronic sources tend to be transitory, printing a hard copy of your sources will make it easier for you to cite accurately and provide evidence for your documentation. MLA style encloses Internet addresses and URLs (Uniform Resource Locators) in angle brackets < >. If you see them around an address, do not use them as part of the address when you attempt to retrieve the source. APA style does not enclose URLs.

Modern Language Association (MLA) Style Guidelines

These guidelines follow the documentation style authorized by the Modern Language Association for electronic sources. Web sources are documented in basically the same way as traditional sources. According to the MLA website, the following items should be included if they are available:

1. Name of the author, editor, compiler, or translator of the source (if available and relevant), reversed for alphabetizing and followed by an abbreviation, such as ed., if appropriate
2. Title of a poem, short story, article, or similar short work within a scholarly project, database, or periodical (in quotation marks); or title of a posting to a discussion list or forum (taken from the subject line and put in quotation marks), followed by the description Online posting
3. Title of a book (underlined)
4. Name of the editor, compiler, or translator of the text (if relevant and if not cited earlier), preceded by the appropriate abbreviation, such as ed.
5. Publication information for any print version of the source
6. Title of the scholarly project, database, periodical, or professional or personal site (underlined); or, for a professional or personal site with no title, a description such as Homepage
7. Name of the editor of the scholarly project or database (if available)
8. Version number of the source (if not part of the title) or, for a journal, the volume number, issue number, or other identifying number
9. Date of electronic publication, of the latest update, or of posting
10. For a posting to a discussion list or forum, the name of the list or forum
11. The number range or total number of pages, paragraphs, or other sections, if they are numbered
12. Name of any institution or organization sponsoring or associated with the website
13. Date when the researcher accessed the source
14. Electronic address, or URL, of the source (in angle brackets)

Examples:

Book

Shaw, Bernard. <u>Pygmalion</u>. 1912. Bartleby Archive. 6 Mar. 1998 <http://www.columbia.edu/acis/bartleby/shaw/>.

Poem

Carroll, Lewis. "Jabberwocky." 1872. 6 Mar. 1998. <http://www.jabberwocky.com/carroll/jabber/jabberwocky.html>.

Article in a Journal
Rehberger, Dean. "The Censoring of Project #17:
    Hypertext Bodies and Censorship." <u>Kairos</u> 2.2
    (Fall 1997): 14 secs. 6 Mar. 1998 <http://
    english.ttu.edu/kairos/2.2/index_f.html>.

Article in a Magazine
Viagas, Robert, and David Lefkowitz. "Capeman Closing
    Mar. 28." <u>Playbill</u> 5 Mar. 1998. 6 Mar. 1998
    <http://www1.playbill.com/cgi-bin/plb/news?cmd
    =show&code=30763>.

Article in a Newspaper
Sandomir, Richard. "Yankees Talk Trades in Broadcast
    Booth." <u>New York Times on the Web</u> 4 Dec. 2001. 5
    Dec. 2001 <http://www.nytimes.com/pages/
    business/media/index.html>.

Article in a Reference Database
"Jupiter." Britannica Online. Vers. 97.1.1 Mar. 1997.
    Encyclopaedia Britannica. 29 Mar. 1998 <http://
    www.eb.com:180>.

Posting to a Discussion List
Grumman, Bob. "Shakespeare's Literacy." Online
    posting. 6 Mar. 1998. Deja News. <humanities.
    lit.author>.

Scholarly Project
<u>Voice of the Shuttle: Web Page for Humanities
    Research</u>. Ed. Alan Liu. Mar. 1998. U of
    California Santa Barbara. 8 Mar. 1998
    <http://humanitas.ucsb.edu/>.

Professional Site
<u>The Nobel Foundation Official Website</u>. The Nobel
    Foundation. 28 Feb. 1998 <http://www.nobel.se/>.

Personal Site
Thiroux, Emily. Home page. 7 Mar. 1998
    <http://academic.csubak.edu/home/acadpro/
    departments/english/engthrx.htmlx>.

Government or Institutional Site
Zebra Mussels in Vermont. Homepage. State of Vermont
    Agency of Natural Resources. 3 May 1998 <http://
    www.anr.state.vt.us/dec/waterq/smcap.htm>.

Synchronous Communications (such as MOOs, MUDs, and IRCs)

Ghostly Presence. Group Discussion. telnet 16 Mar.
1997 <moo.du.org:8000/80anon/anonview/1
4036#focus>.

Gopher Sites

Banks, Vickie, and Joe Byers. "EDTECH." 18 Mar. 1997
<gopher://ericyr.syr.edu:70/00/Listservs/EDTECH/
README>.

FTP (File Transfer Protocol) Sites

U.S. Supreme Court directory. 6 Mar. 1998
<ftp://ftp.cwru.edu/U.S.Supreme.Court/>.

Online Work of Art

Van Gogh, Vincent. The Olive Trees. 1889. Museum of
Modern Art, New York. 5 Dec. 2001 <http://
www.moma.org/docs/collection/paintsculpt/
recent/c463.htm>.

Online Interview

Plaxco, Jim. Interview. Planetary Studies Foundation.
Oct. 1992. 5 Dec. 2001 <http://www.planets.org>.

Online Film or Film Clip

Columbus, Chris, dir. Harry Potter and the Sorcerer's
Stone. Trailer. Warner Brothers, 2001. 5 Dec.
2001 <http://hollywood.com>.

Electronic Television or Radio Program

Chayes, Sarah. "Concorde." All Things Considered.
Natl. Public Radio. 26 July 2000. 7 Dec. 2001
<http://www.npr.com/programs/atc/archives>.

Synchronous Communication

Author's last name, First name. Identifying label.
"Title of work." xx Month 20xx. Name of forum.
xx Month 20xx. <Telnet://lingua.networkname>.

Generally follow the guidelines for other online citations, modifying them
wherever necessary, but always provide as much information as possible. Some
cited material will require identifying labels (e.g., Interview or Online posting),
but such labels should be neither underlined nor set within quotation marks.
When documenting synchronous communications that are posted in MOO
(multiuser domain, object oriented) and MUD (multiuser domain) forums, name
the speaker or speakers; describe the event; provide the date of the event and the
name of the forum (e.g., linguaMOO); and cite the date of access as well as the
network name (including the prefix Telnet://).

Work from an Online Service

```
Author's last name, First name. Publication. 20xx.
    Internet Provider name. xx Month 20xx. Keyword:
    Name.
```

Or

```
Last name, First name. Publication. 20xx. Internet
    Provider name. xx Month 20xx. Path: Name; Name;
    Name.
```

```
Brash, Stephen B. "Bioprospecting the Public Domain."
    Cultural Anthropology 14.4 (1999): 535-56.
    ProQuest Direct. Teaneck Public Library,
    Teaneck, NJ. 7 Dec. 1999 <http://proquest.
    umi.com>.
```

Or

```
Dutton, Gail. "Greener Pigs." Popular Science 255.5
    (1999): 38-39. ProQuest Direct. Teaneck Public
    Library, Teaneck, NJ. 7 Dec. 1999 <http://
    proquest.umi.com>.
```

For works that have been accessed through an online service, either through a library service (e.g., ProQuest Direct or Lexis-Nexis) or through one of the large Internet providers (e.g., America Online), you may not know the URL of the source. In such cases, cite the keyword or path that led to the source, if applicable, and separate each individual item in the path with a semicolon; the keyword or path will be the last item in the citation. For sources accessed through library services, as above, cite the name of the service, the name of the library, the date you assessed the material, and the URL of the service's homepage. If you also know the name of the database used, include that information (underlined) before the name of the online service.

American Psychological Association (APA) Style Guidelines

The most recent (5th) edition of the *Publication Manual of the American Psychological Association* includes general guidelines for citing electronic sources, and the APA has published specific examples for documenting Web sources on its Web page. Go to:

http://www.apastyle.org/elecre.html

In general, document these sources as you do traditional sources, giving credit to the author and including the title and date of publication. Include as much information as possible to help your reader to be able to retrieve the information. Any sources that are not generally available to your readers should be documented within the body of your writing as a personal communication but not included in your reference list. Such sources include material from listservs, newsgroups, Internet relay chats (IRCs), MOOs, MUDs, and e-mail.

According to information at the website for the American Psychological Association entitled "How to Cite Information From the World Wide Web," all references begin with the same information that would be provided for a printed source (or as much of that information as possible). The Web information is then placed at the end of the reference. It is important to use the "Retrieved from" and the date because documents on the Web may change in content, move, or be removed from a site altogether. To cite a website in text (but not a specific document), it's sufficient to give the address (e.g., http://www.apa.org) there. No reference entry is needed.

Use the following guidelines to include a source in your reference list:

```
Name of author [if given]. (Publication date) [in
     parentheses]. Title of the article [following
     APA guidelines for capitalization]. Title of
     periodical or electronic text [italicized].
     Volume number and/or pages [if any]. Retrieved
     [include the date here] from the World Wide Web:
     [include the URL here, and do not end with a
     period]
```

Examples:

Journal Article
```
Fine, M. A. & Kurdek, L. A. (1993, November).
     Reflections on determining authorship credit and
     authorship order on faculty-student
     collaborations. American Psychologist, 48.11,
     1141-1147. Retrieved March 6, 1998 from the
     World Wide Web: http://www.apa.org/journals/
     amp/kurdek.html
```

Newspaper Article
```
Murray, B. (1998, February). Email bonding with your
     students. APA Monitor [Newspaper, selected
     stories online]. Retrieved March 6, 1998 from
     the World Wide Web: http://www.apa.org/monitor/
     bond.html
```

World Wide Web Site
```
Williams, Scott. (1996, June 14). Back to school
     with the quilt. AIDS Memorial Quilt Website.
     Retrieved June 14, 1996, from http://www.
     aidsquilt.org/newsletter/stoires/backto.html
```

File Transfer Protocol (FTP), Telnet, or Gopher Site
```
Altar, T.W. (1993). Vitamin B12 and vegans. Retrieved
     May 28, 1996, from ftp://ftp.cs.yle.edu
```

King, Jr., M.L. (1963, August 28). I have a dream
[speech]. Retrieved January 2, 1996, from
telnet://ukanaix.cc.ukans.edu

Synchronous Communications (MOO, MUD, IRC)
Harnack, A. (1996, April 4). Words [Group
discussion]. Retrieved April 5, 1996, from
telnet://moo.du.org/port=8888

Web Discussion Forum
Holden, J.B. (2001, January 2). The failure of higher
education [Formal discussion initiation].
Message posted to http://ifets.mtu.edu/archives

Listserv (electronic mailing list)
Weston, Heather (2002, June 12). Re: Registration
schedule now available. Message posted to the
Chamberlain Kronsage dormitory electronic
mailing list, archived at http://listserv.
registrar.uwsp.edu/archives/62.html

Newsgroup
Hotgirl (2002, January 12). Dowsing effort fails.
Message posted to news://alt.science.esp3/html